WORLD RUGBY UNION RECORDS

This edition published in 2012

Copyright © Carlton Books Limited 2012

SevenOaks, an imprint of the
Carlton Publishing Group
20 Mortimer Street
London W1T 3JW

A CIP catalogue record for this book is available from the British Library

10 9 8 7 6 5 4 3 2 1

ISBN: 978-1-86200-986-8

Editor: Martin Corteel
Project Art Editor: Luke Griffin
Designers: Sooky Choi & Harj Ghundale
Picture Research: Paul Langan
Production: Maria Petalidou

Printed in Dubai

WORLD RUGBY UNION RECORDS

**REVISED & UPDATED
EDITION**

CHRIS HAWKES

SEVENOAKS

CONTENTS

FROM LEFT TO RIGHT: James O'Connor, Brian
O'Driscoll, Dan Carter, Thierry Dusautoir, Victor
Matfield, Jonny Wilkinson, Richie McCaw,
Bryan Habana, David Pocock, Shane Williams,
Dan Parks and Dimitri Yachvili.

INTRODUCTION

Welcome to the first edition of *World Rugby Union Records*, a book that covers the full breadth of this much loved game, from the traditional 15-a-side international format to sevens, women's and youth international rugby, from an entirely new perspective – from the long list specific moments and achievements that have added extra glitter to the game's long established appeal over the years. The challenge, of course, came in trawling through rugby's numerous and comprehensive archives to find the hidden gems – one's that have made legends out of some individuals and villains out of others. As a passionate fan of the game it was a privileged task, and a process that allowed me to rediscover almost-forgotten rugby-related memories from my earliest days as a fan. The hope is that this book will evoke a similar response in every one of its readers.

The considerable task of compiling such an extensive list of records was made easier by the availability of numerous and comprehensive archives on the game, with match reports and statistics available for every international match that has been played since the very first, when England travelled to Raeburn Place in Edinburgh on 27 March 1871 to play Scotland.

As is the case with all sports in this television money driven era, rugby today is a 12-month-a-year affair, so there had to be a cut-off point. In this instance, all statistics and records in this book are correct as of 23 October 2011, the day New Zealand ended their 24-year wait for a second Rugby World Cup triumph.

Particular thanks for the production of this book are due to Martin Corteel, whose encouragement and assurance while putting a book of this type together remain invaluable, to Lorraine Jerram, for her assiduous eye to detail while editing the book, to Luke Griffin, whose design flair has helped to bring the words to life, to Paul Langan for his meticulous search through rugby's photo archives in an attempt to illustrate even the most obscure of records, and to Maria Petalidou for her considerable skill in ensuring the book's production was achieved in a seamless manner. The various aspects of producing a book of this type would not have come together without their considerable input. Final thanks are due to you, the reader. I hope that the time you spend within the pages of this book will be as enjoyable an experience as it was to put them all together.

Chris Hawkes
Savigny-le-Vieux, October 2011

OPPOSITE: Richie McCaw ends 24 years of agony for New Zealand as he lifts the Webb Ellis Trophy following the All Blacks' 8–7 defeat of France in the 2011 Rugby World Cup final.

OVERLEAF: Peri Weepu leads the All Blacks in their traditional call to battle, the Haka, one of the most stirring and anticipated sights in world rugby.

PART I
THE COUNTRIES

Although a lack of firm evidence suggests that the legendary moment in 1823 when Rugby School pupil William Webb Ellis picked up a ball and ran with it during a game of football to create an altogether different sport may well be apocryphal, no one can dispute the rapid nature of rugby's spread throughout the world.

The first set of rudimentary rules were written in 1845, the first international match took place in March 1871, in which Scotland beat England by one goal to nil at Raeburn Place in Edinburgh, and by 1881 both Ireland and Wales had established international teams. Two years later, in 1883, the world's

first international competition – the Home Nations Championship – was staged and within a few years the rugby gospel had spread beyond the confines of Britain and Ireland.

In 1888, a touring team from the British Isles travelled to Australia and New Zealand, the same year saw a New Zealand side tour Britain for the first time, and by the end of the first decade of the twentieth century, teams from Australia and South Africa had played in the northern hemisphere. And the game's expansion to the furthest reaches of the globe did not stop there: France played its first rugby international in 1906, Argentina in 1910, the USA in 1912, Fiji, Samoa and Tonga in 1924, Japan and Canada in 1932. Many other countries followed and by 2011 the 117 member nations of the International Rugby Board (IRB) – ranging from Andorra to Zimbabwe – had played over 13,800 internationals between them. This section looks not only at the major rugby-playing nations' records in the international arena, but also at the performances of the game's lesser nations, as well as highlighting the players whose performances have made them legendary figures in the game's history.

BELOW: The opening ceremony for the 2011 Rugby World Cup was an explosion of colour and sound.

EUROPE

Europe is the cradle of world rugby. It is the continent in which the game has its origins, in which the laws of the game were first drawn up, in which the world's first international match took place, in which the world's oldest international tournament – the Home Nations Championship – was first contested and from which the game of rugby spread to the furthest reaches of the globe. Europe is also home to some of the world's most powerful rugby-playing nations and features more top-20 ranked countries (nine) than any other continent on the planet.

BELOW: England's home ground, Twickenham, has hosted more international rugby matches (265) than any other stadium on the planet.

ENGLAND

The birthplace of the game, England has more registered players than any other country. They have also achieved considerable success in the international area winning the now Six Nations Championship on 36 occasions: (with 12 grand slams), but their finest moment came in Sydney in 2003, when they beat Australia 20–17 in the final to become the first country from the northern hemisphere to win the Rugby World Cup. England are also two-time finalists in the Rugby World Cup, in 1991 and 2007.

ENGLAND DEMOLISH HAPLESS ROMANIA

When England played Romania at Twickenham on 17 November 2001 it was a day of records. First, Jason Leonard, making his 93rd appearance, became the most capped forward in international rugby history and then his team-mates, as if to celebrate the popular prop's achievement, ran riot. They scored their first try after nine minutes and then overwhelmed their awestruck opponents, scoring 20 tries en route to a staggering 134–0 victory – the biggest win in their history. It was a day to remember for debutant Charlie Hodgson, too: the 21-year-old Sale fly-half bagged 44 points – including two tries – to break Paul Grayson's individual points-scoring record for England, with only the width of a post preventing him from breaking Simon Culhane's world-record haul of 45 points (set while playing for New Zealand against Japan in the 1995 Rugby World Cup).

OVERALL TEAM RECORD

Span	Mat	Won	Lost	Draw	%	For	Aga	Diff	Tries	Conv	Pens	Drop	GfM
1871–2011	646	344	253	49	57.04	10258	7813	+2445	1394	801	998	136	4

BACK TO THE DRAWING BOARD

England may well have pointed to the absence of many of their star players as an excuse for their abject capitulation, but there is no escaping the fact that their side – featuring seven debutants – suffered nothing short of total humiliation against Australia at Brisbane on 6 June 1998. Trailing 33–0 at half-time, they collapsed to a sorry 76–0 loss: it was their largest ever international defeat.

BELOW: Debutant Charlie Hodgson had a day to remember against Romania on 17 September 2001, bagging an England record 44 points.

LOSING START FOR ENGLAND

In December 1870, a group of Scottish players issued a letter of challenge to England in the *Scotsman* and *Bell's Life* newspapers to contest a match in the 'carrying game'. It could hardly be ignored and three months later, on 27 March 1871 at Raeburn Place in Edinburgh, the world's first rugby international took place. Scotland won the 20-a-side affair by scoring one try and a goal to England's solitary try – a points system had still to be devised.

ENGLAND'S RECORD-BREAKING RUN

Few could have questioned England's credentials as favourites to win the 2003 Rugby World Cup. In a period of 18 months leading up to the tournament they strung together 14 consecutive victories between 23 March 2002 and 23 August 2003 – including home-and-away wins over Wales, New Zealand and Australia – to record the longest winning streak in their history. The run came to an end following a slender 17–16 defeat in Marseille on 30 August 2003.

HONOURS

Rugby World Cup:
(best finish) – champions (2003)

Six Nations:
winners – 1883#, 1884#, 1886*, 1890*, 1892#, 1910, 1912*, 1913 (GS), 1914 (GS), 1920*, 1921 (GS), 1923 (GS), 1924 (GS), 1928 (GS), 1930, 1932*, 1934#, 1937#, 1939*, 1947*, 1953, 1954#*, 1957 (GS), 1958, 1960#*, 1963, 1973*, 1980 (GS), 1991 (GS), 1992 (GS), 1995 (GS), 1996#, 2000, 2001, 2003 (GS), 2011

* = shared; (GS) = Grand Slam; # = triple crown

ABOVE: Martin Johnson lifted the Rugby World Cup for England in 2003 and is the team's current head coach.

COACHES

Name	Tenure
Don White	1969–71
John Elders	1972–74
John Burgess	1975
Peter Colston	1976–79
Mike Davis	1979–82
Dick Greenwood	1983–85
Martin Green	1985–87
Geoff Cooke	1988–94
Jack Rowell	1994–97
Sir Clive Woodward	1997–2004
Andy Robinson	2004–06
Brian Ashton	2006–08
Rob Andrew	2008
Martin Johnson	2008–present

MOST TRIES: TOP TEN

Pos	Tries	Player (Span)
1	49	Rory Underwood (1984–96)
2	31	Ben Cohen (2000–06)
=	31	Will Greenwood (1997–2004)
4	30	Jeremy Guscott (1989–99)
5	28	Jason Robinson (2001–07)
6	24	Dan Luger (1998–2003)
7	22	Josh Lewsey (1998–2007)
8	20	Mark Cueto (2004–11)
9	18	Cyril Lowe (1913–23)
10	17	Lawrence Dallaglio (1995–2007)

LONGEST LOSING STREAK

England's longest losing streak is seven consecutive matches, an unfortunate feat achieved on three occasions: between 19 March 1904 and 10 February 1906; between 20 March 1971 and 18 March 1972; and, most recently, between 25 February 2006 and 11 November 2006.

BELOW: A Rugby World Cup winner in 2003, Josh Lewsey stands seventh on England's all-time try-scoring lists with 22 tries.

ON TOP OF THE WORLD

Their detractors may have dubbed them 'Dad's Army' (half of their squad was over the age of 30) and pointed to a one-dimensional style of play based on a muscular pack and the unerring accuracy of Jonny Wilkinson's boot, but England entered the 2003 Rugby World Cup as the world's no.1 ranked team and were supremely confident of victory, having beaten all-comers both home and away in the build-up to the tournament. And they did not disappoint, easing through the group stages before beating Wales in the quarter-finals, France in the semi-finals and edging out Australia 20–17 in a closely contested final (thanks to a last-gasp, extra-time Wilkinson drop goal) to become the first team from the northern hemisphere to win rugby's greatest prize.

ABOVE: 1980 grand slam-winning captain Bill Beaumont is one of four English inductees in the International Rugby Hall of Fame.

ENGLAND HIT NEW HEIGHTS

The 1913 Five Nations Championship – the 31st series of the annual northern hemisphere rugby tournament and the fourth edition of the expanded championship following the inclusion of France in 1910 – was one to remember for England. The defending champions (after sharing the title with Ireland in 1912) beat Wales (12–0, away), France (20–0, home), Ireland (15–4, away) and Scotland (3–0, home) to record the first grand slam (of 12) in their history.

INTERNATIONAL RUGBY HALL OF FAME INDUCTEES

Name	(Span, Caps)
Bill Beaumont	(1975–82, 41 caps)
Martin Johnson	(1993–2003, 92 caps)
Jason Leonard	(1990–2004, 114 caps)
Wavell Wakefield	(1920–27, 31 caps)

MOST TRIES IN A MATCH

The England individual record for the most tries in a match is five, a feat achieved by three players: Daniel Lambert against France at Richmond on 5 January 1907; Rory Underwood against Fiji at Twickenham on 5 November 1989; and Josh Lewsey against Uruguay at Brisbane on 2 November 2003.

EVER-PRESENT LEONARD SETS CAPS LANDMARK

When Jason Leonard won his first cap for England on 28 July 1990, against Argentina, he became his country's youngest ever prop forward: it was the start of a record-breaking career. Capable of scrummaging with equal effect at both loosehead and tighthead, he was a cornerstone of a pack that helped England to the Rugby World Cup final in 1991 and to back-to-back grand slams in 1991 and 1992, and he made the first of five British Lions appearances in 1993. Coaches and players may have come and gone, but Leonard remained an ever-present in the England set-up throughout the 1990s, and in November 2000 passed Rory Underwood's haul of caps to become England's most capped player. By the time he bowed out of international rugby, following England's 2003 Rugby World Cup triumph, he was the most capped player in rugby history with 114 caps – a record since broken by Australia's George Gregan.

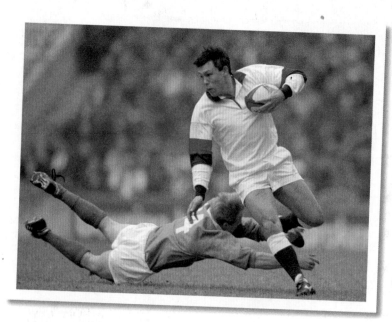

RIGHT: A regular source of points for England for more than a decade, Rory Underwood scored a record 49 tries for his country.

ENGLAND'S YOUNGEST PLAYER

Colin Laird holds the distinction of being the youngest player ever to pull on an England shirt. The fly-half was a mere 18 years and 134 days old when he made his debut during England's 11–9 victory over Wales at Twickenham on 15 January 1927. He went on to make ten appearances for his country (scoring five tries) and was an ever-present in the side when England won their sixth grand slam in 1928.

ENGLAND'S FLIER ON THE WING

An RAF flight lieutenant, Rory Underwood burst on to the international scene in 1984, scoring his first try in only his second Test (against France in Paris); it was an opportunistic effort that highlighted the searing turn of pace that would become the hallmark of his career. Equally comfortable on either wing, he was a constant presence in the England side until his retirement in 1996, during which time he won three grand slams, collected six British Lions caps (scoring one try), and appeared in the 1991 Rugby World Cup final. The first England player to appear in 50 internationals, the quicksilver winger ended his 12-year career with 85 caps – a record for an England back – having scored an all-time national record 49 tries.

LEFT: Jason Leonard is the only player in history to have won more than 100 caps for England.

ALL-TIME LEADING TRY-SCORERS: BY POSITION

Position	Player (Span)	Tries
Full-back	Jason Robinson (2001–07)	13*
Winger	Rory Underwood (1984–96)	49
Centre	Will Greenwood (1997–2004)	31
Fly-half	Charlie Hodgson (2001–11)	6
	Jonny Wilkinson (1998–2011)	6
Scrum-half	Matt Dawson (1995–2006)	16
No.8	Lawrence Dallaglio (1995–2007)	10†
Flanker	Neil Back (1994–2003)	16
Lock	Wade Dooley (1985–93)	3
Prop	Bruno Brown (1911–22)	4
Hooker	Phil Greening (1996–2001)	6

* also scored 15 tries as a winger. † also scored 7 tries as a flanker.

MOST POINTS: TOP TEN

Pos	Points	Player (Span)
1	1179	Jonny Wilkinson (1998–2011)
2	400	Paul Grayson (1995–2004)
3	396	Rob Andrew (1985–97)
4	296	Jonathan Webb (1987–93)
5	259	Charlie Hodgson (2001–11)
6	240	Dusty Hare (1974–84)
7	223	Toby Flood (2006–11)
8	210	Rory Underwood (1984–96)
9	203	Simon Hodgkinson (1989–91)
10	155	Ben Cohen (2000–06)
=	155	Will Greenwood (1997–2004)

RIGHT: Jonny Wilkinson is England's leading points-scorer with 1,179.

BELOW: Clive Woodward celebrates his ultimate achievement, coaching England to Rugby World Cup glory in 2003.

BOTTOM: Will Carling led England 59 times between 1988 and 1996.

CAPTAIN CARLING REVIVES ENGLAND

Appointed England's youngest-ever captain in November 1988 at the tender age of 22, Will Carling played a major role in reviving his country's floundering rugby fortunes, leading them to the Rugby World Cup final in 1991 (which they lost to Australia) and to grand slam success in 1991, 1992 and 1995. He led his country on 59 occasions – a national record – and by the time he relinquished the reins in 1996 he had recorded 44 wins, making him England's most successful captain of all time.

MODERN APPROACH PAYS DIVIDENDS FOR COACH WOODWARD

A talented player in his own right, making 21 appearances for England at centre between 1980 and 1984, Clive Woodward succeeded Jack Rowell as England coach in 1997. Success initially eluded him – and a quarter-final defeat to South Africa at the 1999 Rugby World Cup left many questioning his credentials for the job – but his man-management skills and an innovative approach to pre-match preparation soon brought the best out of the talented group of players he had at his disposal. It culminated, of course, in English rugby's proudest moment: victory at the 2003 Rugby World Cup. When he left the post the following year, England had won 59 of the 83 Tests under his charge – no England coach in history has notched up more wins. He was knighted in 2004.

MOST CAPS: TOP TEN

Pos	Caps	Player (Span)
1	114	Jason Leonard (1990–2004)
2	91	Jonny Wilkinson (1998–2011)
3	85	Lawrence Dallaglio (1995–2007)
=	85	Rory Underwood (1984–96)
5	84	Martin Johnson (1993–2003)
6	78	Joe Worsley (1999–2011)
7	77	Matt Dawson (1995–2006)
8	75	Mike Catt (1994–2007)
=	75	Mike Tindall (2000–2011)
10	73	Steve Thompson (2002–2011)
=	73	Phil Vickery (1998–2009)

WILKINSON PROSPERS FOR ENGLAND

Jonny Wilkinson won his first cap for England against Ireland on 4 April 1998 aged 18 and established himself as a regular within a year. Showing an unerring accuracy with the boot, he helped England to the Six Nations crown in both 2000 and 2001 and by 2003 was considered the best player in world rugby: helping England to back-to-back wins over New Zealand for the first time; playing a leading role in England's first-ever victory on Australian soil; landing the crucial drop goal that secured England the Rugby World Cup; and ending the year as the IRB's Player of the Year. Then injury struck: he missed four years of international rugby, but returned in 2007 to lead England to a second successive Rugby World Cup final. In 2008, he overhauled Neil Jenkins as the leading points-scorer ever in international rugby and is one of only two players in Six Nations Championship history (alongside Ronan O'Gara) to have passed 500 points.

FRANCE

A gold medal in the 1900 Olympic Games apart, France made a stuttering start to international rugby – winning only one of their first 31 matches. It wasn't until the late 1950s that French rugby truly came of age: they won the Five Nations Championship for the first time outright in 1959, claimed a first grand slam in 1968 and have since gone from strength to strength. Three-time finalists in the Rugby World Cup (in 1987, 1999 and 2011), France currently stand third in the International Rugby Board world rankings.

SO NEAR AND YET SO FAR

Rugby World Cup semi-final upsets have been a French speciality over the years: in the inaugural edition of the event in 1987, they stunned hosts and pre-tournament favourites Australia when Serge Blanco dived over the line in the dying moments of the game to secure a 30–24 victory. And they were at it again against much-fancied New Zealand at Twickenham in 1999 – a match described by many as the greatest of all time. Trailing 17–10 at half-time, they rallied in spectacular fashion to secure a memorable 43–31 victory. But that was where the fun ended: France went on to lose the final on both occasions and a third final defeat in 2011 – 8–7 to New Zealand – meant the French had become the first team in history to lose in three Rugby World Cup finals.

MOST TRIES IN A MATCH

The French record for the most tries by one player in a match is four, a feat achieved by two men: Adolphe Jaureguy (against Romania at Colombes on 4 May 1924); and Maurice Celhay (against Italy at Parc des Princes on 17 October 1937).

LEADING LES BLEUS FROM THE FRONT

Two players – both hard men of the French pack in recent times – share the record for being the longest-serving and most successful France captains of all time. Hooker Raphaël Ibanez and lock Fabien Pelous led their country on 41 occasions and both enjoyed 26 wins as captain.

RIGHT: Vincent Clerc scored his 31st try for France in their 26–12 Rugby World Cup 2011 quarter-final victory over England at Auckland, taking him one clear of Philippe Sella and alone in third place in France's all-time try-scorers' list.

EVERY CLOUD HAS A SILVER LINING

In 1931, just when it seemed French rugby was on an upward curve, France made the headlines for all the wrong reasons. Their ferocious style of play had been upsetting their Five Nations rivals for some time, but when rumours of professionalism in French rugby that contradicted the games's strict amateur principals started to emerge, they were summarily thrown out of the tournament and condemned to play matches against the game's lesser nations. They took full advantage: between 6 April 1931 and 17 October 1937, they put together a run of ten consecutive victories – still an all-time record winning streak for France.

HONOURS

Rugby World Cup:
(best finish) – runners-up (1987, 1999, 2011)

Six Nations:
winners – 1955*, 1959, 1960*, 1961, 1962, 1967, 1968 (GS), 1970*, 1973*, 1977 (GS), 1981 (GS), 1983*, 1986*, 1987 (GS), 1988*, 1989, 1993, 1997 (GS), 1998 (GS), 2002 (GS), 2004 (GS), 2006, 2007, 2010 (GS)

* = shared; (GS) = Grand Slam

MOST TRIES: TOP TEN

Pos	Tries	Player (Span)
1	38	Serge Blanco (1980–91)
2	32	Philippe Saint-Andre (1990–97)
3	31	Vincent Clerc (2002–11)
4	30	Philippe Sella (1982–95)
5	26	Philippe Bernat-Salles (1992–2001)
=	26	Emile Ntamack (1994–2000)
7	25	Christophe Dominici (1998–2007)
8	23	Christian Darrouy (1957–67)
9	22	Aurélien Rougerie (2001–11)
10	20	Yannik Jauzion (2001–11)
=	20	Patrique Lagisquet (1983–91)

OVERALL TEAM RECORD

Span	Mat	Won	Lost	Draw	%	For	Aga	Diff	Tries	Conv	Pens	Drop	GfM
1906–2011	677	375	272	30	57.60	12178	9839	+2339	1594	932	1051	217	1

MOST CAPS: TOP TEN

Pos	Caps	Player (Span)
1	118	Fabien Pelous (1995–2007)
2	111	Philippe Sella (1982–1995)
3	98	Raphael Ibanez (1996–2007)
4	93	Serge Blanco (1980–1991)
5	89	Olivier Magne (1997–2007)
6	86	Damien Traille (2001–11)
7	84	Sylvain Marconnet (1998–2011)
8	78	Abdelatif Benazzi (1990–2001)
9	77	Imanol Harinordoquy (2002–11)
10	73	Yannick Jauzion (2001–11)

RECORD-BREAKING TRIUMPH FOR FRANCE IN TOULOUSE

Namibia may not have provided the strongest opposition in their pool but, following a morale-sapping opening-game defeat against Argentina (17–12), France needed to win and win comfortably when they faced off against the African minnows in Toulouse if they wanted to get their 2007 Rugby World Cup campaign back on track. They did not disappoint and thrilled the 35,339 crowd by running in 13 tries en route to a crushing 87–10 victory – the biggest win in their history.

NEW YEAR'S DAY BLUES FOR FRANCE

A crowd of 3,000 people made its way to the Parc des Princes in Paris on New Year's Day 1906 to watch France contest an international rugby match for the first time, against New Zealand, who were playing in the last match of their first-ever tour to the northern hemisphere. It did not turn out to be the happiest of occasions for the home side or the partisan crowd: trailing 18–3 at half-time, they ended up losing the match 38–8, with New Zealand outscoring Les Bleus by ten tries to two.

FAILING TO FIND THE WINNING FORMULA

France made a troubled start to international rugby, managing to win just one of their first 31 matches over a period of 14 years. During that time, between 28 January 1911 (a 37–0 defeat to England) and 17 February 1920 (a slender 6–5 reverse against Wales), they lost 18 matches in a row – the longest streak in international rugby history. It came to an end when France beat Ireland 15–7 in Dublin on 3 April 1920.

ABOVE: Philippe Sella shone at centre for France for 13 years and was the first Frenchman to achieve the 100-cap milestone.

CLASSY CAMBERABERO SHINES FOR FRANCE

After a stuttering performance in their opening match of the inaugural Rugby World Cup in 1987 (a 20–20 draw against Scotland), France bounced back with a dominant victory over Romania (55–12). However, it was still all to play for in the final round of group matches, and only a convincing win against minnows Zimbabwe (who Scotland had beaten 60–21) could guarantee Les Bleus top spot in the pool – and thus avoid a potentially awkward quarter-final tie against hosts New Zealand. They played staggeringly well, crushing the Africans 70–12 to top the group with Didier Camberabero the star of the show. The flamboyant fly-half scored three tries and slotted nine conversions to amass 30 points in the match – an all-time record for France.

BELOW: Didier Camberabero helped France to reach the 1987 Rugby World Cup quarter-final with 30 points against Zimbabwe (three tries and nine conversions in a 70–12 rout). No France player has scored more points in a match.

INTERNATIONAL RUGBY HALL OF FAME INDUCTEES

Name	(Span, Caps)
Serge Blanco	(1980–91, 93 caps)
André Boniface	(1954–66, 48 caps)
Jo Maso	(1966–73, 25 caps)
Jean Prat	(1945–55, 51 caps)
Jean-Pierre Rives	(1975–84, 59 caps)
Philippe Sella	(1982–95, 111 caps)

ALL-TIME LEADING TRY-SCORERS: BY POSITION

Position	Player (Span)	Tries
Full-back	Serge Blanco (1980–91)	38
Winger	Philippe Saint-André (1990–97)	32
Centre	Philippe Sella (1982–95)	30
Fly-half	Alain Penaud (1992–2000)	10
Scrum-half	Jerome Gallion (1978–86)	10
No.8	Imanol Harinordoquy (2002–11)	12
Flanker	Olivier Magne (1997–2007)	14
Lock	Lionel Nallet (2000–11)	9
Prop	Amedée Domenech (1954–63)	8
	Robert Paparemborde (1975–83)	8
Hooker	Raphael Ibanez (1997–2007)	7

FRANCE BLOWN AWAY IN WELLINGTON

A trip to rugby giants New Zealand is not always the best way to prepare for a World Cup campaign and when France travelled to the southern hemisphere to face the All Blacks in June 2007, they returned licking their wounds. If the 42–11 reverse in the first Test at Auckland had been bad, the result of the second Test at Wellington was even worse: France crumbled to a 61–10 loss – the heaviest defeat in their international history.

IF IT ISN'T BROKEN, DON'T FIX IT

France romped to their second-ever grand slam in convincing and record-breaking fashion in the 1977 Five Nations Championship, recording wins over Wales (16–9 in Paris), England (4–3 at Twickenham), Scotland (29–3 in Paris) and Ireland (15–6 in Dublin), but what made their effort all the more laudable was the fact that they used the same 15 players throughout the course of the campaign. It is the only instance of a team remaining unchanged throughout the entire length of the tournament in history.

ABOVE: Philippe Saint-André dazzled on the wing for France in the 1990s, scoring 32 tries – second on the country's all-time try-scoring list. He took over as national coach in 2011.

COACHES

Name	Tenure
Jean Prat	1964–68
Fernand Cazenave	1968–73
Jean Desclaux	1973–80
Jacques Fouroux	1981–90
Daniel Dubroca	1990–91
Pierre Berbizier	1991–95
Jean-Claude Skrela	1995–99
Bernard Laporte	1999–2007
Marc Lièvremont	2007–2011
Philippe Saint-André	2011–present

FRANCE'S MOST CAPPED PLAYER

Fabien Pelous was a formidable line-out jumper and a marauding presence in the loose, who will be remembered as one of the greats of modern rugby. He won his first cap against Romania in 1995 and went on to add another 117 – including a record-equalling 41 appearances as captain – before his retirement following France's Rugby World Cup semi-final defeat against England in 2007. He is the most capped France international of all time.

RIGHT: Fabien Pelous bowed out of international rugby after the 2007 Rugby World Cup semi-final defeat to England as France's most capped player of all time (with 118 caps).

THE LITTLE CORPORAL INSPIRES FRANCE

Nicknamed the 'Little Corporal' because of his diminutive 5ft 3in (1.6m) stature, what Jacques Fouroux may have lacked in height he more than made up for with brawn and an in-your-face attitude, both on the pitch (where he made 27 appearances for France at scrum-half between 1972 and 1977) and as Les Bleus' coach (between 1981 and 1990). His tactical approach as coach, based on a massive pack, may not have been to everyone's liking – removed as it was from France's traditional, free-flowing game – but it was supremely effective: during Fouroux's tenure, France won the Five Nations Championship six times (with two grand slams) and reached the 1987 Rugby World Cup final. No France coach since has come close to matching his achievements.

RIGHT: One of the finest full-backs in rugby history when he was in full flow, Serge Blanco scored a record 38 tries for France during his 11-year international career.

LEFT: Jacques Fouroux was an inspirational figure for France both as a player and a coach.

BELOW: Christophe Lamaison ended his 37-match international career in 2001 as France's all-time leading points scorer with 380.

BRILLIANT BLANCO SETS ALL-TIME TRY-SCORING MARK

In full flow, Serge Blanco was one of the most majestic sights in rugby history. Born in Venezuela, he grew up in France and made his debut for Les Bleus against South Africa in 1980 on the wing, a testament to the searing turn of pace that would become the hallmark of his career. He eventually switched to full-back and went on to make 93 appearances for his country before his retirement in 1991, scoring a national record 38 tries.

THE POINTS MACHINE

Christophe Lamaison made his debut for France against South Africa in November 1996 and went on to become a key member of his country's grand slam-winning sides of 1997 and 1998. His finest hour came during perhaps the most memorable win in France's history – their come-from-behind victory against New Zealand in the 1999 Rugby World Cup semi-final. Producing an inspirational performance at fly-half, Lamaison contributed 28 points (23 of them in the second half) to help his side produce one of the greatest upsets in the tournament's history. Although never the quickest of players, what he lacked in pace he more than made up for with his kicking ability. By the time he made the last of his 37 appearances for Les Bleus, he had scored 380 points (2 tries, 59 conversions, 78 penalties and 6 drop-goals). No player in France's history has scored more.

MOST POINTS: TOP TEN

Pos	Points	Player (Span)
1	380	Christophe Lamaison (1996–2001)
2	367	Thierry Lacroix (1989–97)
3	357	Dimitri Yachvili (2002–11)
4	354	Didier Camberabero (1982–93)
5	267	Gerald Merceron (1999–2003)
6	265	Jean-Pierre Romeu (1972–77)
7	252	Thomas Castaignede (1995–2007)
=	252	Frederic Michalak (2001–10)
9	233	Serge Blanco (1980–1991)
10	232	Morgan Parra (2008–11)

GEORGIA

Georgia gained independence in April 1991 following the break-up of the Soviet Union and the country's development as an international rugby-playing nation is still in its infancy. What Georgia, nicknamed The Lelos, have achieved in such a short space of time, however, has been considerable: they have won the European Nations Cup – the continent's second-tier tournament – on three occasions and have qualified for three successive Rugby World Cups, in 2003, 2007 and 2011.

THE LELOS FIND THEIR FORM

Georgia could not have enjoyed a better build-up to the 2011 Rugby World Cup: they put together the longest winning streak in their history. The run started on 20 November 2010 with an impressive 22–15 home victory over Canada in Tbilisi, included a thumping 60–0 victory over Spain on 12 February 2011 and stretched to eight matches before they suffered a 15–6 defeat to Scotland in their opening game at the 2011 Rugby World Cup.

BELOW: Great versatility helped Malkhaz Urjukashvili to a Georgia record 64 caps.

OVERALL TEAM RECORD

Span	Mat	Won	Lost	Draw	%	For	Aga	Diff	Tries	Conv	Pens	Drop
1989–2011	136	82	49	5	62.13	3113	2546	+567	380	244	222	25

TRY GLUT FOR GEORGIA AGAINST SORRY CZECHS

Georgia proved their tag as the giants of European second-tier rugby in their Six Nations B clash against the Czech Republic at Tbilisi on 7 April 2007. The Lelos raced into a 57–0 half-time lead and ended the match – in which they scored a staggering 17 tries – as 98–3 winners. It remains the largest victory in Georgia's history.

MOST CAPPED PLAYER

A rare figure in international rugby – given that he has represented his country in every position in the backs bar scrum-half – Malkhaz Urjukashvili made his debut for Georgia against Croatia on 12 October 1997. A stalwart in the Lelos' Rugby World Cup campaigns of 2003, 2007 and 2001, he has gone on to collect a national record 69 caps.

MR RELIABLE

In June 2006, Paliko Jimsheladze became the first player in Georgia history to win 50 caps. He made his debut back in 1995, against Romania, and marked the occasion by scoring a hat-trick of tries: from that moment, until his retirement following the 2007 Rugby World Cup, 56 caps later, he was a regular source of points for his country, registering a national record 320.

LONGEST LOSING STREAK

Georgia's longest losing streak is nine matches. It started with a 19–6 defeat to Romania at Tbilisi on 30 March 2003 and continued with a 33–22 reverse against Italy at Asti on 6 September 2003, defeat in all four 2003 Rugby World Cup matches and a 19–14 loss to Portugal in Tbilisi on 14 February 2003. The sorry record-breaking run came to an end when the Lelos mustered a 6–6 draw against Spain in Tarragona on 22 February 2004.

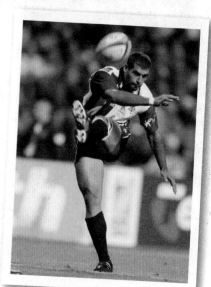

ABOVE: Paliko Jimsheladze played for Georgia for more than a decade, appeared in two Rugby World Cups and scored a record 320 points.

GEORGIA FREEZE ON THE GAME'S BIGGEST STAGE

Matches against world rugby's more powerful nations have proved difficult for Georgia and their inability to cope with the step up in class was never more painfully evident than when the Lelos faced off against England at Perth in the group stages of the 2003 Rugby World Cup. Trailing 34–3 at the interval, the floodgates opened in the second half as England ran in 12 tries en route to a thumping 84–6 victory. It is Georgia's heaviest defeat in international rugby.

MOST POINTS: TOP FIVE

Pos	Points	Player (Span)
1	320	Paliko Jimsheladze (1995–2007)
2	313	Malkhaz Urjukashvili (1997–2011)
3	288	Merab Kvirikashvili (2003–11)
4	104	Nugzar Dzagnidze (1989–95)
5	98	Lasha Malaguradze (2008–11)

LONGEST-SERVING CAPTAIN

A bulky but crafty lock, who can also play at No.8, Ilia Zedginidze made his debut for Georgia as a 21-year-old against Ireland on 14 November 1998, but had to wait until 2000 before establishing himself in the Lelos line-up. Appointed national captain in 2002, he had the distinction of leading his side at both the 2003 and 2007 Rugby World Cups, although his experiences on the game's biggest stage were a bittersweet affair, as both were ended prematurely through injury, the latter of which – a broken kneecap against Ireland in 2007 – forced him to announce his retirement from the international game. However, a return to form and fitness saw him back in the Georgia ranks in February 2009 and, although no longer captain, he holds the national record for having led his side on the most occasions (32).

GEORGIA'S TRY KING

Nicknamed 'Gorgodzilla' by his team-mates because of his imposing 6ft 5in (1.96m) stature, Mamuka Gorgodze made his debut for Georgia as an 18-year-old in March 2003 when he came on as a replacement against Russia. Although he missed out on selection for Georgia's matches at the 2003 Rugby World Cup, he has since gone on to become a

ABOVE: Ilia Zedginidze led Georgia at the 2003 and 2007 Rugby World Cups.

BELOW: Merab Kvirikashvili was on the money against Germany in February 2010, scoring a national record 32 points.

cornerstone of the Lelos pack (at either lock or in the back row), making 41 appearances and scoring a national record 19 tries, including three in a match on two occasions – against the Czech Republic (on 12 June 2005) and against Spain (on 26 April 2008).

CRACKING KVIRIKASHVILI SETS NEW MARK

Merab Kvirikashvili was the main architect behind Georgia's thumping 77–3 victory over Germany in the Rugby World Cup qualifying match at Tbilisi on 6 February 2010. The full-back contributed 32 points to the Lelos cause – two tries and 11 conversions – to set a new national record for the most points by a player in a single match.

MOST TRIES IN A MATCH

The Georgia record for the most tries in a match by a player is three, a feat achieved six times, by five players (Mamuka Gorgodze has done it twice). Those registering a hat-trick of tries in a match are: Paliko Jimsheladze and Archil Kavtarahvili (both against Bulgaria in Sofia on 23 March 1995); Gorgodze (against the Czech Republic in Kutaisi on 12 June 2005 and against Spain at Tbilisi on 26 April 2008); and David Dadunashvili and Malkhaz Urjukashvili (both against the Czech Republic at Tbilisi on 7 April 2007).

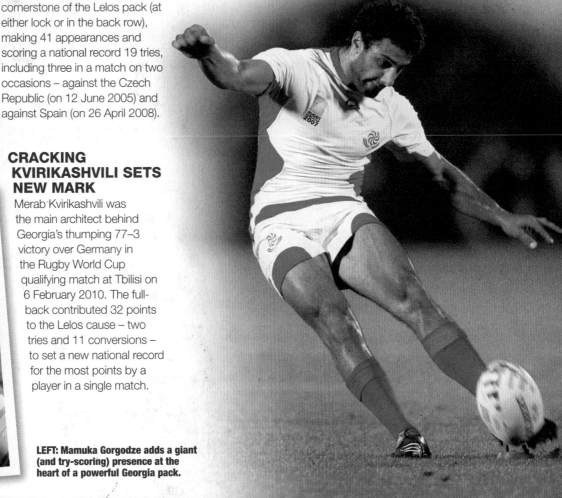

LEFT: Mamuka Gorgodze adds a giant (and try-scoring) presence at the heart of a powerful Georgia pack.

IRELAND

With only 54,500 registered players in Ireland, one could make a strong case that Ireland has continually over-achieved on the rugby pitch over the years. However, because of the glittering array of talent the country has produced, two grand slam wins in over a century of competition and a failure to progress beyond the quarter-finals of the Rugby World Cup mean that the men from the Emerald Isle are forever labelled with the under-achievers' tag.

GRAND SLAM GLORY

A crowd of 32,000 gathered at Belfast's Ravenhill stadium on 13 March 1948 to watch a moment of potential history. Having beaten France (13–6), England (11–10) and Scotland (6–0) in their first three matches of the 1948 Five Nations Championship, Ireland had a shot at registering the first grand slam in their history ... and only Wales stood in their way. The home side took the lead when winger Barney Mullan crossed the line; then Welsh centre Bleddyn Williams scored a try of his own to leave the scores locked at 3–3 at half-time and tensions running as high as ever. Then, seven minutes into the second half, came the most famous moment in Ireland's rugby history: prop John Daly crossed the line to hand his side a lead they would never relinquish and Ireland had won their first ever grand slam.

OVERALL TEAM RECORD

Span	Mat	Won	Lost	Draw	%	For	Aga	Diff	Tries	Conv	Pens	Drop	GfM
1875–2011	611	257	325	29	44.43	8299	8354	-55	1051	603	835	102	3

ENDING THE 61-YEAR DROUGHT

If the Irish rugby-loving public thought that their side's 1948 grand slam success would signal the start of a period of unprecedented success for their team, they were wrong. By the turn of the 21st century, Ireland had won a further seven Five Nations Championship titles (with three triple crowns) but a second grand slam success continued to elude them. That all changed in 2009: having beaten France (30–21), Italy (38–9), England (14–13) and Scotland (22–15), they held their nerve to beat Wales 17–15 in Cardiff and put an end to a frustrating 61-year wait.

ABOVE: Ireland ended 61 years of hurt when they won the Six Nations Championship grand slam in 2009.

LEFT: Denis Hickie is one of three Ireland players to have scored four tries in a match, a feat he achieved in a 2003 Rugby World Cup warm-up match against Italy.

MOST TRIES IN A MATCH

The Ireland record for the most tries in a single match is four, a feat achieved by three players: Brian Robinson (against Zimbabwe at Lansdowne Road on 6 October 1991); Keith Wood (against the United States at Lansdowne Road on 2 October 1999) and Denis Hickie, against Italy at Limerick on 30 August 2003.

MOST TRIES: TOP TEN

Pos	Tries	Player (Span)
1	45	Brian O'Driscoll (1999–2011)
2	29	Denis Hickie (1997–2007)
3	21	Shane Horgan (2000–09)
4	19	Tommy Bowe (2004–11)
=	19	Girvan Dempsey (1998–2008)
5	18	Geordan Murphy (2000–11)
6	17	Brendan Mullin (1984–95)
8	16	Ronan O'Gara (2000–11)
9	15	Kevin Maggs (1997–2005)
=	15	Keith Wood (1994–2003)

RIGHT: Willie John McBride (about to catch the ball) is one of eight Irishmen to be inducted into the International Rugby Hall of Fame.

IRELAND'S LONGEST WINNING STREAK

Ireland's longest winning streak is ten consecutive victories. The run started with a 39–8 victory over Romania at Limerick on 7 September 2002 and featured a significant win over Australia (18–9 at Lansdowne Road on 9 November 2002) and Six Nations Championship victories against Scotland (36–6), Italy (37–13), France (15–12) and Wales (25–24) before coming to an abrupt and definitive end in the grand slam decider against England at Lansdowne Road on 30 March 2003, when the visitors took the spoils following a comprehensive 42–6 victory.

INTERNATIONAL RUGBY HALL OF FAME INDUCTEES

Name	(Span, Caps)
Mike Gibson	(1964–79, 69 caps)
Tom Kiernan	(1960–73, 54 caps)
Jack Kyle	(1947–58, 46 caps)
Willie John McBride	(1962–75, 63 caps)
Syd Millar	(1958–70, 37 caps)
Tony O'Reilly	(1955–70, 29 caps)
Fergus Slattery	(1970–84, 61 caps)
Keith Wood	(1994–2003, 58 caps)

HONOURS

Rugby World Cup:
(best finish) – quarter-finals (1987, 1991, 1995, 2003, 2011)

Six Nations:
winners – 1894#, 1896, 1906*, 1912*, 1926*, 1927*, 1932*, 1935, 1939*, 1948 (GS), 1949#, 1951, 1973*, 1974, 1982#, 1983*, 1985#, 2009 (GS)

* = shared; (GS) = grand slam; # = triple crown

ALL BLACKS RUN RIOT IN WELLINGTON

Having come agonizingly close to recording their first-ever victory on New Zealand soil in the first Test of their 1992 tour to the southern hemisphere (they lost 24–21 in Dunedin), Ireland must have fancied their chances of a win a week later at Wellington when they trailed 15–6 at half-time. However, any Irish hopes of victory soon evaporated when the All Blacks found their stride in the second half, running in 11 tries to condemn the men in green to a 59–6 defeat – the largest in their history.

LEFT: Now the most capped Ireland flanker of all time with 72 appearances, David Wallace has scored 12 tries in more than a decade of action. No Ireland flanker has scored more.

ENDURING THE WORST OF TIMES

Ireland made an inglorious start to international rugby: they lost their first-ever match – a 20-a-side affair against England at The Oval on 15 February 1875 (by two goals to nil) – and went on to lose their next nine matches, before enjoying the taste of victory for the first time following a two goals to nil victory over Scotland at Belfast on 19 February 1881. Not that the victory sparked an immediate upturn in Irish fortunes: after losing against Wales and drawing against England, they then embarked on an 11-match losing streak – the longest in their history. That was not an isolated case of Irish misery, however: they matched their record-breaking losing streak between 12 October 1991 and 20 February 1993.

ALL-TIME LEADING TRY-SCORERS: BY POSITION

Position	Player (Span)	Tries
Full-back	Girvan Dempsey (1999–2008)	15
Winger	Denis Hickie (1997–2007)	29
Centre	Brian O'Driscoll (1999–2011)	45
Fly-half	Ronan O'Gara (2000–11)	14*
Scrum-half	Peter Stringer (2000–11)	6
No.8	Jamie Heaslip (2006–11)	7
Flanker	David Wallace (2000–11)	12
Lock	Malcolm O'Kelly (1997–2009)	8
Prop	Marcus Horan (2000–11)	6
Hooker	Keith Wood (1994–2003)	15

* = Also scored two tries as a replacement;

MOST CAPS: TOP TEN

Pos	Caps	Player (Span)
1	117	Brian O'Driscoll (1999–2011)
2	116	Ronan O'Gara (2000–11)
3	105	John Hayes (2000–11)
4	98	Peter Stringer (2000–11)
5	92	Malcolm O'Kelly (1997–2009)
6	82	Girvan Dempsey (1998–2008)
=	82	Paul O'Connell (2002–11)
8	80	Donncha O'Callaghan (2003–11)
9	72	David Humphreys (1996–2005)
=	72	Geordan Murphy (2000–11)
=	72	David Wallace (2000–11)

COOL-HAND O'GARA HITS HEADY HEIGHTS

American-born, but Irish through and through, it took time for Ronan O'Gara to wrestle the No.10 jersey away from David Humphreys, but by the time the former Under-21 star had established himself in Ireland's senior line-up, he was already a top-level outside-half. An integral part of Ireland's success in the early 2000s, on 20 June 2003 against Samoa in Apia he broke the national record for the most points scored in a match (32), and in Ireland's 2006 Six Nations opener against Italy he overtook Humphreys as his country's all-time leading points-scorer. By 2011, the Munster fly-half had racked up 1,075 international points in 118 appearances (including two caps for the Lions) – only three players in the game's history had scored more.

ABOVE: No international hooker in history has scored more tries than Ireland's Keith Wood (15).

LEFT: Ronan O'Gara is Ireland's all-time time leading points-scorer (1,075), passing the 1,000 points barrier against Wales in the 2011 Six Nations Championship.

WORLD RECORD-BREAKING WOOD

A marauding presence for Ireland for the best part of a decade, hooker Keith Wood made his international debut against Australia in 1994 and went on to win 58 caps for his country (36 of them as captain) before his retirement following the 2003 Rugby World Cup. The inaugural winner of the IRB Player of the Year award in 2001 – he remains the only Irishman to have received the award – he finished his career with 15 international tries to his name, a world record for a hooker.

IRELAND SHOW NO MERCY TO UNCLE SAM

As has become the custom for the game's elite teams in recent years, Ireland used their match against the United States at Manchester, New Hampshire, on 10 June 2000 as a chance to experiment, handing debuts to five players but, regardless of the changes, they still proved far too strong for their hosts. After establishing a 31–3 lead at half-time, the men in green ran riot in the second half en route to a 83–3 victory to record the biggest win in Ireland's history. Ireland ran in a total of 13 tries in the rout.

IRELAND STAR AND BUSINESS MAGNATE

Tony O'Reilly is a unique figure in world rugby. A talented sportsman in his youth and a graduate of University College, Dublin, he excelled at rugby and made his Ireland debut aged 18 against France in 1955. He went on to collect a further 28 caps for his country (and ten for the British and Irish Lions, for whom he scored an all-time record ten tries), with his last outing for Ireland coming in 1970. It is for his successes in the business world, however, that he is better known: he was chairman of Heinz between 1987 and 1998, before going on to establish a media empire and becoming Ireland's first billionaire.

IN B.O.D. IRELAND CONTINUES TO TRUST

Scintillating in attack and dynamic in defence, the qualities that would establish Brian O'Driscoll as the greatest centre in the modern game became apparent to an international audience in only his tenth game, against France in 2000, when he scored a hat-trick of tries to lead Ireland to their first win in Paris for 28 years. A decade later and Ireland's most capped player (with 117 caps) is still the first name on his country's teamsheet: a talismanic leader (he has led Ireland a record 80 times between 2002 and 2011), he is also his country's all-time leading try-scorer (with 45 tries).

COACHES

Name	Tenure
Ronnie Dawson	1971–75
Roly Meates	1975–77
Noel Murphy	1977–80
Willie John McBride	1980–84
Mick Doyle	1984–87
Jim Davidson	1987–90
Ciaran Fitzgerald	1990–92
Gerry Murphy	1993–95
Murray Kidd	1995–97
Brian Ashton	1997–98
Warren Gatland	1998–2001
Eddie O'Sullivan	2001–08
Declan Kidney	2008–present

MOST POINTS: TOP TEN

Pos	Points	Player (Span)
1	1075	Ronan O'Gara (2000–11)
2	560	David Humphreys (1996–2005)
3	308	Michael Kiernan (1982–91)
4	296	Eric Elwood (1993–99)
5	240	Brian O'Driscoll (1999–2011)
6	217	Ollie Campbell (1976–84)
7	161	Jonathan Sexton (2009–11)
8	158	Tom Kiernan (1960–73)
9	145	Denis Hickie (1997–2007)
10	113	Tony Ward (1978–87)

O'SULLIVAN PROMPTS THE GOOD TIMES

Eddie O'Sullivan first cut his teeth as a rugby coach with Galway club Montivea RFC before earning his spurs as a rugby development officer with the Irish RFU and as coach of the 1996 triple crown-winning Ireland Under-21 side. His appointment as national coach in November 2001 – following the IRFU's controversial decision not to renew Warren Gatland's contract – sparked a hugely successful period in Ireland's rugby history. Under his charge they collected three triple crowns and reached as high as third in the world rankings. He resigned following Ireland's poor 2008 Six Nations campaign, but with 51 wins is the most successful Ireland coach of all time.

ITALY

Italy's prize for years of impressive results in the second tier of European rugby was a place in the 2000 Six Nations Championship and a revised status as one of the world's elite rugby-playing nations. It is a billing the Azzurri have struggled to live up to, but there have been many adventures with a string of notable performances (both team and individual) along the way.

20TH TIME LUCKY

By 2007, Italy had recorded three victories in 38 Six Nations matches, but all of them had been at home; an away victory – a result that would have have been a measure of real progress – continued to elude them. That all changed against Scotland at Murrayfield on 24 February 2007. A fine performance, capped by a 22-point display from Andrea Scanavacca, saw Italy run out comprehensive 37–17 winners to register their first-ever Six Nations away win at their 20th attempt.

LEFT: Sergio Parisse (facing camera) celebrates one of Italy's greatest achievements on a rugby field: an away victory (against Scotland at Murrayfield in 2007) in the Six Nations Championship.

THE SWEET TASTE OF SUCCESS

Italy's last-ever involvement in the European Nations Cup – prior to their elevation to the Six Nations Championship in 2000 – provided them with their one moment of triumph in the competition. Prior to that moment, they had developed a habit of falling at the final hurdle, finishing as runners-up on seven occasions. Until 22 March 1997, that is, when they beat France 42–30 in Grenoble – still their only victory on French soil – to win the trophy for the first time.

KINGS OF SECOND-TIER RUGBY

There is no finer example of why Italy's domination of second-tier European rugby in the mid-1990s prompted a growing clamour for their inclusion in what was the Five Nations Championship than their match against the Czech Republic at Viadana on 18 May 1994. Italy put their hapless opponents to the sword, racing to a 71–0 half-time lead before easing to the biggest win in their history, a 16-try, 104–8 romp.

MOST TRIES IN A MATCH

The Italy record for the most tries by a player in a single match is four, a feat achieved by two players: Renzo Cova, against Belgium at Paris on 10 October 1937; and Ivan Francescato, against Morocco at Carcassonne on 19 June 1993.

BELOW: Ivan Francescato is one of only two Italian players to have scored three tries in a match (against Morocco in June 1993). Tragically he died of a heart attack, aged only 31, in January 1999.

MOST TRIES: TOP TEN

Pos	Tries	Player (Span)
1	25	Marcello Cuttitta (1987–99)
2	22	Paolo Vaccari (1991–2003)
3	21	Carlo Checchinato (1990–2004)
=	21	Manrico Marchetto (1972–81)
5	19	Alessandro Troncon (1994–2007)
6	17	Mirco Bergamasco (2002–11)
=	17	Serafino Ghizzoni (1977–87)
=	17	Massimo Mascioletti (1977–90)
9	16	Ivan Francescato (1990–97)
10	14	Mauro Bergamasco (1998–2011)
=	14	Kaine Robertson (2004–10)

COACHES

Name	Tenure
Pierre Villepreux	1978–81
Paolo Paladini/ Marco Pulli	1981–85
Marco Bollesan	1985–88
Loreto Cucchiarelli	1988–89
Bertrand Fourcade	1989–93
Georges Coste	1993–99
Massimo Mascioletti	1999–2000
Brad Johnstone	2000–02
John Kirwan	2002–05
Pierre Berbizier	2005–07
Nick Mallett	2007–11
Jacques Brunel	2011–present

ABOVE: Former Azzuri captain Marco Bollesan held the role as Italy's head coach between 1985 and 1988.

ITALY GET OFF TO A LOSING START

In the 27 matches played between the two countries, Italy have only ever lost to Spain on three occasions, but the first of those defeats could not have come at a more inopportune moment: in Italy's first-ever match. On 20 May 1929 in Barcelona, it was the hosts who celebrated after Italy slipped to a disappointing 9–0 defeat.

ITALY'S LONGEST WINNING STREAK

Inconsistency is a long-standing feature of Italian rugby and has become a watchword of the national team's performances in recent years: they have never been able to string together a significant run of impressive performances that would truly show they have taken a step up to the next level. In 81 years of international rugby their best winning streak is a mere six consecutive victories, between 12 May 1968 (17–3 against Portugal) and 10 May 1969 (30–0 against Belgium).

CRUSHED BY LIFE IN THE FAST LANE

Italy had little time to dwell on the considerable positives they could take from their narrow, but highly creditable, 13–12 victory over Argentina in Cordoba on 28 June 2008 because another 511 days would pass before they tasted victory again. During that time, which included a series of autumn Tests against Australia, Argentina and the Pacific Islanders, a disappointing 2009 Six Nations campaign and a daunting tour to Australia and New Zealand, they lost 13 straight matches – the longest losing streak in their history. The miserable run came to an end when they beat Samoa 24–6 at Ascoli on 28 November 2009.

BOKS DISH OUT THE HARSHEST OF RUGBY LESSONS

Just six months before they were due to make their debut appearance in the Six Nations Championship, Italy received the harshest possible reminder of how tough life would be as a top-tier rugby-playing nation. Against South Africa, on 19 June 1999 at Durban, they found themselves on the wrong end of a hammering: 40 down by half-time, they slipped to a humiliating 101–0 whitewash – it remains the heaviest defeat in their history.

Right: An icon of Italian rugby, Mauro Bergamasco has scored more tries than any other flanker in his country's history.

HONOURS

Rugby World Cup:
(best finish) – group stages (1987, 1991, 1995, 2003, 2007, 2011)

Six Nations:
(best finish) – fifth (2003, 2007)

ALL-TIME LEADING TRY-SCORERS: BY POSITION

Position	Player (Span)	Tries
Full-back	Paolo Vaccari (1991–2003)	5*
Winger	Marcello Cuttitta (1987–99)	25
Centre	Ivan Francescato (1990–97)	11
Fly-half	Diego Dominguez (1991–2003)	9
Scrum-half	Alessandro Troncon (1994–2007)	18
No.8	Carlo Checchinato (1990–2004)	11
Flanker	Mauro Bergamasco (1998–2010)	13
Lock	Carlo Checchinato (1990–2004)	9
Prop	Martin Castrogiovanni (2002–11)	10
Hooker	Fabio Ongaro (2000–11)	5

* also scored 17 tries as a winger.

A CENTURY OF CAPS FOR TRONCON

Alessandro Troncon made his Italy debut when he came on as a replacement against Spain in Parma on 7 May 1994 and soon established himself as a permanent fixture in the side, going on to form a legendary half-back partnership with Diego Dominguez (the pair played together in more than 50 Tests). Captain of his country on 21 occasions, he made his 100th appearance for the Azzurri during Italy's 31–5 victory over Portugal at the 2007 Rugby World Cup, becoming only the seventh player in the game's history to pass a century of caps. He retired at the end of the tournament as Italy's most capped player (with 101 caps) and fifth on his country's try-scoring list (with 19 tries). He is now a member of the Azzuri's coaching staff.

ABOVE: Diego Dominguez is one of only five players in international rugby history to have scored more than 1,000 points.

BELOW: Scrum-half Alessandro Troncon is the only Italy player in history to pass the 100-cap milestone.

MOST CAPS: TOP TEN

Pos	Caps	Player (Span)
1	101	Alessandro Troncon (1994–2007)
2	91	Andrea Lo Cicero Vaina (2000–11)
3	88	Mauro Bergamasco (1998–2011)
=	88	Marco Bortolami (2001–11)
5	85	Mirco Bergamasco (2002–11))
6	83	Carlo Checchinato (1990–2004)
=	83	Sergio Parisse (2002–2011)
=	83	Salvatore Perugini (2000–11)
9	82	Martin Castrogoivanni (2002–11)
10	80	Fabio Ongaro (2000–11)

DIEGO'S SUCCESSFUL RETURN TO THE MOTHERLAND

Frustrated by the lack of opportunities in Argentina – although he played two Tests for the country of his birth (scoring 27 points) – Diego Dominguez turned to Italy, his mother's homeland, for the chance to establish himself in international rugby. And what an impact he had on the Azzurri. He made his debut on 2 March 1991 (against France in Rome), went on to collect a further 73 caps and scored 983 points to become Italy's all-time leading points-scorer. He is one of only five players in history (Dan Carter, Jonny Wilkinson, Neil Jenkins and Ronan O'Gara being the others) to have scored more than 1,000 points in international rugby.

MOST SUCCESSFUL CAPTAIN

Fortunate in some respects to have led the Azzurri when they were the dominant force in the second tier of European rugby, Marco Bollesan is the most successful captain in Italy's history. The No.8 was at the helm for 37 matches between 1968 and 1975 and led his country to 15 wins in that time.

OVERALL TEAM RECORD

Span	Mat	Won	Lost	Draw	%	For	Aga	Diff	Tries	Conv	Pens	Drop
1929–2011	417	167	236	14	41.72	7220	8943	-1723	814	513	784	95

CUTTITTA FINDS HIS TRY-SCORING EDGE

Raised in South Africa by Italian parents and twin brother of prop Massimo (who played for the Azzurri on 60 occasions), Marcello Cuttitta scored a try on his Italy debut, against Portugal in Lisbon on 18 January 1987, and went on to become a regular fixture in the side for the next 12 years. During that time he scored an all-time Italy record 25 tries, including three in a match against Morocco in Casablanca on 19 June 1993.

BETTARELLO FULL HOUSE SEALS BIG ITALY WIN

Stefano Bettarello was Italy's hero of the hour as the Azzurri completed a highly encouraging victory over Canada in Toronto on 1 July 1993. The Rovigo-born fly-half completed the full house, with one try, two conversions, five penalties and two drop goals (for a total of 29 points, an individual record for Italy in a single match) to help his side to a memorable 37–9 victory.

LEFT: Marcello Cuttitta tops Italy's all-time try-scoring list with 25, averaging a try every 2.4 matches.

DOMINGUEZ GETS ITALY OFF TO A FLYER

Italy could not have wished for a better start to life in the top tier of European rugby. On 5 February 2000, in Rome, Diego Dominguez was the hero, kicking an impressive 29 points as Italy thrilled a partisan Stadio Flaminio crowd by securing a memorable 34–20 victory over Scotland In their first-ever Six Nations match.

MOST POINTS: TOP TEN

Pos	Points	Player (Span)
1	983	Diego Dominguez (1991–2003)
2	483	Stefano Bettarello (1979–88)
3	294	Luigi Troiani (1985–95)
4	254	Ramiro Pez (2000–07)
5	250	Mirco Bergamasco (2002–11)
6	147	David Bortolussi (2006–08)
7	133	Ennio Ponzi (1973–77)
8	110	Marcello Cuttitta (1987–99)
9	107	Paolo Vaccari (1991–2003)
10	105	Carlo Checchinato (1990–2004)
=	105	Gert Peens (2002–06)

PARISSE THE PRODIGY

Sergio Parisse was thrown into the deep end when he made his debut for Italy as an 18-year-old against New Zealand in Hamilton on 8 June 2002. Such was the impression he made that he emerged from the 64–10 mauling with his reputation enhanced. It came as no surprise: his supreme handling ability, exceptional line-out skills and a significant presence in both defence and attack – all combined with a supreme work ethic – marked him out as a potentially great player. Appointed captain in 2008, he won his 50th cap in that season's Six Nations and ended the year by becoming the first, and to date only Italian player to have been nominated for the IRB Player of the Year award – a prize ultimately won by Wales's wing wizard Shane Williams.

LEFT: Sergio Parisse, a player who would have graced any international XV, has been a consistent standout performer in a struggling Italian side since he made his debut as an 18-year-old in June 2002.

PORTUGAL

Portugal lost their first-ever international match, against Spain in April 1935, and had to wait 31 years before recording their first win, but long gone are the days when "Os Lobos" (the Wolves) were considered true minnows of the game. A surprise victory at the 2003–04 European Nations Cup and qualification for the 2007 Rugby World Cup both testify to the team's recent upsurge in fortunes.

EARNING THEIR PLACE IN RUGBY'S BIG TIME

A third-place finish in the 2004–06 European Nations Cup, which doubled as the first round of qualifying for the 2007 Rugby World Cup in France, saw Portugal qualify for a three-match series with Italy and Russia in October 2006, with one place going to the winner. A heavy defeat to Italy (83–0) meant they needed to win their match against Russia to keep their hopes alive: they won 26–23 to enter round six.

The Wolves then faced a winner-takes-all, two-legged encounter with Georgia: they lost the first match and drew the second, but there was still a chance – they faced a final repechage round against Uruguay, with the outcome again decided over two legs. Portugal won 12–5 in Lisbon and lost 18–12 in Montevideo, but they had secured the greatest moment in their history: qualification for the Rugby World Cup for the first time, by the slenderest of margins – 24–23 on aggregate.

MOST TRIES: TOP FIVE

Pos	Tries	Player (Span)
1	18	Antonio Aguilar (1999–2011)
2	14	Diogo Mateus (2000–10)
3	10	Vasco Uva (2003–11)
=	10	Goncalo Foro (2007–11)
5	8	Nuno Garvao de Carvalho (2001–05)
=	8	Rohan Hoffman (1996–2002)

MAJOR CONTRIBUTOR FOR THE LOBOS

A civil engineer away from the rugby field, fly-half Goncalo Malheiro made his debut for the Wolves against Morocco in Casablanca as far back as 25 April 1998, but it wasn't until 2003 that he made the Portugal No.10 jersey his own. Since then he became an integral part of the national team (with two appearances in their Rugby World Cup fixtures in 2007), contributing a Portugal all-time record 231 points in 37 matches.

KING OF THE TRIES

Winger Antonio Aguilar made his Portugal debut against the Netherlands in Amsterdam on 6 March 1999 and scored his first try in his third match (in a 33–24 defeat to Uruguay in the 1999 Rugby World Cup repechage match in Lisbon). An ever-present in the squad ever since, he played in three of Portugal's four matches at the 2007 Rugby World Cup and has scored a record 18 international tries for his country.

ABOVE: Goncalo Malheiro tops the points-scoring chart for Portugal with 231 in 37 matches.

BELOW: Antonio Aguilar is Portugal's all-time leading try-scorer with 18.

MOST TRIES IN A MATCH

The Portugal record for the most tries by one player in a match is three, a feat achieved by three players: Nuno Garvao de Carvalho (against Spain at Ibiza on 21 March 2004), Goncalo Malheiro (against the Barbarians at Lisbon on 10 June 2004 – Portugal awarded caps for the game) and Goncalo Foro (against Germany at Heusenstamm on 27 February 2010).

OVERALL TEAM RECORD

Span	Mat	Won	Lost	Draw	%	For	Aga	Diff	Tries	Conv	Pens	Drop
1935–2011	212	87	114	11	43.63	3481	4611	-1130	211	138	229	24

PORTUGAL HIT THEIR STRIDE

Portugal's Six Nations B match against Germany at Heusenstamm on 27 February 2010, which also doubled as a 2011 Rugby World Cup qualifying match, was one to remember. Leading 31–0 at half-time, the Lobos scored nine tries in the match (a joint national record) – three of them by winger Goncalo Foro – en route to a comfortable 69–0 victory, the biggest win in the country's history.

A NEW LEADER FOR A NEW ERA

Portuguese rugby faced difficult times after the 2007 Rugby World Cup, as several long-standing members of the squad saw the end of the tournament as the perfect time to bring down the curtain on their international careers, and a fifth-place showing in the 2006–08 European Nations Cup (their worst-ever finish) and failure to qualify for the 2011 Rugby World Cup testify to the Lobos' subsequent decline. In 2008, veteran hooker Joao Correia was the man appointed to lead Portuguese rugby into a new era, and although results may not have gone his way, Correia has gone on to break the national record for the most matches as captain (20).

FERREIRA'S 14 YEARS AT THE COALFACE

A prop forward or hooker, Joaquim Ferreira made his senior rugby debut in 1990 at the tender age of 17 and went on to take his bow for the Lobos three years later, against Romania in Lisbon on 3 April 1993; aged 20, he was still phenomenally young for a player in that position in international rugby. A loyal servant of the Portugal team, it was fitting that he scored a try in his final match (he was also made captain), during the Wolves' honourable 14–10 defeat to Romania at the 2007 Rugby World Cup in Toulouse. He retired from international rugby having won a national record 84 caps.

ABOVE: Thiery Teixeira scored a national record 30 points against Georgia at Lisbon in 2000, but still ended up on the losing side.

BELOW: Portugal's most-capped player, prop forward Joaquim Ferreira carries the ball against Romania at Toulouse in the 2007 Rugby World Cup, a match in which he made the last of his 84 international appearances.

MOST POINTS: TOP FIVE

Pos	Points	Player (Span)
1	231	Goncalo Malheiro (1998–2007)
2	166	Pedro Cabral (2006–11)
3	110	Pedro Leal (2004–11)
4	109	Joe Gardener (2010–11)
5	107	Duarte Pinto (2003–10)

LONE RESISTANCE FROM TEIXEIRA

Portugal may have suffered the disappointment of an agonizing 32–30 defeat to Georgia in Lisbon on 8 February 2000, in a Six Nations B match, but it was a personal triumph for Thierry Teixeira. Given the defeat, it might not have provided a great deal of comfort for him, but the fly-half kicked all of the Lobos' points (nine penalties and a drop goal) to break the Portugal record for the most points scored in a match by a single player.

STRUGGLING IN THE BIG TIME

Portugal's reward for beating Uruguay in the final round of qualifying for the 2007 Rugby World Cup was a place in Pool C alongside Italy, New Zealand, Romania and Scotland, and nobody thought much of their chances. They lived up to low expectations when they suffered comprehensive defeats in their opening two matches – 56–10 to Scotland and 108–13 to New Zealand, the biggest reverse in their history. But then, with the pressure off, they started to perform. Victory may have eluded them, but there was honour in defeat: 31–5 to Italy (a considerable improvement on the 83–0 drubbing they had suffered against the same opponents a year earlier) and a battling 14–10 loss to Romania. Their first Rugby World Cup experience was over, but the Wolves had done themselves proud.

ROMANIA

A country with a rich rugby history, Romania have been a major force in second-tier European rugby for decades, so much so that in the 1980s there was talk of them being worthy of a place in the Five Nations. But the collapse of Communism in the early 1990s coincided with a downturn in the country's rugby fortunes, and although they have qualified for every one of the seven Rugby World Cups, the Oaks have still to make the breakthrough to claim a place among the game's elite.

OVERALL TEAM RECORD

Span	Mat	Won	Lost	Draw	%	For	Aga	Diff	Tries	Conv	Pens	Drop	GfM
1919–2011	372	204	157	11	56.31	8157	6872	+1285	658	398	449	70	1

EUROPEAN NATIONS CUP BRINGS ON THE GOOD TIMES

Romania have enjoyed the best moments in their history in the many guises of the European Nations Cup. Between 1936 and 1997, a period of French domination, they won five times (in 1968–69, 1974–75, 1976–77, 1980–81 and 1982–83) and finished runners-up on 12 occasions. And, since 2000, the Oaks have been a dominant force in the current, revamped version of the event, winning second-tier European rugby's biggest prize three times (in 2000, 2001–02 and 2004–06).

LEFT: Sorin Socol (reaching for the ball) has captained Romania to victory 20 times in his 34 matches leading the team.

POWERHOUSE LEADER

A stand-out performer in his country's junior international ranks – he was voted Player of the Tournament at the 1996 Under-21 Rugby World Championship – Sorin Socol, a marauding powerhouse of a lock forward, had to bide his time before making his senior international debut (in February 2001) but, once handed the chance, he seized the opportunity with both hands and soon established himself as the ever-present cornerstone of the Oaks' oft-praised pack. Handed the captaincy in 2004, he has since gone on to become Romania's longest-serving captain of all time (leading his country on 36 occasions).

A FAMOUS VICTORY TO SAVOUR

Romania's 64-year wait for a win away against one of the original Five Nations teams finally ended on 10 December 1988 at Cardiff Arms Park. A Gheorghe Ion try and 11 points from fly-half Gelu Ignat stunned Wales and secured a famous 15–9 victory.

DAN IS THE OAKS POINT-SCORING MAN

Dan Dumbrava made his international debut for Romania in a 40–3 defeat against Wales at Wrexham on 1 November 2002, playing at full-back. He played in three of his country's matches at the 2003 Rugby World Cup (including the 37–3 victory over Namibia) and assumed his team's kicking duties the following year, since when he has made consistent points-scoring contributions to the Oaks' cause. Dumbrava switched to fly-half in 2007, and has been an ever-present in the No.10 shirt ever since. At the 2011 Rugby World Cup, he broke Petre Mitu's record as his country's all-time leading points-scorer. His tally, after Romania's exit, stood at 378 points in 62 matches.

LEFT: Dan Dumbrava will be only 34 years old when the Rugby World Cup 2015 comes around and his career points-tally might be out of reach forever by then.

MOST POINTS: TOP FIVE

Pos	Points	Player (Span)
1	378	Dan Dumbrava (2002–11)
2	331	Petre Mitu (1996–2009)
3	316	Ionut Tofan (1997–2007)
4	254	Florin Vlaicu (2006–11)
5	201	Neculai Nichitean (1990–97)

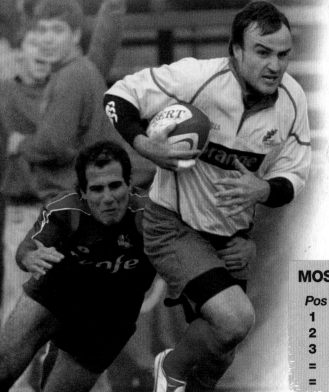

ROMANIA'S VICTORIES IN RUGBY WORLD CUP MATCHES

Year	Opponent	Result
1987	Zimbabwe	21–20
1991	Fiji	17–15
1999	USA	27–25
2003	Namibia	37–7
2007	Portugal	14–10

Note: Romania played in 24 Rugby World Cup matches between 1987 and 2011.

MOST TRIES: TOP FIVE

Pos	Tries	Player (Span)
1	26	Gabriel Brezoianu (1996–2007)
2	22	Catalin Fercu (2005–11)
3	14	Petre Mitu (1996–2009)
=	14	Cristian Sauan (1999–2007)
=	14	Marius Tincu (2002–11)

LEFT: Gabriel Brezoianu crossed the tryline a national record 28 times for Romania in 71 international matches between 1996 and 2007.

AN EVER-PRESENT FOR THE OAKS

Cristian Petre's international career with Romania could not have got off to a worse start as he made his debut for the Oaks in their record-breaking 134–0 rout by England at Twickenham on 17 November 2001. However, the 6ft 5in lock kept his place in the national team and became something of a stalwart of the Romanian pack for the next decade. A veteran of three Rugby World Cup campaigns (in 2003, 2007 and 2011), the AS Béziers second row is the most capped player in Romania's history – with 85 appearances. Three of his five career tries for the Oaks came in the space of four matches in early 2007.

ABOVE: Adrian Lungu won 76 caps for Romania between 1980 and 1995 – a national record until Cristian Petre passed that mark in 2011.

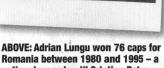

BELOW: Ionut Tofan (10) scored a Romania record 32 points during his country's 2003 Rugby World Cup qualifying match against Spain in October 2002.

SUPREME FINISHER

A 5ft 9in (1.75m) winger who, like many of his compatriots, has spent the majority of his domestic career in the French leagues (mainly with Bordeaux and Dax, Gabriel Brezoianu made his international debut on 20 April 1996 during Romania's 83–5 win over Belgium in Bucharest. An ever-present in the Oaks' line-up since 1998, he appeared in three Rugby World Cups (1999, 2003 and 2007), won 71 caps and went on to become his country's all-time leading try-scorer (with 28 tries) before his retirement in 2007.

MOST TRIES IN A MATCH

The Romania record for the most tries in a match by a player is five, a feat achieved by three players: Gheorgie Rascanu, against Morocco at Bucharest on 2 May 1972; Cornel Popescu, against Portugal at Birlad on 18 October 1986; and Ionel Rotaru, against Portugal at Bucharest on 13 April 1996.

TON UP FOR THE OAKS AGAINST BULGARIA

On 21 September 1976, Romania gave notice of their status as a growing force in the game when they travelled to the Black Sea coastal town of Burgas and proceeded to put their hosts, Bulgaria, to the sword. For the first and only time in their history, they reached three figures, winning the match by the crushing margin of 100–0.

OAKS FELLED AT TWICKENHAM

In 88 matches against the original Five Nations teams (England, France, Ireland, Scotland and Wales), Romania have won only 12 of them, with 11 of those victories coming at home. In short, life on the road in these fixtures has exposed Romanian rugby's greatest weakness over the years: an inability to rise to the challenges posed by a step up in class. And this failing was all too evident when Romania played England at Twickenham on 17 November 2001: they crashed to a thumping 134–0 defeat – the heaviest in their history.

TOFAN'S STAR TURN

Ionut Tofan was the chief architect behind Romania's 67–5 demolition of Spain during the Rugby World Cup qualifying match between the two sides at Iasi on 5 October 2002. The fly-half contributed 32 points to his country's cause – two tries, eight conversions and two penalties – to break the Romania record for the most points scored in a match by one player.

SCOTLAND

One of international rugby's original two, Scotland have enjoyed mixed success on the rugby field. They have won the Home/Five/Six Nations Championship 21 times and in 1991 reached the Rugby World Cup semi-finals, but the years of them punching above their weight appear to be behind them and the glory days (such as the grand slam successes of 1925, 1984 and 1990) are fast becoming a distant memory.

CLASH OF THE TITANS

It is a great sporting occasion at any time, but the Calcutta Cup match of 1990 had added spice: it was the final fixture in that year's Five Nations; both sides were vying for a grand slam; the media hype surrounding the match was unprecedented; and these explosive ingredients combined to produce a classic encounter. It got off to a memorable start: to a chorus of boos, England's players flew out of the tunnel at Murrayfield, confidence oozing after three impressive and comfortable victories; in contrast, the Scots, who had endured a bruising campaign, were greeted by a roar of passionate support as captain David Sole led his team on a slow march towards the pitch. There has perhaps been no stronger statement of intent in sporting history – the Scots, heavy underdogs though they were, were ready for battle. And how they fought. Their 13–7 victory – capped by a Tony Stanger second-half try – remains their most memorable of recent times … and the last grand slam they won.

SCOTLAND OFF TO A WINNING START

The instigators of the world's first rugby international, after a group of their players issued a challenge by letter to their English counterparts in a number of English and Scottish newspapers, Scotland ensured the majority of the 4,000 home crowd went home happy when they beat England by one goal to nil at Raeburn Place in Edinburgh on 27 March 1871. Not that the winning ways continued, however: Scotland would have to wait almost six years before recording their second victory.

LEFT: Ian McGeechan may have won 32 Test caps as a player for Scotland, but he will be remembered best for his skills as a coach.

SCOTS' GRAND SLAM GLORY

It was the perfect way to start life in their new home: having already beaten France (25–4), Wales (24–14) and Ireland (14–8) in their opening three matches of the 1925 Five Nations campaign, Scotland provided a real sense of occasion for what would be the first-ever match at the new Murrayfield stadium – a shot at a first-ever grand slam, with only arch-rivals England standing in their way. The match lived up to its billing, as tries from James Nelson and Johnnie Wallace were enough to secure a famous, if narrow, 14–11 victory.

INTERNATIONAL RUGBY HALL OF FAME INDUCTEES

Name	(Span, Caps)
Gordon Brown	(1969–77, 30 caps)
Gavin Hastings	(1986–95, 61 caps)
Andy Irvine	(1972–82, 51 caps)
Ian McGeechan	(1972–79, 32 caps)
Bill McLaren	Broadcaster

BELOW: Scotland line up before the start of the most famous match in their recent history: a 13–7 victory over England at Murrayfield in the 1990 Five Nations Championship which gave them their third grand slam.

SLAUGHTERED BY THE SPRINGBOKS

Reigning world champions South Africa taught Scotland a demoralizing rugby lesson at Murrayfield on 6 December 1997. The home side may have put in a worthy stint during the first 40 minutes (they trailed only 14–3 at half-time), but to the disappointment of the home crowd capitulated in sorry fashion in the second half, leaking a total of ten tries on their way to a 68–10 defeat – the heaviest in their history).

ALL-TIME LEADING TRY-SCORERS: BY POSITION

Position	Player (Span)	Tries
Full-back	Gavin Hastings (1986–95)	17
Winger	Ian Smith (1924–33)	24
Centre	Alan Tait (1987–99)	16
Fly-half	Gregor Townsend (1994–2003)	12
Scrum-half	Roy Laidlaw (1980–88)	7
No.8	Derek White (1988–92)	9
Flanker	John Jeffrey (1984–91)	11
Lock	Damian Cronin (1988–98)	5
	Stuart Grimes (1998–2005)	5
Prop	Tom Smith (1997–2005)	6
Hooker	Gordon Bulloch (1997–2005)	4

OVERALL TEAM RECORD

Span	Mat	Won	Lost	Draw	%	For	Aga	Diff	Tries	Conv	Pens	Drop	GfM
1871–2011	606	258	316	32	45.21	7770	8516	-746	1033	573	815	145	3

ABOVE: No fly-half has scored more tries (12) for Scotland than Gregor Townsend did in his nine-year, 49-start career in that position. He also scored five tries as a centre.

SCOTS PUT ON A SHOW IN PERTH

A rare home match away from Murrayfield at McDiarmid Park in Perth on 13 November 2004 paid dividends for Scotland when they crushed Japan in front of a thrilled near-capacity 10,200 crowd: 36–8 up by half-time, and in a position of total dominance they went on to run in a total of 15 tries en route to a thumping 100–8 victory, the biggest win in their history.

MOST TRIES: TOP TEN

Pos	Tries	Player (Span)
1	24	Ian Smith (1924–33)
=	24	Tony Stanger (1989–98)
3	22	Chris Paterson (1999–2011)
4	17	Gavin Hastings (1986–95)
=	17	Alan Tait (1987–99)
=	17	Gregor Townsend (1993–2003)
7	15	Iwan Tukalo (1985–92)
8	13	Kenny Logan (1992–2003)
9	12	Arthur Smith (1955–62)
10	11	John Jeffrey (1984–91)
=	11	Johnnie Wallace (1923–26)
=	11	Derek White (1982–92)

HONOURS

Rugby World Cup:
(best finish) – semi-finals (1991)
Six Nations:
winners – 1886*, 1887, 1890*, 1891#, 1895#, 1901#, 1903#, 1904, 1907#, 1920*, 1925 (GS), 1926*, 1929, 1933#, 1938#, 1964*, 1973#, 1984 (GS), 1986*, 1990 (GS), 1999

* = shared; (GS) = grand slam; # = triple crown

RIGHT: Tony Stanger shares the record with Ian Smith as Scotland's all-time leading try-scorer. Stanger scored 24 tries in 52 appearances between 1989 and 1998.

SCOTLAND'S LONGEST LOSING STREAK

If Scottish fans thought a comfortable 19–0 victory over Wales at Murrayfield on 3 February 1951 would signal the start of a winning run, they were sadly mistaken. Instead, the Scots embarked on the worst run in their history: starting with a slender 6–5 defeat in their next fixture against Ireland at Murrayfield on 24 February, they proceeded to lose their next 17 matches. The sorry sequence finally came to an end when they beat France at Colombes on 8 January 1955.

MOST CAPS: TOP TEN

Pos	Caps	Player (Span)
1	109	Chris Paterson (1999–2011)
2	87	Scott Murray (1997–2007)
3	82	Gregor Townsend (1993–2003)
4	77	Jason White (2000–09)
=	77	Nathan Hines (2000–11)
6	75	Gordon Bulloch (1997–2005)
=	75	Mike Blair (2002–11)
8	71	Stuart Grimes (1997–2005)
9	70	Kenny Logan (1992–2003)
10	66	Simon Taylor (2000–09)
=	66	Dan Parks (2004–11)

MR UTILITY FINALLY FINDS HIS ROLE

Chris Paterson made his debut for Scotland against Spain as long ago as the 1999 Rugby World Cup, but his ability to play in a number of positions – fly-half, full-back or wing – often counted against him in his early years, and it wasn't until he took over the side's kicking duties in 2003 that he showed his true worth to the team. Since then he has proved to be a goal-kicker of world-class ability, an essential part of the national side, the first, and to date only, Scotland player to win more than 100 caps (109), and he is his country's all-time leading points-scorer with 809 points.

HASTINGS HITS AN ALL-TIME HIGH

Gavin Hastings was in record-breaking form as he drove Scotland to a comfortable 89–0 victory over minnows Ivory Coast at Rustenberg during the 1995 Rugby World Cup. The veteran full-back, playing in his final tournament for Scotland, scored an all-time national record 44 points in the match, with four tries, nine conversions and two penalties.

ABOVE: Gavin Hastings holds the Scotland record for most points by one player in a match (44 against the Ivory Coast at the 1995 Rugby World Cup).

LEFT: Chris Paterson is Scotland's most capped player (109 caps) and all-time leading points-scorer (809).

RIGHT: Bill McLaren was the voice of rugby for more than half a century

LINDSAY LEADS SCOTLAND TO VICTORY

George Lindsay may only have made four appearances for Scotland (between 1884 and 1887), but his performance in one of them earned him a place in his country's record books. On 26 February 1887 against Wales in Edinburgh, he scored five tries in the match during his country's two goals to nil victory. This match was played in the era when a try carried no points reward – only the right to shoot at goal. The rules may have changed over the years, but Lindsay still holds the Scotland record for the most tries scored in a match by a single player.

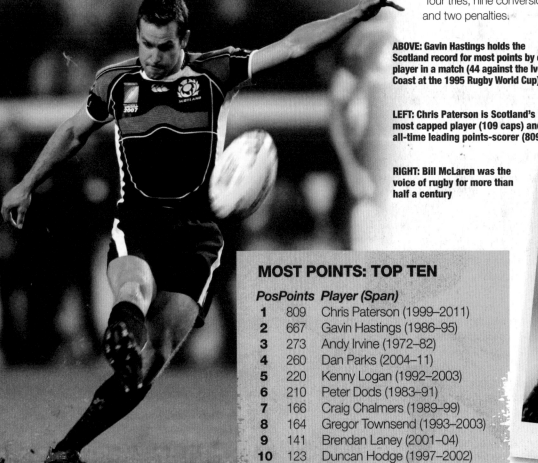

MOST POINTS: TOP TEN

Pos	Points	Player (Span)
1	809	Chris Paterson (1999–2011)
2	667	Gavin Hastings (1986–95)
3	273	Andy Irvine (1972–82)
4	260	Dan Parks (2004–11)
5	220	Kenny Logan (1992–2003)
6	210	Peter Dods (1983–91)
7	166	Craig Chalmers (1989–99)
8	164	Gregor Townsend (1993–2003)
9	141	Brendan Laney (2001–04)
10	123	Duncan Hodge (1997–2002)

BILL MCLAREN: THE VOICE OF RUGBY

An incredible attention to detail coupled with a wonderful turn of phrase helped Bill McLaren to become the BBC's voice of rugby for over 50 years. A talented player whose own career was cut short by a bout of tuberculosis, McLaren drifted into broadcasting via journalism and made his first radio broadcast in January 1952. He soon progressed to BBC Television and became a household name and national institution. In November 2001 he became the first non-international to be inducted into the International Rugby Hall of Fame and, such was the affection in which he was held, that when he made his final broadcast – Scotland against Wales in 2002 – he had to do so amid the deafening chorus of 'For he's a jolly good fellow' being sung in his honour by the crowd. He died, aged 86, in March 2011.

BELOW: David Sole (centre) shone for both Scotland and the British Lions between 1986 and 1992.

COACHES

Name	Tenure
Bill Dickinson	1971–77
Nairn McEwan	1977–80
Jim Telfer	1980–85
Derrick Grant	1986–88
Ian McGeechan	1988–93
Jim Telfer	1994–99
Ian McGeechan	2000–03
Matt Williams	2003–05
Frank Hadden	2005–09
Andy Robinson	2009–present

BELOW: Jim Telfer enjoyed two stints as Scotland coach and led them to a grand slam in 1984.

CAPTAIN GIVES SCOTLAND SOME MUCH-NEEDED SOLE

Born in England, but educated in Scotland and with tartan blood coursing through his veins, prop David Sole made his international debut against France in 1986 and soon established himself as a permanent fixture in the side, with a string of impressive performances earning him a place on the 1989 Lions tour. Appointed national captain in October 1989, he led Scotland to their greatest triumph of modern times (their 1990 Calcutta Cup success against England) and by the time he played in his final international, in 1992, he had become his country's longest-serving (25 matches) and most successful (14 wins) captain of all time.

SCOTLAND'S LONGEST WINNING STREAK

Scotland's longest winning streak is six matches, which has been achieved on two occasions: between 24 January 1925 and 6 February 1926 and between 28 October 1989 and 17 March 1990. Both runs involved grand slam successes in the then Five Nations Championship.

MOST SUCCESSFUL COACH

A back-row forward whose rugged performances brought him 25 caps for Scotland between 1964 and 1970, eight for the British Lions as well as much praise, Jim Telfer went on to achieve even more fame as a coach. He guided Scotland in two spells (1980–85 and 1994–99) and led them to the grand slam in 1984 and to the Five Nations crown in 1999. With 21 wins, he remains the most successful coach in Scotland's long rugby history.

SPAIN

Rugby is a minority sport in Spain – a country with an almost unbridled passion for football – but a growing one and the national team, known as El XV del Leon (the Lion's XV), have enjoyed mixed success over the years. One of the bigger fish in second-tier European rugby, they have knocked on the door of the game's elite for the past two decades without ever quite making the breakthrough needed and have only qualified for the Rugby World Cup once in six attempts.

OVERALL TEAM RECORD

Span	Mat	Won	Lost	Draw	%	For	Aga	Diff	Tries	Conv	Pens	Drop
1927–2011	311	132	167	12	44.37	5659	6753	-1094	316	190	266	17

SPAIN HIT HEADY HEIGHTS

Not surprisingly for a team that in recent decades has established itself among the world's top-30 ranked rugby-playing nations, Spain have enjoyed some of the most successful moments in their history against Europe's lowest-ranked countries, and the Spanish reserved perhaps their finest-ever performance for a European Nations Cup match against the Czech Republic in Madrid on 2 April 1995. Having amassed a comfortable 52–0 lead by half-time, they romped to a 90–8 victory – the biggest in their history.

EUROPEAN NATIONS CUP STRUGGLES

Although they have never won the competition in any one of its many guises over the years, Spain have enjoyed some good times in the European Nations Cup. They have finished third on two occasions (in 1973–74 and 1977–78) and in more recent times provided cause for cheer when they won the Lower Division championship in the 2004–06 edition of the event.

MOST POINTS IN A MATCH BY A PLAYER

The Spain record for the most points in a match by one player is 23, a feat achieved by three players: Andrei Kovalenco (seven penalties and a conversion) against Portugal at Elche on 9 May 1998; Esteban Roque Segovia (four conversions and five penalties) against Hungary at Madrid on 20 November 2004; and Matthieu Peluchon (a try, three conversions and four penalties) against Namibia at Mallorca on 27 November 2010.

SPAIN STAR-STRUCK ON THE GAME'S BIGGEST STAGE

Spain's reward for securing qualification for the 1999 Rugby World Cup was a place in Pool 1 alongside defending champions South Africa, Scotland and Uruguay and a firm reminder of the gulf in class that exists between the game's established nations and the developing ones. El XV del Leon lost their opening game against Uruguay (27–15) – realistically their only winnable match – and were swamped by both South Africa (47–3) and Scotland (48–0). They remain the only side in history to have qualified for the Rugby World Cup and then failed to score a single try during the tournament.

BELOW: Alvar Enciso Fernandez-Valderama is one of three men to have captained Spain on a national record seven occasions.

MOST POINTS: TOP FIVE

Pos	Points	Player (Span)
1	270	Esteban Roque Segovia (2004–07)
2	182	Andrei Kovalenco (1998–2006)
3	124	Cesar Sempere Padilla (2004–10)
4	81	Ferran Velazco Querol (1997–2006)
5	80	Manuel Cascara (2002–03)

SPAIN'S GOLDEN MOMENT

It may have culminated in the greatest moment in Spain's rugby history, but the path to the prize was a far from simple one: El XV del Leon's quest for a place at the 1999 Rugby World Cup started with a place in Pool 3 in Round B of European qualifying against Andorra on 8 November 1997. They eased to a 62–3 victory, went on to beat the Czech Republic, Germany and Portugal and progressed to the next pool round alongside Scotland and Portugal. With all the matches played at Murrayfield, the Scots were considered firm favourites to win the group, but two of the three teams were granted qualification, which meant that Spain's match against neighbours Portugal on 2 December 1998 was the most important in their history. They came through the tense, high-stakes affair 21–17, with six penalties from fly-half Andrei Kovalenco and a drop goal from centre Fernando Diez Molina. It was mission accomplished, and few recall the 85–3 defeat they suffered against Scotland three days later: Spain had qualified for the Rugby World Cup for the first, and to date only, time in their history and that was all that mattered.

SPAIN'S LONGEST-SERVING CAPTAIN

Longevity is not the word when it comes to captaining El XV del Leon and the record for the longest-serving captain is just seven matches, held by three players: Alvar Enciso Fernandez-Valderama (1999–2006), Alberto Malo Navio (1998–99) and Ferran Velazco Querol (2004–06).

MOST TRIES: TOP FIVE

Pos	Tries	Player (Span)
1	22	Cesar Sempere Padilla (2004–10)
2	14	Pablo Feijoo Ugalde (2002–11)
3	13	Ferran Velazco Querol (1997–2006)
4	9	Ignacio Criado Garachana (2002–10)
=	9	Ignacio Martin Goenaga (2000–10)

LEFT: Ferran Velazco Querol (centre, red shirt) is the only player ever to score a hat-trick of tries and kick a penalty goal for Spain in a Rugby World Cup finals match.

MOST TRIES IN A MATCH

The Spanish record for the most tries by one player in a match is three; a feat achieved four times, but only by two players. Ferran Velazco Querol achieved it against the Netherlands at Murcia on 6 April 2002 and Cesar Sempere Padilla did it three times: against Hungary in Madrid on 20 November 2004; Poland in Madrid on 13 November 2005; and the Czech Republic in Prague on 5 May 2007.

MAJOR CONTRIBUTOR TO SPAIN'S CAUSE

Drafted into the national squad to bolster the team's qualifying chances for the 2007 Rugby World Cup, Argentina-born fly-half Esteban Roque Segovia made his debut for El XV del Leon against Hungary in Madrid on 20 November 2004 and contributed 23 points towards his team's comfortable 63–9 victory. He remained a steady source of points through what turned out to be a difficult campaign for the Spanish – one that ultimately failed after successive defeats to Romania, Georgia and Portugal. Segovia returned to Argentina in 2007 as Spain's all-time leading points-scorer (with 270, comprising one try, 53 conversions, 52 penalties and one drop-goal).

LATE STARTER BLOOMS INTO SPANISH MAINSTAY

A relatively late starter to the game – he played his first match at university aged 18 in 1995 – Javier Salazar Lizarraga is one of the few well-travelled Spanish rugby players, having played club rugby in France and provincial rugby in New Zealand. A bulky 6ft 3in (1.9m) prop forward, he made his international debut for Spain against Holland in Mallorca on 5 February 2000 and went on to become the cornerstone of the Spain pack until his retirement on 15 March 2009. By that stage he had become Spain's most capped international of all time, with 57 caps.

THE PYRENEAN MASSACRE

Of the 23 nations that, along with Spain, have qualified for the Rugby World Cup over the years, Spain have only ever recorded victories against Georgia, Italy, Portugal and Zimbabwe. In short, matches against the world's elite rugby-playing nations have proved to be awkward affairs for the Spanish and none more so than their fixture against a French XV on 4 March 1979 at the small town of Oloron, situated in the Pyrenees in the south-west of France. Spain slumped to a 92–0 defeat: the heaviest loss in their history.

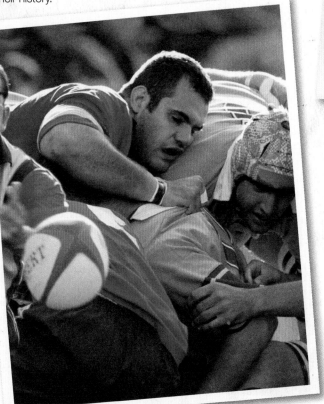

UNIQUE DUO

Fly-half Andrei Kovalenco (15 points against Uruguay) and full-back Ferran Velazco Querol (three points against South Africa) hold a unique place in the annals of Spanish rugby: they are the only two players in their country's history to have scored points in a Rugby World Cup match.

BELOW: Prop forward Javier Salazar Lizarraga won a national record 57 caps for Spain in a nine-year period between February 2000 and March 2009, retiring three months short of his 33rd birthday.

ABOVE: Cesar Sempere Padilla is the only player in Spain's history to have scored three tries in a match on three occasions and he is his country's all-time leading try-scorer with 22.

EL NIÑO PRODIGIO

Perhaps the finest player Spain has ever produced, Cesar Sempere Padilla made his international debut for El XV del Leon against Hungary in Madrid on 20 November 2004 aged just 20 and got off to an explosive start, scoring three tries during his side's emphatic 63–9 victory. A hard-running full-back, he went on to win 34 caps and sits at the top of Spain's all-time try-scoring list with 22, at the excellent average of 0.65 tries per match.

WALES

Rugby is the national sport of Wales and the hype surrounding the national team is matched only in New Zealand. There have been several golden moments in Welsh rugby – most notably in what is now the Six Nations Championship, which they have won outright on 24 occasions (second only to England, with 26 outright victories). But there have been plenty of devastating lows, too, such as the time they failed to make it beyond the group stages of the 1991 and 2007 Rugby World Cups.

OVERALL TEAM RECORD

Span	Mat	Won	Lost	Draw	%	For	Aga	Diff	Tries	Conv	Pens	Drop	GfM
1899–2011	632	325	279	28	53.63	10358	9162	+1196	1376	795	957	122	3

THE GREAT REDEEMER

By 1998 Welsh rugby had hit the depths: the decade had seen just one Five Nations Championship title (in 1994) and a failure to progress beyond the group stages at the last two Rugby World Cups. Wales needed a new direction and chose Kiwi Graham Henry as the man to lead them there. Dubbed the 'Great Redeemer' by the Welsh public, Henry sparked a revival in Welsh fortunes – including leading them on a run of ten straight victories between March and October 1999 – without ever quite bringing back the true glory days, and defeats to Argentina (16–30) and Ireland (10–54) in 2001 and 2002 saw him resign in February 2002. With 20 wins, however, he remains the most successful coach in Wales's history.

ABOVE: Wales won the last of their ten Six Nations grand slams in 2008.

THE FIRST WELSH GOLDEN ERA

When Wales recovered from the 6–3 defeat they had suffered against Scotland to beat Ireland 29–0 in their final match of the 1907 Home Nations Championship to finish second, few would have predicted the greatness that would follow, but the win over Ireland sparked the first golden era in Welsh rugby.

In 1908, the first edition of the Five Nations (following France's inclusion), they won the grand slam, a feat they repeated the following year. Following 11 straight victories (a national record), the magical, 34-month unbeaten run finally came to an end on 15 January 1910 when Wales lost 11–6 to arch-rivals England at Twickenham.

HONOURS

Rugby World Cup:
(best finish) – third (1987)

Six Nations:
winners – 1893#, 1900#, 1902#, 1905#, 1906#, 1908 (GS), 1909 (GS), 1911 (GS), 1920*, 1922, 1931, 1932*, 1936, 1939*, 1947*, 1950 (GS), 1952 (GS), 1954*, 1955, 1956, 1964*, 1965#, 1966, 1969#, 1970#, 1971 (GS), 1973*, 1975, 1976 (GS), 1978 (GS), 1979#, 1988#, 1994, 2005 (GS), 2008 (GS)

* = shared; (GS) = Grand Slam; # = triple crown

WALES'S SECOND GOLDEN ERA

The ten-year period between 1969 and 1979 was a period of almost unprecedented success for Wales and a decade during which the names of JPR Williams, Gerald Davies, John Dawes, Barry John, Phil Bennett and Gareth Edwards, among others, would become permanently etched into Welsh folklore. Remarkably during that time, Wales lost only seven matches in the Five Nations Championship, winning the title eight times, with three triple crowns and three grand slams (in 1971, 1976 and 1978). It is known as Wales's second golden era.

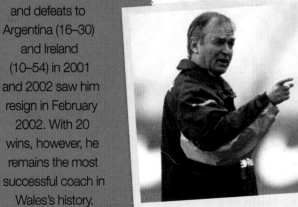

LEFT: Graham Henry, dubbed "the Great Redeemer", may not have brought back the golden times, but he still led Wales to more wins (20) than any other coach in their history.

MOST TRIES: TOP TEN

Pos	Tries	Player (Span)
1	57	Shane Williams (2000–11)
2	40	Gareth Thomas (1995–2007)
3	33	Ieuan Evans (1987–98)
4	22	Colin Charvis (1996–2007)
5	20	Gerald Davies (1966–78)
=	20	Gareth Edwards (1967–78)
=	20	Tom Shanklin (2001–10)
8	18	Rhys Williams (2000–05)
9	17	Reggie Gibbs (1906–11)
=	17	Ken Jones (1947–57)
=	17	Johnny Williams (1906–11)

ALL-TIME LEADING TRY-SCORERS: BY POSITION

Position	Player (Span)	Tries
Full-back	Kevin Morgan (1997–2007)	12
Winger	Shane Williams (2000–11)	57
Centre	Tom Shanklin (2002–10)	13
Fly-half	Arwel Thomas (1996–2000)	11
Scrum-half	Gareth Edwards (1967–98)	20
No.8	Scott Quinnell (1994–2002)	11
Flanker	Colin Charvis (1996–2007)	19
Lock	Alun-Wyn Jones (2007–11)	7
Prop	Gethin Jenkins (2002–11)	4
Hooker	Bryn Meredith (1954–62)	3

BELOW: In an 11-year career, Colin Charvis scored more tries (22) than any other Wales forward in history, 19 of them as a flanker.

RETURN OF THE GOOD TIMES FOR WALES

By the start of the 2005 Six Nations the glory days of Welsh rugby were fast becoming a distant memory – as suggested by their pre-tournament odds of 50–1 against winning the grand slam – but Wales's campaign got off to a pulsating and encouraging start when they edged out England 11–9 in their opening match thanks to a last-gasp long-range Gavin Henson penalty. They then beat Italy (38–8), clawed their way back from being 15–8 down at half-time against France in Paris to win the match 24–18 and went on to beat Scotland 46–22 at Murrayfield to set up their first chance of a grand slam for 32 years and a shot at the title for the first time since 1994. Only Ireland stood in their way but, despite enduring some awkward moments, Wales won 32–20. It was the first time in Six Nations history that a side had won the grand slam after playing the majority of their games away.

WALES FOURTH TO JOIN THE INTERNATIONAL RUGBY CLUB

International rugby between 1871 and 1874 was an exclusive term reserved only for England–Scotland matches, those being the only two countries to have formed national teams. And then Ireland joined the club and the trio continued to play international fixtures against each other for the next seven years. On 19 February 1881, Wales became the fourth international team when they played England at Blackheath. Not that it was a day to remember: Wales lost by eight goals to nil – 82–0 in modern scoring, given that England scored 13 tries, seven conversions and a drop goal.

COACHES

Name	Tenure
David Nash	1967
Clive Rowlands	1968–74
John Dawes	1974–79
John Lloyd	1980–82
John Bevan	1982–85
Tony Gray	1985–88
John Ryan	1988–90
Ron Waldron	1990–91
Alan Davies	1991–95
Alex Evans	1995 (caretaker coach)
Kevin Bowring	1995–98
Dennis John	1998 (caretaker coach)
Graham Henry	1998–2002
Lynn Howells	2001 (caretaker coach)
Steve Hansen	2002–04
Mike Ruddock	2004–06
Scott Johnson	2006 (caretaker coach)
Gareth Jenkins	2006–07
Nigel Davies	2007 (caretaker coach)
Warren Gatland	2007–present

INTERNATIONAL RUGBY HALL OF FAME INDUCTEES

Name	(Span, Caps)
Phil Bennett	(1969–78, 29 caps)
Gerald Davies	(1966–78, 46 caps)
Mervyn Davies	(1969–76, 38 caps)
Gareth Edwards	(1967–78, 53 caps)
Ieuan Evans	(1987–98, 72 caps)
Carwyn James	(1958, 2 caps)
Barry John	(1966–72, 25 caps)
Cliff Morgan	(1951–58, 29 caps)
Gwyn Nicholls	(1896–1906, 24 caps)
JPR Williams	(1969–81, 55 caps)

Note: Only New Zealand (15) has more than Wales's 10 men inducted into the Hall of Fame.

ABOVE: Gareth Edwards was inducted into the International Rugby Hall of Fame in its inaugural year, 1997. The first Welshman to win 50 caps, many consider him to be the greatest scrum-half of all-time.

BOKS TEACH WALES A RUGBY LESSON

Pretoria, 27 June 1998. It will go down as the darkest day in Wales's rugby history. A clinical display from South Africa brutally exposed an inexperienced Wales line-up at Loftus Stadium in Pretoria – with fly-half Arwel Thomas the only shining light, scoring all of his side's points – as the visitors, in the face of wave after wave of attack, conceded 15 tries en route to a shattering 96–13 defeat – the heaviest in their history. Welsh rugby had hit rock bottom.

ABOVE: Shane Williams proved to be one of the best finishers in world rugby in an 11-year career with Wales, scoring 57 tries.

MOST CAPS: TOP TEN

Pos	Caps	Player (Span)
1	104	Stephen Jones (1998–2011)
2	100	Gareth Thomas (1995–2007)
3	99	Martyn Williams (1996–2010)
4	94	Colin Charvis (1996–2007)
5	92	Gareth Llewellyn (1989–2004)
6	87	Neil Jenkins (1991–2002)
7	86	Shane Williams (2000–11)
8	82	Gethin Jenkins (2002–11)
9	76	Dwayne Peel (2001–11)
10	75	Adam Jones (2003–11)

AS GOOD AS IT GETS FOR WALES

Wales travelled to the inaugural Rugby World Cup in 1987 with low expectations, having finished second from bottom in that year's Five Nations Championship with only one win to their name, but they got off to a morale-boosting start when they beat Ireland 13–6 in their opening game. The tone was set, and Wales went on to beat Tonga (29–16) and Canada (40–9) to finish top of the pool and progress to a quarter-final showdown with England – the only side they had beaten in that year's Five Nations. It was a repeat performance for Wales as they cruised to a comfortable 16–3 victory. The dream ended when they crashed to a 49–6 defeat against New Zealand in the semi-finals, but Wales's 22–21 victory over Australia in the third-place play-off match – thanks to a last-gasp Paul Thorburn touchline conversion – meant they went out of the tournament on a high. It remains Wales's best-ever performance at a Rugby World Cup.

WINGER WILLIAMS STANDS TALL

Shane Williams relied on searing pace, a textbook side-step and an uncanny ability to find space where others could not to silence the many doubters who claimed he was too small to play international rugby and develop into one of the most exciting wingers of modern times. He won his first cap when he came on as a replacement against France on 5 February 2000 and scored his first try on his first full appearance two weeks later, against Italy. He became a constant source of points for Wales from that moment on and by 2011 had scored a national record 57 tries (plus two for the British & Irish Lions – to stand third on international rugby's all-time list. In 2008, he became the first, and to date only, Wales player to win the IRB Player of the Year award.

RIGHT: Stephen Jones became Wales's all-time cap-winner at the Rugby World Cup 2011 and further cemented his second place on the points-scoring charts.

MR RELIABLE

Although not hewn from the same golden cast that brought a glittering array of talent to the Welsh No.10 jersey over the years, Stephen Jones's utter reliability made him a standout performer for the Dragons for more than a decade. Not that it started that way: although Jones made his debut as long ago as 1998, it took until 2001 before the metronomic accuracy of his boot and his innate line-breaking abilities secured him the outside-half berth on a regular basis. A key figure in Wales's 2005 Grand Slam success, he was named as captain in 2006, a position he held until the arrival of Warren Gatland as coach in 2007. He was involved in a tussle with James Hook for the Welsh No.10 shirt as Wales won another Grand Slam in 2008, but his performances led to his selection for the Lions tour to South Africa in 2009, during which he played in all three Tests. He spearheaded Wales's 2010 Six Nations campaign, ending the tournament as the leading points-scorer, and, although he lost his place in the starting line-up to Rhys Priestland during Wales's memorable 2011 Rugby World Cup campaign, played an influential role for his team coming off the bench and ended the tournament as the Dragons' most-capped player of all time (104 appearances) and second (behind Neil Jenkins) on his country's all-time points-scoring list (with 917).

WALES'S LONGEST SERVING CAPTAIN

Winger Ieuan Evans was one of the few bright lights in an otherwise disappointing era for Wales. He made his debut on 7 February 1987 against France in Paris in the Five Nations Championship and remained a permanent fixture on the right wing for the next 11 years – going on to score a then national record 33 tries. Evans was appointed captain of Wales in 1991 in the build-up to the Rugby World Cup, and he led them 28 times, more than any other player in Welsh rugby history, until the end of the 1995 Five Nations Championship.

BELOW: Flying winger Ieuan Evans captained Wales 28 times between 1991 and 1995.

JAPAN SURRENDERS IN CARDIFF

It was as close to a no-contest as you could find in rugby as Wales put on a memorable, try-filled show against Japan at the Millennium Stadium on 26 November 2004. Captain Colin Charvis, leading by example, scored four tries, Tom Shanklin three, while Rhys Williams and Shane Williams grabbed two each and Gareth Cooper, Mefin Davies and Gethin Jenkins one apiece (with 14 conversions from the boot of Gavin Henson) as the home side cantered to a 98–0 victory. It remains their biggest victory of all time, although they have scored more points on one occasion, when they beat Portugal 102–11 in Lisbon in a Rugby World Cup qualifying match on 18 May 1994.

THE WORST OF TIMES

The reality of Wales's many shortcomings during an uncomfortable 32–21 victory over Canada at Cardiff on 16 November 2002 was brutally exposed a week later when New Zealand crushed them 43–17. It sparked a miserable run that saw Wales spiral into an unprecedented freefall. They lost all five of their 2003 Six Nations matches – including a demoralizing 30–22 defeat to Italy in Rome – to collect the tournament's wooden spoon; they then lost both of their matches on a tour to the southern hemisphere – New Zealand (3–55) and Australia (10–30); and proceeded to lose to Ireland (12–35) and England (9–43) in their warm-up matches for the 2003 Rugby World Cup. The hapless ten-match losing streak – the longest in Wales's history – spanning a desperate 272 days, finally came to an end when they beat Romania 54–8 in Wrexham on 27 August 2003.

RECORD-BREAKING MOULD-BREAKER

Neil Jenkins was a mould-breaking player who never quite fitted the image of the classical Wales fly-half and, as such, spent an entire international career being shuffled around the back division (he was capped at fly-half, centre and full-back). However, whatever he may have lacked in the incisive-running department – a trademark of the legendary Welsh No.10s of the past (notably Barry John and Phil Bennett) – he more than made up for by possessing one of the most clinical kicking boots in the game's history. In 87 appearances for Wales between 1991 and 2002 he set his country's all-time records for the most points scored (1,049 – he was the first-ever player in international rugby to pass the 1,000-point milestone) and for the most points scored in one match (30, against Italy at Treviso on 20 March 1999).

RIGHT: Neil Jenkins was the first player in international rugby history to break the 1,000-point barrier and is still Wales's leading points-scorer with a total of 1,049.

MOST POINTS: TOP TEN

Pos	Points	Player (Span)
1	1049	Neil Jenkins (1991–2002)
2	917	Stephen Jones (1998–2011)
3	326	James Hook (2006–11)
4	304	Paul Thorburn (1985–91)
5	285	Shane Williams (2000–11)
6	211	Arwel Thomas (1996–2000)
7	200	Gareth Thomas (1995–2007)
8	166	Phil Bennett (1969–78)
9	157	Ieuan Evans (1987–98)
10	152	Steve Fenwick (1975–81)

OTHER EUROPEAN TEAMS

Rugby has flourished more in Europe than on any other continent on earth: of the 93 teams that appear in the current IRB rankings, 38 of them – including Israel – are European. This section looks at the best of the rest from Europe (from Andorra to the Ukraine), those countries outside of the top 10, whose aspirations, for the time being at least, are restricted to the second and third tiers of world rugby and who contest the earliest rounds of Rugby World Cup qualifying matches.

KNOCKING ON THE RUGBY WORLD CUP DOOR

They may never have appeared at a Rugby World Cup, but the Netherlands have won more qualifying matches than any other country in Europe (22 between 1989 and 2009). And the Dutch have come mighty close to appearing on the game's greatest stage over the years, falling at the final qualifying hurdle in 1991, 1995 and 1999.

FIFTH TIME LUCKY FOR RUSSIA

Until recently, Rugby World Cup qualification had become the sore point of Russian rugby: a 30–0 defeat to Romania ended their hopes in 1995; they fell at the final hurdle in 1999; suffered the embarrassment of expulsion in 2003 (for fielding ineligible players); and lost a winner-takes-all showdown with Portugal in 2007 (losing 26–23). It took a change in format to trigger an upturn in Russia's fortunes. Qualification for the 2011 Rugby World Cup would begin with the 2008–10 European Nations Cup, with automatic places given to the top two teams. Russia, playing the best rugby in their history, won seven and drew one of their ten games to finish second and earned a place on world rugby's biggest stage for the first time in their history.

BELOW: 2010 was a great year for Russian rugby. The team qualified for its first ever Rugby World Cup, then won the Bowl final of the Churchill Cup.

BEST OF THE REST: IRB RANKINGS

Russia (21); Belgium (25); Moldova (28); Czech Republic (30); Ukraine (33); Poland (34); Germany (37); Lithuania (38); Sweden (39); Netherlands (42); Croatia (50); Malta (53); Switzerland (56); Andorra (58); Latvia (59); Israel (67); Serbia (68); Denmark (69); Slovenia (70); Hungary (71); Austria (79); Bulgaria (80); Bosnia and Herzegovina (87); Monaco (89); Norway (90); Luxembourg (92): Finland (93)

Note: ranking correct as of 23 October 2011.

SWEDEN RUN IN THE TRIES

The earliest rounds of Rugby World Cup qualifying in Europe have seen a plethora of one-sided results, but none more so than Sweden's 116–3 away victory over Luxembourg on 5 May 2001 and Germany's 108–0 home win over Serbia and Montenegro on 12 November 2005: both Sweden and Germany ran in 18 tries during their impressive triumphs.

RUGBY WORLD CUP QUALIFYING WOE FOR GERMANY

Germany have lost more Rugby World Cup qualifying matches than any other European nation. In the 33 ties they have played between 1989 and 2010 they have lost 18 of them, with their heaviest defeat coming against Georgia at Tbilisi on 6 February 2010 when they crashed to a 77–3 reverse.

WINS OVER SIX NATIONS TEAMS

Team	Result	Opponent	Venue	Date
Germany	17–16	France	Frankfurt	15 May 1927
Germany	19–8	Italy	Berlin	14 May 1936
Germany	6–3	Italy	Milan	1 Jan 1937
Germany	10–0	Italy	Stuttgart	6 Mar 1938
Germany	3–0	France	Frankfurt	27 Mar 1938
Germany	12–3	Italy	Milan	11 Feb 1939
Czechoslovakia	14–6	Italy	Prague	22 May 1949
Poland	12–6	Italy	Warsaw	23 Oct 1977

ABOVE: England winger Dan Luger (carrying the ball against Uruguay in the 2003 Rugby World Cup) is the son of the former head of the Croatian rugby federation, but he is just one of numerous international rugby stars who have links to the Balkan state.

GERMAN RUGBY'S GLORY DAYS

German rugby was at its strongest between the two World Wars. Between 1927 and 1938 – a period during which they recorded regular victories over Italy (including a 6–3 win in Milan on 1 January 1937) and enjoyed two defeats of France (17–16 in Frankfurt on 15 May 1927 and 3–0 in Frankfurt on 27 March 1938) – they established themselves among the best of continental Europe's teams.

A DAY TO REMEMBER FOR THE CZECHS

Five successive failed Rugby World Cup qualifying campaigns, coupled with a long-established position among the third-tier teams in world rugby, mean that Czech fans have had little reason to celebrate over the years, but they certainly had something to shout about on 22 May 1949. In what still ranks as the most notable victory in Czech rugby history (and their only win over a Six Nations opponent), they beat Italy 14–6 in Prague.

LIFE AT ROCK BOTTOM FOR FINLAND

Finland played their first match, against Switzerland in Helsinki, on 22 May 1982 and lost 60–0. This defeat set the tone for a miserable start to life in international rugby; the Finns had to wait until 29 September 1991 – their ninth international (against Norway in Karlskrona) – before they could celebrate a victory (18–3). Since then, however, Finland have won only seven of 29 matches and are currently the bottom-ranked team (93rd) in world rugby.

ONE MOMENT OF TRUE RUGBY GLORY

Poland may not have set international rugby alight in the 52 years that have passed since they played their first match – against East Germany in 1958 – but for a period in the 1970s, a surge in form saw them arouse a degree of interest. During that time they recorded wins over the Netherlands, Morocco, Czechoslovakia and the Soviet Union; suffered narrow defeats to a France XV and Italy; and went on to record the greatest win in Poland's rugby history: a 12–6 victory over Italy in Warsaw on 23 October 1977. Sadly, they have not hit such heights since.

BACK IN THE BIG TIME

When Ukraine lost all ten of their matches in the 2004–06 European Nations Cup (with a sorry points difference of –499) and suffered the ignominy of relegation to the second division of the competition (essentially the third tier of European rugby), it could have triggered a collapse in the country's rugby fortunes; instead, it triggered a mini-revival, albeit a slow one. In 2006–08, they finished second from bottom in Division 2A, narrowly missing out on a second successive relegation. In the following competition (2008–10), however, they won five out of eight games to gain promotion (as Division 2A champions) back into the top tier of continental European rugby. It remains the greatest achievement in Ukraine's rugby history.

CROATIAN BLOOD COURSES THROUGH THEIR VEINS

Croatia are currently the 50th ranked team in international rugby and have never qualified for the Rugby World Cup. However, over the years, there have been several players with ancestral links to the country (and thus were qualified to play for it) but who appeared on the international stage for other countries. Most notable is England winger Dan Luger (38 caps), whose father was the head of Croatia's rugby federation. Frano Botica, who won seven caps for New Zealand, had grandparents from Croatia, while New Zealanders Sean Fitzpatrick (92 caps), Mark Carter (seven caps) and Mike Brewer (32 caps) and Australian Matthew Cooper (seven caps) all have Croatian heritage.

ONWARDS AND UPWARDS FOR LITHUANIA

Although rugby is still very much a minority sport in Lithuania, playing second and third fiddle to football and basketball, the performances of its national team in recent years has made people sit up and take notice. In the 2006–08 European Nations Cup they won all eight of their Division 3B matches to win promotion to Division 3A. In 2008–10 they recorded their second successive 100 per cent campaign – with seven wins out of seven – to gain promotion to Division 2. Currently ranked 38th in the world, Lithuania are a team undeniably on the up.

SCORED 100 POINTS OR MORE IN A MATCH

Team	Opponent	Result	Venue	Date
Sweden	Luxembourg	116–3	Luxembourg City	5 May 2001
Germany	Serbia & Mon	108–0	Heidelberg	12 Nov 2005
Sweden	Luxembourg	116–3	Luxembourg City	5 May 2001
Russia	Denmark	104–7	Copenhagen	13 May 2000
Denmark	Finland	100–0	Eskilistuna	10 Oct 1987

ASIA AND OCEANIA

Oceania is home to two of the powerhouses of the world game: Australia, the two-time Rugby World Cup winners, who have a rugby heritage dating back to the 1860s; and New Zealand, home of the legendary All Blacks, the team that captures the essence of the game more than any other. European settlers took rugby with them to the Pacific Islands and Fiji, Samoa and Tonga were all playing international rugby by 1924. Rugby has yet to achieve lift-off in Asia, although Japan, the kings of Asian rugby, have appeared in all seven Rugby World Cups.

BELOW: Samoa fans entered into the party spirit as they cheered on their heroes during their country's 49–12 victory over Namibia at Rotorua in the 2011 Rugby World Cup.

AUSTRALIA

Rugby has a rich heritage in Australia, but although the Wallabies have been playing international rugby since the 1880s, it wasn't until the 1980s – and in particular a grand-slam winning tour to the British Isles in 1984 – that they became established as a truly dominant force in the world game, a position they have maintained ever since. They won the Rugby World Cup in 1991 and became the first team to win the trophy for a second time when they triumphed in 1999.

OVERALL TEAM RECORD

Span	Mat	Won	Lost	Draw	%	For	Against	Diff	Tries	Conv	Pens	Drop	GfM
1880–2011	532	270	247	15	52.16	10908	8729	+2179	1391	822	1009	78	2

WALLABIES CONFIRM STATUS AS WORLD'S NO.1

Australia lost their first-ever Tri-Nations match, against New Zealand in Wellington on 6 July 1996, 43–6, and the heavy defeat seemed to set the tone for the Wallabies' struggles in the competition in its earliest years: they finished bottom in 1996 and 1997 and second in 1998 and 1999. As such, the newly crowned world champions had a point to prove going into the 2000 campaign, but got off to the worst possible start when they lost a thrilling match against New Zealand (39–35). They rallied a fortnight later in Brisbane to beat South Africa (26–6), and edged out the All Blacks in Wellington (24–23). It meant that victory in their final match, against South Africa in Durban, would bring the Wallabies their first-ever Tri-Nations crown: they lived up to their billing as the best team in the world when they won a gripping match 19–18.

WALLABIES' RECORD-BREAKING STATEMENT OF INTENT

Australia's crushing 142–0 win over Namibia at Adelaide in the 2003 Rugby World Cup will always be remembered as a classic example of the massive gulf in class that exists between the game's haves and have-nots rather than the hard-hitting statement of intent from a team playing at the top of its game – form that would take them to the final – that it was. The Wallabies ran in 22 tries – five of them by Chris Latham (an all-time national record) – en route to the biggest-ever win in a Rugby World Cup match, their largest victory of all time and the only time in their history that they have scored 100 points in a match.

ABOVE: Bob Dwyer masterminded Australia's victory at the 1991 Rugby World Cup.

BELOW: Mat Rogers runs in one of Australia's 22 tries against the minnows of Namibia at the 2003 Rugby World Cup.

DEFYING THE ODDS FOR RUGBY WORLD CUP GLORY

Australia's 2–1 series defeat to the British and Irish Lions in 1989 was a moment of revelation for their coach Bob Dwyer: it made him recognize the absolute importance of a dominant pack, and he set about addressing what, in truth, had been an Australian weakness for years. The results were encouraging if not spectacular and the Wallabies travelled to the 1991 Rugby World Cup as nobody's pick to win the tournament. They struggled through the group stages, winning all three games but in less than spectacular fashion, and survived a huge scare in the quarter-finals in Dublin before a last-gasp Michael Lynagh try saw off the spirited Irish 19–18. Two tries from David Campese and another from Lynagh inspired them to a 16–6 semi-final win over New Zealand and only England stood in the way of an unlikely victory. And it was a resilient pack that won the day for Australia in the final at Twickenham on 2 November. Tony Daley's first-half try, coupled with heroic defence – repelling wave after wave of England attacks – helped the Wallabies to a 12–6 victory and the first Rugby World Cup win in their history.

TAKING THEIR TIME TO TAME THE LIONS

Between 1899 and 1989, Australia had played 17 matches against the British and Irish Lions and had won only three of them. What's more, no Australia side had ever recorded a series victory over the northern-hemisphere tourists. That all changed in 2001, even though the Wallabies got off to the worst of starts, losing 29–13 in the opening Test in Brisbane. The defending world champions bounced back in style a week later in Melbourne, winning 35–14 before making history on 14 July 2001, when they edged a tense deciding Test in Sydney, 29–23.

UNDERDOGS MAKE RUGBY WORLD CUP HISTORY

Australia may have beaten New Zealand 28–7 at Sydney in their final match of what had otherwise been a disappointing 1999 Tri-Nations campaign to retain the Bledisloe Cup, but few fancied their chances of success in the forthcoming Rugby World Cup later in the year, especially as it was to be held in Europe. The Wallabies, however, would silence the doubters in style, marching to the final with ruthless efficiency. They cruised through Pool 5, beating Romania (57–9), Ireland (23–3) and the United States (55–19), battled to an efficient if not convincing 24–9 victory over hosts Wales in the quarter-final in Cardiff,

and edged a tense semi-final against South Africa to reach the Rugby World Cup final for a second time. On 6 November 1999, at the Millennium Stadium in Cardiff, Australia proved too strong for France and won the match 35–12 to become the first team to lift the Webb Ellis Cup for a second time.

BELOW: Fly half Mark Ella is one of seven Australian inductees into the International Rugby Hall of Fame. He was in the inaugural class of 1997.

LEFT: Australia's players celebrate on the pitch at Sydney in July 2001 following the 29–23 victory that gave the Wallabies their first-ever series victory over the British & Irish Lions.

COACHES

Name	Tenure
Bob Dwyer	1982–84
Alan Jones	1984–87
Bob Dwyer	1988–96
Greg Smith	1996–97
Rod Macqueen	1997–2001
Eddie Jones	2001–05
John Connolly	2006–07
Robbie Deans	2007–present

MOST TRIES: TOP TEN

Pos	Tries	Player (Span)
1	64	David Campese (1982–96)
2	40	Chris Latham (1998–2007)
3	30	Tim Horan (1989–2000)
=	30	Drew Mitchell (2005–11)
=	30	Joe Roff (1995–2004)
=	30	Lote Tuqiri (2003–08)
7	29	Matt Burke (1993–2004)
=	29	Matt Giteau (2002–11)
=	29	Stirling Mortlock (2000–09)
10	25	Stephen Larkham (1996–2007)

SPRINGBOKS HAND AUSTRALIA RECORD-BREAKING DEFEAT

Australia's fine start to the 2008 Tri-Nations campaign – they had won three of their opening four games (against South Africa in Perth, 16–9, and Durban, 27–15, and against New Zealand in Sydney, 34–19) – came to a crashing and record-breaking end on 30 August 2008 against a Springbok side who lived up to their world-champion status in front of a passionate home crowd in Johannesburg. The Boks ran riot, scoring eight tries (five of them converted) and a penalty to win 53–8. It remains Australia's biggest-ever defeat.

LONGEST WINNING STREAK

Australia's longest winning streak is ten matches, a feat achieved on three occasions: between 4 October 1991 and 19 July 1992 (a period that included the Wallabies' first Rugby World Cup success); between 29 August 1998 and 24 July 1999; and between 28 August 1999 and 8 July 2000 (a period that saw them lift the Webb Ellis trophy for the second time).

INTERNATIONAL RUGBY HALL OF FAME INDUCTEES

Name	(Span, Caps)
David Campese	(1982–96, 101 caps)
Ken Catchpole	(1961–68, 27 caps)
John Eales	(1991–2001, 86 caps)
Mark Ella	(1980–84, 25 caps)
Nick Farr-Jones	(1984–93, 63 caps)
Tim Horan	(1989–2000, 80 caps)
Michael Lynagh	(1984–95, 72 caps)

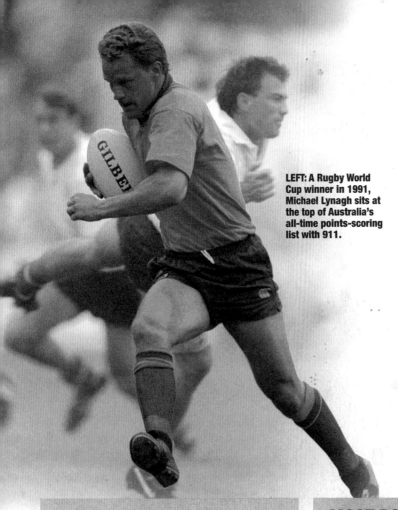

LEFT: A Rugby World Cup winner in 1991, Michael Lynagh sits at the top of Australia's all-time points-scoring list with 911.

AUSTRALIA'S MR RELIABLE

Michael Lynagh made his debut for Australia at inside-centre against Fiji at Suva on 9 June 1984 and did enough in the match – he slotted three penalties – to retain his place in the Wallabies' line-up for the forthcoming tour of Britain and Ireland, going on to play a full part in his team's grand slam success (scoring 42 points in the four Test matches). He switched to fly-half after the tour and directed operations for the Wallabies for the next decade, guiding them to Rugby World Cup success in 1991. When he retired, after 72 appearances, in 1995 – following the Wallabies' Rugby World Cup quarter-final defeat to England – he did so as the world's all-time leading points-scorer (with 911 points). That mark has since been overtaken by others, but Lynagh remains Australia's leading points-scorer of all time.

LONGEST LOSING STREAK

Australia's longest losing run is ten matches, a feat achieved on two occasions: between 22 July 1889 and 3 August 1907 (when the game was still in its infancy in the country); and between 26 June 1937 and 14 June 1947 (when the game of rugby took a back seat in the country before, during and after the Second World War).

SECOND TIME LUCKY FOR DWYER

Bob Dwyer's two stints as Australia coach could not have been more different. The first ended after a disappointing two years when Alan Jones replaced him in February 1984. The second (1988–96), on the other hand, coincided with arguably the greatest period in Australia's rugby history, notably the Wallabies' Rugby World Cup win in 1991. When he left his post in 1996, this time of his own volition, he did so with a sky-high global reputation and as Australia's most successful coach of all time.

BELOW: Chris Latham in record-breaking form against Namibia at the 2003 Rugby World Cup. The full-back ran in five tries during the 142–0 victory, a record for Australia.

MOST CAPS: TOP TEN

Pos	Caps	Player (Span)
1	139	George Gregan (1994–2007)
2	110	George Smith (2000–09)
3	102	Stephen Larkham (1996–2007)
4	101	David Campese (1982–96)
5	100	Nathan Sharpe (2002–11)
6	92	Matt Giteau (2002–11)
7	86	John Eales (1991–2001)
=	86	Joe Roff (1995–2004)
9	81	Matt Burke (1993–2004)
10	80	Tim Horan (1989–2000)
=	80	Stirling Mortlock (2000–09)

MOST POINTS: TOP TEN

Pos	Points	Player (Span)
1	911	Michael Lynagh (1984–95)
2	878	Matt Burke (1993–2004)
3	684	Matt Giteau (2002–11)
4	489	Stirling Mortlock (2000–09)
5	315	David Campese (1982–96)
6	260	Paul McLean (1974–82)
7	244	Joe Roff (1995–2004)
8	200	Chris Latham (1998–2007)
9	199	James O'Connor (2008–11)
10	182	Elton Flatley (1997–2005)

ALL-TIME LEADING TRY-SCORERS: BY POSITION

Position	Player (Span)	Tries
Full-back	Chris Latham (1998–2007)	36[†]
Winger	David Campese (1982–96)	52[*]
Centre	Tim Horan (1989–2000)	26
Fly-half	Stephen Larkham (1998–2007)	20
Scrum-half	George Gregan (1994–2007)	18
No.8	Tim Gavin (1988–96)	9
	Toutai Kefu (1997–2003)	9
Flanker	Rocky Elsom (2005–11)	14
Lock	Nathan Sharpe (2002–11)	7
Prop	Tony Daly (1989–95)	4
Hooker	Phil Kearns (1989–99)	8
	Jeremy Paul (1998–2006)	8

* Scored 12 tries as full-back.
† Scored 4 tries as winger.

HUNTING A HISTORIC GRAND SLAM

When Alan Jones became Australia coach in February 1984, he did so with the intention of taking the Wallabies to the pinnacle of world rugby. A Bledisloe Cup defeat to New Zealand may not have signalled the best of starts, but Jones knew the upcoming tour to Britain and Ireland in late autumn 1984 presented his young charges with a fantastic opportunity to become the first Australian team in history to win all four tour matches. They opened up with a 19–3 victory over England at Twickenham on 3 November; beat Ireland 16–9 in Dublin a week later; eased past Wales 28–9 at Cardiff on 24 November and rounded off the tour in style with a commanding 37–12 victory over Scotland at Murrayfield. They had won the grand slam, and in some style: fly-half Mark Ella scored a try in each match and the Wallabies had become the first side in history to score more than 100 Test points on a tour to Britain and Ireland.

BELOW: George Gregan shone for Australia in a 13-year career that saw him amass a world-record 139 international caps.

SHOWSTOPPER CAMPESE IS THE WALLABIES' TRY KING

Although he amassed as many critics as admirers over the years (for his brashness off the field rather than his skills on it), there is little doubt that David Campese is the finest player Australia has ever produced. He made a try-scoring debut against New Zealand in 1982 and crossed the line again in his second match. He made his name on the Wallabies' 1984 grand-slam winning tour to Britain and Ireland, thrilling the crowd with a magnificent solo try against the Barbarians. The highlight of his career came at the 1991 Rugby World Cup, when his six tries saw him voted Player of the Tournament. He retired in 1996 with 101 caps and a then world record 64 tries.

GREGAN IN FOR THE LONG HAUL

In 1994, his first full season with the Wallabies, George Gregan became a part of Australia's rugby folklore when he pulled off one of the greatest try-saving tackles of all time – against the All Blacks' Jeff Wilson – to help his side to a famous Bledisloe Cup win. He appeared in the first of three Rugby World Cups in 1995, with the tournament ending in the disappointment of a quarter-final defeat to England. As vice-captain, the Lusaka-born scrum-half enjoyed better fortune during Australia's victorious 1999 Rugby World Cup campaign, scoring a try against Wales in the quarter-finals. He inherited the captaincy in 2001, led his country to the Rugby World Cup final in 2003, won his 100th cap in 2005 and passed Jason Leonard's all-time appearance record in 2006. He won the last of his international record 139 caps during the 2007 Rugby World Cup.

ABOVE: David Campese's outstanding talents on a rugby pitch saw him notch up an Australian record 64 tries in 101 appearances from 1982 to 1996. He was the first Australian player to reach the 100-cap mark.

BELOW: Australia's most successful captain, John Eales, shows off the Rugby World Cup in 1999.

MOST SUCCESSFUL CAPTAIN

John Eales is the most successful captain in the history of Australian rugby, leading his country to 41 wins in 55 matches as captain between 1996 and 2001. One of only six players in the game's history to have won the Rugby World Cup on two occasions, he ended his career in eighth place on Australia's all-time points-scoring list (a phenomenal achievement for a lock forward). He made his debut in 1991 as a 21-year-old and played a full part in his side's Rugby World Cup victory that year. Five years later he was made Australia's captain and fought his way back from a serious shoulder injury to lead his side to a second Rugby World Cup success in 1999.

There are few countries with as much passion for the game of rugby as Fiji and the national team, currently ranked 16th in the world, has enjoyed considerable success over the years. They won the South Pacific Championship (the forerunner of the Pacific Nations Cup) on four occasions, have reached the Rugby World Cup quarter-finals twice (in 1987 and 2007) and, what's more, have stuck to their principles of playing a thrilling brand of attacking rugby.

BIG PERFORMANCES ON THE BIGGEST STAGE

It is Fiji's record in the Rugby World Cup over the years, and the attacking brand of rugby they have brought to the tournament, that mark the islanders out as being the most thrilling and spectacular of the Pacific Island nations' teams. In the inaugural event in 1987, a 28–9 opening game win over Argentina proved enough to see them through a tough group completed by Italy and New Zealand, although the dream ended following a 31–16 quarter-final defeat to France. Tough years then followed, including failing to qualify for the 1995 Rugby World Cup, but they were back in the quarter-finals in 2007 – thanks in no small part to a pulsating 38–34 victory over Wales in Nantes – only to lose yet again, this time 37–20 to South Africa.

RIGHT: Waisale Serevi, a legend on the Sevens circuit, performed with distinction for Fiji in the 15-a-side game, too, scoring 221 points in 38 Tests between 1989 and 2003.

OVERALL TEAM RECORD

Span	Mat	Won	Lost	Draw	%	For	Aga	Diff	Tries	Conv	Pens	Drop
1924–2011	286	135	142	9	48.77	5846	5853	-7	836	491	425	35

FIJI DUMP WALES OUT OF THE RUGBY WORLD CUP

Victories over Japan (35–31) and Canada (29–16) followed by an expected defeat to Australia (55–12) meant that Fiji's final 2007 Rugby World Cup Pool B match against Wales – who had produced an identical record – at Nantes on 29 September had become a straight knockout clash for a quarter-final place. Fiji raced into a 25–10 lead at half-time; Wales rallied in the second half and reclaimed the lead with minutes remaining; and then came the most famous moment in Fiji's rugby history. In the final throes of the game, prop Graham Dewes bundled his way over the line and Fiji secured a memorable 38–34 victory.

ABOVE: Severo Koroduadua Waqanibau notched an all-time Fiji best 36 points during the country's record-breaking 120–4 rout of Nieu Island in 1983.

TOUGH TIMES AGAINST THE ALL BLACKS

Fiji have endured some difficult times in matches against New Zealand. In the ten matches they have played against the All Blacks, they have lost them all, scored just 75 points (7.5 per match) and conceded a mighty 519 (51.9 per match). Their heaviest defeat against New Zealand – and the worst in Fiji's history – came at North Shore City on 10 June 2005, when the All Blacks cruised to a 91–0 win.

FIJI'S RECORD-BREAKING WIN

Fiji's match against Niue Island, a tiny Polynesian nation with a population of 1,398, at the South Pacific Games (the tournament first took place in 1963 and, like the Olympic Games, is staged every four years) at Apia (Samoa's capital) on 10 September 1983, was as one-sided a game of rugby as you'll ever find. Fiji scored 20 tries in the match on the way to a crushing 120–4 victory – the largest win in their history – with full-back Severo Koroduadua Waqanibau contributing a national record 36 points to Fiji's cause.

MOST POINTS: TOP FIVE

Pos	Points	Player (Span)
1	670	Nicky Little (1996–2011)
2	268	Severo Koroduadua Waqanibau (1982–91)
3	223	Seremaia Baikeinuku (2000–11)
4	221	Waisale Serevi (1989–2003)
5	103	Taniela Rawaqa Maravunawasawasa (2007–11)

FIJI'S LEADING TRY-SCORER

Sanivalati Laulau made his debut for Fiji during the 22–9 defeat against Australia at Suva on 24 May 1980 and scored his first international try in his third match later in the year against the New Zealand Maoris. Equally capable at centre or wing, he went on to win 32 caps for his country between 1980 and 1985 and holds the Fiji record for the most tries scored (20).

ABOVE: Winger Sanivalati Laulau is Fiji's all-time leading try-scorer, crossing the line 20 times in 32 appearances between 1980 and 1985.

MOST TRIES: TOP FIVE

Pos	Tries	Player (Span)
1	20	Sanivalati Laulau (1980–85)
2	16	Fero Lasagavibau (1997–2002)
=	16	Norman Ligairi (2000–10)
=	16	Viliame Satala (1999–2005)
5	13	Aisea Tuilevu Kurimudu (1996–2004)

BELOW: The only Fiji player in history to score more than 500 points (670), Nicky Little enjoyed a 15-year career in international rugby.

SMITH PROVES A TOP-CLASS RECOMMENDATION

A born-and-bred New Zealander, Greg Smith switched his allegiance to Fiji – for whom he qualified to play through his father – following a recommendation by Waikato's John Boe to then Fiji coach Brad Johnstone. A stocky hooker, he made his debut against Wales in November 1995 and remained a cornerstone of the Fiji pack for the next eight years. Appointed captain in 1996, he went on to lead his country a record 30 times (recording 17 wins) before relinquishing the captaincy in 2002. He retired as a player after the 2003 Rugby World Cup

BELOW: New Zealand-born hooker Greg Smith captained his adopted Fiji a record 30 times between 1996 and 2002.

FIJI'S MISERABLE RUN OF FORM

The darkest days in Fiji's rugby history started with a 28–12 home defeat to England at Suva on 20 July 1991; they then lost all three of their group matches at the 1991 Rugby World Cup to finish bottom of their pool (which contained Canada, France and Romania) for the first, and to date only, time in their history. The miserable run continued with defeats to Samoa (20–16) and Tonga (13–9) in the 1992 Pacific Tri-Nations championship and stretched into 1993 following four defeats in 12 months. Fiji's ten-match losing streak – the longest in their history – finally ended three days short of two years since it began, with a 15–10 victory over Tonga at Nufu A'lofa on 17 July 1993.

LITTLE BY NAME, BUT A BIG PERFORMER

The nephew of former All Blacks centre Walter Little, Nicky Little was born and educated in New Zealand and played provincial rugby there, before taking up the option of playing for Fiji, for whom he qualified through his father. A dependable kicker and a fly-half with good distribution skills, he made his international debut aged 19 against South Africa in Pretoria on 2 July 1996 and remained a constant in the Fiji line-up for the next 13 years. A veteran of four Rugby World Cups – he appeared in the 1999, 2003, 2007 and 2011 tournaments (the latter at the age of 35) – he held his country's record for the most caps (71) and for the most points scored (670).

MIXED FORTUNES

The Pacific Tri-Nations tournament (contested annually between Fiji, Samoa and Tonga) provided Fiji with a mixture of triumph and disappointment over the years. Winners of the inaugural competition in 1982, they went on to win the event a further nine times before it evolved into the expanded Pacific Nations Cup in 2006. They have endured difficult times in the latter, with a best-place finish of second (in 2009 and 2010).

FIJI'S LONGEST WINNING STREAK

Progress for Fiji has been hindered by the islanders' inability to string together a run of consistent performances. The longest winning streak in their history is five matches, a feat they have achieved on two occasions: between 21 September 1928 and 8 August 1934; and between 24 August 1999 and 9 October 1999.

MOST TRIES IN A MATCH

The Fiji record for the most tries by a player in a single match is six, a feat achieved by two players: Tevita Makutu, against Papua New Guinea at Suva on 30 August 1979; and Sanivalati Laulau, against Solomon Islands at Apia on 8 September 1983.

JAPAN

Japan may be the undisputed kings of Asian rugby – they have won the Asian Five Nations Championship each of the three times the competition has been contested – but the Cherry Blossoms have always struggled against non-Asian opponents. One of only 12 teams to have appeared in every one of the six Rugby World Cups, they have struggled on rugby's greatest stage, winning only one of 24 matches, drawing two and suffering some thumping defeats along the way.

OVERALL TEAM RECORD

Span	Mat	Won	Lost	Draw	%	For	Aga	Diff	Tries	Conv	Pens	Drop
1930-2011	273	101	163	9	38.64	6993	8249	-1256	973	613	394	23

LIFE IN A BIGGER RUGBY POND

In 1991, teams from Asia and Oceania were placed in the same Rugby World Cup qualifying group for the first and only time and, although Japan finished second and progressed through the group containing Tonga, Korea and Western Samoa, they lost a Rugby World Cup qualifying match for the first, and to date only, time in their history – 37–11 against Western Samoa in Tokyo. Rugby life, it seemed, was tougher for Japan against the physical Pacific islanders. So when, in 2006, the Cherry Blossoms were invited to play in the Pacific Nations Cup, there was great interest in how they would cope against rivals that over the years have included the Junior All Blacks, Fiji, Tonga and Samoa. They have held their own:, winning two matches in 2010 to finish third and then beating Tonga and Fiji in 2011 to claim the title from Samoa on points difference.

TOKYO TRY-FEST FOR JAPAN AGAINST CHINESE TAIPEI

Everyone was expecting a win for Japan when they played Chinese Taipei at Tokyo on 7 July 2002 in a qualifying match for the 2003 Rugby World Cup and the Cherry Blossoms lived up to pre-match expectations in record-breaking style. Having established a comfortable 71–3 lead by half-time, the onslaught continued into the second half, as Japan ran in a match total of 23 tries – eight of them from Daisuke Ohata (a national record for any player in one match) – to complete a thumping 155–3 victory. In international rugby history, only Argentina (152–0 against Paraguay on 1 May 2002) have matched the Cherry Blossoms' 152-point margin of victory.

UNDISPUTED KINGS OF ASIAN RUGBY

If Japan's status as the best team in Asia was already well established by the time the Asian Five Nations Championship was contested for the first time in 2008 – they had, after all, never lost a Rugby World Cup qualifying match against an Asian opponent – then the new competition merely confirmed it. The Cherry Blossoms' record in the tournament is a perfect one (played 16, won 16) and they took the overall spoils in 2008, 2009, 2010 and 2011.

BELOW RIGHT: Katsuhiro Matsuo goes over for a try during Japan's 52–8 rout of Zimbabwe in a 1991 Rugby World Cup match in Belfast, the Cherry Blossoms' only tournament win to date.

JAPAN'S RUGBY WORLD CUP STRUGGLES

Japan may have qualified for every one of the seven Rugby World Cups (bar the inaugural tournament, which was an invitation-only affair), but that is where the Cherry Blossoms' success in the competition has ended. They have endured numerous miserable and morale-sapping moments in matches against the world's elite rugby-playing nations, recording only one victory in 24 matches – 52–8 against Zimbabwe at Belfast on 14 October 1991. There have been many painful defeats along the way, but none more so than the 145–17 drubbing they received at the hands of New Zealand in Bloemfontein on 4 June 1995 – it remains not only the heaviest defeat in Japan's history but also the highest ever score in the Rugby World Cup.

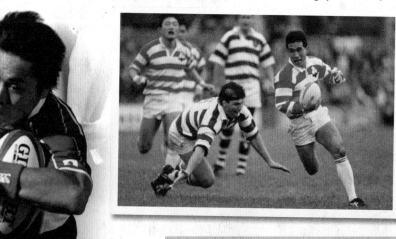

ABOVE LEFT: The world's all-time leading international try-scorer Daisuke Ohata touched down a record eight times against Chinese Taipei on 7 July 2002.

MOST POINTS: TOP FIVE

Pos	Points	Player (Span)
1	422	Keiji Hirose (1994–2005)
2	347	Toru Kurihara (2000–03)
3	345	Daisuke Ohata (1996–2006)
4	286	James Arlidge (2007–11))
5	215	Hirotoki Onozawa (2001–11)

MOST TRIES: TOP FIVE

Pos	Tries	Player (Span)
1	69	Daisuke Ohata (1996–2006)
2	43	Hirotoki Onozawa (2001–11)
3	29	Terunori Masuho (1991–2001)
4	23	Takashi Kikutani (2005–11)
5	20	Toru Kurihara (2000–03)
=	20	Alisi Tupuailei (2009–11)

LEFT: Takuro Miuchi, a former Oxford Blue, was an inspired leader for Japan in 41 Tests between 2002 and his retirement in 2008.

RUGBY'S MOST PROLIFIC TRY-SCORER

Japan may not be one of the superpowers of world rugby, but they possess the most prolific try-scorer ever to have played international rugby. On 14 May 2006, Daisuke Ohata scored three tries in Japan's victory over Georgia to take his tally to 65 tries in 55 Tests and past David Campese's world record which had stood for a decade. He broke on to the scene at the 1999 Hong Kong Sevens, a spawning ground for the game's biggest names, and was voted the tournament's most valuable player – an accolade once afforded to Campese. By the time he retired in 2006 after 58 matches, Ohata had stretched his world record try tally to 69.

WAITING FOR THE RUGBY WORLD CUP PARTY TO BEGIN

Even though Japan were considered to have the stronger bid, they suffered the disappointment of losing out to New Zealand for the right to host the 2011 Rugby World Cup, but the IRB could not ignore the Cherry Blossoms' strong claims to host the tournament for long. Having successfully co-hosted the 2002 FIFA World Cup, they possessed both the experience and infrastructure to hold an event of such magnitude. In July 2007, the IRB announced that England would host the 2015 Rugby World Cup and that Japan would become the tournament's first Asian hosts in 2019. The countdown has already started.

BELOW: Keiji Hirose is top of Japan's all-time points-scoring list with 422, garnered over an 11-year span from 1994 to 2005.

WINNING AND LOSING STREAK RECORDS

Throughout history, the start of a Japanese losing streak tends to coincide with the moment they play a team from world rugby's top tier and the Cherry Blossoms' winning ways tend to re-emerge the instant they have returned to the comfort of Asian rugby or to other internationals against second-tier nations. As such, it comes as little surprise that Japan's longest-ever losing streak came when they played a host of touring teams at home between 1952 and 1958 – they lost 11 straight matches. Conversely, their longest winning run – six matches between 16 November 2008 and 23 May 2009 – came during two Tests against the United States and a 100 per cent qualifying campaign for the 2011 Rugby World Cup.

MIUCHI'S LEADERSHIP QUALITIES

A former Oxford Blue, Takuro Miuchi made his debut for Japan as a flanker during the Cherry Blossoms' 59–19 victory over Romania at Tokyo on 19 May 2002. Remarkably, he was appointed national captain in only his second Test appearance, but soon settled into the role and led Japan to the 2003 Rugby World Cup and beyond. Controversially, new coach Jean-Pierre Elissalde relieved him of the captaincy in February 2006, but Miuchi's stint among the ranks was a short one: John Kirwan reappointed him as captain the moment he took over the coaching reins on 1 January 2007. By the time of his final appearance, against Samoa at Apia on 5 July 2008, Miuchi had led his country on 42 occasions, an all-time record for Japan.

KURIHARA SETS NEW WORLD-BEST MARK

On 7 July 2002, Japan hammered Chinese Taipei 155–3 in Tokyo – their 152-point winning margin is the joint highest in international rugby history. Two weeks later, they travelled to Tainan for the reverse fixture and romped to not only another comfortable victory but also a record-breaking one: winger Toru Kurihara, with six tries and 15 conversions, scored 60 points in the match to break Eduardo Morgan's long-standing all-time record (50 points for Argentina against Paraguay in October 1973) for the most points scored by a single player in an international match.

HIROSE HITS THE HIGH NOTES

Keiji Hirose, a diminutive, 5ft 7in (1.7m) fly-half, made a points-scoring international debut (four penalties and two conversions) during Japan's 26–11 victory over Korea at Kuala Lumpur on 29 October 1994 and quickly established himself as the Cherry Blossoms' first choice No.10. A reliable goal-kicker, by the time he won the last of his 40 caps, against Australia A in Tokyo on 8 June 2003, he had scored 422 points – an all-time record for a Japan player.

LEFT: Toru Kurihara amassed a breathtaking 60 points (six tries and 15 conversions) for Japan against Chinese Taipei in Tainan on 21 July 2002 to break a world record that had stood since 1973. Japan won the Rugby World Cup qualifier 120–3.

New Zealand are to rugby what Brazil are to football: they capture the very heart and soul of the game and have a team that lives up to the country's unbridled passion for the sport. Like Brazil, the All Blacks start every competition among the pre-tournament favourites; but unlike their South American football counterparts, New Zealand have not necessarily translated year-on-year dominance into Rugby World Cup success: the ten-time Tri-Nations champions have won the game's greatest prize only twice.

SECOND STRING ALL BLACKS PUT ON A RECORD SHOW

Given that victory in the group had all but been assured following convincing opening wins over Ireland (43–19) and Wales (34–9), New Zealand made 11 changes to their side for their final Pool C fixture at the 1995 Rugby World Cup – against Japan at Bloemfontein on 4 June. The results were explosive: finally given an opportunity to display their talent, what was essentially a second-string All Blacks XV blew Japan apart, scoring 21 tries – with winger Marc Ellis scoring six tries and fly-half Simon Culhane slotting 45 points (both All Blacks records) – on the way to a stunning 145–17 victory. It is the largest win in New Zealand's history.

OVERALL TEAM RECORD

Span	Mat	Won	Lost	Draw	%	For	Aga	Diff	Tries	Conv	Pens	Drop	GfM
1903–2011	484	364	103	17	76.96	12568	6128	+6440	1654	1060	1001	87	5

ALL BLACKS TAME THE LIONS

New Zealand won their first-ever match against a touring team from Britain – 9–3 in a one-off encounter at Wellington on 13 August 1904 – and have maintained the upper hand over the men from the northern hemisphere ever since. In 38 matches against the British and Irish Lions, the All Blacks have won 29 of them and have collected nine series wins in the 11 contested, with one drawn and one lost (in 1971). Most recently, in 2005, New Zealand trounced the Lions 3–0.

BIGGEST DEFEAT

Of their 472 international matches – the first being a 22–3 win over Australia at Sydney on 15 August 1903 – New Zealand have only ever lost 101 and, remarkably, only one of them by more than 20 points. The heaviest defeat in New Zealand's history came against Australia at Sydney on 28 August 1999, when they slipped to a 28–7 reverse.

AGAINST-THE-ODDS RUGBY WORLD CUP SUCCESS

New Zealand rugby was in turmoil in the build-up to the inaugural Rugby World Cup in 1987. The year before, a rebel tour to South Africa had resulted in several star players being banned. This shook the All Blacks to their very core and, disenfranchised, the country's passionate supporters were starting to turn their backs on the national team in their droves. The 1987 Rugby World Cup provided the All Blacks with an opportunity to win back those supporters … and they did it in some style. They won their pool comfortably, beat Scotland 30–3 in the quarter-finals and thumped Wales 49–6 in the semi-finals to take their place in the final against France in front of an adoring crowd at Eden Park, Auckland. Then, in what remains one of the New Zealand's greatest days in rugby, they ran in three tries to France's one to win the match 29–9 and claim the game's greatest prize for the first time in their history.

ABOVE: One of the finest ever All Blacks, Richie McCaw led his team to Rugby World Cup glory in 2011.

BELOW LEFT: Marc Ellis scored a New Zealand record six tries in the 145–17 dismantling of Japan at the 1995 Rugby World Cup.

THE LONG WAIT ENDS

In 2011, New Zealand finally brought an end to 24 years of deep Rugby World Cup frustration and often misery. The All Blacks, tournament hosts and – as often before – hot favourites for the title, romped to the top of their first round pool with comfortable victories over Tonga (41–10), Japan (83–7), France (37–17) and Canada (79–15), outlasted Argentina in the quarter-finals (33–10), outclassed Australia in the semi-finals (20–6) and edged to the narrowest of victories (8–7) over France in a tense final at Eden Park, Auckland, to lift the Webb Ellis trophy for a second time.

HONOURS

Rugby World Cup:
(best finish) – champions (1987, 2011)
Tri-Nations:
(best finish) – champions (1996, 1997, 1999, 2002, 2003, 2005, 2006, 2007, 2008, 2010)

INTERNATIONAL RUGBY HALL OF FAME INDUCTEES

Name	(Span, Caps)
Fred Allen	(1946–49, 6 caps)
Don Clarke	(1956–64, 31 caps)
Sean Fitzpatrick	(1986–97, 92 caps)
Grant Fox	(1985–93, 46 caps)
David Gallaher	(1903–06, 6 caps)
Michael Jones	(1986–98, 56 caps)
Ian Kirkpatrick	(1967–77, 39 caps)
John Kirwan	(1984–94, 63 caps)
Brian Lochore	(1964–71, 25 caps)
Jonah Lomu	(1994–2002, 63 caps)
Terry McLean	(journalist)
Colin Meads	(1957–71, 55 caps)
Graham Mourie	(1977–82, 21 caps)
George Nepia	(1924–30, 9 caps)
Wilson Whineray	(1957–65, 32 caps)

TRI-NATIONS TRIUMPHS

In recent years, it is their electric form in the Tri-Nations, the toughest competition in the game, that has established New Zealand's credentials as the no.1 side in world rugby. They won the inaugural competition in 1996 with a 100 per cent record, repeated the feat the following year and have gone on to win ten of the 15 tournaments contested, most recently in 2010, when they won all six of their matches.

ABOVE: A slender 23–22 victory over Australia in Sydney on 11 September 2010 saw New Zealand win their tenth Tri Nations crown.

MOST TRIES: TOP TEN

Pos	Tries	Player (Span)
1	49	Doug Howlett (2000–07)
2	46	Christian Cullen (1996–2002)
=	46	Joe Rokocoko (2003–10)
4	44	Jeff Wilson (1993–2001)
5	37	Jonah Lomu (1994–2002)
6	36	Tana Umaga (1997–2005)
7	35	John Kirwan (1984–94)
8	34	Mils Muliaina (2003–11)
9	29	Dan Carter (2003–11)
=	29	Sitiveni Sivivatu (2005–11)

THE ALL BLACKS' WINNING WAYS

New Zealand tasted victory in all of their first six internationals (between 1903 and 1905) and have gone on to win three of every four matches played and record a remarkable win percentage of 76.80. There have been plenty of lengthy winning streaks along the way, but the longest stretched to 17 matches from September 1965 to June 1969 and came to an end following a 17–6 defeat to South Africa in Pretoria. The All Blacks' longest unbeaten streak is 23 matches: the run of wins, which started with a 70–6 victory over Italy at Auckland on 22 May 1987 and included the country's first, and to date only, Rugby World Cup win, ended at ten after a 19–19 draw against Australia at Brisbane on 16 July 1988. But the unbeaten run stretched a further 12 games before New Zealand lost 21–9 to Australia at Wellington on 18 August 1990.

RIGHT: An electrifying performer for New Zealand on 58 occasions between 1996 and 2002, Christian Cullen scored 46 tries for his country. Only Doug Howlett has scored more for the All Blacks.

ALL BLACKS' LONGEST LOSING STREAK

For a country so used to the sweet taste of victory on the rugby pitch, losing streaks are hard to find in the annals of New Zealand rugby and when they do occur, they tend to trigger a national crisis. The worst losing streak the All Blacks ever suffered (six consecutive losses) started with a 2–0 series defeat to South Africa in July–August 1949 and stretched a further five games before they went on to enjoy a 2–0 series win over the British Lions in 1950.

ALL-TIME LEADING TRY-SCORERS: BY POSITION

Position	Player (Span)	Tries
Full-back	Christian Cullen* (1996–2002)	40*
Winger	Joe Rokocoko (2003–10)	46
Centre	Frank Bunce (1991–97)	20
Fly-half	Dan Carter (2003–11)	24
Scrum-half	Justin Marshall (1995–2005)	24
No.8	Zinzan Brooke (1990–97)	14
Flanker	Richie McCaw (2001–10)	19
Lock	Ian Jones (1990–99)	9
Prop	Kees Meeuws (1998–2004)	8
	Tony Woodcock (2002–11)	8
Hooker	Sean Fitzpatrick (1986–97)	12

* scored six tries as a centre or wing.

A LEADING LIGHT FOR NEW ZEALAND

One of the finest players ever to emerge from the land of the long white cloud, hooker Sean Fitzpatrick experienced both the highs and lows of New Zealand's rugby fortunes. His swift rise to international rugby – he made his debut against France at Christchurch in June 1986, shortly after his 23rd birthday – had been accelerated by the blanket ban imposed on New Zealand players who had appeared in the 1986 rebel tour to South Africa, and Fitzpatrick became part of the 'Baby Blacks' – a new generation of players charged with restoring the All Blacks' fortunes and with winning over an increasingly frustrated New Zealand rugby public. An integral part of the 1987 Rugby World Cup-winning team, he was appointed captain in 1992 and took his side to the 1995 Rugby World Cup final against South Africa – only to suffer the anguish of defeat. By the time he bowed out of international rugby in 1997 after his 92nd cap, he was New Zealand's most capped player – a record that stood until 2010.

MOST CAPS: TOP TEN

Pos	Caps	Player (Span)
1	103	Richie McCaw (2001–11)
2	100	Mils Muliaina (2003–11)
3	92	Sean Fitzpatrick (1986–97)
=	92	Keven Mealamu (2002–110)
5	85	Dan Carter (2003–11)
6	83	Tony Woodcock (2002–11)
7	81	Justin Marshall (1995–2005)
8	79	Ian Jones (1990–99)
9	74	Tana Umaga (1997–2005)
10	73	Ali Williams (2002–11)

LEFT: Long-time skipper and hooker Sean Fitzpatrick (lifting the Bledisloe Cup in 1995) became the first All Black in history to win 90 Test caps. He was also the first player to captain New Zealand 50 times (51 in total).

DAN'S THE MAIN MAN FOR NEW ZEALAND

A player whose reputation transcends both hemispheres, Dan Carter made his debut for New Zealand aged 21 against Wales at Hamilton on 21 June 2003 and scored 20 points in the match (one try, six conversions and a penalty). But it took a disastrous Rugby World Cup campaign in 2003 – in which New Zealand lost 22–10 to Australia in the semi-finals, with Carter watching on from the sidelines – before he was given a chance to establish himself as the All Blacks' first-choice No.10. Showing raw speed, a natural side-step, huge defensive strength and a metronomic left boot, he grabbed the opportunity with both hands, played a starring role in New Zealand's 3–0 series victory over the British Lions in 2005 and has gone on to become arguably the most complete fly-half in the game's history. By 2011, aged 29 and a winner of 85 caps, he has scored 1,250 international points (with 29 tries) to become the all-time leading points-scorer in international rugby.

BELOW: Dan Carter has been a regular source of points for the All Blacks (1,188 of them) since he made his debut in 2003

COACHES

Name	Tenure
Alex McDonald	1949
Tom Morrison	1950
Len Clode	1951
Arthur Marslin	1953–54
Tom Morrison	1955–56
Dick Everest	1957
Jack Sullivan	1958–60
Neil McPhail	1961–65
Ron Bush	1962
Fred Allen	1966–68
Ivan Vodanovich	1969–71
Bob Duff	1972–73
John Stewart	1974–76
Jack Gleeson	1977–78
Eric Watson	1979–80
Peter Burke	1981–82
Bryce Rope	1983–84
Sir Brian Lochore	1985–87
Alex Wyllie	1988–91
Laurie Mains	1992–95
John Hart	1996–99
Wayne Smith	2000–01
John Mitchell	2002–03
Graham Henry	2004–11

DEADLY DOUG HITS NEW HEIGHTS

A player blessed with searing pace (he once clocked 10.68 for the 100m in his youth), Doug Howlett made his first appearance for New Zealand, as a replacement, against Tonga in June 2000 and helped himself to two tries – the first just 20 seconds after coming on to the pitch. Remarkably, he went on to score a try in each of his next six internationals setting the tone for the rest of his successful career: he was a try-scoring regular in the All Blacks line-up and appeared at both the 2003 and 2007 Rugby World Cups. By the time he was sensationally dropped from the squad, after causing alleged criminal damage during a drunken night out in Cardiff (for which he issued a grovelling apology), he had scored 49 tries in 62 matches to become New Zealand's leading try-scorer of all time. Howlett's international career may have ended on a sour note, but he will always be remembered as one of the greatest finishers in rugby history.

BELOW: Three-time IRB International Player of the Year, flanker Richie McCaw is not only New Zealand's longest-serving captain, he is also the nation's most successful skipper and the second All Black to lift the Rugby World Cup, which he did in 2011.

MAGICAL McCAW LEADS THE WAY

When Richie McCaw burst on to the international scene in 2001 aged 20 there was immediate talk that New Zealand had unearthed another potential legend. Super strong in both attack and defence, he fulfilled those heady expectations to become the best active openside flanker in the world and, maybe, the best of all time. He is the only player ever to win the IRB Player of the Year award three times (in 2006, 2009 and 2010). McCaw was appointed New Zealand captain in 2004 and has enjoyed a highly successful stint at the helm, leading the All Blacks in 66 matches, winning 58, including the memorable 8–7 victory over France in the 2011 Rugby World Cup final.

ABOVE: Doug Howlett was New Zealand's supreme finisher, scoring a national record 49 tries in 62 Tests between 2000 and 2007.

Above: Graham Henry's place in New Zealand rugby history was secured when he led the All Blacks to victory in the 2011 Rugby World Cup final.

HENRY LEADS ALL BLACKS TO GAME'S HOLY GRAIL

When Graham Henry was appointed New Zealand coach in 2004, following the country's disastrous semi-final collapse at the 2003 Rugby World Cup, he was charged with the task of bringing back the Webb Ellis trophy to the land of the long white cloud for the first time since 1987. And although New Zealand enjoyed plenty of good times under Henry, notably five Tri-Nations triumphs, Rugby World Cup glory eluded them for 20 years. The task was completed in 2011. Once again overwhelming pre-tournament favourites, especially as New Zealand were the hosts, Henry guided the All Blacks to the top of their pool, and victories over Argentina (33–10), Australia (20–6) and France in the final (8–7) to leave an indelible mark on his country's rugby history.

MOST POINTS: TOP TEN

Pos	Points	Player (Span)
1	1250	Dan Carter (2003–11)
2	967	Andrew Mehrtens (1995–2004)
3	645	Grant Fox (1985–93)
4	291	Carlos Spencer (1997–2004)
5	245	Doug Howlett (2000–07)
6	236	Christian Cullen (1996–2002)
7	234	Jeff Wilson (1993–2001)
8	230	Joe Rokocoko (2003–10)
9	207	Don Clarke (1956–64)
10	201	Allan Hewson (1981–84)

PACIFIC ISLANDERS

Born out of the formation of the Pacific Islands Rugby Alliance (PIRA) in 2003 and created to ease the considerable financial constraints under which teams from the South Pacific operate, the Pacific Islanders, made up, initially, of players from Fiji, Samoa and Tonga, played their first international match in 2004. An oddity in rugby because they do not appear at the Rugby World Cup – in which each individual nation represents itself – to date they have undertaken a tour every four years.

ENDING THE LONG WAIT FOR VICTORY

The Pacific Islanders endured a torrid start to life in international rugby, losing each of their first eight matches, but their ninth fixture, against Italy at Reggio Emilia on 22 November 2008, finally presented them with a realistic chance of success. They went on to take it with both hands: two tries from winger Vilimoni Delesau and one from full-back Kameli Ratuvou were enough to see them to a slender 25–17 victory – the first, and to date only, win in their history.

OVERALL TEAM RECORD

Span	Mat	Won	Lost	Draw	%	For	Aga	Diff	Tries	Conv	Pens	Drop
2004–08	9	1	8	0	11.11	178	339	-161	25	13	9	0

A SORRY SWANSONG FOR THE ISLANDERS

The Pacific Islanders' match against Ireland at Dublin on 26 November 2006 will principally be remembered for being the last international played at Lansdowne Road before the stadium underwent extensive redevelopment, but for the Pacific Islanders it will go down as the worst performance in their short history. Ireland swamped them, running in eight tries en route to a comprehensive 61–17 victory.

BELOW: Seremaia Baikeinuku is the Pacific Islanders' all-time leading scorer with 35 points.

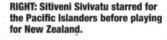

RIGHT: Sitiveni Sivivatu starred for the Pacific Islanders before playing for New Zealand.

CROSSING THE DIVIDE

One of the PIRA's intentions when setting up the Pacific Islanders team was to safeguard the region's players against the prying eyes of the southern hemisphere's biggest rugby nations and to provide them with financial incentives to abstain from the temptation of the Australia or New Zealand dollar. Instead of protecting the players, however, Pacific Islanders matches have, in two instances, merely showcased them. Both previously uncapped, Fiji's Sitiveni Sivivatu and Tonga's Sione Lauaki made their international debuts for the Islanders in July 2004 and impressed, with winger Sivivatu scoring two tries against both New Zealand and South Africa and Lauaki putting together a string of solid performances at No.8. Soon after, the All Blacks came calling and Sivivatu and Lauaki made their New Zealand debuts in June 2005.

BAI A NATURAL PICK AT NO.10

Seremaia Baikeinuku – otherwise known as 'Bai' – made his international debut when he came on as a replacement during Fiji's 47–22 victory over Japan in Tokyo on 20 May 2000, and soon became a first-choice selection for his national side (at either fly-half or centre). He was also a natural choice to wear the No.10 jersey in the Pacific Islanders' first-ever match, against Australia at Adelaide on 3 July 2004, contributing four points during the 29–14 defeat. He played in the Islanders' next seven matches and is both their all-time leading points-scorer, with 35, and the record holder for the most points in a match by a single player – 12 (four penalties) against France at Sochaux-Montbéliard on 15 November 2008

MOST POINTS: TOP FIVE

Pos Points Player (Span)

1	35	Seremaia Baikeinuku (2004–08)
2	20	Kameli Ratuvou (2006–08)
=	20	Sitiveni Sivivatu (2004)
4	19	Seru Rabeni (2004–08)
5	15	Sione Lauaki (2004)

PACIFIC ISLANDERS REPRESENTATION

Country	No. of Players
Samoa	20
Fiji	19
Tonga	17
Cook Islands	1

THE EVER-PRESENTS

Centre Seru Rabeni and scrum-half Moses Rauluni (both from Fiji) are the only two players to have played in all nine of the Pacific Islanders' internationals.

MOST TRIES

Two players hold the record for the most tries by a Pacific Islanders player: Kameli Ratuvou, with four tries in six matches between 2006 and 2008; and Sitiveni Sivivatu, with four tries in three matches in 2004.

ABOVE: Fijian centre Seru Rabeni (white shirt) is one of only two players to have appeared in all nine of the Pacific Islanders' matches.

LEFT: Another Fijian, Kameli Ratuvou (with ball), tops the Pacific Islanders' all-time try-scoring list (alongside compatriot Sitiveni Sivivatu) with four, in six matches between 2006 and 2008.

MOST TRIES: TOP FIVE

Pos	Tries	Player (Span)
1	4	Kameli Ratuvou (2006–08)
=	4	Sitiveni Sivivatu (2004)
3	3	Sione Lauaki (2004)
=	3	Seru Rabeni (2004–08)
5	2	Sireli Bobo (2004)
=	2	Vilimoni Delasau (2008)

IN AT THE DEEP END

The Pacific Islanders could not have chosen three tougher opponents for their first-ever internationals: three matches in three weeks against Australia, New Zealand and South Africa. And although they lost all three, they put in a trio of commendable performances in defeat, losing 29–14 to the Wallabies, 41–26 to the All Blacks and 38–24 to the Springboks. It may not have been a winning start to international rugby life for the Islanders, but it had been a worthy one.

NORTHERN HEMISPHERE BLUES

Many believed the Pacific Islanders' second tour – to Wales, Scotland and Ireland, their first to the northern hemisphere, in November 2006 – would bring with it their first victory. Instead the Islanders struggled, losing 38–20 to Wales and 34–22 to Scotland before suffering a 61–17 collapse against Ireland. The Pacific Islanders' record now stood at played six lost six, and the long wait for that elusive victory continued.

LONGEST-SERVING CAPTAIN

Tonga lock forward Inoke Afeaki holds the distinction of having captained the Pacific Islanders in their first-ever outing in international rugby, against Australia in July 2004. He also holds the record as the Islanders' longest-serving captain (three matches) along with Fiji lock Simon Raiwalui, who led them on their tour to the northern hemisphere in 2006.

FROM THREE TO TWO

In July 2009, following the International Rugby Board's announcement that they would only sanction a Pacific Islanders' tour every four years rather than every two, Samoa quit PIRA claiming that the union had failed to bring the expected financial rewards. As of March 2011, plans for the Islanders' fourth tour have yet to be announced and the future of the Pacific Islanders as a team remains in doubt.

SAMOA

Known as 'Manu Samoa' in their own land, after a famous warrior, Samoa can justifiably lay claim to being the best of the Pacific island rugby-playing nations. Their hard-hitting, physical style has brought them plenty of success over the years: nine Pacific Tri-Nations championships, the Pacific Nations Cup in 2010, qualification for every Rugby World Cup for which they were eligible and a place in the last eight of the game's biggest tournament in 1991 and 1995.

PNG PULPED IN APIA

Samoa's punishment for what by their standards had been a disappointing 2007 Rugby World Cup campaign – they lost three of their four matches – was to pass through the Oceania qualifying section and earn a place at the 2011 tournament. Not that this presented Samoa with too difficult a hurdle: qualification, it transpired, hinged on a winner-takes-all, home-and-away tie against Papua New Guinea. It was a no-contest: in the first match, at Apia on 11 July 2009, Samoa ran in 17 tries with Gavin Williams scoring a national record 30 points during a thumping 115–7 victory – the biggest in their history – and they went on to win the tie 188–19 on aggregate.

OVERALL TEAM RECORD

Span	Mat	Won	Lost	Draw	%	For	Aga	Diff	Tries	Conv	Pens	Drop
1924–2011	182	87	90	5	49.17	3806	3895	-89	402	238	264	9

TOUGH TIMES AGAINST THE ALL BLACKS

Given the close, albeit tense, association between the two countries, it seems strange that Samoa and New Zealand have only ever contested five Tests over the years and, for Samoa, the results make disappointing reading. They have lost all five, conceded 50 points or more in four of them and, on 3 September 2008 at New Plymouth, the two sides' most recent encounter, crashed to a sorry 101–14 away defeat – the heaviest in their history.

BELOW: Gavin Williams contributed 30 points in Samoa's 115–7 rout of Papua New Guinea in July 2009.

POLICY CHANGE REAPS REWARDS FOR SAMOA

Qualification for the 1991 Rugby World Cup ultimately triggered an upturn in fortunes for Samoa, but not before they had embarked on a radical change of policy. Back in the 1960s and 1970s, there had been a mass migration of Samoans to New Zealand; 20 years later, and the offspring of these migrants were starting to make waves in New Zealand domestic rugby, and the Samoan coaching staff spotted an opportunity to call on the island's lost sons to play for their homeland. In came New Zealand-born players such as Pat Lam, Stephen Bachop, Frank Bunce and Apollo Perelini, and the improvement was instantaneous. In 1991, thanks

in no small part to a stunning 16–13 opening victory over Wales in Cardiff, Samoa reached the quarter-finals; they repeated the feat in 1995, but since then – and the advent of professionalism – it has become harder for them to attract such players, and they have failed to progress beyond the group stages at the last four Rugby World Cups.

SUCCESS ON THE HOME FRONT

Samoa have enjoyed considerable success in the Pacific Tri-Nations championship over the years, winning the annual event against Fiji and Tonga 12 times in 22 attempts between 1982 and 2005. When the tournament evolved into the Pacific Five Nations Championship the following year, Samoa finished a creditable second behind the Junior All Blacks. It remained their best result in the expanded competition until 2010, when they won the renamed Pacific Nations Cup for the first time in their history.

NOTABLE SAMOA VICTORIES

Team	Score	Venue	Date
Wales	16–13	Cardiff	6 Oct 1991 (RWC)
Argentina	35–12	Pontypridd	13 Oct 1991 (RWC)
Wales	34–9	Moamoa	25 Jun 1994
Ireland	40–25	Dublin	12 Nov 1996
Wales	38–31	Cardiff	14 Oct 1999 (RWC)
Argentina	28–12	Buenos Aires	3 Dec 2005
Australia	32–23	Sydney	17 Jul 2011

SAMOA SHOCK IRELAND IN DUBLIN

Samoa have not reserved the champagne moments of their rugby history – the victories against top-tier nations – exclusively for the Rugby World Cup. On 12 November 1996 (just three months after losing 60–0 to Fiji), at Lansdowne Road, Dublin, they outscored Ireland by five tries to one to record a stunning 40–25 victory. During what was perhaps the most notable result in their history, they had put 40 points past a top-tier opponent for the first, and to date only, time in their history.

VA VA VOOM FOR VA'A

A former rugby league player – he was part of Samoa's squad for the 1995 Rugby League World Cup, although did not play – Earl Va'a made his international rugby union debut for Samoa during their memorable 40–25 win over Ireland in Dublin, a game in which the debutant scored 15 points. Although he may be short by modern standards, standing at just 5ft 6in (1.68m), it soon became clear that whatever he may have lacked in height, he more than made up for with raw power and a sublime kicking touch. When he bowed out of international rugby following Samoa's 2003 Rugby World Cup exit, he did so as his country's all-time leading points-scorer (with 172 points).

MOST TRIES: TOP FIVE

Pos	Tries	Player (Span)
1	29	Brian Lima (1991–2007)
2	17	Semo Sititi (1999–2009)
3	15	Afato So'oalo (1996–2001)
=	15	Alesana Tuilagi (2002–11)
5	14	Lome Fa'atau (2000–07)

THE CHIROPRACTOR STARS FOR SAMOA

Nicknamed 'The Chiropractor' because of his bone-crunching tackles, Brian Lima's formidable defence became the stuff of rugby legend – just ask South Africa's Derick Hougaard. Lima legitimately flattened him during the 2003 Rugby World Cup and left the Springbok fly-half visibly dazed for several minutes, prompting one commentator to describe the scene as a 'car crash'. But Lima has brought much more to Samoa rugby than defensive brawn: an incisive runner, he made his debut as a 19-year-old against Tonga in May 1991, went on to appear in every one of his country's Rugby World Cup appearances (and is the only player in the game's history to appear in the tournament five times) and bowed out of international rugby in 2007 as his country's most capped player (64 caps) and leading try-scorer (29 tries).

ABOVE: Brian Lima was a standout performer for Samoa for more than a decade and a half and he scored a national record 29 tries in his 62 appearances.

LONG-TIME LEADER

A back-row forward who is equally comfortable on the flank or at No.8, Semo Sititi made his Samoa debut against Japan at Apia in May 1999 and did enough in his first few internationals to earn a place in the 1999 Rugby World Cup squad – he was the only Samoa-based player to do so. He took over the captaincy following Pat Lam's retirement after the Rugby World Cup and led the islanders a record 39 times, until 2007, at which point he relinquished the leadership and returned to the playing ranks until his retirement later that year.

CHANGING SIDES

The rugby relationship between Samoa and New Zealand is a thorny and complex one, with the standard argument being that New Zealand feasts upon the islands for rugby talent. The situation, however, is far from that simple. Born out of politics (and a mass migration of Samoans to New Zealand in the 1960s and 1970s), by the early 1990s a new generation of New Zealand-born Samoans were starting to make waves in domestic rugby and, quite naturally, both Samoa and New Zealand laid claim to them. The choice for the players was straightforward: an easier path into international rugby with Samoa or the chance to pull on the famous All Black jersey. Unfortunately, to the detriment of Samoa rugby (and making a mockery of the IRB's player qualification rules), some did both. Over the years Samoa has lost quality players such as Michael Jones, Frank Bunce, Ofisa Junior Tonu'u, Va'aiga Tuigamala, Stephen Bachop, Alama Ieremia, Pat Lam, John Schuster and Andrew Blowers to the All Blacks.

LEFT: Earl Va'a adds a few more points to his all-time Samoa record, which now stands at 172.

MOST POINTS: TOP FIVE

Pos	Points	Player (Span)
1	172	Earl Va'a (1996–2003)
2	145	Silao Leaegailesolo (1997–2002)
3	140	Brian Lima (1991–2007)
4	137	Darren Kellett (1993–95)
5	119	Roger Warren (2004–08)

MOST TRIES IN ONE MATCH BY A PLAYER

The Samoa record for the most individual tries in a match is four, a feat achieved by three players. All three came during this century and all three were achieved in the capital, Apia: Elvis Seveali'i, against Japan, on 10 June 2000; Alesana Tuilagi, against Tonga, on 2 July 2005; and Esera Lauina, against Papua New Guinea, on 11 July 2009.

TONGA

Missionaries brought rugby to Tonga in the early twentieth century and the islanders were playing international matches by 1924. Their early games were restricted to fixtures against South Pacific neighbours Fiji and Samoa and were often brutal affairs, which goes some way to explaining the physicality for which the Sea Eagles have become renowned. Tonga's uncompromising style may have its critics, but it has brought them two Pacific Tri-Nations titles and six Rugby World Cup appearances.

TONGA REACH RUGBY WORLD CUP IN RECORD-BREAKING STYLE

With a place at the 2003 Rugby World Cup all but assured following their 75–0 away victory in the first leg of their repechage showdown with Korea, Tonga gave their fans even more reason to celebrate when they produced a record-breaking performance in the return fixture at Nuku A'lofa on 22 March 2003. The Sea Eagles raced into a 56–0 half-time lead and went on to register 17 tries in the one-sided match (four of them from No.8 Benhur Kivalu and two from fly-half Pierre Hola, who also slotted 17 conversions – his 44 points in the match is a national record) en route to a 119–0 victory – the biggest in their history.

OVERALL TEAM RECORD

Span	Mat	Won	Lost	Draw	%	For	Aga	Diff	Tries	Conv	Pens	Drop
1924–2011	222	80	137	5	37.16	3993	5078	-1085	467	271	228	7

OUT OF THEIR DEPTH

Tonga have played four matches against the All Blacks and have lost all of them, scoring only 26 points and conceding a mighty 279. The heaviest of those defeats – and the heaviest in the Sea Eagles' history – came at North Shore City, Auckland, on 16 June 2000, when they were crushed 102–0.

BELOW: Tonga's record points-scorer (with 317) Pierre Hola shone for the Sea Eagles for more than a decade.

SORRY TIMES FOR TROUBLED TONGA

Their first match at the 2003 Rugby World Cup triggered the most miserable run of form in Tonga's history. The Sea Eagles slumped to a 36–12 defeat to Italy and went on to lose all four games. The barren spell continued when they endured disappointing Pacific Tri-Nations campaigns in 2004 and 2005 (they lost all six matches) and a difficult tour to the northern hemisphere that saw them lose to Italy (48–0) and France (43–8). The sorry losing streak, stretching to 12 matches, finally came to an end when the Sea Eagles beat Japan 57–16 at Fukuoka on 4 June 2006 – two years and eight months after it had started.

LACK OF CONSISTENCY KEY TO STILTED PROGRESS

The ability to put together a string of consistent performances has eluded Tonga over the years. In 222 internationals played since 1924, they have only won three consecutive matches on five occasions and four consecutive matches twice: a pair of victories over both the New Zealand Maoris and Samoa in 1969; and between 30 November 2002 and 22 March 2003, when they beat Papua New Guinea (twice) and Japan (twice).

BELOW: Tongan captain Nili Latu tries to break through the Samoa defence during the Sea Eagles' 19–15 2003 Rugby World Cup victory.

MOST POINTS: TOP FIVE

Pos	Points	Player (Span)
1	317	Pierre Hola (1998–2009)
2	190	Sateki Tuipulotu (1993–2003)
3	187	Kurt Morath (2009–11)
4	118	Josh Taumalolo (1996–2007)
5	114	Gustavo Tonga (1996–2001)

TONGA'S TRIUMPHS

The golden times in Tonga's rugby history are hard to find, but the Pacific Tri-Nations tournament provided the Sea Eagles with their greatest moments: victory in 1983 and 1986 – during the latter they won both of their matches (31–13 against Samoa and 13–6 against Fiji) for the only time in their history. Their best performance in the expanded Pacific Nations Cup came in 2011, when they finished second to Japan on points-difference

ALL-TIME LEADING POINTS-SCORER

Pierre Hola made a points-scoring debut for Tonga (he slotted one conversion) against Samoa at Sydney on 18 September 1998, but missed out on a place in Tonga's 1999 Rugby World Cup squad and had to wait until 2002 before becoming a permanent fixture in the national side. A fans' favourite, the fly-half appeared at the 2003 and 2007 Rugby World Cups (and topped the Sea Eagles' points list in both), has gone on to win 39 caps (to stand joint-second on Tonga's all-time appearance list) and has scored a national record 317 points.

TONGA'S BEST PERFORMANCE AT THE RUGBY WORLD CUP

Tonga have appeared in six of the first seven Rugby World Cups (failing to qualify only in 1991). But they have struggled to make a serious breakthrough on rugby's biggest stage, never progressing beyond the group stages and winning only six of 21 matches. However, the Sea Eagles' performances appear to be on the up: they won twice at the tournament for the first time in 2007 and repeated the feat in New Zealand in 2011, including a 19–14 victory over France – arguably the most famous victory in the team's 87-year history.

TAUMALOLO IS TONGA'S TRY-SCORING KING

Although he only ever played in one Rugby World Cup match for his country – a 45–9 defeat against New Zealand at Bristol in 1999, in which he kicked all of his side's points – Siua 'Josh' Taumalolo nevertheless made a big impact on Tonga rugby over a period of 11 years. He made a try-scoring debut during Tonga's 30–15 defeat against Samoa on 13 July 1996 and, playing at centre or fly-half, went on to win 26 caps. When he bowed out of international rugby, in June 2007, he did so as Tonga's all-time leading try-scorer, with 14 tries.

MOST TRIES: TOP FIVE

Pos	Tries	Player (Span)
1	14	Josh Taumalolo (1996–2007)
2	11	Pierre Hola (1998–2009)
3	10	Fepiku Tatafu (1996–2002)
4	9	Vunga Lilo (2007–11)
5	8	Benhur Kivalu (1998–2005)
=	8	Elisi Vunipola (1990–2005)

THIRD TIME LUCKY FOR VUNIPOLA

Elisi Vunipola made his Tonga debut on 24 March 1990, against Fiji, collected his second cap three weeks later, against Korea, but then had to wait over three years before winning his third cap, against Samoa on 29 May 1993. But it proved to be third time lucky for the diminutive fly-half and he was ever-present in the Sea Eagles' line-up for the next decade, appeared at the 1995 and 1999 Rugby World Cups and ended his international career in November 2005 as Tonga's most capped player of all time (with 41 caps).

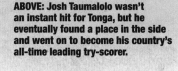

ABOVE: Josh Taumalolo wasn't an instant hit for Tonga, but he eventually found a place in the side and went on to become his country's all-time leading try-scorer.

LATU LEADS BY EXAMPLE

Big-tackling flanker Nili Latu was appointed Tonga captain in only his third international – a 77–10 victory over the Cook Islands on 24 June 2006 – and went on to become a source of inspiration for the Sea Eagles. He led from the front during their successful 2007 Rugby World Cup campaign (they won two matches for the first time during the tournament) and by 2011 he had led Tonga on 19 occasions to become his country's longest-serving captain of all time.

LEFT: Tonga's players celebrate after their stunning 19–14 defeat of finalists-to-be France at the 2011 Rugby World Cup.

OTHER ASIA AND OCEANIA TEAMS

Rugby in Asia and Oceania may be dominated by the gargantuan presence of Australia and New Zealand (on the global scene) and Japan (in Asia), but rugby life beneath those top-tier teams is alive and kicking in both regions, each of which stages its own Rugby World Cup qualifying tournament. In Asia, teams also compete in the various divisions of the Asia Five Nations Championship; in Oceania, second-tier teams and below compete for the Oceania Cup.

RECORDS SHATTERED IN KUALA LUMPUR

Hong Kong's greatest moment on a rugby field came against Singapore at Kuala Lumpur, Malaysia, in an Asia Pool 2 Rugby World Cup qualifying match on 27 October 1994. They won the match 164–13 to break the all-time record for the most points scored in an international match and set a new mark for the most tries scored with 27; their full-back, Ashley Billington, scored ten of them – another international all-time record for a player in a single match.

KOREA'S RUGBY WORLD CUP QUALIFYING WOES

It may be due to their regular forays into the latter stages of the tournament, but Korea have lost more Rugby World Cup qualifying matches (24) than any other nation and some of those defeats have been particularly painful: against Japan in the qualification final for the 2005 tournament and against Tonga in three repechage matches (for the 1999, 2003 and 2007 tournaments).

A RUGBY WORLD CUP WORST FOR VANUATU

Vanuatu, currently 91st in the IRB world rankings, hold the unenviable record of having played in the most Rugby World Cup qualifying matches without ever recording a win. Their record reads: played five, lost five, points for 40, points against 246. And there have been some hefty defeats along the way, the worst of which came at Port Moresby on 20 August 2005 when they lost 97–3 to Papua New Guinea.

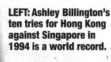

LEFT: Ashley Billington's ten tries for Hong Kong against Singapore in 1994 is a world record.

ABOVE: Korea's 21–17 defeat of Japan in the final of the 1998 Asian Games in Bangkok was one of the country's finest moments on a rugby field. They repeated their success on home soil in 2002.

CHINESE TAIPEI TROUNCED IN TOKYO

The vast difference between Asian rugby's haves and have-nots is best shown when one of the region's second-tier nations pays a visit to Japan, the undisputed kings of Asian rugby – they are the only team from the continent to play in the Rugby World Cup and have not lost a home qualifying match against an Asian opponent in 13 attempts. On 1 May 2002, in Tokyo, Chinese Taipei became Japan's latest victims, losing 155–3; the 152-point losing margin is the joint highest in international rugby history (matched only by Paraguay's miserable 152–0 defeat to Argentina in Mendoza on 1 May 2002).

GOLDEN MOMENTS FOR KOREA

Korea's finest rugby moments both came at the Asian Games. In 1998, in Bangkok, they beat arch-rivals Japan 21–17 in the final to take gold; four years later, in Busan, South Korea, they overcame Japan in the semi-finals (24–7) before going on to beat Chinese Taipei 33–21 in the final to retain their crown. These are the only two occasions a 15-a-side tournament was contested at the event.

100-PLUS POINTS SCORED IN A MATCH

Team	Opponent	Result	Venue	Date
Hong Kong	Singapore	164–13"	Kuala Lumpur	27 Oct 1994
Korea	Malaysia	135–3	Hong Kong	20 Sep 1992
Korea	Chinese Taipei	119–7	Seoul	30 Jun 2002
Hong Kong	Chinese Taipei	114–12	Taipei	9 Nov 1996
Korea	Malaysia	112–5	Taipei	5 Nov 1996
Hong Kong	Sri Lanka	108–0	Taipei	9 Nov 1980
Hong Kong	Malaysia	103–5	Taipei	3 Nov 1996
Korea	Malaysia	102–0	Hong Kong	12 Nov 1988

ASIAN FIVE NATIONS – CHAMPIONS

Year	Top div	Div 1	Div 2	Div 3	Div 4	Region 1	Region 2	Region 3
2008	Japan	Singapore	Thailand	-	-	Indonesia	Philippines	Iran
2009	Japan	Arabian Gulf	Malaysia	Philippines	-	Laos	-	Uzbekistan
2010	Japan	Sri Lanka	Philippines	Iran	Jordan	-	-	-
2011	Japan	South Korea	Taiwan	China	Qatar	-	-	-

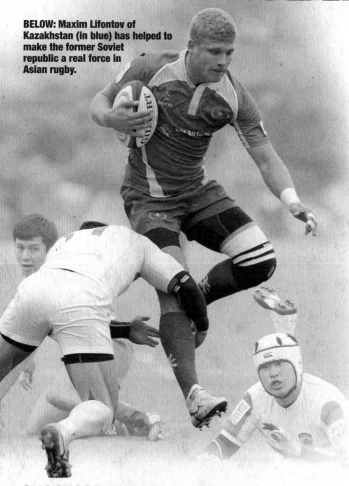

BELOW: Maxim Lifontov of Kazakhstan (in blue) has helped to make the former Soviet republic a real force in Asian rugby.

KAZAKHS ON THE UP

With the exception of Georgia, Kazakhstan are the most successful of the ex-Soviet nations and one of the fastest rising teams in world rugby. They finished runners-up in both the 2009 and 2010 Asia Five Nations Championship – won, convincingly, on both occasions by Japan – to stake their further claim (backed up by their current world ranking of 31) to being among the best teams in Asia.

YO-YO TIMES FOR SINGAPORE

Singapore, currently 49th in the IRB world rankings, have struggled to cross the divide between the first and second tier of Asian rugby. As Asia Five Nations Division 1 champions in 2008, they earned promotion to the top flight of the championship but lost all four of their matches the following year and were relegated back to Division 1. They are the only promoted team in the tournament's brief history (dating back to 2008) not to have retained their top-flight status.

Best of the rest: IRB world rankings

Hong Kong (27); Kazakhstan (31); Korea (32); Sri Lanka (45); Papua New Guinea (46); Singapore (49); Cook Islands (54); Chinese Taipei (57); China (61); Malaysia (62); Thailand (64); Niue Island (66); India (75); Solomon Islands (77); Tahiti (85); Guam (86); Vanuatu (91).

MAGIC MOMENT FOR NIUE ISLAND

The Niue Island's national rugby team played their first international match on 10 September 1983 against Fiji at Apia and suffered a comprehensive 124–4 defeat – still the heaviest in their history. They had to wait another 18 years before contesting their second international fixture and even when they returned in 2001 they enjoyed little success. Until, that is, 1 September 2008, when they beat New Caledonia 27–5 in the FORU Oceania Cup final to win the only title in their history.

SUCCESSFUL SWANSONG FOR ARABIAN GULF

The Arabian Gulf international rugby team, consisting of players from Bahrain, Kuwait, Oman, Qatar, Saudi Arabia and the United Arab Emirates, was formed in 1993 and took part in Rugby World Cup qualifying tournaments and the Asia Five Nations until 2010, when it was announced that each nation would compete individually. They combined team bowed out in style: relegated from the top tier in 2008, they won promotion at the first time of asking and then, in 2010, won two top-tier games out of four to finish fourth and become the first promoted team in history to avoid relegation. But the team then disbanded.

THE PAPUA NEW GUINEA SHOW

The Federation of Oceania Rugby Unions Cup, otherwise known as the FORU Oceania Cup, has been contested on annually since 2007 between teams from nine nations or territories: American Samoa, the Cook Islands, New Caledonia, Niue Island, Papua New Guinea, Solomon Islands, Vanuatu and Wallis and Fortuna. There is no doubt about who have been the stars of the show: Papua New Guinea have collected the title twice in the four editions of the event (in 2007 and 2009).

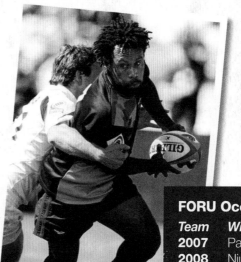

LEFT: Papua New Guinea have been the dominant team in the FORU Oceania Cup, winning the competition twice since its inception in 2007.

FORU Oceania Cup winners

Team	Winners
2007	Papua New Guinea
2008	Niue Island
2009	Papua New Guinea

AFRICA

Although rugby had been around in Africa since the 1850s, it wasn't until 1891 – when Governor Cecil Rhodes's preference for the sport over football prompted him to invite a British touring team to South Africa – that interest in the game started to grow in southern Africa and, helped by the presence of troops in the various colonies, it did not take long before the rugby gospel was spread to the far corners of the continent. Not that everyone listened: of Africa's 54 countries, only 14 of them are listed in the current IRB world rankings.

Ellis Park Stadium in Johannesburg is one of the world's great rugby stadiums and was the venue for the 1995 Rugby World Cup final.

IVORY COAST

The Federation Ivoirienne de Rugby was formed as recently as March 1990, so it came as a huge surprise when the Ivory Coast qualified for the Rugby World Cup for the first time in their history in 1995. The tournament itself, however, was a disaster. The Elephants lost all three matches, endured the agony of seeing one of their players horrifically injured and have not qualified for the event since. In recent times, they have played in the continent's annual Africa Cup competition.

TOUGH START FOR THE ELEPHANTS

The Ivory Coast's first recognized match in international rugby came against Zimbabwe at Harare on 5 May 1990 in a Rugby World Cup qualifying match: they lost 22–9. Two further defeats over the next seven days (12–7 against Tunisia on 8 May and 11–4 against Morocco on 12 May) left their Rugby World Cup dreams in tatters and a further three years would pass before the Elephants contested another international fixture.

ABOVE: The Ivory Coast came up short against Scotland at the 1995 Rugby World Cup, especially against line-out jumpers such as Doddie Weir.

HOME COMFORTS

The Ivory Coast national team may only be a relative newcomer to the international rugby scene, but the Elephants have already established an impressive home record, winning eight and drawing two of the 13 fixtures played in Abidjan. Of those victories, the most impressive came against Tunisia on 12 May 2001, when they won the African CAR Championship match 46–0 – the biggest win in their international history.

THE LONG ROAD TO SOUTH AFRICA

The Ivory Coast's third international match – three years after their second – would lead them on the path towards the greatest moment of their short rugby history. A 19–16 Rugby World Cup qualifying round one victory over Tunisia in Tunis on 26 October 1993 (their first-ever win) virtually assured them of a safe passage to the next round, a position that was confirmed four days later following a comfortable 25–3 win over Morocco (who had also beaten Tunisia). The Elephants progressed into the final qualifying group, containing Morocco, Namibia and Zimbabwe, with the winner of the round-robin tournament, staged in Casablanca in June 1994, earning qualification to the 1995 Rugby World Cup. The Ivory Coast got off to the worst of starts, losing 17–9 to a Morocco side revitalized by playing in front of their home crowd. Instead of

ABOVE: Max Brito's tragic story is the darkest spot on the Rugby World Cup's history.

capitulating, the Elephants rallied in style, beating Namibia (13–12) and Zimbabwe (17–10) to top the group and win one of the biggest prizes in the game – a coveted place at the sport's biggest event – the Rugby World Cup.

HARD TIMES FOR THE IVORY COAST

A major consolation for the Ivory Coast was that their Rugby World Cup appearance in 1995 guaranteed them a place in the final round of qualifying for the 1999 tournament (a group of four teams). They lost all three matches to finish bottom and have endured nothing but Rugby World Cup disappointment since. They failed to make it beyond the initial group stages in 2003 and fell in the second round in 2007. There was a glimmer of hope in June 2009 when they advanced to the semi-finals of the 2011 qualification tournament, but that was soon extinguished following a 67–27 aggregate defeat to Namibia.

THE RUGBY WORLD CUP'S DARKEST MOMENT

Max Brito, who played club rugby in south-west France, was 24 years old when he travelled to South Africa to play in the 1995 Rugby World Cup. A committed winger, he made his debut in the Ivory Coast's opening-game against Scotland (an 89–0 defeat), coming on as a replacement, and played a full part in the Elephants' much improved performance against France (a 54–18 defeat). In the third minute of the Ivory Coast's final group match, against Tonga, Brito made an impressive defensive catch on the run and advanced towards the massed Tonga defence. Disaster struck: he was tackled, ended up at the bottom of a ruck and was left motionless on the ground, paralyzed from the neck down: 3 June 1995 remains the darkest day in Rugby World Cup history.

CHASTENED ON THE BIG STAGE

The Ivory Coast's reward for securing qualification for the 1995 Rugby World Cup in South Africa was a place in Pool D alongside France, Scotland and Tonga. It proved too tough a proposition for the Elephants. In their opening match they crashed to an 89–0 defeat against Scotland in their opening match (still the biggest defeat in their history). They fared a little better against France, scoring two tries in a 54–18 reversal, then battled to a 29–11 defeat to Tonga (scoring one try in the match) to finish bottom of the group. The Ivory Coast's first, and to date only, Rugby World Cup experience had been a chastening one.

NAMIBIA

Rugby has been played in Namibia since 1916, when South African soldiers invaded the German colony, but the country did not play its first international match until 1990, when it gained independence. Since then, the Namibia national team – known as the Welwitschias – has gone on to establish itself as one of Africa's strongest second-tier sides: they have qualified for the Rugby World Cup on four occasions and have won the Africa Cup three times.

OFF TO A FLYER

There have been several newcomers to the world rugby fold since the early 1990s and Namibia, hardened by years of playing in South Africa's domestic Currie Cup competition (as South-west Africa), were the most prepared to cope with the rigours of the international game. Between March 1990 and May 1992, the Welwitschias won 16 of their first 18 internationals, which included recording a memorable pair of home victories over Italy (17–7 and 33–19) and Ireland (15–6 and 25–15).

BELOW: The most famous name in Namibia rugby, Gerhard Mans captained the Weltwischias in the first-ever international and scored a national record 27 tries.

THIRD TIME LUCKY FOR NAMIBIA

Independence came too late for Namibia to participate in the qualifying tournament of the 1991 Rugby World Cup and they fell at the final hurdle in 1995, losing to the Ivory Coast (13–12) and drawing with Morocco (16–16), but they finally found the winning formula at the third time of asking. They progressed to the final round of the 1999 qualifying tournament on points difference (following a surprise 20–17 defeat to Tunisia), but went on to win all three of their round-robin matches – against the Ivory Coast (22–10), Morocco (17–8) and Zimbabwe (39–14) – to earn a place on the game's biggest stage for the first time. They have qualified for every Rugby World Cup since.

A VICTORY TO REMEMBER

Namibia have become the kings of African Rugby World Cup qualifying tournaments over the years, winning all but five of 27 matches and progressing through the various rounds of the competition to qualify for 1999, 2003, 2007 and 2011

editions. There have been some thumping victories along the way, but none more so than their 18-try, 116–0 romp against Madagascar at Windhoek on 15 June 2002 – the biggest win in the Welwitschias' history.

STRUGGLING ON THE BIG STAGE

Namibia may have discovered the knack of qualifying for the Rugby World Cup, but once they have get there they struggle. The Weltwischias have played 15 matches on rugby's biggest stage (in four separate tournaments) and lost every single one of them, including eight by 50 points or more. The worst of those defeats came on 25 October 2003, when they lost 142–0 to Australia in Adelaide – the heaviest defeat in both Namibia's and the tournament's history.

NAMIBIA'S AFRICA CUP SUCCESS

Namibia have enjoyed considerable success in the Africa Cup, which has been played on an annual basis since 2000. In 2002, the Welwitschias won the competition on tries scored following their 43–43 aggregate tie against Tunisia in the two-legged final. They lost to Morocco in the final the following year (27–7), but gained revenge over the North Africans in the 2004 final, winning 39–22 to claim the cup for a second time. They tasted the bitterness of a final defeat once more in 2006 (losing 29–27 to South African Amateurs) before claiming the title for the third time in 2008–09 with a 40–23 aggregate victory over Tunisia in the final.

ABOVE: Jaco Coetzee's 335 points is a record total for a Namibian player.

NAMIBIA'S LEADING POINTS-SCORER

Jaco Coetzee won his first cap for Namibia on 21 April 1990 when he came on as a replacement during the Welwetschias' thumping 88–9 victory over Portugal. He made his first full start in Namibia's next match, against Wales, and scored his first international points during the narrow 34–30 defeat. Playing at either full-back or No.10, Coetzee became a mainstay of the Namibia line-up, winning 28 caps (his last coming in 1995) and scoring a national record 335 points.

LEGEND MANS LEADS TRY-SCORING LIST

Gerhard Mans is a legend in Namibia rugby. A winger with deadly finishing skills, he was a leading member of the South West Africa side that defied the odds to finish third in the 1988 Currie Cup. He was captain of Namibia in their first post-independence international, against Zimbabwe on 24 March 1990 (he scored a try in the 33–18 victory), and carried on playing until 1994, by which time he had scored an impressive 27 tries (a national record) in 27 matches.

SOUTH AFRICA

In 1891, South Africa became the first team from the southern hemisphere to play international rugby and it was not long before the Springboks became established as one of the world's leading sides. Barred from competing in IRB-sanctioned matches between 1984 and 1992 as a result of their government's apartheid policy, they returned to the world stage as a dominant force, winning the Rugby World Cup in 1995 and 2007 and the Tri-Nations championship in 1999, 2004 and 2009.

THE BOKS AGAINST THE LIONS

British representative sides have been touring South Africa since 1891, providing the opposition for the Springboks when they played their first-ever international match (at Port Elizabeth on 30 July 1891) and recorded their first-ever win (5–0 at Cape Town on 5 September 1896), but it wasn't until 1955 that a representative team dubbed the British Lions came to town. The Boks won the final match 22–8 to level the series … and a legendary rivalry was born. Of the six series played since then, South Africa have won four of them (in 1962, 1968, 1980 and, most recently, 2009) and lost only two (in 1980 and 1997).

HONOURS

Rugby World Cup:
(best finish) – champions (1995, 2007)
Tri-Nations:
(best finish) – champions (1998, 2004, 2009)

RIGHT: South Africa's inspired Rugby World Cup victory on home turf in 1995 is the proudest moment in the country's rugby history.

OVERALL TEAM RECORD

Span	Mat	Won	Lost	Draw	%	For	Aga	Diff	Tries	Conv	Pens	Drop	GfM
1891–2011	404	255	130	19	65.47	9167	6198	+2969	1137	738	797	95	1

THE BOKS BECOME A WORLD FORCE

If South Africa's first tour to the northern hemisphere in 1906–07 had been a political attempt to ease the strained relations that prevailed in the aftermath of the Boer War, then the Springboks' second tour to Britain, France and Ireland in 1912–13 was about showing the world what a true rugby force they had become. They won all five matches – against Scotland (16–0), Ireland (38–0), Wales (3–0), England (9–3) and France (38–5) to achieve the northern hemisphere grand slam for the first time in their history.

SOUTH AFRICA'S WILDERNESS YEARS

The murmurs of dissatisfaction directed towards South Africa's national rugby team as a result of the country's apartheid policy had been growing into a worldwide clamour for more than a decade and a half (the Gleneagles Treaty discouraging sporting contact with South Africa had been signed by Commonwealth-member countries as early as 1976), but South Africa continued to play in IRB-sanctioned international matches until 1984. And then came the wilderness years, when the Springboks were restricted to playing matches against rebel touring teams. Their first match back in the international fold came against New Zealand at Johannesburg on 15 August 1992 – they lost a thriller 27–24.

SPRINGBOKS BATTER URUGUAY IN EAST LONDON

Nobody had expected Uruguay to pose South Africa too many problems when the two sides met in a one-off Test in East London on 11 June 2005, but few could have predicted the abject capitulation that followed. The Springboks raced into a 56–3 half-time lead and continued to run riot in the second half, scoring a total of 21 tries in the match – Tonderai Chavhanga scored six of them (a national record) – on the way to completing a crushing 134–3 victory – the biggest in their history.

ABOVE: Tonderai Chavhanga scored a national record six tries against Uruguay on 11 June 2005.

SOUTH AFRICA HIT ROCK BOTTOM

From England's perspective, their match against South Africa at Twickenham on 23 November 2002 provided further proof of their claims that they would travel to the following year's Rugby World Cup as one of the pre-tournament favourites; for South Africa, however, their sorry showing merely confirmed how far they had fallen since the heady days of 1995. Trailing 18–3 at half-time, the Springboks slumped in the second half and went on to suffer a humiliating 55–3 defeat – the heaviest in their history.

UNITING THE RAINBOW NATION

The 1995 Rugby World Cup provided the world with one of the greatest moments of modern times and one of the most iconic images in sporting history. The tournament was the first major sporting event to take place in post-apartheid South Africa and the first Rugby World Cup in which the hosts had competed. The Springboks got off to a blistering start, beating defending champions Australia 27–18 in their opening match, and when they followed that up with hard-fought victories over Romania (21–8) and Canada (20–0) an entire nation started to believe. Fuelled by an increasingly vociferous support, the Boks beat Samoa 42–15 in the quarter-finals and defied appalling conditions in Durban to see off France in the semis (19–15). All that stood between them and rugby immortality was a powerful New Zealand side playing at the peak its powers and brimming with confidence following a 45–29 demolition of England in the last four. It was a final nobody expected South Africa to win, but they succeeded in stifling All Black giant Jonah Lomu, where others had failed and, thanks to the boot of Joel Stransky, secured a 15–12 victory after extra-time. Few who saw it will forget the moment when Nelson Mandela, wearing a No.6 Springbok shirt (so often the symbol of white supremacy in the country), handed the Rugby World Cup trophy to Francois Pienaar and, moments later, as the Webb Ellis trophy was hoisted aloft, an entire nation danced in the streets.

ABOVE: Arguably the most iconic moment in sporting history as Nelson Mandela hads the Webb Ellis Trophy to Francois Pienaar after South Africa's 1995 Rugby World Cup final victory over New Zealand at Ellis Park, Johannesburg.

PARADISE IN PARIS FOR SOUTH AFRICA

South Africa had won only two of their previous five matches (against Namibia and Scotland) going into the 2007 Rugby World Cup in France and few thought they had any chance of winning the trophy for a second time. The Springboks, however, quickly found their stride, beating Samoa (59–7), England (36–0), Tonga (30–25) and the USA (64–15) to win their pool with ease. They then beat Fiji in the quarter-finals (37–20) and downed Argentina in the last four (37–13) before ending England's spirited title defence with a 15–6 victory in the final in Paris. South Africa had joined Australia as a two-time world champion.

ON A RECORD-BREAKING ROLL

A 61–12 demolition of Australia in Pretoria on 23 August 1997 sparked the richest vein of form in the Springboks' history. They travelled to the northern hemisphere three months later and won all five matches; they beat Ireland, Wales and England in matches at home; they went on to record a 100 per cent record in the 1998 Tri-Nations; and travelled to Britain and Ireland off the back of 14 consecutive wins. The record-breaking winning streak ended at 17 matches following a 13–7 defeat to England at Twickenham on 5 December 1998.

LEFT: (left to right) Bryan Habana, Jake White and John Smit celbrate South Africa's 2007 Rugby World Cup triumph.

THE BOKS' LONGEST LOSING STREAK

For a period of 13 months in the mid-1960s South Africa could not buy a win. The slump began with an 8–6 home defeat against France at Springs on 25 July 1964 and continued with away defeats to Ireland (9–6) and Scotland (8–5) in 1965. The Springboks lost four further Tests – two apiece to Australia and New Zealand – before ending the longest losing run in their history at seven matches when they beat the All Blacks 19–16 in the third Test at Christchurch on 4 September 1965.

SPRINGBOKS ROMP TO TRI-NATIONS GLORY

New Zealand had grabbed the headlines in the opening years of the Tri-Nations, winning the first editions of the tournament (in 1996 and 1997) without losing a single match. In 1998, however, it was South Africa's turn to steal the glory. The Springboks, who had ended the first two series as runners-up to the All Blacks, opened their 1998 campaign with a tense 14–13 victory over Australia in Sydney on 18 July, beat the All Blacks 13–3 in Wellington a week later (to record their first win on New Zealand soil since 1981), edged a nervy encounter against New Zealand in Durban on 15 August (24–23) and beat Australia 29–15 in their final match at Johannesburg a week later to win the Tri-Nations crown for the first time in their history. The Springboks won the trophy for a second time in 2004 and again in 2009.

INTERNATIONAL RUGBY HALL OF FAME INDUCTEES

Name	(Span, Caps)
Naas Botha	(1980–92, 28 caps)
Danie Craven	(1931–38, 16 caps)
Morne du Plessis	(1971–80, 22 caps)
Frik du Preez	(1961–71, 38 caps)
Danie Gerber	(1980–92, 24 caps)
Hennie Muller	(1949–53, 13 caps)
Benny Osler	(1924–33, 17 caps)
Francois Pienaar	(1993–96, 29 caps)
Joost van der Westhuizen	(1993–2003, 89 caps)

MONTGOMERY SETS THE BOKS' ALL-TIME POINTS MILESTONE

Namibia-born Percy Montgomery made his debut for South Africa (at centre) during the Boks' series-losing 18–15 defeat to the British and Irish Lions at Durban on 28 June 1997, scoring one of his side's three tries in the match. An incisive runner with a steady boot, he switched to full-back later in the year and went on to make the Springbok No.15 jersey his own for the best part of a decade (although he did make a handful of appearances at fly-half or centre). A veteran of three Rugby World Cups, he bowed out of international rugby in August 2008 after 102 caps (he was the first South African in history to pass the 100-cap landmark) as South Africa's all-time leading points-scorer (with 893). He also holds the South Africa record for the most points in a match (35 – one try, 12 conversions and a penalty – against Namibia at Cape Town on 15 August 2007).

BELOW: Percy Montgomery, South Africa's all-time leading points scorer, in full flow.

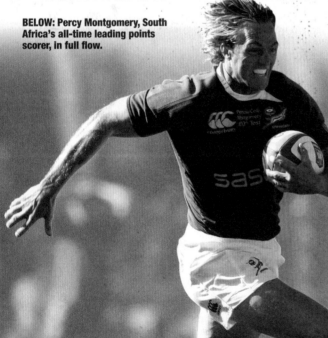

MOST CAPS: TOP TEN

Pos	Caps	Player (Span)
1	111	John Smit (2000–11)
2	105	Victor Matfield (2001–10)
3	102	Percy Montgomery (1997–2008)
4	89	Joost van der Westhuizen (1993–2003)
5	80	Os du Randt (1994–2007)
6	77	Mark Andrews (1994–2001)
7	76	Bakkies Botha (2002–11)
8	74	Bryan Habana (2004–11)
9	73	C.J. van der Linde (2002–11)
10	72	Jean de Villiers (2002–11)

INSPIRATIONAL LEADER

John Smit won his first cap (at hooker) for South Africa against Canada on 10 June 2000 at the age of 22, but it wasn't until coach Jake White made him captain in 2004 that he established himself as a real force in the team and proved his true worth to his country. Smit was an inspirational choice as captain and by 2011 had led South Africa on 83 occasions (an all-time record in international rugby) and to some of the greatest moments in the Springboks' history: two Tri-Nations wins (in 2004 and 2009), a series victory over the British Lions (in 2009) and, most notably, the Rugby World Cup in 2007. He also became South Africa's most-capped player, with 111, one ahead of long-time teammate Victor Matfield.

ABOVE: South Africa's hooker and captain John Smit put in some storming performances during the 2011 Rugby World Cup, but the defending champions lost their crown in the quarter-final, when Australia beat the Springboks, 11–9, at the Westpac Stadium, Wellington.

ALL-TIME LEADING TRY-SCORERS: BY POSITION

Position	Player (Span)	Tries
Full-back	Percy Montgomery (1997–2008)	18
Winger	Bryan Habana (2004–11)	39
Centre	Jaque Fourie (2003–11)	28
Fly-half	Morne Steyn (2009–11)	6
	Joel Stransky (1993–96)	6
	Piet Visagie (1967–71)	6
Scrum-half	Joost van der Westhuizen (1993–2003)	38
No.8	Pierre Spies (2006–11)	7
Flanker	Schalk Burger (2003–11)	13
Lock	Mark Andrews (1994–2001)	12
Prop	Gurthro Steenkamp (2004–11)	6
Hooker	John Smit (2000–11)	6

MOST POINTS: TOP TEN

Pos	Points	Player (Span)
1	893	Percy Montgomery (1997–2008)
2	410	Morne Steyn (2009–11)
3	312	Naas Botha (1980–92)
4	240	Joel Stransky (1993–96)
5	221	Braam van Straaten (1999–2001)
6	200	Bryan Habana (2004–11)
7	190	Joost van der Westhuizen (1993–2003)
8	181	Jannie de Beer (1997–99
9	171	Andre Pretorius (2002–07)
10	160	Jacque Fourie (2003–11)

THE COACH WHO COAXED THE BOKS TO RUGBY WORLD CUP SUCCESS

It is hard to argue against Kitch Christie's claims to be the most successful coach in South Africa's rugby history. Appointed to the position in mid-1994, following the Springboks' 2–0 series defeat against New Zealand, the former Transvaal coach was charged with turning a team that had won just four of its previous ten internationals into serious challengers for the following year's Rugby World Cup, which South Africa was hosting. He did just that: the Springboks won every one of their 14 matches under Christie's charge, including the Rugby World Cup, before ill-health forced him to step down from the position in March 1996. Tragically, he died two years later, aged 58.

COACHES

Name	Tenure
Danie Craven	1949–56
Basil Kenyon	1958
Hennie Muller	1960–61, 1963, 1965
Boy Louw	1960–61, 1965
Izak van Heerden	1962
Felix du Plessis	1964
Ian Kirkpatrick	1967, 1974
Avril Malan	1969–70
Johan Claassen	1964, 1970–74
Nelie Smith	1980–81
Cecil Moss	1982–89
John Williams	1992
Ian McIntosh	1993–94
Kitch Christie	1994–96
Andre Markgraaff	1996
Carel du Plessis	1997
Nick Mallett	1997–2000
Harry Viljoen	2000–02
Rudolph Straeuli	2002–03
Jake White	2004–07
Peter de Villiers	2008–11

ABOVE: Bryan Habana's eight tries at the 2007 Rugby World Cup did much to guide the Springboks to a second world title.

BRILLIANT BURGER ON TOP FORM FOR THE SPRINGBOKS

A member of South Africa's IRB Under-21 World Championship-winning side in 2002, it did not take long before Schalk Burger was catapulted into the senior side. He made his try-scoring international debut (as a replacement) against Georgia at the 2003 Rugby World Cup at the tender age of 20, and his first full start against Ireland in 2004, going on to enjoy a magical year, during which he established a reputation as one of the rising stars of the game, helped the Springboks to their second Tri-Nations title and ended the year by becoming the first South Africa player in history to be voted the IRB's Player of the Year. He overcame a career-threatening neck injury to play a full part in the Springboks' 2007 Rugby World Cup success and by 2011 had won 68 caps for his country.

MOST TRIES: TOP TEN

Pos	Tries	Player (Span)
1	40	Bryan Habana (2004–11)
2	38	Joost van der Westhuizen (1993–2003)
3	32	Jaque Fourie (2003–11)
4	26	Breyton Paulse (1999–2007)
5	25	Percy Montgomery (1997–2008)
6	21	Pieter Rossouw (1997–2003)
7	20	James Small (1992–97)
8	19	Danie Gerber (1980–92)
=	19	Stefan Terblanche (1998–2003)
=	19	Jean de Villiers (2002–11)

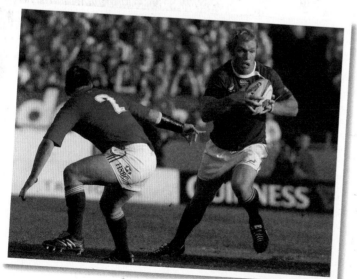

ABOVE: Schalk Burger made a spectacular start to his international career for South Africa in 2004 and ended his first season as the IRB's Player of the Year.

FLYING HABANA SHOWS A LETHAL TRY-SCORING TOUCH

A player blessed with an electric turn of pace (he once clocked a time of 10.2 for the 100m), Bryan Habana was a star of the IRB Under-21 World Championship in 2004 (in which South Africa finished third) and went on to make his senior debut against England at Twickenham on 20 November later that year, sensationally scoring a try with his first touch of the ball. His reputation as one of the most lethal finishers in the game's history was cemented at the 2007 Rugby World Cup, in which his eight tries in seven matches did much to lead South Africa to the country's second title; he ended the season as the IRB's Player of the Year. By 2011, still aged only 27, he had made 74 appearances for his country and scored a South Africa record 40 tries, two more than previous mark, set by 1995 Rugby World Cup winning scrum-half Joost van der Westhuizen.

ZIMBABWE

Zimbabwe has a long rugby history dating back to the 1890s, when British soldiers first brought the game to the country (which was then known as Rhodesia). Nicknamed the Sables, they have competed as Zimbabwe since 1981 and participated in the first two Rugby World Cups, 1987 and 1991, without winning a single match. In recent times, the nation's political problems have seen both a downturn in fortunes on the rugby pitch and an increasing exodus of players to other countries.

SABLES HIT THE HEIGHTS

Zimbabwe produced the best performance in their history when Botswana came to Bulawayo on 7 September 1996: the Sables won the match 130–10 to record the biggest victory in their history and the only time they have won a match by more than 100 points.

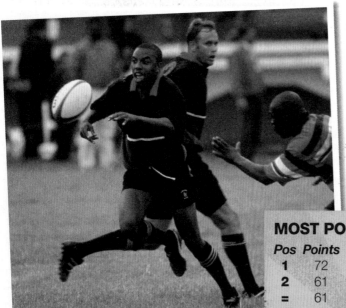

BELOW: Kenny Tsimba made only six appearances for Zimbabwe before turning his back on international rugby to forge a successful career on South Africa's domestic circuit.

OVERALL TEAM RECORD

Span	Mat	Won	Lost	Draw	%	For	Aga	Diff	Tries	Conv	Pens	Drop
1981–2011	123	47	76	0	38.21	2901	3258	-357	238	129	167	10

WALLOPED IN WINDHOEK

Back in 1987, Zimbabwe's national rugby team was considered strong enough to receive one of the 16 invitations to the inaugural Rugby World Cup; less than a decade and a half later, however, their fortunes had spiralled downwards to such an extent that they were considered one of world rugby's third-tier nations. A measure of just how far they had fallen came in their Africa Cup match against near neighbours Namibia in Windhoek on 25 September 2004: they crashed to a 68–8 defeat – the heaviest in their history.

SABLES' LONGEST WINNING STREAK

Victories have been hard to come by for the Sables – of the 123 internationals they have played since the formation of the Zimbabwe Rugby Union in 1981 they have won just 47 of them. Their longest winning streak during that time is four matches, achieved in the build-up to the 1987 Rugby World Cup when they beat Russia (26–10), Nigeria (111–12) and Portugal twice (35–9 and 50–9).

THE ONE THAT GOT AWAY

Once considered one of the most promising No.10s in world rugby, Kennedy Tsimba made only six appearances for the Sables between 1997 and 1998 – scoring a national record 72 points – before he turned his back on Zimbabwe rugby at the age of 24 to pursue a domestic career in South Africa, where he further enhanced his reputation with a string of stirring performances for the Free State Cheetahs in the Currie Cup.

ZIM'S LONGEST LOSING STREAK

Zimbabwe used a five-match home-and-away series of games against Namibia as preparation for the 1991 Rugby World Cup. It was a disaster: they lost all five matches, went winless in the Rugby World Cup (losing all three fixtures) and then lost three two-match series against a France XV (42–15 and 37–16), Namibia (55–23 and 69–26) and Wales (35–14 and 42–13). The Sables' miserable 13-game losing streak – stretching over two years – finally came to an end on 3 July 1993 when they beat Kenya 42–7 at Nairobi.

RUGBY WORLD CUP WOE FOR ZIMBABWE

Zimbabwe received one of the 16 invitations to appear in the inaugural Rugby World Cup in 1987 and, although the Sables got off to a commendable start – losing only narrowly to Romania (21–20) – the remainder of the tournament proved a chastening experience as they suffered heavy defeats to Scotland (60–21) and France (70–12). They qualified for the tournament in 1991, but suffered three consecutive defeats for a second time – against Ireland (55–11), Scotland (51–12) and, disappointingly, against Japan (52–8). Zimbabwe have not competed at a Rugby World Cup since.

MOST POINTS: TOP FIVE

Pos	Points	Player (Span)
1	72	Kennedy Tsimba (1997–98)
2	61	Marthinus Grobler (1987–94)
=	61	Ian Noble (1993–94)
4	54	Andy Ferreira (1987–91)
5	48	Anthony Papenfus (1997–98)

MOST TRIES: TOP FIVE

Pos	Tries	Player (Span)
1	8	Victor Olonga (1993–98)
2	7	Shaun Landman (1993–98)
3	4	Kennedy Tsimba (1997–98)
4	3	Brendon Dawson (1990–98)
=	3	Aaron Jani (1994–97)
=	3	Ian Noble (1993–94)
=	3	Anthony Papenfus (1997–98)
=	3	Doug Trivella (1997–98)
=	3	Richard Tsimba (1987–91)

ZIMBABWE'S ALL-TIME LEADING TRY-SCORER

Victor Olonga – the older brother of Henry, who, at the 2003 Cricket World Cup, famously wore a black armband to mourn the death of democracy in Zimbabwe (and was subsequently forced into hiding) – made a try-scoring debut for the Sables during their 35–14 defeat to Wales in Bulawayo on 22 May 1993. A diminutive 5ft 8in (1.73m) full-back, he went on to make a further 13 appearances for his country (the last coming against Namibia in Casablanca on 19 September 1998) and scored a national record eight tries.

RIGHT: Victor Olonga, brother of former international cricketer Henry, tops the Sables' all-time try-scorers list with eight.

GENEROUS HOSTS

From 1910, the Zimbabwe national team (playing under its former name Rhodesia) hosted touring sides from Britain and Ireland, but with little success. They lost every one of the eight matches played (the last in 1974), scoring a total of 83 points and conceding a mighty 265.

BELOW: Andy Ferreira scored 54 points in his Zimbabwe international career which ended against Ireland in the 1991 Rugby World Cup.

EXODUS OF PLAYERS

Presented with ever-decreasing opportunities to further their careers in their homeland, thanks to an increasingly fraught political situation and a general lack of money, a growing number of players have left Zimbabwe to pursue their rugby careers in other countries. Among the most notable of these exiles are Gary Teichmann, Bobby Skinstad and Tonderai Chavange (who went on to play for South Africa), and David Pocock (who has become a star of the Australia side in recent times).

MOST POINTS IN A MATCH

The Zimbabwe record for the most points by a player in a match is 27, achieved by Doug Trivella (two tries, four conversions and three penalties) during the Sables' 52–39 victory over Italy A at Harare on 21 June 1997.

BELOW: Bobby Skinstad is one of a number of Zimbabwe-born players who have left the country to find fame with other rugby-playing nations, in his case South Africa.

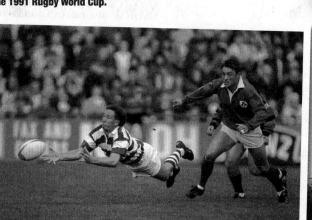

OTHER AFRICA TEAMS

Of all the African nations (14) to appear in the IRB world rankings, only two-time world champions South Africa could be considered as a force in the world game. There is, however, an increasingly active rugby scene on the continent, with the lesser nations competing on a four-year basis for Africa's one available Rugby World Cup qualification spot and on an annual basis for the Africa Cup, organized by the Confederation of African Rugby (CAR) and contested since 2000

KENYA'S BRIGHTEST MOMENT

Kenya entered the African section of the 2011 Rugby World Cup qualifying tournament having enjoyed little previous success in the competition: only once had they progressed beyond the initial group stages (in 2007) and they had never recorded more than one victory. However, they got off to a flying start, beating Cameroon 76–8 in Nairobi on 13 July 2008 to record the most comprehensive Rugby World Cup qualifying campaign by a second-tier African nation in history. Any thoughts of going through to the second round were soon dashed, however, when they crashed to a 44–15 defeat to Tunisia in Tunis three weeks later.

SOUTH AFRICA AMATEURS A MAJOR AFRICA CUP FORCE

South Africa may have sent an amateur side to compete in the Africa Cup to promote a level of fairness, but they have still proved the team to beat in the tournament, emerging victorious in 2000 (beating Morocco 44–14 in the final), 2001 (beating Morocco 36–20 in the final) and again in 2006 (when they beat Namibia 29–27 in the final to become the competition's first three-time winners).

NEAR MISSES FOR MADAGASCAR

It's been a case of almost but not quite for Madagascar in the Africa Cup. In 2005, they enjoyed a commendable 33–31 victory over perennial challengers South Africa Amateurs in the semi-final, only to lose out to Morocco in the final in Paris (43–6). It was a similar story in 2007: they beat the Ivory Coast 32–25 in the semi-final and, despite having home advantage in the final, lost out to Uganda (32–22).

MOROCCO MAD FOR THE AFRICA CUP

The highest ranked African team not to have appeared at a Rugby World Cup – although they have come mighty close, falling in the final repechage round on two occasions (1999 and 2003) – Morocco (currently ranked 26 in the world) have reserved their best rugby moments for the Africa Cup. They finished as runners-up to South Africa Amateurs in 2000 and 2001, beat Namibia in the 2003 final (27–7) to win the trophy for the first time, lost out 39–22 to the same opponents in the 2004 final (to finish runners-up for a record third time) and enjoyed their second tournament victory in 2005 following a comprehensive 43–6 victory over Madagascar in the final.

AFRICA CUP

Year	Winner	Runners-up
2000	South Africa Amateurs	Morocco
2001	South Africa Amateurs	Morocco
2002	Namibia	Tunisia
2003	Morocco	Namibia
2004	Namibia	Morocco
2005	Morocco	Madagascar
2006	South Africa Amateurs	Namibia
2007	Uganda	Madagascar
2008–09	Namibia	Tunisia
2010	*tournament cancelled*	

Best of the rest: IRB world rankings

Morocco (26); Tunisia (36); Kenya (40); Uganda (43); Senegal (52); Madagascar (55); Zambia (72); Cameroon (78); Swaziland (81); Botswana (82); Nigeria (88).

Ranking as of 23 October 2011.

RIGHT: Sydney Ashioya of Kenya avoids a Scottish tackler on his way to scoring a try during the 2010 Commonwealth Games in India.

CAR DEVELOPMENT TROPHY WINNERS

Year	North section winners	South section winners
2004	Mali	Botswana
2005	Burkina Faso	Mauritius
2006	Niger	Tanzania
2007	Nigeria	Botswana
2008	Niger	Réunion

RIGHT: Uganda (with Allan Musoke Senkindu in black) had to wait a long time for recognition on the contintental stage.

LEFT: Benoit Nicolas wins a line-out for Morocco, the best African nation not to have played in the Rugby World Cup.

80 AND OVER POINTS SCORED IN A MATCH

Team	Opponent	Result	Venue	Date
Zambia	Rwanda	107–9	Lusaka	9 Sep 2003
Uganda	Burundi	100–0	Lusaka	9 Sep 2003
Kenya	Nigeria	96–3	Nairobi	10 Aug 1987
Cameroon	Mauritania	81–0	Bamako	10 Oct 2003
Cameroon	Togo	80–3	Bamako	5 Oct 2003
Kenya	Botswana	80–9	Gaberone	2 Aug 2003

NEAR MISSES FOR TUNISIA

Tunisia contested their first international match against the Netherlands on 1 July 1979; they lost 12–0, and it would take three years before they tasted success for the first time (beating Portugal 16–13 on 17 April 1982). Since then, they have become one of the most improved rugby nations on the planet and are currently ranked 36th in the world. Yet to qualify for the Rugby World Cup, their best moments have been reserved for the Africa Cup, where they reached the final in 2002 (only to lose to Namibia) and in 2008–09 (when the Welwitschias got the better of them for the second time). Along with Madagascar, they are the only side to have appeared in two Africa Cup finals without winning the competition.

THE CRANES HIT NEW HEIGHTS

A member of the international rugby brotherhood since 1958 (the year in which they played their first match, against Kenya), Uganda – nicknamed the Cranes – had to wait 44 years before they enjoyed any significant success, when they won the second division of the Africa Cup. Five years later they were the toast of the continent after beating Madagascar 42–11 in the final to win the Africa Cup proper for the first time in their history.

TWO-TIME WINNERS

Established in 2004 to help develop the game among Africa's lesser nations, the CAR Development Trophy, which is split into two sections (north and south), is essentially the second division of the Africa Cup. Each of the sections has produced a two-time winner: Botswana (2004 and 2007) in the south; and Niger (2006 and 2008) in the north.

OVER 100 POINTS CONCEDED

Team	Opponent	Result	Venue	Date
Botswana	Zimbabwe	10–130	Bulawayo	7 Sep 1996
Madagascar	Namibia	0–116	Windhoek	15 Jun 2002
Nigeria	Zimbabwe	12–111	Bulawayo	7 Sep 1996
Tunisia	France XV	3–104	Split	18 Sep 1979

THE AMERICAS

Rugby has been played in the Americas since the late nineteenth century, but, perhaps more than in any other part of the world, has struggled to establish itself in the face of the passion felt for other sports, notably American football, baseball, basketball and ice hockey in the North and football in the South. Nevertheless the game remains in good health in the region: Argentina and Canada have been ever-presents at each of the seven Rugby World Cups (with the Pumas reaching the semi-finals in 2007 and quarter-finals in 1999 and 2011, and the Canucks reaching the quarter-finals in 1991) and there are annual competitions staged in both the North and the South.

BELOW: Argentina's finest hour on the world stage came in the 2007 Rugby World Cup when they reached the semi-final, then stunned hosts France 34–10 at the Parc des Princes, Paris, in the third-place play-off.

ARGENTINA

Although the game in Argentina has long been overshadowed by the country's deep and unbridled passion for football, the Pumas have achieved considerable success on the rugby pitch over the years. In recent times, they have developed into a real force on the world stage, with their tough, forward-dominated game taking them to the Rugby World Cup semi-finals in 2007 and, in the same year, to as high as third in the IRB world rankings.

PUMAS GET OFF TO A LOSING START

Argentina's first international fixture came against a Great Britain touring side at Flores on 12 June 1910, but it was a disappointing day for the Pumas as the tourists ran out 28–3 winners. Argentina did not contest another international fixture for 17 years and had to wait until September 1936 (their ninth match – the eight-match losing streak is the longest in Argentina's history) before registering their first victory – 29–0, away against Chile at Valparaiso.

OVERALL TEAM RECORD

Span	Mat	Won	Lost	Draw	%	For	Aga	Diff	Tries	Conv	Pens	Drop	GfM
1910–2011	345	194	142	9	57.53	10067	6395	+3672	1330	826	707	86	1

THE MENDOZA MASSACRE

Argentina may have fielded a virtual second-string side in their South American Championship clash against Paraguay at Mendoza on 1 May 2002 – of the 15 who played in the match only two would line up for the Pumas in their opening match of the 2003 Rugby World Cup – but they still proved far too strong for their near neighbours. They ran in 24 tries in the match to complete a crushing 152–0 victory, the joint-highest winning margin in international rugby history (equalled by Japan when they beat Chinese Taipei 155–3 in Tokyo on 7 July 2002).

WELLINGTON WOE FOR THE PUMAS

Argentina have endured some torrid times against New Zealand over the years. Of the 13 official matches played between the countries (the first in Buenos Aires in October 1985), they have lost 12 of them and drawn one. Of those defeats, the heaviest – the biggest reverse in their history – came at Wellington on 21 June 1987, when the All Blacks ran in 14 tries en route to a thumping 93–8 victory.

BELOW: Only England and South Africa did better than Argentina at the 2007 Rugby World Cup. The Pumas lost 37–13 to the Springboks in their first-ever semi-final, but they went on to win their third-place playoff against France.

RIGHT: A legendary figure in Argentina's rugby history, stand-off Hugo Porta scored a record 592 points for his country in a stellar career that spanned 59 Tests across three decades.

PUMAS SHOCK LES BLEUS

The stage was set. Tournament hosts France, playing in front of an expectant public, were favourites to beat Argentina in the opening match of the 2007 Rugby World Cup in the Stade de France in Paris. The only problem was that Argentina hadn't read the script. The Pumas, dominating an error-strewn French side, led 17–9 at half-time – thanks to an Ignacio Corleto try and four Felipe Contepomi penalties – and held on to win 17–12 and record the most sensational result in their history. It was only the second time in the Rugby World Cup that the tournament hosts failed to win their opening game (England lost to New Zealand in 1991).

DOMINATING THE AMERICAS' RUGBY SCENE

The Pumas confirmed their status as the Americas' no.1 team with their performances in the Pan-American Championship, a tournament staged on five occasions between 1995 and 2003 and contested against Canada, the United States and Uruguay. Argentina won the event every time it was held (1995, 1996, 1998, 2001 and 2003).

HONOURS

Rugby World Cup:
(best finish) – third (2007)
South American Championship:
(best finish) – champions (1951, 1958, 1961, 1964, 1967, 1969, 1971, 1973, 1975, 1977, 1979, 1983, 1985, 1987, 1989, 1991, 1993, 1995, 1998, 2000, 2001, 2002, 2003, 2004, 2005, 2006, 2007, 2008, 2009, 2010, 2011)
Pan-American Championship:
(best finish) – champions (1995, 1996, 1998, 2001, 2003)

SOUTH AMERICAN GIANTS

Argentina are the undisputed kings of South American rugby, winning the South American Championship 31 out of the 32 times it has been contested. The only occasion they did not win the competition was in 1981 – it was the only time they did not take part in the tournament.

MOST POINTS: TOP TEN

Pos	Points	Player (Span)
1	590	Hugo Porta (1971–99)
2	588	Felipe Contepomi (1998–2011)
3	486	Gonzalo Quesada (1996–2003)
4	365	Santiago Meson (1987–97)
5	256	Federico Todeschini (1998–2008)
6	188	Lisandro Arbizu (1990–2005)
7	158	Juan Fernandez Miranda (1997–2007)
8	145	Jose Nunez Piossek (2001–08)
9	138	Jose Cilley (1994–2002)
10	129	Jose Luna (1995–97)

ARGENTINA'S GREATEST OF ALL TIME

Argentina's rise in world rugby can be attributed to the deeds of one man: Hugo Porta. A fly-half with a deadly boot – perhaps the deadliest of all time – he made his debut against Chile on 10 October 1970 (aged 20) and, phenomenally, went on to enjoy a 16-year stint as his country's first choice fly-half. There were plenty of highlights along the way: in October 1979, he kicked all of the Pumas' points in their 24–13 victory over Australia in Buenos Aires – the greatest result in their history to that point; six years later, he kicked all of the Pumas' points in their historic 21–21 draw against the All Blacks. He retired after Argentina's 1987 Rugby World Cup campaign but returned, briefly, in 1990 and for one match against a World XV in 1999. He is his country's all-time leading points-scorer (with 590 points) and remains Argentina's only player to been inducted into the International Rugby Hall of Fame.

THE PUMAS' RECORD-BREAKING RUN

The longest winning streak in Argentina's history started in September 1992 with home-and-away victories over Spain (38–10 in Buenos Aires and 43–34 in Madrid) and continued with two more away wins over Romania (21–18) and France (24–20) and a pair of triumphs on home soil against Japan (30–27 and 45–20). The Pumas then won all four matches in the 1993 South American Championship (culminating in a 19–10 victory over Uruguay in the final) before the run of wins came to an end at ten after a 29–26 defeat to South Africa in Buenos Aires.

PUMAS TAME THE WALLABIES

This was the moment the rugby world sat up and took notice of Argentina. Five weeks after beating a star-studded World XV (containing David Campese and Mark Ella) 28–20 in Buenos Aires, the Pumas travelled to Brisbane on 31 July 1983 to play Australia. Their 18–3 victory – thanks to tries from Buenaventura Minguez and Tomas Petersen, coupled with ten points from the boot of Hugo Porta – marked the moment Argentina emerged as a true force in international rugby and remains their most famous away victory of all time.

RECORD-BREAKING TIMES AGAINST PARAGUAY

Argentina have played Paraguay on 16 occasions and have won every one of the matches – scoring 1,311 points (with 225 tries) and conceding a mere 58. And what's more, the Pumas have reserved some of their record-breaking moments for the fixture, including their largest ever victory (152–0) and the most points in a match by one player: 50 by Eduardo Morgan (six tries and 13 conversions) in the South American Championship clash at Sao Paulo, Brazil, on 14 October 1973.

BELOW: Jose Nunez Piossek notched a national record 29 tries in 28 appearances for Argentina between 2001 and 2008.

PIOSSEK TOPS THE PUMAS' ALL-TIME TRY-SCORING LIST

Winger Jose Nunez Piossek made a try-scoring debut for the Pumas in their 32–27 victory over Uruguay in their Pan-American Championship match at Kingston, Jamaica, on 19 May 2001. He finally established himself in the Argentina side in 2003 – a year that saw him score nine tries in a match against Paraguay in Montevideo (a record for an Argentina player in a single match) and win a place in his country's Rugby World Cup squad for the tournament in Australia (in which he played all three matches). He made his 28th and final appearance for the Pumas on 9 August 2008 (a 63–9 loss to South Africa in Johannesburg) and bowed out of international rugby as his country's all-time leading try-scorer, with 29 tries.

MOST CAPS: TOP TEN

Pos	Caps	Player (Span)
1	86	Lisandro Arbizu (1990–2005)
=	86	Rolando Martin (1994–2003)
3	84	Mario Ledesma Arocena (1996–2011)
4	78	Pedro Sporleder (1990–2003)
5	75	Felipe Contepomi (1998–2011)
6	73	Federico Mendez Azpillaga (1990–2004)
7	71	Agustin Pichot (1995–2007)
8	65	Ignacio Fernandez Lobbe (1996–2008)
=	65	Omar Hasan Jalil (1995–2007)
10	63	Diego Cuesta Silva (1983–95)

ABOVE: Argentina's most-capped player, Lisandro Arbizu led his side on 48 occasions between 1993 and 2005.

LONG-TIME LEADER

Lisandro Arbizu brought a dash of flair and invention to Argentina's back division for 15 years. Equally comfortable at fly-half or centre, he made his international debut aged 19 when he came on as a replacement during the Pumas' slender 20–18 defeat to Ireland at Lansdowne Road on 27 October 1990. He appeared at the 1991 Rugby World Cup (the first of his three appearances in the tournament) and became his country's youngest-ever captain (aged 21) when he led the Pumas to a 38–10 victory over Spain in September 1992. He went on to captain Argentina on 48 occasions (a national record) and retired from international rugby in June 2005 after collecting his 86th cap (having equalled the national record with long-serving flanker Rolando Martin).

MOST TRIES: TOP TEN

Pos	Tries	Player (Span)
1	29	Jose Nunez Piossek (2001–08)
2	28	Diego Cuesta Silva (1983–95)
3	24	Gustavo Jorge (1989–94)
4	18	Rolando Martin (1994–2003)
=	18	Facundo Soler (1996–2002)
6	17	Lisandro Arbizu (1990–2005)
=	17	Hernan Senillosa (2002–07)
8	14	Guillermo Alvarez (1975–77)
=	14	Federico Mendez Azpillaga (1990–2005)
=	14	Lucas Borges (2003–10)
=	14	Felipe Contepomi (1998–2011)
=	14	Ignacio Corleto (1998–2007)
=	14	Guillermo Morgan (1977–79)
=	14	Uriel O'Farrell (1951)
=	14	Pedro Sporleder (1990–2003)

LOFFREDA LEADS THE PUMAS TO DIZZY NEW HEIGHTS

Marcelo Loffreda won 46 caps for Argentina between 1978 and 1994 (12 of them as captain) – playing at centre outside legendary fly-half Hugo Porta – and switched to coaching when his playing career ended. Appointed coach of the national side in 2000, he led the Pumas to five South American Championship titles, to prestigious series victories over France (in 2003) and Wales (in 2006), to a first-ever victory over England at Twickenham (25–18 on 11 November 2006) and to within a whisker of his country's first-ever victories over South Africa (33–37 on 12 November 2000) and New Zealand (20–24 on 1 December 2001). His crowning moment, however, came when he led the Pumas to an unexpected third place at the 2007 Rugby World Cup. He left his role after the tournament to take up a coaching position with Leicester Tigers, but will be remembered as Argentina's greatest coach of all time.

RIGHT: An outstanding player, Marcelo Loffreda achieved even more fame as a coach when he led Argentina to third place at the 2007 Rugby World Cup, a run that saw two spectacular victories over hosts France.

PICHOT: THE PUMAS' LITTLE MASTER

Though small in stature, at 5ft 9in (1.75m), Agustin Pichot was a giant for Argentina on the rugby pitch for over a decade. A talented scrum-half capable of sniping runs through the smallest of gaps, he made his debut against Australia in April 1996, was appointed captain in 2000 and led the Pumas to some of the greatest moments in their history, culminating in a third-place finish at the 2007 Rugby World Cup. He retired from international rugby in 2008, and in the same year received the IRB Special Merit award for his role in leading the Pumas towards the top of the world game. He is the only Argentina player in history to be presented with such an award from the IRB.

BELOW: Scrum-half Agustin Pichot's 71-match, 12-year career did much to propel Argentina towards the top of the rugby world.

INTERNATIONAL RECOGNITION

Argentina's reward for finishing third at the 2007 Rugby World Cup (a tournament in which they recorded two victories over hosts France and one over Ireland) was to see two of their players nominated for the IRB Player of the Year award – Felipe Contepomi and Juan Hernandez. South Africa's Bryan Habana eventually took the spoils, but Contepomi and Hernandez remain the only Argentina players in history to have made it on to the award's shortlist.

BELOW: Juan Hernandez's superb performances at the 2007 Rugby World Cup saw him end the year amont the nominees for the IRB Player of the Year award.

ALL-TIME LEADING TRY-SCORERS: BY POSITION

Position	Player (Span)	Tries
Full-back	Ignacio Corleto (1999–2007)	10
Winger	Jose Nunez Piossek (2001–08)	29
Centre	Diego Cuesta Silva (1983–95)	21
Fly-half	Hugo Porta (1971–99)	11
Scrum-half	Agustin Pichot (1995–2007)	10
No.8	Pablo Camerlinckx (1989–99)	7
Flanker	Rolando Martin (1994–2003)	17
Lock	Pedro Sporleder (1990–2003)	12
Prop	Rodolfo Ventura (1975–83)	6
	Martin Scerzo (1996–2011)	6
Hooker	Federico Mendez Azpillaga (1994–2004)	10

CANADA

One of only 12 nations to have competed at every one of the six Rugby World Cups (they reached the quarter-finals in 1991), Canada has a rich rugby history dating back to the late nineteenth century, although the Canucks did not contest their first international fixture until 1932. Considered one of the game's second-tier nations (they are currently ranked 13th in the world), they are the second strongest team in the Americas, behind Argentina.

CANUCKS COAST TO RECORD-BREAKING VICTORY

Canada eased past Barbados in their Rugby World Cup qualifying match at Bridgetown on 24 June 2006 in record-breaking style. They led 45–0 at half-time and ran in a total of 11 tries in the match on the way to a comprehensive 69–3 victory. The 66-point winning margin is the best in their history, although they have scored more points on one occasion – when they beat Namibia 72–11 in Toulouse during the pool stages of the 1999 Rugby World Cup.

RIGHT: Powerful flanker Al Charron was a massive force for Canada in a 13-year, national record 76-cap career.

THUMPED AT TWICKENHAM

Canada have only ever tasted victory once against England in 11 attempts, 15–12 at Burnaby Lake on 29 May 1993, but that was against England's second-string XV. Matches against a full-strength England side have proved altogether tougher affairs, and none more so than at Twickenham on 13 November 2004. England ran in 12 tries – three of them by Jason Robinson – to complete a 70–0 drubbing. It remains the heaviest defeat in Canada's history.

CANADA STUN WALES IN CARDIFF

Trailing by nine points to six at half-time during their match against Wales at Cardiff on 10 November 1993, most expected Canada to fall to yet another defeat against their loftier opponents. But the Canucks had other ideas: second-half tries from Al Charron and Scott Stewart, both converted by Gareth Rees (who also added three penalties), saw them march to a surprise 26–24 win. It was Canada's first-ever victory over one of rugby's top-tier nations fielding a full-strength side.

RECORD-BREAKING RUN OF DEFEATS

Ironically, Canada's bid to break their record for the most consecutive wins ended not only in defeat but also triggered their longest ever losing streak. The Canucks played Argentina in Buenos Aires on 22 August 1998 seeking a record-breaking seventh successive win, but lost 54–28. They then lost to Japan (23–21), Samoa (17–13), the USA (18–17) and Tonga (18–10) before embarking on an unsuccessful tour to Britain that saw them lose both matches – against Wales (33–19) and England (36–11). It was far from ideal preparation for the 1999 Rugby World Cup, and Canada lost their opening two games – to France (33–20) and Fiji (38–22) – before bringing their record-breaking losing streak to an end at ten matches when they beat Namibia 72–11 in their final group game.

LAST EIGHT AS GOOD AS IT GETS FOR CANADA

Canada were one of the 16 teams invited to take part in the inaugural Rugby World Cup in 1987, but an opening-game victory over Tonga in Napier (37–4) was as good as it got for the Canucks as subsequent defeats to Ireland (46–19) and Wales (40–9) saw them fail to progress beyond the group stages. They qualified for the 1991 tournament and got off to a flyer, beating Fiji 13–3 in their opening match and following up with a hard-fought 19–11 victory over Romania. A narrow 19–13 defeat to France mattered little: Canada had qualified for the quarter-finals. But that is where their journey ended: the All Blacks proved too strong for the Canucks and ran out 29–13 winners in Lille. It still ranks as Canada's best-ever performance at a Rugby World Cup: they failed to progress beyond the group stages in 1995, 1999, 2003, 2007 and 2011, and did not win more than one game in any tournament.

OVERALL TEAM RECORD

Span	Mat	Won	Lost	Draw	%	For	Aga	Diff	Tries	Conv	Pens	Drop
1932–2011	202	84	113	5	42.82	4073	5192	-1119	413	274	447	34

MOST POINTS: TOP FIVE

Pos	Points	Player (Span)
1	487	Gareth Rees (1986–99)
2	419	Bobby Ross (1989–2003)
3	400	James Pritchard (2003–11)
4	227	Mark Wyatt (1982–91)
5	226	Jared Barker (2000–04)

LEFT: Canada's all-time record points-scorer, Gareth Rees appeared in every one of the first four Rugby World Cups.

CANADA'S LONGEST WINNING STREAK

Winning hasn't come easily to Canada over the years and they got off to the worst of starts: it took them until 1977 (45 years and 12 matches after they had played their first international) before they recorded their first victory and a further six years before they won back-to-back games for the first time. The Canucks' longest winning streak is six matches, a feat achieved on two occasions – between 16 June 1990 and 9 October 1991 and between 23 May 1998 and 18 August 1998.

MOST CAPS FOR CHARRON

Back-row forward Al Charron made his debut for Canada in 1990 and went on to become a vital member of the strongest Canucks' team in history. He played a key role in his country's march to the Rugby World Cup quarter-finals in 1991 and scored the try that handed Canada a famous victory over Wales in Cardiff in 1993. He appeared at both the 1995 and 1999 Rugby World Cups and was awarded his country's captaincy on a permanent basis (having led them in four matches in 1996) in 2000. He retired from international rugby following Canada's group-stage elimination at the 2003 Rugby World Cup as his country's most capped player of all time (with 76 caps).

THE MAN WITH THE GOLDEN BOOT

Born in Canada and educated at the world-famous Harrow School and then Oxford University (in England), Gareth Rees made his debut for the Canucks at the age of 21 against the USA in November 1986, scoring a drop goal in his side's 27–16 victory. A deadly place-kicker, he was a regular feature in his country's line-up, when fit, for the next 13 years. Rees made the first of his four Rugby World Cup appearances in 1987, did much to help Canada to the quarter-finals in 1991 and, in 1995, ended the tournament with a 30-day suspension after being sent off in his side's infamous group match against South Africa, which was later dubbed the 'Battle of Boet Erasmus'. He retired after the 1999 tournament – he is one of only a select group of players to have appeared in the first four Rugby World Cups – having won 55 caps (25 of them as captain, a joint national record) and scored a Canada all-time record 487 points.

MOST TRIES: TOP FIVE

Pos	Tries	Player (Span)
1	24	Winston Stanley (1994–2003)
2	13	Morgan Williams (1999–2008)
3	12	James Pritchard (2003–10)
=	12	D.T.H. van der Merwe (2006–10)
5	10	Kyle Nichols (1996–2002)

CANADA'S SINGLE GAME RECORDS

The Canada record for the most tries in a match is four, by Kyle Nichols against Japan at Markham on 15 July 2000. The Canucks' record for the most points in a single match is 36, by James Pritchard (three tries, six conversions and three penalties) against the USA at St John's on 12 August 2006.

STANLEY SETS TRY-SCORING MARK

A tall winger with an incisive turn of speed, Winston Stanley made his first appearance for Canada against the USA on 21 May 1994 and scored his first tries for the Canucks (two of them) in his fifth match, against Argentina, ten months later. He remained a regular source of points for his country from then on, appearing in 66 matches (his last in 2003) and scoring a Canada all-time record 24 tries.

BELOW: Winston Stanley's brawn on the wing brought him 24 tries for Canada – a national record.

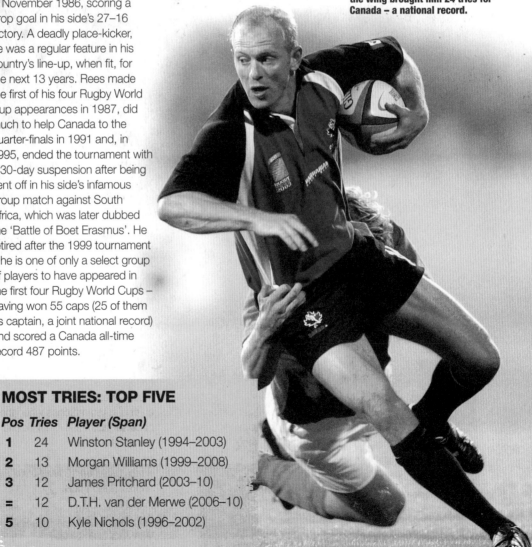

UNITED STATES

Rugby was introduced to the United States as far back as the mid-nineteenth century, but it has always struggled to compete against American football, baseball, basketball and ice hockey and is considered a minority sport in the country. The national team, known as the Eagles, played its first international match in 1912, has appeared in six of the seven Rugby World Cups contested and is currently placed 17th in the IRB world rankings.

GOLDEN MOMENTS FOR UNCLE SAM

One has to go back many years to find the United States' greatest moments on a rugby pitch. They were one of only two teams to enter the rugby tournament at the 1920 Olympic Games in Antwerp and they beat France 8–0 in the 'final' to take gold. Four years later, in Paris, they beat Romania (37–0) and France (17–3) in the three-team tournament to defend their title. Rugby has not featured at the Games since and the United States remain the only country in history to win two gold medals for rugby at the Olympics.

OVERALL TEAM RECORD

Span	Mat	Won	Lost	Draw	%	For	Aga	Diff	Tries	Conv	Pens	Drop	GfM
1912–2011	187	60	125	2	32.62	3570	5192	-1622	408	266	341	18	1

RUGBY FIRSTS FOR UNCLE SAM

The United States played their first international match against Australia at Berkeley on 16 November 1912, but the day ended in disappointment when they slipped to a narrow 12–8 defeat. Their first victory came in their third match, when they beat Romania 21–0 in a warm-up match at Colombes, France, prior to the 1920 Olympic Games.

UNITED STATES' RECORD VICTORY

Of the United States' 55 wins in international rugby, all bar two of them – both against France (on 5 September 1920 and 18 May 1924) – have come against the rugby world's second- or third-tier nations. The biggest of those victories came against Barbados in a Rugby World Cup qualifying match at Santa Clara on 1 July 2006. Leaging 49–0 at half-time, the USA romped to a 13-try, 91–0 victory.

TROUNCED AT TWICKENHAM

The United States have lost 52 of the 54 matches they have played against world rugby's top-tier nations (Argentina, Australia, England, France, Ireland, New Zealand, Scotland and Wales) and lost 21 of those fixtures by a margin of 30 points or more. The heaviest defeat in their history came against England at Twickenham on 21 August 1999, when they crashed to a 106–8 reverse – it is the only time the Eagles have ever conceded more than 100 points in a match.

RECORD WINNING AND LOSING STREAKS

The United States have always struggled to put together consistent runs of good performances. It took them until 1991 (having played 79 years of international rugby) before they won three consecutive matches and until 2003 before they won four matches in a row for the first time in their history (between 12 April and 18 June). Losing, on the other hand, has come altogether more easily to the Eagles: they have recorded one six-game losing streak, one of seven games and twice they have lost eight in a row, but their longest run of consecutive losses is ten, between 18 May 2007 and 21 June 2008.

RUGBY WORLD CUP RECORD

The Eagles have appeared in six of the seven Rugby World Cups (they failed to qualify for the 1995 tournament), but have never progressed beyond the group stages. Of the 121 matches they have played, they have only recorded three wins, two against Japan – 21–18 at Brisbane in 1987 and 39–26 at Gosford in 2003 – and one against Russia, 13–6 at New Plymouth in 2011.

HERCUS HEADS ALL-TIME POINTS LIST

Born in the USA (in Virginia on 6 June 1979) but brought up and educated in Sydney, Mike Hercus progressed through the junior ranks of Australian rugby (appearing for their Schoolboy and Under-21 sides) before answering the call from the country of his birth. He made his debut for the Eagles (at fly-half) in a 65–23 defeat to Scotland in San Francisco on 22 June 2002 and went on to be his country's key playmaker for the next seven years. He appeared at both the 2003 and 2007 Rugby World Cups, and made the last of his 48 international appearances against Uruguay in November 2009. Hercus bowed out of international rugby as the United States' all-time leading points-scorer with 465.

LEFT: The United States team took the Antwerp 1920 Olympic Games by storm when they beat France 8–0 in the final to claim the gold medal. They defended their title four years later, also against France, winning 17–3 in Paris.

SUCCESSFUL IMPORT

Born in Tonga on 20 September 1970, Vaea Anitoni moved to California as a 21-year-old student in 1991 and made his debut for the Eagles the following year, coming on as a replacement against Canada and scoring his first international try. A short but powerful winger, he did not become a regular in the side until 1994, but when he did he soon proved himself as the best finisher in USA rugby history. When he retired from international rugby in 2000, he had scored an impressive 26 tries in 46 matches – no other American player has ever scored more than 10 tries.

BELOW: Prop Mike MacDonald has been a loyal servant to the Eagles' cause, winning a USA record 65 caps between 2000 and the Rugby World Cup 2011.

MOST TRIES: TOP FIVE

Pos	Tries	Player (Span)
1	26	Vaea Anitoni (1992–2000)
2	15	Paul Emerick (2003–11)
3	11	Todd Clever (2003–11)
4	10	Phillip Eloff (2000–07)
5	9	David Fee (2002–05)
=	9	Mike Hercus (2002–09)
=	9	Riaan van Zyl (2003–04)

ABOVE: Vaea Anitoni is the best finisher in American rugby history, scoring a national record 26 tries in 46 matches between 1992 and 2000.

RIGHT: An incredibly versatile player, Dave Hodges led the United States a record 28 times.

MACDONALD MAKES HIS MARK FOR THE EAGLES

Prop Mike MacDonald made his international debut as a replacement in the Eagles' 37–21 defeat to Fiji at Apia on 30 June 2000. He made his first start against Canada in 2001 and has been a cornerstone of the USA pack ever since. A veteran of three Rugby World Cups (2003, 2007 and 2011), with 65 caps, he became his country's most capped player at the 2011 tournament.

THE USA'S LONGEST-SERVING CAPTAIN

A 6ft 4in (1.93m) back-row forward who, unusually, played in every forward position in international rugby bar hooker, Dave Hodges made his debut for the Eagles against Uruguay in September 1996. He was appointed captain in May 2000 and went on to lead his side on 28 occasions (a national record).

MOST POINTS IN A MATCH

The USA record for the most points scored by a player in a match is 26, achieved three times, by two players. Chris O'Brien did it against Uruguay at Montevideo on 5 November 1989, and Mike Hercus did it twice, against Russia at Tokyo on 30 May 2004 and against Barbados at Santa Clara on 1 July 2006.

MOST POINTS: TOP FIVE

Pos	Points	Player (Span)
1	465	Mike Hercus (2002–09)
2	286	Matt Alexander (1995–98)
3	144	Chris O'Brien (1988–94)
4	143	Mark Williams (1987–99)
5	130	Vaea Anitoni (1992–2000)

URUGUAY

Rugby has been growing steadily in popularity in Uruguay since the country contested its first international match in August 1948, against Chile. Now considered the second best team in South America, after Argentina, Los Teros (the Lapwings) won the South American Championship for the first and only time in their history in 1981 and appeared at the 1999 and 2003 Rugby World Cups. They are currently 21st in the IRB world rankings.

CONTINENTAL CHAMPIONS

Argentina's decision not to enter the 1981 South American Championship – the only occasion the 32-time champions have not taken part in the tournament (which has been staged on 33 occasions) – provided the continent's other rugby-playing nations with a golden opportunity to lay their hands on the trophy for the first time. And, despite suffering a defeat to Chile (33–3), Uruguay took full advantage of the Pumas' absence, recovering to beat both Paraguay (54–14) and Brazil (77–0) to win the title for the first and only time in their history. They have finished runners-up on 22 occasions and third on ten.

RIGHT: Full-back Alfonso Cardoso holds the distinction of having scored Uruguay's first-ever Rugby World Cup try – their their 27–15 victory over Spain in 1999.

OVERALL TEAM RECORD

Span	Mat	Won	Lost	Draw	%	For	Aga	Diff	Tries	Conv	Pens	Drop
1948–2011	181	76	102	3	42.81	3841	4601	-760	264	155	229	18

URUGUAY'S RUGBY WORLD CUP MATCH WINS

Uruguay have qualified for two Rugby World Cups – 1999 and 2003 – and have recorded a single victory on both occasions: 27–15 against Spain at Galashiels on 2 October 1999 (in their first-ever match in the tournament) and 24–12 against Georgia at Sydney on 28 October 2003.

RECORD WINNING AND LOSING STREAKS

Uruguay's longest-ever winning streak is five matches: it started with a surprise 25–23 victory over Canada in Montevideo on 24 August 2002 (arguably the greatest victory in the country's history) and continued with home wins over the USA (10–9), Chile twice (34–23 and 20–13) and Paraguay (53–7) and came to an end on 3 May 2003 following a 32–0 defeat to Argentina in Buenos Aires. Their worst-ever losing streak is seven matches, recorded between 18 November 2000 and 1 September 2001.

LAPWINGS BATTERED BY THE SPRINGBOKS

Matches against the world's top-ranked rugby nations have always proved at least one step too far for Uruguay: they have lost all 43 contests against Argentina, Australia, England, France, Ireland, New Zealand, Scotland, South Africa and Wales, and 13 of these defeats hae been by more than 50 points. The worst of those reversals – and the heaviest in Uruguay's history – came against South Africa at East London on 11 June 2005, when Los Teros capitulated to a 134–3 defeat, which was also South Africa's biggest victory. The 131-point losing margin is the ninth heaviest in international rugby history.

FIRSTS FOR URUGUAY

Uruguay contested their first international fixture against Chile in Buenos Aires, Argentina, on 5 August 1948, although it did not turn out to be a day to remember for Los Teros: they lost the match 21–3. Their first victory came in their third match, when they beat the same opponents 8–3 on 13 September 1951.

RUGBY WORLD CUP HEARTACHE

Uruguay's dreams of making a third successive appearance at the Rugby World Cup in 2007 ended in heartbreaking fashion. They faced off against Portugal in the final repechage round, with the aggregate winner of the two-legged tie earning a Rugby World Cup spot. They lost the first leg 12–5 in Lisbon on 10 March and, despite winning the second leg 18–12 two weeks later, lost out 24–23 on aggregate.

LOS TEROS PUT PARAGUAY TO THE SWORD

Every one of Uruguay's 11 50-points-plus victories has come against opponents from South American and seven of those have been in matches against Paraguay. The largest was in the South American Championship contest at Cataratas on 14 May 2011, when Los Teros ran out comprehensive 102–6 winners.

MOST TRIES: TOP FIVE

Pos	Tries	Player (Span)
1	16	Diego Ormaechea (1979–99)
2	8	Nicolas Grille (1996–2007)
3	7	Alfonso Cardoso (1996–2003)
=	7	Federico Sciarra (1991–99)
=	7	Leandro Leivas (2008–10)

THE LAPWINGS' ALL-TIME LEADING POINTS-SCORER

Small in stature at 5ft 9in (1.75m), but with a deadly kicking boot, Juan Menchaca made his debut for Uruguay at full-back against Portugal in March 1999 and won his next three caps during his country's first-ever Rugby World Cup campaign later in the year. On 7 September 2002, in a match against Chile, he scored 27 points (one conversion, five penalties and four drop goals) to break the national record for the most points scored by a player in a single match. He played in all four of Uruguay's matches at the 2003 Rugby World Cup and finally bowed out of international rugby in 2007 (with 38 caps) – after the repechage-round defeat to Portugal – as his country's all-time leading points-scorer (with 222 points).

RIGHT: Juan Menchaca was a major contributor to Uruguay's cause, scoring 222 points in a 36-match career that spanned eight years.

LEFT: When the biggest name in Uruguay's rugby history, Diego Ormaechea bowed out of international rugby in 1999, after his country's first appearance at the Rugby World Cup, he held a host of national records.

URUGUAY LEGEND

Considered the greatest player ever to emerge from Uruguay, Diego Ormaechea was a stalwart for his country for 20 years between 1979 and 1999. A powerful No.8, he is his country's most capped player (with 73 caps), Uruguay's longest-serving captain (he led Los Teros on 25 occasions, including during their first-ever appearance at the Rugby World Cup in 1999 – aged 40, he is the oldest player to have played at the tournament) and is also his country's all-time leading try-scorer (with 16 tries).

MOST POINTS: TOP FIVE

Pos	Points	Player (Span)
1	222	Juan Menchaca (1999–2007)
2	167	Federico Sciarra (1991–99)
3	89	Diego Aguirre (1995–2007)
4	79	Diego Ormaechea (1989–99)
5	70	Matias Arocena (2005–10)

OTHER AMERICAS TEAMS

Argentina, Canada, the United States and Uruguay may well be the only countries from the Americas to have qualified for the Rugby World Cup, with their presence in the continent's other competitions casting a giant shadow over the rest of the teams, but rugby is alive and well in the region. Nations compete in Rugby World Cup qualifying rounds on a four-yearly basis and in domestic competitions (both in the North and South) on an annual basis.

CHILE: BEST OF THE REST

Chile, 23rd in the IRB world rankings, can rightfully claim to be the third best team in South America, the fifth best team in the Americas and the best team from either North or South never to have qualified for the Rugby World Cup. They have finished as runners-up in the South American Championship (a tournament dominated by Argentina) on nine tenoccasions and third on 20 occasions. They have also scored more points in Rugby World Cup qualifying matches (611) than any other team in the region.

Best of the rest: IRB World Rankings

Chile (23); Brazil (29); Paraguay (41); Bermuda (47); Trinidad and Tobago (48); Venezuela (51); Guyana (60); Peru (63); Cayman Islands (65); Colombia (73); St Vincent and the Grenadines (74); Barbados (76); Jamaica (83); Bahamas (84).

As of 23 October 2011.

FIRING ON BLANKS

St Vincent and the Grenadines are one of only six teams to hold an unusual rand unenviable record in rugby history. They have never won a Rugby World Cup qualifying match.

BRIGHT MOMENTS FOR BRAZIL ON THE RUGBY PITCH

Brazil's national rugby team, who have contested international matches since November 1951, have had to compete under the giant shadow cast by their successful national football team, but they have still found cause to celebrate: in 1964, they finished as runners-up in the South American Championship (losing out, predictably, to Argentina) and, despite never having qualified for the Rugby World Cup, have won more qualifying matches (15) than any other team in the Americas that has not qualified for the tournament proper.

ABOVE: Brazil (yellow shirts) beat Paraguay 36–21 in a RWC qualifier in Montevideo in May 2009, but they were unable to advance to the 2011 Rugby World Cup.

BELOW: Sergio Valdes of Chile is about to kick downfield during a 2003 Rugby World Cup qualifying match against United States of America in Salt Lake City. Chile, the best team in the Americas never to have qualified for main tournament of the Rugby World Cup, lost this match 35-22.

PARAGUAY HIT AN ALL-TIME LOW

Paraguay hold the unfortunate distinction of having suffered the joint highest margin of defeat in international rugby history. Unlike Chinese Taipei, however, who lost 155–3 to Japan on 7 July 2002, Paraguay failed to score a single point during their history-making 152–0 capitulation to Argentina in Mendoza on 1 May 2002.

MORE THAN 100 POINTS CONCEDED

Team	Opponent	Result	Venue	Date
Paraguay	Argentina	0–152	Mendoza	1 May 2002
Paraguay	Argentina	0–144	Montevideo	27 Apr 2003
Venezuela	Argentina	7–147	Santiago	1 May 2004
Brazil	Argentina	3–114	Sao Paulo	2 Oct 1993
Brazil	Argentina	3–109	Santiago	9 Oct 1979
Paraguay	Chile	0–102	Montevideo	3 May 2003
Paraguay	Uruguay	6–102	Cataratas	14 May 2011
Brazil	Argentina	9–103	Montevideo	3 Oct 1989
Paraguay	Argentina	9–103	Asuncion	24 Sept 1995

CARIBBEAN'S BEST RUGBY WORLD CUP QUALIFYING PERFORMERS

Trinidad and Tobago have played in more Rugby World Cup qualifying matches (18) and have notched up more victories in the tournaments (eight) than any other of the Caribbean nations. They progressed the furthest of the Caribbean section of qualifying in 1999, 2003 and for 2011, although they have yet to qualify for the tournament proper.

CARIBBEAN'S LEADING POINTS-SCORERS

Bermuda have scored more points in international matches than any other of the Caribbean rugby-playing nations: 1,205 points in 44 matches since 1975.

BELOW: Trinidad & Tobago celebrate after beating their hosts, Cayman Islands, in the opening match of their 2011 Rugby World Cup qualifying campaign.

BOTTOM OF THE PILE

The Bahamas hold the unenviable honour of being the lowest ranked team in the Americas – 89th in the IRB world rankings out of 93 teams.

WAITING TO GET OFF THE MARK

Four teams in the Americas region are still waiting for their first-ever victory in international rugby: Costa Rica (no wins in 14 matches); Guadeloupe (no wins in three matches); St Vincent and the Grenadines (no wins in three matches); and the Turks and Caicos Islands (no wins in two matches).

RIGHT: A line-out contested between the most prolific points-scorers in Caribbean rugby, Bermuda (blue shirts), and the lowest ranked Americas team, Bahamas. The match, a RWC qualifier in the Cayman Islands in 2008, went the way of Bermuda, 29–13 the final score.

80 AND OVER POINTS SCORED IN A MATCH

Team	Opponent	Result	Venue	Date
Chile	Paraguay	102–0	Montevideo	3 May 2003
Guyana	St Lucia	97–0	Port-of-Spain	10 Aug 2005
Brazil	Costa Rica	95–0	Caracas	16 Oct 2006
Chile	Venezuela	95–3	Santiago	28 Apr 2004
Paraguay	Venezuela	92–7	Asuncion	28 Sep 2005
Barbados	St Lucia	87–0	Port-of-Spain	13 Aug 2005
Trinidad & Tobago	St Lucia	82–0	Port-of-Spain	7 Aug 2005
Paraguay	Colombia	82–8	Asuncion	23 Sep 2005

PART II
BRITISH AND IRISH LIONS

A team from Britain has been touring the southern hemisphere since 1888, although the first tour to New Zealand and Australia – comprising 35 matches – was an unofficial affair and, as such, does not form part of the team's official records. Three years later, a British representative team toured South Africa with official backing and a further five tours took place before 1910, when, for the first time, the touring party was selected by a committee represented by England, Ireland, Scotland and Wales; prior to that, only one of the six official tours had featured players from all of the four Home Unions.

The British Lions – the name was coined by British and South African journalists during the side's 1924 tour there – came of age in the 1950s, with a 2–2 series draw against South Africa in 1955, but the golden era came in the 1970s, when the Lions recorded their one, and to date only, series victory over New Zealand (2–1 in 1971) and then beat a powerful South Africa side 3–0 three years later. Interest waned in the early 1980s but a revival followed their memorable come-from-behind 2–1 series victory over Australia in 1989, and any fears that the onset of professionalism in the mid-1990s would threaten this most amateur of traditions were blasted away by a compelling 2–1 series win over reigning world champions South Africa in 1997. The Lions were here to stay and their last three tours – to Australia (2001), New Zealand (2005) and South Africa (2009) – have attracted massive attention, with thousands of fans (30,000 of them travelled to New Zealand) roaring their support.

Today, British Lions tours are the stuff of legend, the highlight of a player's career and, with the exception perhaps of the Rugby World Cup, are the most eagerly anticipated fixtures on the rugby calendar.

BELOW: The latest batch of British Lions line up to face South Africa in 2009. The series ended in a 2–1 defeat.

TEAM RECORDS

OVERALL RECORD

Country (Span)	Mat	Won	Lost	Draw	%	For	Aga	Diff	Tries	Conv	Pens	Drop	GfM
South Africa (1891–2009)	46	17	23	6	43.47	516	600	-84	68	30	59	13	1
Australia (1899–2001)	20	15	5	0	75.00	335	195	+140	51	30	26	7	1
New Zealand (1904–2005)	38	6	29	3	19.73	345	634	-289	41	18	51	6	0
Argentina (2005)	1	0	0	1	50.00	25	25	0	1	1	6	0	0

SPREADING THE RUGBY GOSPEL

If the first tour by a British representative team to the southern hemisphere – to New Zealand in 1888 – had principally been an ad hoc affair (brought together by Alfred Shaw and Arthur Shrewsbury, the tourists played both rugby and Aussie Rules football), then the first official tour, to South Africa three years later, was largely a promotional one. Financially underwritten by Cecil Rhodes, then governor of Cape Colony Province, its main purpose was to promote the game in the colony. The 22-man touring party (featuring 18 Englishmen and four Scotsmen, including captain Bill MacLagan) played a total of 20 matches – including three Tests – and won every one of them, scoring 224 points and conceding just one.

RIGHT: British Lions captain Mike Campbell-Lamerton (with ball) leads from the front during his side's 11–0 opening Test triumph over Australia in Sydney in 1966.

RECORD AS BRITAIN AND IRELAND (FROM 1891 TO 1938)

Prior to 1950, the Home Nations touring side was known as Britain and Ireland. They made 12 official tours to the southern hemisphere between 1891 and 1938, winning four series – including the first three (two against South Africa and one against Australia). Their overall record in that time was: played 36, won 15, lost 17, drew 4 (a winning percentage of 41.67).

LIONS ROMP TO VICTORY IN BRISBANE

The British Lions ended their two-match tour to Australia in 1966 on a record-breaking high. Having edged the first Test 11–8 in Sydney on 28 May, they put their hosts to the sword in Brisbane a week later, scoring five unanswered tries – two of them from centre Ken Jones – on the way to recording a 31–0 victory. It is the biggest margin of victory for a British Lions team.

ABOVE: The British and Irish Lions class of 2009 assemble for a team huddle prior to kick-off in the first Test against South Africa in Durban on 20 June. They lost s thrilling encounter 26–21.

CHANGING COLOURS OF THE LIONS

The Lions may have become synonymous with their famous red jerseys, but that has not always been the case. Between 1891 and 1896, the team wore red and white hooped jerseys with dark blue shorts; in 1899 and 1904 they wore blue hooped jerseys with thin red and white bands; 1908 saw the reintroduction of red and white hooped jerseys; and from 1910 to 1938 the team took to the field wearing dark blue jerseys. The Lions wore the red shirt, white shorts and green and blue socks – the four colours of the Home Nations – for the first time in 1950 and have continued to do so ever since.

SERIES

Year	Opponent	Result
TOURS AS GREAT BRITAIN		
1891	South Africa	3–0
1896	South Africa	3–1
1899	Australia	3–1
1903	South Africa	0–1
1904	Australia	3–0
1904	New Zealand	0–1
1908	New Zealand	0–2
1910	South Africa	1–2
1924	South Africa	0–3
1930	New Zealand	1–3
1930	Australia	0–1
1938	South Africa	1–2
TOURS AS THE BRITISH LIONS		
1950	New Zealand	0–3
1950	Australia	2–0
1955	South Africa	2–2
1959	Australia	2–0
1959	New Zealand	1–3
1962	South Africa	0–3
1966	Australia	2–0
1966	New Zealand	0–4
1968	South Africa	0–3
1971	New Zealand	2–1
1974	South Africa	3–0
1977	New Zealand	1–3
1980	South Africa	1–3
1983	New Zealand	0–4
1989	Australia	2–1
1993	New Zealand	1–2
1997	South Africa	2–1
2001	Australia	1–2
2005	Argentina	0–0*
2005	New Zealand	0–3
2009	South Africa	1–2

* One-off match, played in Cardiff, prior to the tour of New Zealand

HONOURS EVEN

Britain and Ireland's 1955 tour to South Africa – the 15th in their history and their second as the British Lions – was a record-breaking one and did much to foster the team's legendary status in the years to come. In what turned out to be a yo-yo series, the Lions won the first Test in Johannesburg on 6 August (23–22), lost the second in Cape Town two weeks later (25–9), edged out the Springboks 9–6 in the third Test in Pretoria on 3 September, but lost the final match of the series (22–8) in Port Elizabeth on 24 September. It is the only time the Lions have drawn a Test series in their history.

BIRTH OF THE BRITISH LIONS

The term British Lions was first used by journalists on the 1924 tour to South Africa (because of the emblem the tourists wore on their ties and jackets); and the name was used officially for the first time on the 1950 tour to Australia and New Zealand. This tour also saw the players wear the now-famous red jerseys for the first time.

LIONS' FIRST SERIES DEFEAT

The British Isles' first three official tours had all ended with a series victory – 3–0 against South Africa in 1891, 3–1 against the same opponents five years later and 3–1 against Australia in 1899 – but the tourists' series-winning ways came to an end during their 1903 tour to South Africa. The first two Tests were drawn – 10–10 in Johannesburg and 0–0 in Kimberley – before the Springboks won the deciding Test 8–0 in Cape Town to become the first nation in history to win a series against a British touring side.

LEFT: A 2–1 series defeat to South Africa in 2009 made it three unsuccessful tours in a row for the British and Irish Lions.

ABOVE: Scrum-half Dave Loveridge tries to go past John Rutherford during the All Blacks' 15–8 third Test win at Dunedin in July 1983.

LAMENTABLE LIONS CRASH TO RECORD-BREAKING DEFEAT

The Lions endured a miserable tour to New Zealand in 1983, suffering narrow defeats in the first three Tests – 16–12 in Christchurch, 9–0 in Wellington and 15–8 in Dunedin – before capitulating 38–6 in the fourth and final Test in Auckland. Not only had they suffered a series whitewash for only the second time in their history (bar one-off Tests, that is), but the 32-point losing margin was the largest in their history.

RECORD AS THE BRITISH LIONS (FROM 1950)

The British Lions have undertaken 20 tours to the southern hemisphere (and played in a one-off Test against Argentina prior to their 2005 tour to New Zealand) and won only seven of them, with one series drawn (against South Africa in 1955). Their overall playing record is played 69, won 23, lost 40 and drawn 6 – a winning percentage of 33.33.

BIGGEST VICTORIES: TOP FIVE

Score	Opponent	Venue	Date
31–0	Australia	Brisbane	4 Jun 1966
24–3	Australia	Sydney	26 Aug 1950
24–3	Australia	Sydney	13 Jun 1959
28–9	South Africa	Pretoria	22 Jun 1974
28–9	South Africa	Johannesburg	4 Jul 2009

LEFT: Jeremy Guscott (right) celebrates hi last-gasp drop-goal which saw the Lions snatch an 18–15 second Test victory over South Africa in Durban in 1997. It laid the foundations for the tourists' last series win over the Springboks.

RECORD AGAINST SOUTH AFRICA

The British Lions provided South Africa with their first international opposition and, not surprisingly, the tourists eased to victory in the first two series played (winning 3–0 in 1891 and 3–1 five years later), but the British tourists' early supremacy over the Springboks did not last long. South Africa won the next four series (in 1903, 1910, 1924 and 1938), drew in 1955 (2–2) and have lost only two of the six series played since then – in 1974 and 1997. The Lions' overall record against South Africa reads: played 46, won 17, lost 23 and drawn 6.

WINNING WAYS AGAINST THE WALLABIES

Ever since their 13–3 victory at Sydney on 24 June 1899 – the first match played between the two sides – the Lions have enjoyed the upper hand in contests against Australia. Of the seven series played, the Lions have won five of them, losing only in 1930 (1–0) and in 2001 (the Wallabies won the most recent series 2–1 after losing the first Test). The Lions' overall record against Australia is a pretty impressive one and reads: played 20, won 15 and lost 5.

THE LIONS' STRUGGLES AGAINST THE ALL BLACKS

Matches against New Zealand have always been a tough proposition for the British Lions. In the 11 series contested between the two sides (the first in 1904), the All Blacks have won ten of them, with the Lions' only series success coming in 1971 (2–1).

The tourists' overall record against New Zealand reads: played 38, won 6, lost 29 and drawn 3. The two sides' most recent encounters, in 2005, ended with the All Blacks cruising to a 3–0 series whitewash; in the second Test in Wellington on 2 July, the Lions crashed to a 48–18 defeat – they have never conceded more points in a match.

BIGGEST DEFEATS: TOP FIVE

Score	Opponent	Venue	Date
6–38	New Zealand	Auckland	16 Jul 1983
18–48	New Zealand	Wellington	2 Jul 2005
0–29	New Zealand	Auckland	25 Jul 1908
5–32	New Zealand	Dunedin	6 Jun 1908
14–35	Australia	Melbourne	7 Jul 2001

WILKINSON SAVES LIONS' BLUSHES

What was expected to be a comfortable victory against an under-strength Argentina side, as well as a gentle warm-up for the upcoming challenging tour to New Zealand in 2005, almost turned into a major embarrassment for the Lions and it took the unerring boot of Jonny Wilkinson to save their blushes. With the Lions trailing 25–22 going into the final moments of the one-off match at Cardiff on 23 May 2005, Wilkinson nailed a last-gasp penalty from the left touchline to secure a face-saving 25–25 draw. It is the only fixture contested between the two sides.

LEFT: Australia celebrates a 2–1 series victory over the British and Irish Lions in 2001 – only the second the Wallabies have recorded in seven attempts.

MOST DEFEATS AT A SINGLE GROUND

The Lions have suffered a record eight defeats at two separate venues: at Lancaster Park, Christchurch, New Zealand (where they have lost eight of the nine matches played – the only victory coming on 9 July 1977); and at Newlands Stadium, Cape Town, South Africa (where they have lost eight of the 12 matches played). Ironically, the Lions have scored more points at Newlands (116) than at any other venue.

MAKING HISTORY IN SOUTH AFRICA

The British Lions' 1974 tour to South Africa is considered by many to be the most famous of their illustrious history – and with good reason. They won the first Test in Cape Town (12–3) and eased to victory in both the second (28–9 in Pretoria) and third (26–9 in Port Elizabeth) before drawing the fourth and final Test (13–13 in Johannesburg). Their 3–0 series victory meant they had become the first touring team in the twentieth century to win a four-Test series in South Africa, and the 79 points they scored in the process is still an all-time Lions record.

WHITEWASHES – FOR

Of the 32 series the Lions have contested since 1891, four of them have ended in a series whitewash: against South Africa in 1891 (3–0) and against Australia in 1904 (3–0), 1950 (2–0) and 1959 (2–0).

WHITEWASHES – AGAINST

The British Lions have been on the receiving end of a series whitewash on only two occasions, both times against New Zealand – in 1983 (0–4) and 2005 (0–3). They also lost a one-off Test against the All Blacks in 1904 and against Australia in 1930.

MOST SUCCESSFUL VENUE FOR THE LIONS

The Lions have enjoyed more success at the Sydney Cricket Ground in Australia than at any other venue. They have played there on eight occasions between 1899 and 1966 and recorded six victories, scoring 100 points and conceding 40.

BELOW: Winger J.J. Williams (right) impressed with four tries when the British Lions secured a memorable 3–0 series triumph over South Africa in 1974.

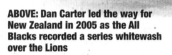

ABOVE: Dan Carter led the way for New Zealand in 2005 as the All Blacks recorded a series whitewash over the Lions

WON OPENING GAME AND GONE ON TO LOSE THE SERIES

The Lions have won the opening game but then gone on to lose the series on two occasions: against New Zealand in 1930, when they won 6–3 in Christchurch but went on to lose the next three Tests; and against Australia in 2001, when they won the opening game in Brisbane (29–13), but then lost in Melbourne (35–14) and Sydney (29–23) to lose the series 2–1.

LOST OPENING GAME AND COME BACK TO WIN THE SERIES

As a general rule of thumb, if the Lions lose the first Test, the chances are they will go on to lose the series. Only once have they disproved that theory: during their 1989 tour to Australia they lost the opening game 30–12 in Sydney, but then, remarkably, went on to win in Melbourne (35–14) and Sydney (29–23) to take the series 2–1.

BATTERED BY THE ALL BLACKS

The British Lions travelled to New Zealand in 2005 on a wave of optimism: their squad contained 15 members of England's 2003 Rugby World Cup-winning squad; Sir Clive Woodward, the only coach from the northern hemisphere to lift the Webb Ellis trophy, was head coach; and they had the support of an estimated 30,000 fans. The tour, however, was an unmitigated disaster: the Lions slipped to a 21–3 defeat in the opening Test in Christchurch; crashed 48–18 in the second Test in Wellington; and lost 38–19 in the final match in Auckland to suffer their first series whitewash since 1983. What's more, the 107 points they conceded in the three Tests was the most in their history.

LEFT: The 1989 British and Irish Lions made history when they became the first team to lose the opening Test (against Australia) and then gone on to win the series.

O'REILLY DISPLAYS LETHAL TRY-SCORING TOUCH

Before achieving success in the business world – he went on to become Ireland's first billionaire – Tony O'Reilly made his name on the rugby pitch. On 6 August 1955, aged 19 years 91 days, the Irish winger made a try-scoring debut for the British Lions during their narrow 23–22 victory over South Africa at Johannesburg. He was not only the youngest British Lion of all time, but also the side's youngest-ever try-scorer. He played in all four matches during the drawn series, scoring a try in the lost final Test at Port Elizabeth. He was back in a Lions shirt four years later for their tour to Australia and New Zealand and scored two tries during their 2–0 series win over the Wallabies and a further two during their 3–1 series defeat to the All Blacks. His six tries for the Lions is an all-time record.

MOST TRIES IN A MATCH (TEAM)

The British Lions team record for the most tries scored in a match is five, achieved on five occasions: against Australia at Sydney on 26 August 1950; against South Africa at Johannesburg on 6 August 1955; against Australia at Sydney on 13 June 1959; against Australia at Brisbane on 4 June 1966; and against South Africa at Pretoria on 22 June 1974.

MOST TRIES IN A MATCH (PLAYER)

Only two players have scored two tries in a match for the British Lions on two occasions: Malcolm Price (against Australia at Sydney on 13 June 1959 and against New Zealand at Dunedin on 18 July 1959); and J.J. Williams (against South Africa at Pretoria on 22 June 1974 and against the same opponents at Port Elizabeth on 13 July 1974).

MOST TRIES BY A PLAYER AT A SINGLE GROUND

Two players, hold the British Lions record for the most tries scored by a player at a single ground: Alfred Bucher (in 1899) and Willie Llewellyn (in 1904) both scored three tries at the Sydney Cricket Ground.

ABOVE: Willie Llewellyn's four tries for Britain and Ireland in the 1904 series has been equalled but never bettered.

MOST TRIES IN A SERIES (PLAYER)

The British Lions record for the most tries by a single player in a series is four, a feat achieved by four players: Willie Llewellyn (on the 1904 tour to Australia and New Zealand); Tony O'Reilly (on the 1959 tour to Australia and New Zealand); Malcolm Price (on the 1959 tour to Australia and New Zealand); and, most recently, J.J. Williams (on the 1974 tour to South Africa).

MOST TRIES IN A SERIES (TEAM)

The British Lions record for the most tries in a series is ten, a feat achieved on three occasions: against Australia in 1904 (they won the series 3–0); and twice against South Africa – in 1955 (the series ended in a 2–2 draw) and in 1974 (when the Lions won the four-match series 3–0).

ABOVE: MOST TRIES: TOP TEN
Gerald Davies is one of six players to have scored three tries in his British Lions career.

LEFT: No player has scored more tries for the British Lions than Tony O'Reilly, with six on his two tours, in 1955 and 1959.

MOST TRIES: TOP TEN

Pos	Tries	Player (Span)
1	6	Tony O'Reilly (1955–59)
2	5	J.J. Williams (1974–77)
3	4	Willie Llewellyn (1904)
=	4	Malcolm Price (1959)
5	3	Carl Aarvold (1930)
=	3	Alfred Bucher (1899)
=	3	Jeff Butterfield (1955)
=	3	Gerald Davies (1968–71)
=	3	Ken Jones (1962–66)
=	3	Jack Spoors (1910)

LEFT: One of an elite group of players to have played on three tours, Dickie Jeeps (far left) played in 13 matches for the Lions without scoring a try.

FIRST TRY

Randolph Aston holds the distinction of scoring the first-ever try by an official touring team from Britain – he scored the opening try in his side's 4–0 victory over South Africa at Port Elizabeth on 30 July 1891.

FIRST TRY SCORED AS BRITISH LIONS

Ken Jones holds the honour of scoring the first try in a British Lions Test (post-1950): he scored his side's opening try in their 9–9 draw against New Zealand at Dunedin on 27 May 1950.

TRYLESS JEEPS SETS ALL-TIME MARK FOR THE BRITISH LIONS

One of an elite group of players to have made their international debut for the Lions before making a first appearance for their country, scrum-half Dickie Jeeps forged a memorable half-back partnership with Welsh fly-half Cliff Morgan during the Lions' 1955 tour to South Africa (which ended in a 2–2 draw). He was back in a Lions shirt for their 1959 tour to Australia and New Zealand (playing in five of the six matches) and again in 1962, when he appeared in all four Tests during the Lions' 3–0 series defeat. His final match for the Lions – in the fourth Test of the 1962 tour against South Africa – was also his final international appearance and he retired from the game's big stage with an unwanted landmark: he holds the Lions all-time record for having made the most appearances (13) without scoring a single try.

MOST TRIES SCORED AS CAPTAIN

Only six (of 37) British Lions captains have scored tries in Tests: Bill MacLagan (against South Africa at Cape Town on 5 September 1891); Teddy Morgan (against Australia at Sydney on 30 July 1904); Carl Aarvold (against New Zealand at Auckland on 26 July 1930); Bleddyn Williams (against Australia at Brisbane on 19 August 1950). Ronnie Dawson (against Australia at Sydney on 13 June 1959); and Gareth Thomas (against New Zealand at Wellington on 2 July 2005).

MOST TRIES IN A LOSING CAUSE

The British Lions record for the most tries scored by a player in a match the team went on to lose is two, a feat achieved by four players: Carl Aarvold (against New Zealand at Christchurch on 5 July 1930); Malcolm Price (against New Zealand at Dunedin on 18 July 1959); Gerald Davies (against New Zealand at Christchurch on 10 July 1971); and, most recently, Tom Croft (against South Africa at Durban on 20 June 2009).

OLDEST TRY-SCORER

Bill MacLagan set two new records when he scored Great Britain's second try during their 4–0 victory over South Africa at Cape Town on 5 September 1891: he was the first-ever Lions captain to score a try and, at 32 years 330 days, became the oldest try-scorer for the Lions of all time.

BELOW: Tom Croft's two tries in the first Test at Durban on 20 June 2009 failed to prevent the British and Irish Lions falling to a 26–21 defeat against South Africa.

LIONS TRY-SCORERS: BY NATIONALITY

England	37
Ireland	23
Scotland	18
Wales	36

BRITISH AND IRISH LIONS:
POINTS-SCORING RECORDS

MOST POINTS IN A MATCH

The British Lions all-time record for the most points in a match by a single player is 20, achieved by two players: Jonny Wilkinson, against Argentina at Cardiff on 23 May 2005; and Stephen Jones, against South Africa at Pretoria on 27 June 2009. Jones's haul in Pretoria set another all-time leading mark for the Lions: it is the most points scored by a Lions player in a losing cause – they lost the match 28–25. Wilkinson and Jones also hold the record for the most conversions by a Lions player (both have nailed seven conversions in six Lions appearances).

FULL-BACK JENKINS PROVES HIS WORTH

He may not have been everyone's first choice for the full-back role during the British Lions' 1997 tour to South Africa, but the unerring accuracy of Neil Jenkins' boot played a massive role in the tourists' unexpected 2–1 series victory over the reigning world champions. The Welshman kicked five penalties during the 25–16 win in the first Test in Cape Town; bagged five more during the series-clinching 18–15 second Test victory in Durban; and rounded off the tour with three penalties and a conversion during the 35–16 defeat in Johannesburg. His 13 penalties and 41 points in the three Tests are both all-time records for a British Lions player in a series.

RIGHT: Neil Jenkins's record series haul did much to help the Lions to an unexpected 2–1 series victory against South Africa in 1997.

BELOW: Stephen Jones equalled Jonny Wilkinson's record haul of 20 points in the British and Irish Lions' 28–25 defeat to South Africa in 2005.

LEADING ALL-TIME POINTS-SCORERS AGAINST EACH OPPONENT

Opponent	Points	Player
Argentina	20	Jonny Wilkinson
Australia	36	Jonny Wilkinson
New Zealand	38	Gavin Hastings
South Africa	41	Neil Jenkins

ALL-TIME LEADING POINTS-SCORERS: BY POSITION

Position	Player (Span)	Points
Full-back	Gavin Hastings (1989–93)	66
Winger	J.J. Williams (1974–77)	20
Centre	Dave Hewitt (1959–62)	16
Fly-half	Jonny Wilkinson (2001–05)	64
Scrum-half	Matt Dawson (1997–2001)	10
No.8	John Faull (1959)	5
	Scott Quinnell (2001)	5
Flanker	Tom Croft (2009)	10
Lock	Gordon Brown (1971–77)	8
Prop	John Robins (1950)	10
Hooker	Ronnie Dawson (1959)	3
	Ken Kennedy (1966)	3
	Bryn Meredith (1955–62)	3
	Dai Parker (1930)	3

THE BRITISH LIONS' ALL-TIME LEADING POINTS-SCORER

Jonny Wilkinson made a barnstorming debut for the British Lions, notching up three conversions and a penalty during the tourists' impressive 29–13 win in the first Test of the 2001 series against Australia at Brisbane. However, despite the mercurial fly-half's best efforts (he contributed 27 points in the next two Tests, including one try), the Wallabies rallied to claim the series 2–1. Sidelined for 18 months after his Rugby World Cup-winning exploits for England in 2003, Wilkinson returned to the international rugby fold in a British Lions shirt and showed he had lost none of his formidable kicking prowess – contributing 20 points to save the Lions' blushes during their 25–25 draw against Argentina on 23 May 2005. His performance earned him a place on the Lions tour to New Zealand a month later and, though not at his best, contributed 11 points in two Tests before a shoulder injury prematurely ended his tour. He has not appeared for the Lions since, although he remains their all-time leading points-scorer, with 67 points.

THE LIONS' SERIAL RECORD-BREAKER

A stalwart of two British and Irish Lions tours (to Australia in 1989 and New Zealand in 1993, the latter as captain), Gavin Hastings set several all-time records for the British Lions: he has kicked the most penalties (20); he shares the record with Jonny Wilkinson for the most penalties in a match – six, against New Zealand at Christchurch on 12 June 1993 (Wilkinson kicked six penalties against Argentina at Cardiff on 23 May 2005); his haul of 18 points in the match against New Zealand at Christchurch is a record for a Lions captain and the most by a Lions player in a match against the All Blacks; and he has scored the most points by a British and Irish Lions player at a single ground (21 in two matches at the Sydney Football Stadium in 1989).

BELOW: International rugby's all-time leading points-scorer, fly-half Jonny Wilkinson continued his England form in a Lions shirt, scoring a record 67 points in six matches between 2001 and 2005.

UNUSED WEAPON

It may be that British Lions sides have decided on a more attacking, ball-in-hand game plan over the years, but surprisingly, given their considerable points value (they have been worth three points since 1891) and their frequency in the modern game (England's Jonny Wilkinson has scored 33 in 86 internationals – 2.6 per game), drop goals have been a rarity in Lions matches. The record for the most drop goals in a Lions career is two, achieved by five players: Percy Bush, David Watkins, Barry John, Phil Bennett and Rob Andrew. John and Bennett did it in the same game, against South Africa at Port Elizabeth on 13 July 1974.

ABOVE: Scotland's Gavin Hastings was an outstanding performer on the two tours for the British Lions (in 1989 and 1993) and he broke host of records along the way.

WILSON'S RECORD-BREAKING DEBUT

Former Oxford Blue Stewart Wilson made a record-breaking contribution in his Test debut for the British and Irish Lions. During the comprehensive 31–0 second Test victory over Australia at Lang Park, Brisbane, on 4 June 1966, the Scotland full-back nailed five conversions (out of five) – the most conversions by any Lions player in a single match.

MOST POINTS IN A MATCH AGAINST EACH OPPONENT

Opponent	Points	Player	Venue	Date
Argentina	20	Jonny Wilkinson	Cardiff	23 May 2005
Australia	18	Jonny Wilkinson	Brisbane	14 July 2001
New Zealand	18	Gavin Hastings	Christchurch	12 Jun 1993
South Africa	20	Stephen Jones	Pretoria	27 Jun 2009

MOST POINTS: TOP TEN

Pos Points Player (Span)

Pos	Points	Player (Span)
1	67	Jonny Wilkinson (2001–05)
2	66	Gavin Hastings (1989–93)
3	53	Stephen Jones (2005–09)
4	44	Phil Bennett (1974–77)
5	41	Neil Jenkins (1997–2001)
6	35	Tom Kiernan (1962–68)
7	30	Barry John (1968–71)
=	30	Stewart Wilson (1966)
9	28	Andy Irvine (1974–80)
10	26	Ollie Campbell (1980–83)
=	26	Lewis Jones (1950)

MOST CONVERSIONS IN A SERIES

The Lions all-time record for the most conversions in a series is six, by Stephen Jones against South Africa in 2009.

REPLACEMENTS DRAW A BLANK

The British Lions have used 38 replacements in matches over the years, but, remarkably, not one of them has come on to the pitch and contributed a point to their team's cause.

WILLIE-JOHN MCBRIDE: THE ULTIMATE LION

A latecomer to the game – he did not pick up a rugby ball until well into his teens – Willie-John McBride made his international debut (at lock) during Ireland's second match of the 1962 Five Nations – against England at Twickenham – kept his place in the side and performed well enough in his country's final two matches of the campaign to earn selection for that year's British Lions tour to South Africa, making his first appearances for the tourists in the final two matches of the series. For McBride, it was the start of an enduring love affair with the Lions: he was back in a red shirt for the 1966 tour to Australia and New Zealand and was a key member of the tourists' series-winning performances against New Zealand in 1971 (as pack leader) and against South Africa in 1974 (as captain in his final tour). With 17 caps – gathered over five tours – he is the most capped British Lion of all time.

THE BRITISH LIONS' OLDEST PLAYER

Supreme fitness allied to a tireless work rate made Neil Back a stand-out performer in international rugby – but not before he had silenced his critics. He made his debut for England in 1994, but struggled to shake off the widely held notion that, at 5ft 10in (1.78m), he was too small for an international flanker, and made only four more appearances for his country over the next two years. It was during the Lions' 1997 tour to South Africa, however, that the rugby world started to appreciate his true worth: he made a decisive contribution when he came on as a replacement during the series-clinching win in the second Test and was an ever-present in international rugby from that moment on: touring Australia with the Lions in 2001; helping England to the Rugby World Cup in 2003; and bowing out of international rugby after the Lions' 2005 tour to New Zealand, during which – in the third Test at Christchurch – he became, aged 36 years 160 days, their oldest-ever player.

BELOW: No one has embodied the British and Irish Lions' spirit better than Willie-John McBride, who made a record-breaking 17 Test appearances in the famous red shirt.

ABOVE: Still in the thick of it (lying on the ground, bottom right) in his 37th year, Neil Back has the distinction of being the British Lions' oldest player.

LIONS PLAYERS: BY COUNTRY	
England	186
Ireland	107
Scotland	78
Wales	141
TOTAL	**512**

MOST APPEARANCES IN A WINNING SIDE

The British Lions all-time record for the most appearances in a winning side is six, held by two players: Froude Hancock (in seven matches between 1891 and 1896) and Blair Swannell (in seven matches between 1899 and 1904). Of the 20 players who have played in four or more matches for the Lions, all of them have tasted defeat at least once.

MOST LIONS TOURS

5	Willie-John McBride (Ireland)
3	Neil Back (England)
3	Gordon Brown (Scotland)
3	Matt Dawson (England)
3	Gareth Edwards (Wales)
3	Ieuan Evans (Wales)
3	Mike Gibson (Ireland)
3	Jeremy Guscott (England)
3	Richard Hill (England)
3	Andy Irvine (Scotland)
3	Dickie Jeeps (England)
3	Martin Johnson (England)
3	Jason Leonard (England)
3	Syd Millar (Ireland)
3	Brian O'Driscoll (Ireland)
3	Graham Price (Wales)
3	Derek Quinnell (Wales)
3	Jeff Squire (Wales)
3	Phil Vickery (England)

MOST APPEARANCES: TOP TEN

Pos	Caps	Player (Span)
1	17	Willie-John McBride (1962–74)
2	13	Dickie Jeeps (1955–62)
3	12	Mike Gibson (1966–71)
=	12	Graham Price (1977–83)
5	10	Gareth Edwards (1968–74)
=	10	Tony O'Reilly (1955–59)
=	10	Rhys Williams (1955–59)
8	9	Andy Irvine (1974–80)
=	9	Syd Millar (1959–68)
10	8	*15 players*

PRICE ENDURES THE BITTER TASTE OF DEFEAT

A legend in Welsh rugby and one of the most celebrated prop forwards in international rugby history, Pontypool's Graham Price suffered more than anyone in a British Lions shirt. A stalwart of three tours (1977, 1980 and 1983) and a veteran of 12 appearances (only Willie-John McBride and Dickie Jeeps have made more), he tasted victory only twice – against New Zealand at Christchurch on 9 July 1977 and against South Africa at Pretoria on 12 July 1980. His ten appearances on a losing Lions side are an all-time record.

ABOVE: Graham Price has suffered the misery of defeat more often than any other Lions player, being on the losing side in ten Test matches.

ALL-TIME LEADING APPEARANCES: BY POSITION

Position	Player (Span)	Appearances
Full-back	J.P.R. Williams (1971–74)	8
Winger	Tony O'Reilly (1955–59)	9
Centre	Mike Gibson (1966–71)	8
	Jeremy Guscott (1989–97)	8
Fly-half	Phil Bennett (1974–79)	8
Scrum-half	Dickie Jeeps (1955–62)	13
No.8	Mervyn Davies (1971–74)	8
Flanker	Noel Murphy (1959–66)	8
Lock	Willie-John McBride (1962–74)	17
Prop	Graham Price (1977–83)	12
Hooker	Bryn Meredith (1955–62)	8

MOST APPEARANCES: BY OPPONENT

Opponent	Player	Appearances
Australia	Blair Swannell	6
New Zealand	Mike Gibson	8
South Africa	Willie-John McBride	10

LEFT: Ronnie Dawson (left, carrying the Lion mascot) shares the honour (with Martin Johnson) of having the captained the British Lions on the most occasions (six).

BELOW: No player in the history of the Lions has made more Test replacement apperances than Ireland winger Shane Horgan, who made four, all in 2005.

MOST APPEARANCES AS CAPTAIN

The all-time British Lions record for the most appearances as captain is six, held by two players: Ronnie Dawson (in 1959) and Martin Johnson (between 1997 and 2001). Johnson, however, is the only player in history to have led the Lions on two separate tours (in 1997 and 2001).

ONE-CAP WONDERS

Of the 512 players to have represented the British Isles (and then the British Lions) over the years, 116 of them have made only one appearance – a surprising 22.66 per cent.

MOST APPEARANCES AS A REPLACEMENT

No player has made more appearances for the British Lions as a replacement than Shane Horgan. The Ireland winger came off the bench in every one of the Lions' matches in 2005 (against Argentina in the drawn match at Cardiff and in all three Tests of the losing series against New Zealand).

IAN McGEECHAN: A LIONS LEGEND

Ian McGeechan would have possessed a distinguished rugby resumé even without his exploits as coach of the British Lions. He was good enough as a player to win 32 caps for Scotland (at centre between 1972 and 1979) and eight caps for the Lions (on the 1974 and 1977 tours), and as Scotland coach he led his side to a historic grand slam in 1990 and to the Rugby World Cup semi-finals a year later. But it is his role as Lions coach that propelled him to legendary status: he has coached them on an unprecedented four tours: to a 2–1 series win over Australia in 1989; to a 1–2 series reverse against New Zealand in 1993; to a 2–1 series win over reigning world champions South Africa in 1997; and to South Africa again in 2009 (the Lions lost the gripping series 2–1).

ABOVE: Ian McGeechan's legend in the game was enhanced by his exploits with the British Lions.

RIGHT: Graham Henry is one of only two non-British or Irish coaches to have led the Lions.

FAR RIGHT: England Rugby World Cup-winning coach Sir Clive Woodward could not find the winning formula with the British Lions in 2005; his side lost the series against New Zealand 3–0.

COACHES AND CAPTAINS

Year	Opponent	Head coach	Captain
1891	South Africa	Edwin Ash	Bill MacLagan
1896	South Africa	Roger Walker	Johnny Hammond
1899	Australia	Matthew Mullineux	Matthew Mullineux (1)/ Frank Stout (3)
1903	South Africa	Johnny Hammond	Mark Morrison
1904	Australia	Arthur O'Brien	David Bedell-Sivright
1904	New Zealand	George Harnett	Arthur Harding
1908	New Zealand/Australia	W. Cail/Walter Rees	Tommy Smyth
1910	South Africa	R.V. Stanley	John Raphael
1924	South Africa	Harry Packer	Ronald Cove-Smith
1930	New Zealand	James Baxter	David MacMyn
1930	New Zealand/Australia	James Baxter	Doug Prentice
1938	South Africa	B.C. Hartley	Sam Walker
1950	New Zealand/Australia	L.B. Osborne	Karl Mullen
1955	South Africa	Jack Siggins	Robin Thompson
1959	Australia/New Zealand	O.B. Glasgow	Ronnie Dawson
1962	South Africa	Harry McKibbin	Arthur Smith
1966	Australia/New Zealand	John Robins	Mike Campbell-Lamerton (4)/ David Watkins (2)
1968	South Africa	Ronnie Dawson	Tom Kiernan
1971	New Zealand	Carwyn James	John Dawes
1974	South Africa	Syd Millar	Willie-John McBride
1977	New Zealand	John Dawes	Phil Bennett
1980	South Africa	Noel Murphy	Bill Beaumont
1983	New Zealand	Jim Telfer	Ciaran Fitzgerald
1989	Australia	Ian McGeechan	Finlay Calder
1993	New Zealand	Ian McGeechan	Gavin Hastings
1997	South Africa	Ian McGeechan/Jim Telfer	Martin Johnson
2001	Australia	Graham Henry	Martin Johnson
2005	New Zealand	Clive Woodward	Brian O'Driscoll (1)/ Martin Corry (1)/ Gareth Thomas (1)
2009	South Africa	Ian McGeechan	Paul O'Connell

(Campbell-Lamerton and O'Driscoll were tour captains, but did not play in every Test match because of injury. The figure in brackets is the number of Tests they were captain.)

GUIDED BY A FOREIGN HAND

Of the 25 men to have coached the British Lions since their first official tour (to South Africa in 1891), only two of them have not come from Britain or Ireland: New Zealand's Arthur O'Brien (who led the Lions to Australia and New Zealand in 1904); and another Kiwi, Graham Henry (who was coach during the Lions' 2001 tour to Australia).

CAPTAIN FANTASTIC

Martin Johnson may have been an unexpected choice as captain for the British Lions' 1997 tour to South Africa (he had, after all, not yet captained his country – that would come in 1999), but it was an inspirational one. He led the Lions to a memorable 2–1 series victory over the reigning world champions. His appointment to lead the Lions to Australia in 2001 was the complete reverse – it was completely expected and the tour ended in a 2–1 series defeat – but it was, nonetheless, a history-making moment: Johnson is the only player ever to lead the Lions on two tours.

CAPTAINS BY NATIONALITY

England	12
Ireland	10
Scotland	8
Wales	5

LIONS SEEING YELLOW OR RED

No British Lion has ever received a red card, but four have spent time in the sin bin for a yellow-card offence: Martin Corry and Phil Vickery (against Australia at Brisbane on 30 June 2001); Paul O'Connell (against New Zealand at Christchurch on 25 June 2005); and Simon Shaw (against South Africa at Johannesburg on 4 July 2009).

COACHES BY NATIONALITY

England	12
Ireland	6
Scotland	2
Wales	6
Other	2

THE LIONS AT HOME

The British and Irish Lions have made only three official appearances on British soil: against the Barbarians at Twickenham in 1977 (a charity fundraiser held as part of the Queen's Silver Jubilee celebrations, which they won 23–14); against a Rest of the World XV at Cardiff in 1986 (to celebrate the IRB's centenary – they won the match 15–7); and against Argentina at Cardiff in May 2005 (which ended in a surprising 25–25 draw). Only the last of these three matches was given international status.

NATURAL-BORN LEADER

Sydney John Dawes has a special place in the British Lions' roll of honour. In 1971, he marshalled perhaps the greatest backline ever assembled – Gareth Edwards, Barry John, David Duckham, Mike Gibson, Dawes, Gerald Davies and J.P.R. Williams – to a 2–1 series win over New Zealand. It is still the Lions' only series success in the Land of the Long White Cloud. Dawes retired as a player after the series, but wasn't out of international rugby for long. In 1974, he became Wales coach; and three years later he was handed the Lions' coaching reins for their tour to New Zealand. This series may have ended in defeat (3–1), but Dawes became, and remains, the only person to captain the Lions on one tour and be coach on another tour.

CHANGING SIDES

Only two players have appeared in matches playing both for and against the British Lions: Tom Reid, who played for the tourists on their 1955 tour to South Africa and against the 1959 Lions for East Canada; and Riki Flutey, who played against the 2005 Lions for Wellington and, having qualified for England through residency, was selected and played for the Lions during their 2009 tour to South Africa.

ABOVE: John Dawes is the only man in history to have been both captain and coach of the British Lions.

THE LIONS' ONLY PLAYER-COACH

An ordained deacon off the rugby pitch and a scrum-half on it (he played with distinction for Cambridge University), Matthew Mullineux was selected for the British Isles' 1896 tour to South Africa and made his international debut in the first Test at Port Elizabeth. Three years later, for the Lions' first-ever tour to Australia, he was captain and coach – the only man to fill both roles on the same tour – though he played in only the first Test. The tourists won the series 3–1.

MIDWEEK SIDE

The midweek side, made up of those selected for the touring party but who have failed to make it into the test team, are charged with the honour of representing the Lions against state or regional sides. It has become an increasingly important part of British Lions tours. Only three times in history has it recorded a 100 percent record during a tour: in 1959 (to Australia/New Zealand), 1971 (New Zealand) and 2005 (New Zealand).

OVERSEAS-BORN LIONS

Player (Span)	Place of birth	Appearances
Cuthbert Mullins (1896)	South Africa	2
Pat McEvedy (1904–08)	New Zealand	5
Arthur O'Brien (1904)	New Zealand	4
Tom Richards (1910)	Australia	2
Brian Black (1930)	New Zealand	5
Mike Catt (1997)	South Africa	1
Ronan O'Gara (2005–09)	United States	2
Riki Flutey (2009)	New Zealand	1
Jamie Heaslip (2009)	Israel	3
Simon Shaw (2009)	Kenya	2

LEFT: Rikki Flutey is one of only two men in history to have played for and against the British Lions.

PART III

RUGBY WORLD CUP

If one day in 1823, when William Webb Ellis picked up a ball and ran with it during a football match on a playing field at Rugby School, provided the game of rugby with its most apocryphal moment, then a meeting of the IRB committee at Paris in 1985 provided it with its most pivotal one.

On 21 March 1985, votes were cast to decide whether a Rugby World Cup should take place: Australia, New Zealand and France were in favour of the idea; the Home Nations – keen to preserve the game's amateur ideals – were against it and the inevitable commercialism that would come with

such a tournament; but South Africa still had to vote. Whether or not the prospect of facing years in the international sporting wilderness – as a result of its government's oppressive apartheid policy – had any influence on its decision will never be known, but South Africa voted in favour of the idea, and the votes were locked at 4–4. It was a stalemate and the process started all over again. First England rescinded, Wales soon followed, and the die had been cast. The Rugby World Cup was born, with the first tournament, hosted by Australia and New Zealand, to be staged in 1987.

The inaugural Rugby World Cup was an invitation-only, 16-team affair that saw New Zealand stroll to victory over France in the final. Australia took the spoils in 1991, beating England in a closely contested final at Twickenham. The third edition of the event, 1995, was the year the tournament came to life: hosts South Africa, competing for the game's biggest prize for the first time, prompted a previously disharmonious nation to dance in the streets in united celebration when they beat New Zealand in the final. In 1999, Australia became the first team to win the trophy for the second time; it was another first in 2003, when England became the first team from the northern hemisphere to be crowned world champions. South Africa took the top prize in 2007 and, in 2011, New Zealand broke their tournament jinx as they beat France 8–7 in the final to lift the Webb Ellis Trophy for a second time.

BELOW: Richie McCaw holds aloft the Webb Ellis trophy at the end of the 2001 Rugby World Cup final, ending the All Blacks' 24-year wait to be crowned World Champions.

RUGBY WORLD CUP 2011

The 2011 Rugby World Cup had all the ingredients of a magnificent tournament: a raft of highly competitive matches; feverish support from the host nation; and some hugely memorable action on the pitch, including a nail-biting final that concluded with hosts New Zealand ending a 24-year hoodoo to win the Webb Ellis trophy for the second time..

ALL BLACKS ON TOP OF THE WORLD

Following a catalogue of calamitous near-misses in the past, hosts New Zealand had every right to treat their pre-tournament favourites tag with extreme caution – although, as things turned out, they need not have been concerned. The standout team in the competition, the All Blacks topped the tournament's statistical charts in terms of points scored (301), tries scored (40), points per match (43.0) and most tries scored in a match (13 against Japan) en route to becoming world champions for the first time since 1987.

MOST POINTS: TOP TEN

Pos	Points	Player (Country)
1	62	Morne Steyn (South Africa)
2	52	James O'Connor (Australia)
3	45	Kurt Morath (Tonga)
4	44	Ronan O'Gara (Ireland)
5	41	Piri Weepu (New Zealand)
6	39	Dimitri Yachvili (France)
7	37	Morgan Parra (France)
8	36	Colin Slade (New Zealand)
9	34	James Arlidge (Japan)
10	30	Chris Ashton (England)
=	30	Vincent Clerc (France)

MOST TRIES IN A MATCH

The record for the most tries in a match by a single player at the 2011 Rugby World Cup was four, a feat achieved by two players: Fiji's Vereniki Goneva against Namibia at Rotorua on 10 September 2011; and New Zealand's Zac Guildford against Canada at Wellington and 2 October 2011.

TOUGH TIMES CONTINUE FOR NAMIBIA

Namibia's Rugby World Cup record entering the 2011 tournament was a miserable one – played 11, lost 11 – and things barely improved for the Welwitschias in New Zealand. Drawn in a tough pool, they lost their opening match of the campaign (49–25 to Fiji), followed

ABOVE: Morne Steyn enhanced his reputation as a great goalkicker with his 2011 Rugby World Cup tournament best 62 points.

it up with a 49–12 defeat to Samoa and then succumbed to a pair of thrashings: 89–0 against South Africa (the heaviest defeat in the competition) and 81–7 to Wales. The 266 points conceded in four matches was also a tournament high.

BELOW: One of the biggest parties ever known in New Zealand was about to start wehn the All Blacks won the 2011 Rugby World Cup.

MOST TRIES: TOP TEN

Pos	Tries	Player (Country)
1	6	Chris Ashton (England)
=	6	Vincent Clerc (France)
3	5	Adam Ashley-Cooper (Australia)
=	5	Israel Dagg (New Zealand)
=	5	Keith Earls (Ireland)
6	4	Mark Cueto (England)
=	4	Vereniki Goneva (Fiji)
=	4	Zac Guildford (New Zealand)
=	4	Richard Kahui (New Zealand)
=	4	Jerome Kaino (New Zealand)
=	4	Scott Williams (Wales)
=	4	Sonny Bill Williams (New Zealand)

ABOVE: Vincent Clerc finished the tournament as the top try-scorer with six, including this effort which broke England hearts in the quarter-final.

SPOILS SHARED

Having already lost their first three group matches, against France (47–21), New Zealand (83–7) and Tonga (31–18), Japan's final Pool A match at the 2011 Rugby World Cup, against Canada, represented their final opportunity to register a first victory at the tournament since 1991. For Canada, having already beaten Tonga (25–20) and lost to France (46–19) – and with a final encounter against hosts New Zealand looming, victory in the match would have represented a successful campaign (the first time they would have won two matches at the tournament since 1991). Neither side got their wish: Canada may have outscored Japan by three tries to two, but the match ended in a 23–23 stalemate. It was the tournament's only draw and only the third in the competition's history.

MOST POINTS IN A MATCH

The most points in a match by a player at the 2011 Rugby World Cup was 23, a feat achieved by two players: New Zealand's Colin Slade (a try and nine conversions against Japan at Hamilton on 16 September); and France's Morgan Parra (four conversions and five penalties against Canada at Napier on 18 September).

RED MIST

Two players were shown red cards at the 2011 Rugby World Cup (the same number as in 2007). Samoa's Paul Williams was sent off in the 69th minute of his side's 13–5 defeat to South Africa (for striking Heinrich Brussow); and Welsh captain Sam Warburton was given his marching orders in the 18th minute of his side's 9–8 semi-final defeat to France (for an illegal tackle on Dimitri Yachvili). The record for the most red cards in a tournament is four, in 1995 and 1999.

BELOW: Colin Slade scored 23 points against Japan, but his tournament was ended early because of injury.

ONE-POINT WINS

Apart from a number of predictable mismatches (eight of the 48 matches saw a 50-point-plus winning margin, compared to nine in 2007), one notable feature of the 2011 Rugby World Cup was how closely matched the top-tier teams were. The tournament saw four games ending in a one-point winning margin – South Africa-Wales in Pool D (17–16), Argentina-Scotland in Pool B (13–12), France-Wales in the semi-final (9–8) and New Zealand-France in the final (8–7), the most in the event's history.

YOUNGEST AND OLDEST

He may have been the youngest player in the tournament, aged 19 years 151 days when he played against South Africa, but George North proved a massive hit for Wales at the 2011 Rugby World Cup. The giant winger scored three tries during a campaign that saw his country reach the semi-finals for the first time since 1987. The tournament's oldest player was Russia's Vyacheslav Grachev, who was 38 years 162 days when he played in his country's Pool C match against Australia at Nelson.

FAR RIGHT: Wales winger George North looks for a gap in Australia's defence in the third-place play-off, but the Wallabies won 21–18.

RUGBY WORLD CUP ALL-TIME RECORDS

Since the first tournament was staged in 1987, 25 countries have contested 281 matches in seven separate Rugby World Cups – and there have been numerous ground-breaking moments along the way. This section takes a comprehensive look at the tournament's all-time records (both team and individual), from points scored and penalties kicked to the most matches played and the stadiums that have been host to the most games.

BELOW: Ellis Park, Johannesburg, hosted the 1995 Rugby World Cup final, the last time the hosts had been triumphant until New Zealand in 2011. Before the match, fans saw a South African Airways jet flying overhead, bearing the message, "Good Luck Bokkie".

TEAM RECORDS

OVERALL RECORD

Country (Span)	Mat	Won	Lost	Draw	%	For	Aga	Diff	Tries	Conv	Pens	Drop
Argentina (1987–2011)	30	15	15	0	50.00	742	605	+137	74	49	85	9
Australia (1987–2011)	41	33	8	0	80.48	1423	528	+895	181	132	91	8
Canada (1987–2011)	25	7	16	2	32.00	469	707	-238	49	29	52	8
England (1987–2011)	40	29	11	0	72.50	1246	633	+613	131	97	121	20
Fiji (1987–2011)	24	9	15	0	37.50	538	762	-224	59	45	48	6
France (1987–2011)	43	30	12	1	70.93	1354	770	+584	158	109	121	10
Georgia (2003–11)	12	2	10	0	16.66	144	401	-257	9	9	26	1
Ireland (1987–2011)	30	17	13	0	56.66	819	584	+235	96	73	64	9
Italy (1987–2011)	24	9	15	0	37.50	455	811	-356	47	32	53	3
Ivory Coast (1995)	3	0	3	0	0.00	29	172	-143	3	1	4	0
Japan (1987–2011)	24	1	21	2	8.33	428	1159	-731	51	29	42	3
Namibia (1999–2011)	15	0	15	0	0.00	144	974	-830	16	11	10	4
New Zealand (1987–2011)	43	37	6	0	86.04	2012	584	+1428	272	198	98	8
Portugal (2007)	4	0	4	0	0.00	38	209	-171	4	3	3	1
Romania (1987–2011)	24	5	19	0	20.83	305	939	-634	33	14	40	1
Russia (2011)	4	0	4	0	0.00	57	196	-139	8	4	2	1
Samoa (1991–2011)	24	11	13	0	45.83	585	608	-23	68	47	51	2
Scotland (1987–2011)	33	19	13	1	59.09	972	620	+352	113	82	85	10
South Africa (1995–2011)	29	25	4	0	86.20	1009	378	+631	115	88	73	13
Spain (1999)	3	0	3	0	0.00	18	122	-104	0	0	6	0
Tonga (1987–2011)	21	6	15	0	28.57	335	731	-396	36	25	35	1
United States (1987–2011)	21	3	18	0	14.28	300	736	-436	32	24	31	2
Uruguay (1999–2003)	7	2	5	0	28.57	98	352	-254	10	6	12	0
Wales (1987–2011)	32	18	14	0	56.25	919	633	+286	115	83	61	6
Zimbabwe (1987–91)	6	0	6	0	0.00	84	309	-225	11	5	10	0

ENGLAND AND FRANCE RECOVER FROM SETBACKS

England were the first team to lose a Rugby World Cup pool match and recover to reach the final. In 1991, they lost to New Zealand (18–12), but rallied to reach the final (in which they lost 12–6 to Australia). In 2007, South Africa crushed them 36–0, but England went to play in the final, only to lose to the Springboks for a second time (15–6). In 2011, France lost two pool games (37–17 to New Zealand and 19–14 to Tonga), but still got to the final, where the All Blacks again beat them 8–7.

1987: ALL BLACKS REVEL IN HOME COMFORTS

New Zealand rugby was in turmoil as they entered the inaugural Rugby World Cup in 1987. An unsanctioned rebel tour to South Africa the previous year had left many of their star players facing a ban and the New Zealand rugby public was becoming disillusioned with its team. Their performances in the World Cup changed that: they easily won all three pool matches against Italy (70–6), Fiji (74–13) and Argentina (46–15) to top the group; cruised past Scotland in the quarter-finals (30–3); found their try form to crush Wales 49–6 in the semi-finals and went on to face France in the final. It was a no-contest: the All Blacks – in front of a now passionate home crowd – cantered to a much-deserved 29–9 victory to become rugby's first world champions.

ABOVE: David Kirk was the first New Zealand captain to have lift the Rugby World Cup.

TOURNAMENT WINNERS

1987	New Zealand
1991	Australia
1995	South Africa
1999	Australia
2003	England
2007	South Africa
2011	New Zealand

1991: WALLABIES BATTLE TO WORLD CROWN

Having entered the 1987 Rugby World Cup among the favourites to win the tournament, only to see France dash their hopes in the semi-finals, Australia went to Europe for the 1991 competition with a point to prove ... and, despite a few wobbles along the way, how they proved it. They battled to victory in their pool, beating Argentina (32–19), Western Samoa (9–3) and Wales (38–3); needed a last-gasp try to see off a dogged Ireland side in the quarter-finals (19–18); and found form in the semi-finals to defeat New Zealand (16–6). In the final, against England at Twickenham, a Tony Daly try ultimately proved the difference as the Wallabies edged a closely fought contest 12–6. Australia were on top of the world.

1995: SPRINGBOKS LIVE THE DREAM

South Africa's fairytale began with a confidence-boosting 27–18 opening victory over defending champions Australia in Cape Town and simply carried on from there. They beat Romania (21–8) and Canada (20–0) to win their pool; beat Western Samoa (42–14) in the quarter-finals and dug deep to see off France (19–15) in a rain-soaked semi-final in Durban. Few, however, thought they could beat New Zealand in the final, but some things, it seems, are simply meant to be. The Springboks were resolute in defence; their fly-half, Joel Stransky, was deadly with the boot; and the whole of South Africa danced in the streets following a 15–12 victory.

MOST RUNNERS-UP FINISHES

The record for the most runners-up finishes in the Rugby World Cup is three, by France. In 1987, they lost 29–9 to New Zealand, in 1999 it was a 35–12 defeat to Australia), and in 2011, New Zealand broke French hearts by the narrowest of margins, 8–7.

ABOVE: The second Australian captain to lift the Rugby World Cup trophy John Eales led the Wallabies to a 35–12 victory over France in 1999.

1999: THE WALLABIES' SECOND RUGBY WORLD CUP WIN

A 28–7 home victory over New Zealand in their final match of the 1999 Tri-Nations (in which they finished second) meant that Australia travelled to the Home Nations and France for that year's Rugby World Cup in high spirits. Their good form continued in the group stages, with comfortable victories over Romania (57–9), Ireland (23–3) and the United States (55–19). They cruised past Wales in the quarter-finals (24–9) and then needed extra time – and the boot of Matthew Burke (with eight penalties) – to end South Africa's reign as world champions with a 27–21 victory in the semi-finals. The Wallabies then outclassed France in the final, scoring two unanswered tries during a comfortable 35–12 victory that saw them become the first team in history to lift the Rugby World Cup for a second time.

ABOVE: Martin Johnson becomes the first and, to date, only captain from the northern hemisphere to lift the Webb Ellis trophy after England beat Australia in the 2003 final in Sydney.

2003: ENGLAND LIVE UP TO PRE-TOURNAMENT BILLING

England travelled to the 2003 Rugby World Cup off the back of a Six Nations grand slam, away victories over New Zealand (15–13) and Australia (25–14), and ranked as the best team in the world – and they duly lived up to their pre-tournament billing. Blessed with a mighty pack and the unerring boot of Jonny Wilkinson, they won their pool – beating Georgia (84–6), South Africa (25–6), Samoa (35–22) and Uruguay (111–13) – beat Wales in the quarter-finals (28–17), France in the semi-finals (24–7) and defending champions and hosts Australia in the final (20–17) to become the first team from the northern hemisphere to lift the Rugby World Cup.

2007: SPRINGBOKS DOWN ENGLAND TO CLAIM SECOND TITLE

South Africa started their 2007 Rugby World Cup campaign with two serious statements of intent: a 59–7 victory over a dangerous Samoa side in their opening match and, even better, a 36–0 demolition of defending champions England in their second. It set the tone for the rest of the tournament. Victories over Tonga (30–25) and the United States (64–15) saw them win their pool; they beat Fiji in the quarter-finals (37–20) and Argentina in the semi-finals (37–13) to face England in the final. It was a much closer affair this time round, but South Africa won the battle of the boot 15–6 to win the Rugby World Cup for the second time in their history.

2011: MISSION ACCOMPLISHED FOR NEW ZEALAND

If ever New Zealand were to break the most talked-about hoodoo in the game – their 24-year Rugby World Cup jinx – then 2011 seemed the perfect time to do it. The All Blacks would be hosting the event for the first time since 1987, the last time they had lifted the trophy. And home comforts, coupled with passionate support, seemed to do the trick: they romped through the pool stage – beating Tonga (41–10), Japan (83–7), France (37–17) and Canada (79–15), beat Argentina in the quarter-finals (33–10) and trans-Tasman rivals Australia in the semi-finals (20–6) to reach the final for the first time since 1995. And although they did not have it all their own way in the final showdown – France surpassed them in many of the match's statistical categories, including metres run with the ball (309 to 238), defenders beaten (13 to 7) and offloads (12 to 2), New Zealand won the only battle that mattered, the one on the scoreboard, to win 8–7 and become world champions for the second time in their history.

LEFT: Chris Latham was the star of the show for Australia during their ecord-breaking 142–0 victory over Namibia in 2003. The full-back ran in five tries.

TOP FIVE: BIGGEST VICTORIES

Pos	Score	Team	Opponent	Venue	Date
1	142–0	Australia	Namibia	Adelaide	25 Oct 2003
2	145–17	New Zealand	Japan	Bloemfontein	4 Jun 1995
3	101–3	New Zealand	Italy	Huddersfield	14 Oct 1999
=	111–13	England	Uruguay	Brisbane	2 Nov 2003
5	108–13	New Zealand	Portugal	Lyon	15 Sep 2007

ALL BLACKS FAIL TO MAKE THEIR DOMINANCE PAY

Before 2011, New Zealand had the tag of being the Rugby World Cup's great chokers and statistics alone highlight how the All Blacks have failed to convert world dominance into tournament success. In 2003, for example, they scored 361 points and 52 tries (both records for a team in one tournament), but lost to Australia in the semi-finals. New Zealand also hold the all-time records for the most victories (37), the most tries scored (272) and the most points scored (2.012). The All Blacks have won rugby's greatest prize twice (in 1987 and 2011), but suffered many low points in the intervening 24 years.

RIGHT: Dejected England players reflect on their 36–0 pool match defeat to Stouh Africa at the 2007 Rugby World Cup.

WALES VALIANT IN DEFEAT

By dint of winning their opening three matches both New Zealand and Wales had already qualified for the knockout stages of the 2003 Rugby World Cup, so, on paper, the final Group D match between the two sides at Sydney on 2 November was a simple showdown to decide which team would top the group. The match turned out to be both an entertaining and record-breaking one: New Zealand won as expected (53–37), but the 37 points scored by Wales are an all-time Rugby World Cup record for a team that has gone on to lose the match.

FAILING TO SHINE ON THE BIG STAGE

Qualifying for the Rugby World Cup has become a matter of course for Namibia in recent years: they have secured qualification for the last four tournaments (in 1999, 2003, 2007 and 2011). Once on the game's biggest stage, however, they appear to freeze in the limelight: they have not won a single game in 15 attempts and in 2003 conceded a demoralizing 310 points – a record for a team in a single tournament.

TOUGH GOING FOR NEW BOYS SPAIN

A hard-fought 21–17 victory over Portugal at Murrayfield on 2 December 1998 represented the greatest moment in Spain's rugby history: it meant that they had secured qualification for the following year's Rugby World Cup. However, they were drawn in a tough group, lost all three matches (27–15 to Uruguay, 47–3 to South Africa and 48–0 to Scotland) and remain the only team ever to have played in the Rugby World Cup and not scored a single try.

FAILING TO SCORE A SINGLE POINT

Team	Opponent	Score	Venue	Date
Ivory Coast	Scotland	0–89	Rustenberg	26 May 1995
Canada	South Africa	0–20	Port Elizabeth	3 Jun 1995
Spain	Scotland	0–48	Murrayfield	16 Oct 1999
Namibia	Australia	0–142	Adelaide	25 Oct 2003
England	South Africa	0–36	Paris	14 Sep 2007
Romania	Scotland	0–42	Murrayfield	18 Sep 2007
Scotland	New Zealand	0–40	Murrayfield	23 Sep 2007
Namibia	Georgia	0–30	Lens	26 Sep 2007
Namibia	South Africa	0–87	North Shore City	22 Sep 2011
Fiji	Wales	0–66	Hamilton	2 Oct 2011

GAMES DECIDED BY A SINGLE POINT

Score	Winner	Opponent	Venue	Date
22–21	Wales	Australia	Rotorua	18 Jun 1987
19–18	Australia	Ireland	Dublin	20 Oct 1991
24–23	Ireland	Wales	Johannesburg	4 Jun 1995
19–18	Fiji	USA	Brisbane	15 Oct 2003
16–15	Ireland	Argentina	Adelaide	26 Oct 2003
17–16	Australia	Ireland	Melbourne	1 Nov 2003
17–16	South Africa	Wales	Wellington	11 Sep 2011
13–12	Argentina	Scotland	Wellington	25 Sep 2011
9–8	France	Wales	Auckland	15 Oct 2011
8–7	New Zealand	France	Auckland	23 Oct 2011

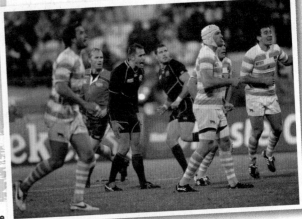

RIGHT: Dan Parks (third left) watches his drop goal miss the posts, condemning Scotland to a 13–12 loss to Argentina.

CHERRY BLOSSOMS WILT IN WORLD CUP LIMELIGHT

Japan are the unrivalled kings of Asian rugby: they received an invitation to appear at the inaugural Rugby World Cup in 1987 and have qualified for every one of the six tournaments since – the only Asian nation to do so. That, however, is where the good news ends for the team known as the Cherry Blossoms: no side in Rugby World Cup history has suffered more defeats (21 in 24 matches) or conceded more points (1,159).

WALES SLUMP TO LAST-GASP DEFEAT

It was one of the most memorable matches in Rugby World Cup history. Shortly before half-time in the final Pool B match at Nantes on 29 September 2007 (with the winner guaranteed a place in the quarter-finals), Fiji led Wales 25–3 and the Welsh needed to dig deep to keep their tournament dreams alive. They rallied in spectacular fashion, scoring five unanswered tries to edge into a 34–31 lead with just six minutes remaining. But, three minutes from time, disaster struck when Fiji's Graham Dewes crashed over the line and Nicky Little slotted the conversion to secure a 38–34 victory and send Wales crashing out of the competition. The fact that they had scored the most tries by a team in a losing cause in Rugby World Cup history would have come as little consolation to the Welsh – it was the third time in six attempts that they had failed to progress beyond the group stages at a Rugby World Cup.

SORRY ROMANIA HIT RECORD-BREAKING LOW

Romania hold the distinction of being one of only 12 teams to have appeared in all seven Rugby World Cups, and have recorded one victory in every tournament bar two – 1995 and 2011. But 1995, in particular, was forgettable for Romania: paired with hosts South Africa, Canada and Australia, they lost all three matches and scored only 14 points – the lowest in a Rugby World Cup tournament.

BELOW: Fiji's players celebrate after Graham Dewes's last-gasp try secured a famous 38–34 victory over Wales at the 2007 Rugby World Cup.

HONOURS EVEN

There have been three draws in the Rugby World Cup. First France drew 20–20 with Scotland at Christchurch in 1987. And Japan and Canada have drawn twice, at Bordeaux in 2007 (12–12), and at Napier in 2011 (23–23).

WAITING TO GET OFF THE MARK

Six countries are still waiting to record their first Rugby World Cup victory: Namibia (in four tournament appearances), Portugal, Russia, Spain, Ivory Coast and Zimbabwe (in one tournament appearance).

WINNING MARGINS BREAKDOWN

Margin (points)	No. of matches
1–10	82
11–20	57
21–30	51
31–40	29
41–50	23
51 plus	36

RECORDS TUMBLE AS THE ALL BLACKS RUN RIOT

With their progression to the quarter-finals all but assured following comfortable opening wins over Ireland (43–19) and Wales (34–9), New Zealand opted to give their second-string XV a run-out for their final pool match of the 1995 Rugby World Cup against Japan in Bloemfontein. It was one-way traffic: the All Blacks won the match 145–17 (the most points ever scored by a team in a Rugby World Cup match), notching up 21 tries – six of them were scored by Marc Ellis, an all-time Rugby World Cup record for a player in one match.

MOST TRIES: TOP TEN

Pos	Tries	Player (Country, Span)
1	15	Jonah Lomu (New Zealand, 1995–99)
2	13	Doug Howlett (New Zealand, 2003–07)
3	11	Vincent Clerc (France, 2007–11)
=	11	Chris Latham (Australia, 1999–2007)
=	11	Joe Rokocoko (New Zealand, 2003–07)
=	11	Rory Underwood (England, 1987–95)
7	10	David Campese (Australia, 1987–95)
=	10	Bryan Habana (South Africa, 2007–11)
=	10	Brian Lima (Samoa, 1991–2007)
=	10	Drew Mitchell (Australia, 2007–11)
=	10	Shane Williams (Wales, 2003–11)

THE YOUNGEST TRY-SCORER

Japan's Terunori Masuho is the youngest try-scorer in the Rugby World Cup. The winger was aged 19 years and 107 days when he scored twice against Zimbabwe at Belfast on 14 October 1991.

BELOW: Terunori Masuho is the youngest ever try-scorer in Rugby World Cup history – he was 19 years and 107 days old when he scored against Zimbabwe in 1991.

THE MOST DESTRUCTIVE PLAYER IN RUGBY HISTORY

Jonah Lomu made his international debut for New Zealand against France in Christchurch on 26 June 1994 (becoming the youngest-ever All Black), but it wasn't until the following year's Rugby World Cup in South Africa in 1995 that the world got its first glimpse of the most destructive player ever to appear on a rugby pitch. The 6ft 5in (1.96m) winger may have scored two tries against Ireland in the All Blacks' opening match and once against Scotland in the quarter-finals, but it was his single-handed, bulldozing, four-try destruction of England in the semi-finals – a performance that left defeated England captain Will Carling labelling him a 'freak' – that made an indelible impression on the game of rugby and led to Lomu becoming the sport's first true icon. That South Africa managed to find a way of shackling him in the final was the principal reason they won the competition. Ironically, that was the best the world would see of Lomu. Health problems struck in 1996; he missed all of 1997, and struggled back to form and near total fitness for the 1999 Rugby World Cup. Once again he provided the All Blacks with a formidable attacking option, scoring seven tries in the tournament, including two in the semi-final defeat to France. His tally of 15 tries in Rugby World Cup matches is an all-time tournament record.

ABOVE: Marc Ellis scored a Rugby World Cup record six of New Zealand's 21 tries against Japan at Bloemfontein in 1995.

LEFT: Jonah Lomu was at his destructive best against England in New Zealand's 45–29 semi-final victory at Cape Town in 1995.

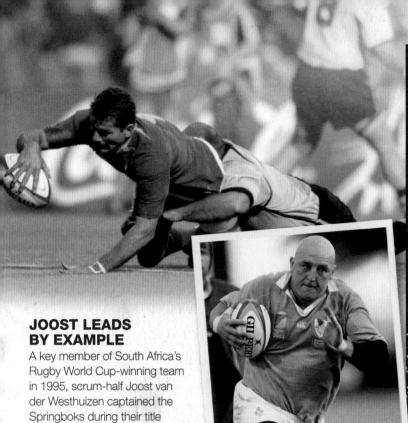

ALL-TIME LEADING TRY-SCORERS: BY POSITION

Position	Player (Country, Span)	Tries
Full-back	Chris Latham (Aus, 1999–2007)	11
Winger	Jonah Lomu (NZ, 1995–99)	15
Centre	Jaque Fourie (SA, 2003–11)	9
Fly-half	Michael Lynagh (Aus, 1987–95)	4
	Carlos Spencer (NZ, 2003)	4
Scrum-half	Joost van der Westhuizen (SA, 1995–2003)	6
No.8	Pablo Bouza (Arg, 2003)	4
	Adriaan Richter (SA, 1995)	4
	Brian Robinson (Ire, 1991)	4
	Laurent Rodriguez (Fr, 1987)	4
Flanker	John Jeffrey (Sco, 1987–91)	6
Lock	Lionel Nallet (Fr, 2007–11)	4
Prop	Nigel Popplewell (Ire, 1991–95)	3
	Rod Snow (Can, 1995–2007)	3
Hooker	Keith Wood (Ire, 1995–2003)	5

JOOST LEADS BY EXAMPLE

A key member of South Africa's Rugby World Cup-winning team in 1995, scrum-half Joost van der Westhuizen captained the Springboks during their title defence in 1999 (scoring three tries in five matches) and once during the 2003 tournament (against Uruguay – a match in which he scored three tries). His total of six tries is an all-time record for a captain in Rugby World Cup matches.

TOP: South Africa's captain and scrum-half Joost van der Westhuizen scores against Uruguay in 2003

ABOVE: No hooker has scored more tries the Rugby World Cup than Ireland's Keith Wood (with five).

LEONARD DRAWS A RECORD-BREAKING TRY-SCORING BLANK

A veteran of four Rugby World Cups (1991–2003) and one of 18 players to appear in two finals (in 1991 and when he collected a winners' medal in 2003), England prop Jason Leonard holds the tournament record for having made the most appearances (22) without scoring a try.

MOST TRIES IN A SINGLE TOURNAMENT

The record for the most tries in a single tournament is eight, achieved by two players: New Zealand's Jonah Lomu (in five matches in 1995) and South Africa's Bryan Habana (in seven matches in 2007).

MOST TRIES BY A PLAYER IN A MATCH IN A LOSING CAUSE

The most tries by a player in a single match for a team that has gone on to lose is two, a feat achieved by 20 players.

OLDEST TRY-SCORER

Uruguay's Diego Ormaechea holds the distinction of being the oldest try-scorer in Rugby World Cup history. The veteran No.8 was 40 years 13 days old when he touched down against Spain at Galashiels on 2 October 1999.

BELOW: Bryan Habana's eight tries in the 2007 Rugby World Cup did much to guide South Africa to victory in the tournment.

RUGBY WORLD CUP TRY-SCORING FIRSTS

One of the stranger footnotes to New Zealand's 70–6 victory over Italy in the first-ever Rugby World Cup match, at Eden Park, Auckland, on 22 May 1987, was that the first-ever try in the tournament's history was a penalty try. Flanker Michael Jones added New Zealand's second try, and so holds the distinction of being the first individual try-scorer in Rugby World Cup history. Jones was also the first-ever try-scorer in a Rugby World Cup final, registering the first of the All Blacks' three tries (David Kirk and John Kirwan added the others) during the co-hosts' 29–9 victory over France.

LEADING TRY-SCORERS: BY TOURNAMENT

Year	Player (Country)	Tries
1987	Craig Green (New Zealand)	6
	John Kirwan (New Zealand)	
1991	David Campese (Australia)	6
	Jean-Baptiste Lafond (France)	
1995	Marc Ellis (New Zealand)	7
	Jonah Lomu (New Zealand)	
1999	Jonah Lomu (New Zealand)	8
2003	Doug Howlett (New Zealand)	7
	Mils Muliaina (New Zealand)	
2007	Bryan Habana (South Africa)	8
2011	Chris Ashton (England)	6
	Vincent Clerc (France)	

POINTS-SCORING RECORDS

FANTASTIC MR FOX SPOT ON FOR NEW ZEALAND

Grant Fox may not have been the greatest of fly-halves when he had the ball in his hands, but he was a true master of the art of goal-kicking and few could question the major contribution he made to New Zealand's Rugby World Cup-winning cause in 1987. The New Plymouth-born No.10 nailed a tournament record 30 conversions and scored 126 points (42.3 per cent of the All Blacks' overall points total) during the tournament – another record.

ABOVE: Grant Fox made an enormous contribution to New Zealand's Rugby World Cup triumph in 1987.

BELOW: Argentina's Gonzalo Quesada holds the record for the most penalties kicked at a single Rugby World Cup, with 31 in 1999.

MOST POINTS: TOP TEN

Pos	Points	Player (Country, Span)
1	277	Jonny Wilkinson (England, 1999–2011)
2	227	Gavin Hastings (Scotland, 1987–95)
3	195	Michael Lynagh (Australia, 1987–95)
4	170	Grant Fox (New Zealand, 1987–91)
5	163	Andrew Mehrtens (New Zealand, 1995–99)
6	140	Chris Paterson (Scotland, 1999–2011)
7	135	Gonzalo Quesada (Argentina, 1999–2003)
8	125	Matt Burke (Australia, 1995–2003)
=	125	Nicky Little (Fiji, 1999–2011)
=	125	Felipe Contepomi (Argentina, 1999–2011)

CULHANE SHINES IN RARE STARTING ROLE

As New Zealand ran in try after try (21 of them) during their record-breaking 145–17 rout of Japan at Bloemfontein during the 1995 Rugby World Cup, debutant Simon Culhane, the All Blacks' understudy fly-half (who would only win a total of six caps for his country), had a day to remember as he kicked his way into the record books: as well as scoring a try, he slotted 20 conversions (out of 21) and contributed 45 points to his team's cause – both are all-time Rugby World Cup records for a player in a single match.

MOST POINTS BY A REPLACEMENT

Veteran fly-half Nicky Little, his country's most capped player, embarked on a 70-minute journey that would end up with him earning an obscure place in the record books when he replaced Waisale Serevi in the tenth minute of Fiji's 2003 Rugby World Cup Pool B match against Japan at Townsville. He ended up scoring 13 points (three penalties and two conversions) during Fiji's 41–13 win – not a substantial amount, but, remarkably, the most points ever scored by a replacement in a Rugby World Cup match.

SPEEDY GONZALO HAS THE LAST LAUGH

The often-cutting English press may have dubbed him 'Speedy Gonzalo' because of it, but Gonzalo Quesada's meticulous at best – spectacularly slow at worst – preparation before attempting a kick at goal paid dividends during the 1999 Rugby World Cup. The Argentina fly-half nailed a record 31 penalties during the course of the tournament.

MOST POINTS: BY POSITION

Position	Player (Span)	Points
Full-back	Gavin Hastings (Sco, 1987–95)	227
Winger	Chris Paterson (Sco, 2003–07)	83
Centre	Thierry Lacroix (Fra, 1991–95)	112
Fly-half	Jonny Wilkinson (Eng, 1999–2011)	277
Scrum-half	Dimitri Yachvili (Fra, 2003–11)	50
No.8	Pablo Bouza (Arg, 2003)	20
	Ariaan Richter (SA, 1995)	20
Flanker	Neil Back (Eng, 1995–2003)	25
Lock	Lionel Nallet (Fra, 2007–11)	20
Prop	Rod Snow (Can, 1995–2007)	15
Hooker	Keith Wood (Ire, 1995–2003)	25

HASTINGS MAKES HIS MARK

Gavin Hastings will always be remembered for, and almost certainly haunted by, his glaring, in-front-of-the-posts miss in the final moments of Scotland's 1991 Rugby World Cup semi-final match against England (a brutal encounter the Auld Enemy went on to win 9–6), but, that lapse apart, the full-back proved a reliably consistent goal-kicker over the years. In 13 Rugby World Cup matches between 1987 and 1995 – in which he scored 227 points – he slotted a tournament all-time record 39 conversions. He is also one of four players to have kicked eight penalties in a Rugby World Cup match – a feat he achieved against Tonga at Pretoria on 30 May 1995. The others to have equalled Hastings' feat are: Thierry Lacroix (France) against Ireland at Durban on 10 June 1995; Gonzalo Quesada (Argentina) against Samoa at Llanelli on 10 October 1999; and Matt Burke (Australia) against South Africa at Twickenham on 30 October 1999.

BELOW: Gavin Hastings enjoyed spectacular highs and lows in a Scotland shirt in Rugby World Cup matches.

DE BEER STRIKES DROP-GOAL GOLD

Jannie de Beer produced a performance that neither his country nor opponents England would forget during South Africa's 44–21 1999 Rugby World Cup quarter-final at the Stade de France, Paris. The occasional fly-half became a national hero when he kicked a remarkable – and tournament record – five drop goals during the match.

ABOVE: South Africa's Jannie de Beer was in inspired form against England in the 1999 Rugby World Cup quarter-final, dropping five goals.

BELOW: England's Jonny Wilkinson has enjoyed some magical moments at the Rugby World Cup and he has set all-time numerous records.

HUMPHREYS GOES DOWN FIGHTING

Thankfully used only once, the 1999 Rugby World Cup's ill-conceived and much criticized format saw Ireland (the runners-up in Pool 5) having to appear in a play-off match for one of the three remaining quarter-final places against Argentina (the third-placed team in Pool 4). And although the match at Lansdowne Road proved a calamity for the men in green – they lost 28–24 to crash out of the tournament – no one could have pointed the finger of blame in the direction of David Humphreys. The Ulster fly-half scored all 24 of Ireland's points – seven penalties and a drop goal – the most by any player to end up on the losing side in Rugby World Cup history.

ENGLAND'S NO.10 KICKS HIS WAY INTO THE RECORD BOOKS

Jonny Wilkinson was only 20 years 130 days old when he made his Rugby World Cup debut in England's opening pool match against Italy at the 1999 tournament and scored a try, 11 conversions and a penalty (a haul of 32 points) during their comfortable 67–7 victory. He was dropped following England's 30–16 defeat to New Zealand in their next match and sat out the remainder of the pool matches, but returned for their quarter-final play-off victory over Fiji, scoring 23 points. He was controversially left out of England's starting XV for their quarter-final defeat against South Africa, and many cite his absence as a big factor in England's loss. By 2003, however, and now established as the best fly-half in world rugby, no one would have dreamt of leaving Wilkinson out of a starting line-up. He contributed 113 points in five matches during the tournament – including a last-gasp, match-winning drop goal in the final – to help England to the world crown. He returned from an injury nightmare in time for the 2007 Rugby World Cup and his 67 points in five matches did much to help England reach a second successive final (in the process he became the only player in history to have scored in two finals). The mercurial fly-half also played at the 2011 tournament and holds the all-time Rugby World Cup records for: the most points (277), the most penalties (58), the most drop goals in a tournament (8 in 2003) and the most drop goals overall (14).

LEADING POINTS-SCORERS: BY TOURNAMENT

Year	Player (Country)	Points
1987	Grant Fox (New Zealand)	126
1991	Ralph Keyes (Ireland)	68
1995	Thierry Lacroix (France)	112
1999	Gonzalo Quesada (Argentina)	102
2003	Jonny Wilkinson (England)	113
2007	Percy Montgomery (South Africa)	105
2011	Morne Steyn (South Africa)	62

APPEARANCE RECORDS

THE RUGBY WORLD CUP'S OLDEST PLAYER

Having battled for Uruguay's cause for a decade and one day, Diego Ormaechea chose to bow out of international rugby after his country's greatest hour – their first appearance at the Rugby World Cup, for which Ormaechea was captain. He did so not only with his status as his country's greatest-ever rugby player assured, but also as a record-breaker: when he made his final appearance, against South Africa in Uruguay's last Pool A match in 1999, he was 40 years 26 days old – the oldest player ever to appear in the tournament.

PALAMO IS THE RUGBY WORLD CUP'S YOUNGEST PLAYER

A junior international for Samoa, powerful winger Thretton Palamo chose to play for the country of his birth, the United States, and made history when he came off the bench to make his international debut for the Eagles during their Pool A match against South Africa at Montpellier during the 2007 Rugby World Cup. Aged just 19 years 8 days, he became the youngest player in Rugby World Cup history.

LOMU BREAKS RECORD IN DEFEAT

Having made such an enormous impact on both the tournament, and the game of rugby itself, during the 1995 Rugby World Cup, Jonah Lomu would have wanted to end the tournament with a winners' medal around his neck, which was no less than his barnstorming performances deserved. It wasn't to be: South Africa found a way to shackle his explosive power and the match ended in defeat for the All Blacks. At 20 years 43 days, however, Lomu remains the youngest-ever player to have appeared in a Rugby World Cup final.

HISTORY-MAKING WORLD CUP FINAL

There were plenty of records at stake when England faced off against South Africa in the 2007 Rugby World Cup final: England were looking to become the first team in history to make a successful defence of their title; their veteran back Mike Catt (at 36 years 33 days) was seeking to usurp Jason Leonard (35 years 100 days) as the oldest-ever Rugby World Cup winner; and the Springboks' young tyro Francois Steyn (at 20 years 159 days) was attempting to become the youngest Rugby World Cup winner in history. As it was, Steyn and South Africa took the spoils following a hard-fought 15–6 victory, although Catt did have the consolation, scant though it may have been, of becoming the oldest player ever to appear in a Rugby World Cup final.

ABOVE: South Africa's 15–6 victory over England in the 2007 final at the Stade de France in Paris saw Francois Steyn become the youngest-ever winner of the Rugby World Cup.

BELOW: When he faced South Africa aged 40 years and 26 days old in 1999, Uruguay's Diego Ormaechea became the oldest player to appear in the Rugby World Cup match

MOST APPEARANCES: TOP TEN

Pos	Apps	Player (Country, span)
1	22	Jason Leonard (England, 1991–2003)
2	20	George Gregan (Australia, 1995–2007)
3	19	Mike Catt (England, 1995–2007)
=	19	Jonny Wilkinson (England, 1999–2011)
5	18	Raphael Ibanez (France, 1999–2007)
=	18	Martin Johnson (England, 1995–2003)
=	18	Mario Ledesma Arocena (Argentina, 1999–2011)
=	18	Brian Lima (Samoa, 1991–2007)
=	18	Lewis Moody (England, 2003–11)
10	17	Felipe Contepomi (Argentina, 1999–2011)
=	17	Lawrence Dallaglio (England, 1999–2007)
=	17	Sean Fitzpatrick (New Zealand, 1987–95)
=	17	Brian O'Driscoll (Ireland, 1999–2011)
=	17	Jean-Baptiste Poux (France, 2003–11)
=	17	Aurelien Rougerie (France, 2003–11)
=	17	John Smit (South Africa, 2003–11)

LEONARD IN FOR THE LONG HAUL

Just 17 days short of his 22nd birthday when he packed down at prop for England for the first time in an international match, against Argentina in Buenos Aires on 28 July 1990, Jason Leonard appeared in his first Rugby World Cup match just over a year later, during England's 18–12 opening-game defeat to New Zealand. He remained the cornerstone of the impressive pack that inspired their rally to the final, which they lost 12–6 to Australia after inexplicably abandoning their forward-oriented approach. Leonard recovered from a serious neck injury to earn selection for England's squad at the 1995 Rugby World Cup and played in four matches as they reached the semi-finals. He was first choice in 1999 (making five appearances) and, three months after his 35th birthday and by now the most capped player in the game's history, appeared in all seven of England's games at the 2003 Rugby World Cup, ending his fourth tournament with a winners' medal around his neck. He has appeared in more Rugby World Cup matches than any other player (22) and holds the record, shared with Australian scrum-half George Gregan, for having made the most Rugby World Cup appearances on a winning side (16).

MOST RUGBY WORLD CUP FINAL APPEARANCES

Eighteen players have appeared in two Rugby World Cup finals, but only six of them have ended up on the winning side on both occasions: Dan Crowley, John Eales, Tim Horan, Phil Kearns and Jason Little (for Australia in 1991 and 1999) and Os du Randt (for South Africa in 1995 and 2007).

MOST APPEARANCES AS A REPLACEMENT

No player has made more Rugby World Cup replacement appearances than Australia's Jeremy Paul. Of his 11 appearances in the tournament between 1999 and 2003, ten of them came off the replacements' bench, including both the 1999 and 2003 finals.

ONE MATCH ONLY

Of the 2,440 players to have played in a Rugby World Cup match, 389 of them appeared in one match only – a surprising 15.94 per cent.

BELOW: A winner in 2003, England's Jason Leonard has appeared in more Rugby World Cup matches (22) than any other player.

NO RUGBY WORLD CUP LOVE FOR ROMEO

A regular presence at centre for Romania in four Rugby World Cups (1995, 1999, 2003 and 2007), Romeo Gontineac holds the record for having appeared on the losing side in the tournament on more occasions than other player in history (11). It has not all been bad news for Gontineac, however: he tasted victory on three occasions – against the United States in 1999 (27–25), against Namibia in 2003 (37–7) and against Portugal in 2007 (14–10).

ABOVE: Centre Romeo Gontineac experienced defeat in 11 of his 14 Rugby World Cup matches for Romania – an all-time tournament record.

ABOVE: England centre Will Carling (with ball) is one of four captains to have led their team in 11 Rugby World Cup matches.

MOST APPEARANCES AS CAPTAIN

The record for most Rugby World Cup appearances as captain is 11, achieved by four players: Will Carling (for England, in 1991 and 1995), Raphael Ibanez (for France, 1999–2007), Martin Johnson (for England, in 1999 and 2003) and John Smit (ror South Africa 2003–11).

DISCIPLINE AND REFEREES

MOST ILL-DISCIPLINED TEAM

As is the custom with teams from that part of the world, Tonga engage in a war dance before the start of a match. Their dance – known as the 'kailao' – calls for players 'to maul and loose forwards shall I know and crunch any fierce hearts I know'. The players, it appears, take the words literally: the Sea Eagles are the most ill-disciplined team in Rugby World Cup history, having received three red cards and seven yellow cards in 17 matches in the tournament between 1987 and 2007.

RED CARDS: BY COUNTRY

3 Canada, Tonga
2 Samoa South Africa, Wales
1 Argentina, Australia, Fiji, Namibia

THE FIRST MAN TO REFEREE A RUGBY WORLD CUP MATCH

Australia's Bob Fordham has the distinction of refereeing the first-ever Rugby World Cup match. He was in charge when New Zealand played Italy at Eden Park, Auckland, on 22 May 1987. The All Blacks won 70–6.

CONTEPOMI THE FIRST TO SEE RUGBY WORLD CUP YELLOW

Sixty-five yellow cards have been issued in Rugby World Cup matches since they were introduced in 2003. The first of them was shown to Argentina's Manuel Contepomi (for an illegal tackle on the Wallabies' Mat Rogers) in the Pumas' match against Australia at Sydney on 10 October 2003.

MOST YELLOW CARDS

The record for the most yellow cards received by a player in Rugby World Cup matches is three, a fate suffered Italy's Fabio Ongaro. The hooker was sent to the sin-bin twice during the 2007 tournament and once more in 2011.

RICHARDS GETS THE RUGBY WORLD CUP'S FIRST RED CARD

Wales's Huw Richards infamously became the first player to be given his marching orders in a Rugby World Cup match as a result of throwing a punch at New Zealand's Guy Whetton in the 1987 semi-final. In the subsequent melee, the All Blacks' Buck Shelford flattened Richards, but only the Welshman, after he had recovered his senses, was shown the red card. There have been a further 15 instances of a player being shown a red card in the Rugby World Cup.

LEFT: Wales's Huw Richards holds the unfortunate distinction of being the first player in the Rugby World Cup to be sent off.

BELOW: Scotsman Jim Fleming is the Rugby World Cup's most experienced referee, having taken charge of 11 matches between 1987 and 1999.

LEFT: Argentina's Manuel Contepomi made history against Australia in 2003 when he became the first player in the Rugby World Cup to receive a yellow card.

RUGBY WORLD CUP FINAL REFEREES

Year	Name (country)
1987	Kerry Fitzgerald (Australia)
1991	Derek Bevan (Wales)
1995	Ed Morrison (England)
1999	Andre Watson (South Africa)
2003	Andre Watson (South Africa)
2007	Alain Rolland (Ireland)
2011	Craig Joubert (South Africa)

MOST MATCHES AS REFEREE

Jim Fleming has refereed more matches than any other official in Rugby World Cup history. The Scot took charge of 11 matches in four tournaments (1987, 1991, 1995 and 1999).

MOST YELLOW CARDS FOR A TEAM THAT HAS GONE ON TO WIN THE MATCH

The most yellow cards received by a team that has gone on to win a Rugby World Cup match is two, and it has happened five times: to Wales (Colin Charvis and Sonny Parker), during their 41–10 victory over Canada at Melbourne on 12 October 2003; Australia (Drew Mitchell and Nathan Sharpe), during their 32–20 triumph against Wales at Cardiff on 15 September 2007; South Africa (Bryan Habana and Francois Steyn), in their 30–25 win against Tonga at Lens on 22 September 2007; Argentina (Rimas Alvarez Kairelis and Juan Manuel Leguizamon), during their 34–10 third-place play-off win over France at the Parc des Princes, Paris, on 19 October 2007; and Tonga (Halani Aulika and Lua Lokotui) in their 31–18 defeat of Japan at Whangarai on 21 September 2011.

ONLY MAN TO REFEREE TWO RUGBY WORLD CUP FINALS

An engineer by trade who left his profession to become a full-time referee, South Africa's Andre Watson went on to become the most capped referee of all time (taking charge of 27 internationals) and is the only man in history to have officiated at two Rugby World Cup finals: in 1999 (Australia against France at Cardiff) and in 2003 (England against Australia in Sydney).

THE FAMOUS WHISTLE

The opening game of every Rugby World Cup has been started by a shrill blast from the same whistle. The chosen whistle is more than a century old and was used for the first time by referee Gil Evans in the international between New Zealand and England at Dunedin in December 1905 (the All Blacks won 15–0). A true piece of rugby history, the whistle was also used, it is believed, during the 1924 Olympic final (when the USA beat hosts France 17–13) and in January 1925 for England's match against New Zealand at Twickenham (during which England's Cyril Brownlie became the first person in international rugby history to be sent off).

BELOW: South Africa's Andre Watson is the only official in history to referee two Rugby World Cup finals – in 1999 and 2003.

RIGHT: The fiery match between South Africa and Canada at Port Elizabeth in 1995 culminated in three players being sent off.

MOST YELLOW CARDS IN A MATCH

The record for the most yellow cards in a match is three, a total that has been reached on four occasions: Tonga against Italy at Canberra on 15 October 2003 (Ipolito Fenukitau and Milton Ngauamo for Tonga, and Fabio Ongaro for Italy); United States against England at Lens on 8 September 2007 (Paul Emerick and Vaha Esikia for the United States and Lawrence Dallaglio for England); South Africa against Tonga at Lens on 22 September 2007 (Bryan Habana and Francois Steyn for South Africa, and Sefa Vaka for Tonga); and Argentina against France at Parc des Princes, Paris, on 19 October 2007 (Rimas Alvarez Kairelis and Juan Manuel Leguizamon for Argentina, and Raphael Ibanez for France).

THE BATTLE OF BOET ERASMUS

It was the most inglorious moment of South Africa's fairytale march to glory at the 1995 Rugby World Cup. An ill-disciplined, often brutal, Pool A match between the Springboks and Canada at the Boet Erasmus Stadium in Port Elizabeth degenerated into a mass brawl ten minutes from time. When the dust settled, Canada's Gareth Rees and Rod Snow and South Africa's John Dalton were given their marching orders. It is the only time in history that three players have been shown a red card in a single Rugby World Cup match. For the record, South Africa went on to win 20–0.

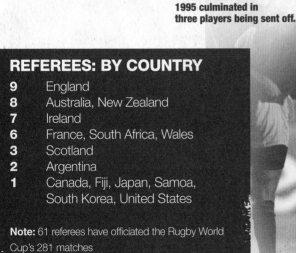

ALL BLACK BLOOD IN HIS VEINS

One of the best No.8s the All Blacks have ever produced and one of his country's finest captains, Brian Lochore won 20 caps for New Zealand between 1964 and 1971. He switched to coaching at the end of his playing career and achieved considerable success at club level before being appointed a national selector in 1983 and then coach of the national team in 1985. In 1987, he achieved the finest moment of his career, leading the All Blacks – known as the 'Baby Blacks' at the time – to Rugby World Cup glory. He will be remembered as the first coach in the tournament's history to lay his hands on the game's greatest prize.

ABOVE: Alex Wyllie was coach of the New Zealand in 1991 and led Argentina to the Rugby World Cup quarter-finals eight years later.

FIRST TO COACH TWO TEAMS AT A RUGBY WORLD CUP

A Canterbury legend (he made 210 appearances for the province over 15 years between 1964 and 1979, then became their coach in 1982 and achieved instant success), Alex Wyllie was assistant coach to Brian Lochore as New Zealand won the Rugby World Cup in 1987. He succeeded Lochore as coach of the national team in 1988 and enjoyed enormous success, losing only two games in 23 – both defeats to Australia. With a Rugby World Cup looming, back-to-back defeats to the Wallabies made the New Zealand Rugby Union nervous and they appointed Wyllie's Auckland rival, John Hart, as joint coach for the 1991 tournament. It was an uncomfortable pairing: the All Blacks lost to Australia in the semi-finals and Laurie Mains took over the coaching reins. That was not the last the competition saw of Wyllie, however. In 1999 he became the first person in history to coach two sides at a Rugby World Cup, leading the Pumas to the quarter-finals. Others to have achieved the feat are: Pierre Berbizier (France and Italy), Graham Henry (Wales and New Zealand) and John Kirwan (Italy and Japan).

ABOVE: A great All Black as a player, Brian Lochore added to his legacy as New Zealand's victorious coach in the inaugural Rugby World Cup in 1987.

CAPTAIN FANTASTIC AS WELL AS A FIERY COACH

Daniel Dubroca, a hard-nosed hooker, was appointed France captain for the 1986 Five Nations, led Les Bleus to the final of the 1987 Rugby World Cup and retired as a player the following year. But his nous and passion for the game were not lost to French rugby and in 1990, following the resignation of Jacques Fouroux, he was appointed coach of the national team, leading them at the 1991 Rugby World Cup (and becoming the first person in history to have played in one Rugby World Cup and then coached a team in the next). His final act in a Rugby World Cup match will linger long in the memory: having seen his side crash out to England (19–10) in a brutal clash in Paris in the quarter-finals, he manhandled referee David Bishop in the tunnel shortly after the final whistle and resigned soon afterwards.

RIGHT: Rod Macqueen was coach of Australia during a golden run that started with victory at the 1999 Rugby World Cup.

MACQUEEN LEADS WALLABIES ON GOLDEN RUN

Rod Macqueen was appointed coach of Australia's national team in September 1997 and, although he did not get off to the most blistering of starts (the Wallabies lost 18–16 to Argentina in Buenos Aires in his second match in charge), he would ultimately lead them on one of the greatest runs in their history. It all started at the 1999 Rugby World Cup when he led Australia to their second tournament triumph (thus becoming the first nation to win the cup twice); in 2000 they won the Tri-Nations for the first time in their history; and in 2001 they secured a memorable 2–1 series win over the British Lions.

WHITE NURSES WOUNDED SPRINGBOKS BACK TO HEALTH

A former schoolteacher who made a name for himself when he coached South Africa U21 to Rugby World Cup glory in 2002, Jake White was appointed coach of the senior Springbok side in early 2004, at a time when South African rugby was in turmoil: they had endured a disappointing 2003 Rugby World Cup campaign, had slipped to sixth in the world rankings and were having to fend off damaging revelations about their controversial preparations for the tournament. Renowned throughout the game for his technical acumen, White set about revitalizing the Springboks: he led them to Tri-Nations glory in 2004, and by 2007 had assembled a squad capable of challenging for that year's Rugby World Cup. They were the best team in the tournament and beat England 15–6 in the final to regain the world title and claim the no.1 spot in the rankings for the first time. His job done, White duly stepped down.

PLAYER WITH ONE TEAM AND THEN COACH OF TWO DIFFERENT TEAMS

Two men have appeared in the Rugby World Cup as players and then gone on to coach two different teams in the tournament: John Kirwan, who played for New Zealand at the 1987 and 1991 Rugby World Cups and then coached Italy (in 2003) and Japan (in 2007); and Pierre Berbizier, who played for France at the 1987 tournament and then went on to coach France (in 1995) and Italy (in 2007).

RUGBY WORLD CUP-WINNING COACHES	
Year	Coach (country)
1987	Brian Lochore (New Zealand)
1991	Bob Dwyer (Australia)
1995	Kitch Christie (South Africa)
1999	Rod Macqueen (Australia)
2003	Clive Woodward (England)
2007	Jake White (South Africa))
2011	Graham Henry (New Zealand)

COACHING THE DEFENDING CHAMPIONS

The best result achieved by a coach leading the defending champions into a Rugby World Cup is to finish as runners-up: Eddie Jones (with Australia in 2003) and Brian Ashton (with England in 2007). The worst performance is to reach the quarter-finals: first by Bob Dwyer (with Australia in 1995) and then by Peter de Villiers (with South Africa in 2011).

MOST TOURNAMENTS AS COACH

Two coaches hold the record for overseeing the most Rugby World Cup matches as coach: Jim Telfer (for Scotland in 1991, 1995 and 1999); and Bryan Williams (for Samoa, also in 1991, 1995 and 1999).

HENRY ENDS NEW ZEALAND'S RUGBY WORLD CUP HOODOO

New Zealand enjoyed success after appointing Graham Henry as coach in 2004, winning five Tri-Nations titles and spending years at the top of the IRB world rankings, but one entry was missing from the Auckland coach's CV: a Rugby World Cup triumph. When the All Blacks lost sensationally to France in a 2007 quarter-final, the 2011 tournament represented Henry's final chance to secure a permanent place in his country's rugby history. His players responded magnificently, winning all four pool matches, before beating Argentina in the quarter-finals (33–10), Australia in the semi-finals (20–6) and France in the final (8–7) to bring the impatient wait for rugby's most passionate nation to an end.

RUGBY WORLD CUP COACHES: BY NATIONALITY	
21	New Zealand
10	France
9	England
8	Argentina, Australia
7	South Africa
4	Ireland, Japan
3	Romania, Scotland, United States, Wales
2	Canada, Fiji, Namibia, Tonga, Uruguay
1	Georgia, Italy, Ivory Coast, Portugal, Russia, Samoa, Spain

RUGBY WORLD CUP
STADIUMS, HOSTS AND ATTENDANCES

JOINT EFFORT RESULTS IN FIRST RUGBY WORLD CUP

The idea of staging a World Cup-style tournament for rugby had first been mooted in the 1950s, but was rejected on the grounds that it would threaten the amateur spirit of the game, and so lay dormant for the next three decades. By the 1980s, however, things were about to change: in the early years of the decade two companies approached the IRB with proposals for a World Cup – both were rejected.

In 1983, Gideon Lloyd International and London-based sports promoter Neil Durden-Smith put forward another proposal – again it was rejected. Later that year, the rugby unions of Australia and New Zealand lodged separate bids to stage the tournament – both were rejected, but this time with a caveat: the IRB suggested the two countries pool their resources and come up with a tournament feasibility study. In March 1985, in a hotel in Paris, the results of that study were put to the IRB vote: the outcome was that, in 1987, Australia and New Zealand would co-host rugby's first World Cup.

HIGHEST ATTENDANCES (MATCH): TOP FIVE

Pos	Attendance	Match	Venue	Date
1	82,957	Australia v England	Telstra Stadium, Sydney	22 Nov 2003
2	82,444	Australia v New Zealand	Telstra Stadium, Sydney	15 Nov 2003
3	82,346	England v France	Telstra Stadium, Sydney	16 Nov 2003
4	80,430	England v South Africa	Stade de France, Paris	20 Oct 2007
5	80,283	France v England	Stade de France, Paris	13 Oct 2007

A RUGBY WORLD CUP OF FIRSTS AND LASTS

The 1995 Rugby World Cup in South Africa (which would mark the country's debut appearance in the tournament) was a ground-breaking one: it was the first major sporting event ever to take place on African soil; it was the first time the tournament was staged within the boundaries of one country; and was the last Rugby World Cup of the game's amateur era.

FUTURE HOSTS

On 28 July 2009, the IRB announced that England had beaten off bids from Italy, Japan and South Africa for the right to host the Rugby World Cup in 2015. At the same time, the IRB declared that Japan, who many had expected to be given the tournament in 2011 (rather than New Zealand), would host the 2019 tournament. It will mark the first time that rugby's biggest tournament will have been staged in Asia.

LOWEST-EVER CROWD FOR A RUGBY WORLD CUP FINAL

The least attended Rugby World Cup in history – just 448,318 spectators attended the 32 matches of the 1987 tournament – culminated in the lowest-ever attendance for a Rugby World Cup final: 48,035 spectators gathered at Eden Park, Auckland, on 20 June 1987 to watch New Zealand beat France 29–9 and become the competition's inaugural winners.

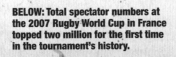

BELOW: Total spectator numbers at the 2007 Rugby World Cup in France topped two million for the first time in the tournament's history.

RUGBY WORLD CUP HOST NATIONS

1987	Australia, New Zealand
1991	England, France, Ireland, Scotland, Wales
1995	South Africa
1999	Wales, England, France, Ireland, Scotland
2003	Australia
2007	France
2011	New Zealand

RUGBY WORLD CUP: AVERAGE ATTENDANCES

Year	Match average	Spectators total	Matches total
1987	14,010	448,318	32
1991	33,127	1,060,065	32
1995	29,281	936,990	32
1999	37,965	1,556,572	41
2003	38,263	1,836,607	48
2007	46,786	2,245,731	48
2011	30,711	1,474,126	48

BELOW: The 2003 Rugby World Cup final between Australia and England at the Telstra Stadium in Sydney on 22 November 2003 was the most watched match in the tournament's history.

BELOW: Huge crowds turned up at River Plate's stadium in Buenos Aires to watch Argentina's unexpected progress to the semi-finals of the 2007 Rugby World Cup.

INCREASING APPEAL

It didn't take long for the Rugby World Cup to find both its public appeal and its commercial bite: by 1991, the number of spectators reached over one million for the first time (the figure would rise to two million-plus in 2007); by 1999, the tournament had grossed over £70 million; and by 2007, the same year it attracted a worldwide television audience of over four billion, it made an operating profit of £122.4 million.

CROWDS FLOCK TO WATCH THE RUGBY WORLD CUP SHOW

If any proof were needed to show just how far the Rugby World Cup has grown in stature, look no further than Australia. In 1987, as co-hosts of the inaugural tournament, the country hosted nine matches at two stadiums – the Concord Oval in Sydney (with a capacity of 20,000) and Ballymore Stadium in Brisbane (24,000 capacity) – with an average attendance of just 9,501 spectators per match. Sixteen years later, this time as sole tournament hosts, the country staged 48 matches in 11 state-of-the-art stadiums and attracted an average crowd of 38,263 (a dramatic 402.7 percent increase from 1987) – including the highest-ever attendance for a Rugby World Cup final, when England triumphed 20–17 against Australia at the Telstra Stadium in Sydney on 22 November 2003 in front of 82,957 spectators.

LOWEST ATTENDANCES (MATCH): TOP FIVE

Pos	Attendance	Match	Venue	Date
1	3,000	Tonga v Ireland	Ballymore, Brisbane	3 Jun 1987
=	3,000	USA v Romania	Lansdowne Road, Dublin	9 Oct 1999
=	3,000	Uruguay v South Africa	Hampden Park, Glasgow	15 Oct 1999
4	3,761	Spain v Uruguay	Netherdale, Galashiels	2 Oct 1999
5	4,000	Zimbabwe v France	Eden Park, Auckland	2 June 1987

THE LONG AND THE SHORT OF IT

The longest Rugby World Cup was the 2011 tournament, which covered 44 days (from 9 September to 23 October). The shortest tournament was the first, in 1987. It lasted a mere 29 days (between 22 May and 20 June 1987).

RIGHT: The deserted Hampden Park stands in the background attest to the fact that South Africa's game against Uruguay at the 1999 Rugby World Cup shares the record as the least attended match in the tournament history

A VENUE FOR EVERY STAGE OF THE RUGBY WORLD CUP

Only one stadium in history has hosted a match at every stage of a Rugby World Cup: the Stade de France in Paris (which was built for the FIFA World Cup in 1998) hosted pool matches (in 2007), England's quarter-final against South Africa in 1999, the two semi-finals and the final won by South Africa against England in 2007.

BELOW: Murrayfield in Edinburgh, is the only stadium to have been used at three Rugby World Cups (in 1991, 1999 and 2007).

MOST SEMI-FINAL MATCHES STAGED

Four stadiums hold the record for staging the most Rugby World Cup semi-final matches (two apiece): Twickenham, London (both last-four matches in the 1999 tournament); the Telstra Stadium, Sydney (both semi-final clashes in 2003); the Stade de France, Paris (which hosted both semi-finals in 2007); and Eden Park, Auckland (which hosted both semi-finals in 2011).

ABOVE: The Stade de France in Paris is the only stadium in Rugby World Cup history to have hosted a match at every stage of one tournament.

MOST MATCHES HOSTED (BY STADIUM): TOP TEN

Pos	Matches	Stadium (Years)
1	16	Eden Park, Auckland (1987, 2011)
2	13	Murrayfield, Edinburgh (1991, 1999, 2007)
3	11	Millennium Stadium, Cardiff (1999, 2007)
4	10	Twickenham, London (1991, 1999)
5	9	Lansdowne Road, Dublin (1991, 1999)
=	9	Suncorp Stadium, Brisbane (2003)
7	8	Stade de France, Paris (1999, 2007)
=	8	Westpac Stadium, Wellington (2011)
9	7	Telstra Stadium, Sydney (2003)
=	7	Telstra Dome, Melbourne (2003)

LARGEST STADIUM

Built in 1999 as the centrepiece for the 2000 Olympic Games in Sydney (for which it had a capacity of 110,000), Stadium Australia, then the Telstra Stadium, now the ANZ Stadium, is the largest used (by capacity) in Rugby World Cup history. It could seat a massive 83,500 spectators in 2003.

POPULAR VENUE

A multi-sport stadium in every sense – it is the home of the All Blacks, has hosted a Rugby League World Cup final (in 1988) and has been a Test venue for New Zealand's national cricket team since 1930 – the 61,079-capacity Eden Park in Auckland is a Rugby World Cup record-breaking stadium. It is the only ground in the tournament's history: to have hosted three quarter-finals (France v. Fiji in 1987 and France v. England and New Zealand v. Argentina in 2011), to have been the venue for two Rugby World Cup finals (in 1987 and 2011) and has accommodated more Rugby World Cup matches (16) than any other stadium in history (across the 1987 and 2011 tournaments).

BELOW: No stadium has hosted more Rugby World Cup matches than Auckland's Eden Park, with 16 in two tournaments, 1987 and 2011.

ABOVE: The venue for the 2003 Rugby World Cup final, the Telstra Stadium in Sydney is the largest stadium, by capacity in the tournament's history.

MOST STADIUMS USED

The most stadiums used in a single Rugby World Cup tournament is 19, in 1991; the fewest stadiums used in a single tournament is nine, in 1995, when the tournament was staged inside one country (South Africa) for the first time.

SMALLEST STADIUM

Once the venue for a famous victory by the North of England against the mighty All Blacks (21–9 on 17 November 1979), Otley RUFC's rustic ground, Cross Green, in West Yorkshire, England, is the smallest-ever ground to host a Rugby World Cup match. Not that this deterred the fans because, when Italy played the United States in a pool match there at the 1991 Rugby World Cup – a fixture the Azzurri won 30–9, the match was a complete sell-out.

MULTIPLE RUGBY WORLD CUP FINAL HOST STADIUMS

Two stadiums used in Rugby World Cup matches have hosted World Cup finals in different sports. The Stade de France in Paris, hosted the 1998 FIFA World Cup (France 3 Brazil 0) and 2007 Rugby World Cup (South Africa 15 England 6), and Eden Park, Auckland, which hosted the 1987 and 2011 Rugby World Cup finals and 1988 Rugby League World Cup final (Australia 25 New Zealand 12).

RUGBY WORLD CUP FINAL VENUES

1987	Eden Park, Auckland
1991	Twickenham, London
1995	Ellis Park, Johannesburg
1999	Millennium Stadium, Cardiff
2003	Telstra Stadium, Sydney
2007	Stade de France, Paris
2011	Eden Park, Auckland

MATCHES STAGED BY COUNTY

1	70	New Zealand (1987)
2	58	Australia (1987–2003)
=	58	France (1991–2007)
4	32	South Africa (1995)
5	20	Wales (1991–2007)
6	16	England (1991–99)
7	15	Scotland (1991–2007)
8	12	Ireland (1991–99)

RUGBY WORLD CUP
QUALIFYING TOURNAMENT RECORDS

Regional qualifying tournaments for the Rugby World Cup were staged for the first time for the 1991 tournament and are now not only an integral and much-anticipated part of the sporting calendar for rugby's lower-ranked nations, but also an invaluable means of assisting the game's growth throughout the world. And how it has grown: in 1991, 25 teams battled it out for eight available spots; for the 2011 Rugby World Cup, 86 teams participated in the regional qualifying tournaments.

RIGHT: Will Greenwood in action for England against Italy in a qualifying match for the 1999 Rugby World Cup – the only time England have been forced to qualify.

MOST AVAILABLE QUALIFYING SPOTS

It is the only time in Rugby World Cup history that such a qualifying tournament has been used, but only four teams were granted automatic entry into the 1999 competition, the three top-placed teams from the 1995 event (South Africa, New Zealand and France) and tournament hosts Wales. For the rest, they would have to participate in an elongated – and as it turned out entirely unnecessary – qualification process. As a result, 16 places were up for grabs for the 1999 Rugby World Cup – the most in history.

Thankfully, this particular format was abandoned for the 2003 tournament and has not been used since.

GULF IN CLASS

The vast difference between the game's haves and have-nots is not restricted to the Rugby World Cup finals but it is also evident in the regional qualifying tournaments. There have been 15 instances of teams scoring more than 100 points in a match in Rugby World Cup qualifying matches (but only six in the tournament itself). The biggest victory (155–3 – the joint-highest winning margin in international rugby history) recorded by Japan against Chinese Taipei in Tokyo on 7 July 2002.

SPAIN SET ALL-TIME MARK FOR MOST MATCHES AND MOST VICTORIES

Although they have earned entry into the tournament on only one occasion (in 1999, courtesy of a 21–17 victory over Portugal in the final stages of qualifying at Murrayfield on 2 December 1998), Spain have played in and won more Rugby World Cup qualifying matches than any other nation – 28 in 50 matches between 1989 and 2010 (with 21 defeats and one draw).

RIGHT: Romania's Madalin Lemnaru surges through Uruguay's defence in the 21–21 draw in the 2011 Rugby World Cup final repechage round in Montevideo.

OVERALL POINTS FOR AND AGAINST

The all-time Rugby World Cup qualifying record for the fewest points scored in all matches played is five, set by Pakistan (in two matches in 2008). The record for the fewest points conceded by a team in all Rugby World Cup qualifying matches is 15, set by England (in two matches in 1998).

FINAL REPECHAGE RESULTS (PIC)

Year	Qualifier	Opponent	Home	Away	Aggregate
1999	Tonga	Korea	58–26	82–15	140–41
	Uruguay	Morocco	18–3	18–21	36–24
2003	United States	Spain	58–13	62–13	120–26
	Tonga	Korea	119–0	75–0	194–0
2007	Portugal	Uruguay	12–5	12–18	24–23
	Tonga	Korea	–	–	85–3*
2011	Romania	Uruguay	39–12	21–21	60–33

one-off match played in Auckland, New Zealand

Note: repechage matches were first introduced for the 1999 tournament.

LEFT: Wales (playing Italy at Cardiff in 1994) are one of only four countries never to have lost a Rugby World Cup qualifying match.

ASIA'S RUGBY WORLD CUP NEARLY MEN

Stymied by the fact that there is only one Rugby World Cup place on offer for Asian teams – which Japan has eagerly grabbed on every occasion – Korea are the nearly men of Rugby World Cup qualifying. In 1991, the only time the Asia and Oceania qualifying competition was combined, they lost all three matches in a tough group containing Western Samoa, Japan and Tonga. In 1995, they lost to Japan in the final qualifying round. In 1999, they lost to Tonga in the final repechage round – a fate they would also suffer in both 2003 and 2007. Exasperated, perhaps, by their lack of fortune, they slumped to four straight defeats in the 2010 Asian Five Nations, which served as a qualifying tournament for the 2011 Rugby World Cup. Overall, because they have gone so far into the process on so many occasions, Korea hold two unwanted records: they have lost more matches (24) and have conceded more points (1,469) than any other team in Rugby World Cup qualifying history.

FEWEST DEFEATS

Four sides have never lost a Rugby World Cup qualifying match: Australia (three matches in 1998); England (two matches in 1998); Ireland (four matches between 1998 and 2002); and Wales (four matches in 1994).

RIGHT: Fernando Diez drives Spain forward during their 21–17 Rugby World Cup qualifying victory over Portugal at Murrayfield in December 1998.

BELOW: Georgia's David Zirakishvili (with ball) in action during his country's 17–9 victory over Spain in a 2011 Rugby World Cup qualifyng match in Tbilisi.

WAITING TO GET OFF THE MARK

The following sides have never won a Rugby World Cup qualifying match: Finland (played two, lost two in 2004); Nigeria (played three, lost three between 2004 and 2008); Pakistan (played two, lost two in 2008); St Vincent and Grenadines (played two, lost two between 2005 and 2008); and Vanuatu (played five, lost five between 2001 and 2009).

FEWEST AVAILABLE QUALIFYING SPOTS

The eight quarter-finalists from the 1991 Rugby World Cup, plus tournament hosts South Africa, all received automatic entry into the 1995 edition of the tournament. Consequently, as this was the last of the 16-team Rugby World Cups (tournament entry was increased to 20 for 1999), it meant that only seven qualifying places were up for grabs – the fewest in history.

RECORD FOR BIGGEST HALF-TIME LEAD

Hong Kong did not take long to show their supremacy over Singapore in the Asian section Rugby World Cup qualification match at Kuala Lumpur on 27 October 1994: they raced into an 83–3 lead by half-time (the biggest interval lead in international rugby history) and went on to win the match 164–13 (the most points ever scored by an international team in a single match).

CHERRY BLOSSOMS ARE THE WORLD CUP QUALIFYING KINGS

Along with Romania, Japan are the only side in history to have qualified for every Rugby World Cup, and they have set records along their trailblazing way: no side in history has scored more points (1,740) or more tries (259 in 27 matches – a staggering 9.6 tries per match) in Rugby World Cup qualifying history.

QUALIFIERS BY YEAR

Year	Qualifiers (Continent)
1987	None – entry to the tournament was by invitation only
1991	Zimbabwe (Africa); Western Samoa, Japan (Asia and Oceania); Italy, Romania (Europe); Argentina, Canada, United States (Americas)
1995	Ivory Coast (Africa); Argentina (Americas); Japan (Asia); Wales, Italy, Romania (Europe); Tonga (Oceania)
1999	Namibia (Africa); Argentina, Canada, United States, Uruguay (Americas); Japan (Asia); England, Ireland, Italy, Romania, Scotland, Spain (Europe); Australia, Fiji, Tonga, Western Samoa (Oceania)
2003	Namibia (Africa); Ireland, Italy, Romania, Georgia (Europe); Japan (Asia); Canada, Uruguay, United States (Americas); Fiji, Samoa, Tonga (Oceania)
2007	Namibia (Africa); Italy, Romania, Portugal, Georgia (Europe); Japan (Asia); Argentina, Canada, United States (Americas); Fiji, Samoa, Tonga (Oceania)
2011	Namibia (Africa); Georgia, Romania, Russia (Europe); Japan (Asia); Canada, United States (Americas); Samoa (Oceania)

MOST CONVERSIONS (IN A WORLD CUP QUALIFYING MATCH)

The record for the most conversions in a Rugby World Cup qualifying match is 17, held by two players: J. McKee, for Hong Kong against Singapore at Kuala Lumpur on 27 October 1994; and Pierre Hola, for Tonga against Korea at Nuku A'lofa on 22 March 2003.

MOST QUALIFYING ROUND APPEARANCES

The record for the most appearances in Rugby World Cup qualifying matches is 24, held by two Spanish players: Alvar Enciso Fernandez-Valderama (between 1993 and 2006); and Pablo Feijoo Ugalde (between 2002 and 2010).

MOST POINTS (INDIVIDUAL): TOP TEN

Pos	Points	Player (Country, Span)
1	206	Esteban Roque Segovia (Spain, 2004–06)
2	196	Mike Hercus (USA, 2002–09)
3	170	Daisuke Ohata (Japan, 1998–2006)
4	140	Federico Sciarra (Uruguay, 1993–99)
5	130	Pierre Hola (Tonga, 1998–2006)
6	129	Toru Kurihara (Japan, 2002)
7	119	Petre Mitu (Romania, 1997–2009)
8	117	Diego Dominguez (Italy, 1994–98)
9	115	Yuriy Kushnarev (Russia, 2006–10)
10	101	Juan Menchaca (Uruguay, 1999–2007)

BELOW: International rugby's all-time leading try-scorer, Daisuke Ohata has prospered in Rugby World Cup qualifying matches, scoring a record 34 for Japan.

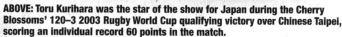

ABOVE: Toru Kurihara was the star of the show for Japan during the Cherry Blossoms' 120–3 2003 Rugby World Cup qualifying victory over Chinese Taipei, scoring an individual record 60 points in the match.

LETHAL FINISHER

Those who question the real value of Daisuke Ohata's status as the leading try-scorer in international rugby history (with 69 tries) will point to the fact that he played the majority of his games against lesser opponents (of those 69 tries only 14 of them came against teams that have appeared at the Rugby World Cup), but you can only play the cards you are dealt and there is no doubt that Ohata played them exceptionally well, particularly in qualifying matches: he holds the all-time qualifying records for the most tries scored (34) and for the most tries scored in a single qualifying tournament (17 in Japan's successful 2007 Rugby World Cup qualifying campaign).

CLINICAL KURIHARA PROSPERS AGAINST CHINESE TAIPEI

In the space of two weeks in July 2002, Japan played two matches against Chinese Taipei (at home and away) and scored 275 points to Chinese Taipei's six. In the first match, at Tokyo on 7 July, the Cherry Blossoms won 155–3 to record the joint-highest winning margin in international rugby history. The return match (a 120–3 victory at Tainan on 21 July) saw another record-breaking performance: winger, Toru Kurihara, contributed 60 points (six tries and 15 conversions) to his team's cause – an all-time record for a player in a single Rugby World Cup qualifying match.

MOST TRIES (INDIVIDUAL): TOP TEN

Pos	Tries	Player (country, span)
1	34	Daisuke Ohata (Japan, 1998–2006)
2	15	Cesar Sempere Padilla (Spain, 2004–10)
3	14	Ashley Billington (Hong Kong, 1994–98)
=	14	Hirotoki Onozawa (Japan, 2002–09)
5	10	Toru Kurihara (Japan, 2002)
6	9	Kosuke Endo (Japan, 2006–10)
=	9	Pablo Feijoo Ugalde (Spain, 2002–10)
=	9	Diego Ormaechea (Uruguay, 1993–99)
9	8	*six players*

LEFT: Juan Menchaca of Uruguay celebrates victory his four drop goals helped his country to defeat Chile 34–23 in Montevideo in September 2002.

THE YOUNGEST TRY-SCORER

Robin Bredbury holds the distinction of being the youngest player to score a try in the history of the Rugby World Cup qualifying competition. The young fly-half, making his debut for Hong Kong aged 17 years and 145 days, scored the first of his team's 14 tries in their thumping 93–0 victory over Thailand in Kuala Lumpur on 25 October 1994. He made just five further appearances for his country.

SEGOVIA IS A SERIAL RECORD-BREAKER

It took time for diminutive fly-half Esteban Roque Segovia to get his chance to play for Spain – he was 30 years 188 days old when he made his debut against Hungary in Madrid on 20 November 2004 – but when he was finally handed his opportunity he grabbed it with both hands, particularly in Rugby World Cup qualifying matches. In 14 qualifying matches between 2004 and 2006, he set all-time records for: the most points scored (206); the most penalties (36); the most conversions (45); and the most points in a single qualifying tournament (206 during the qualification campaign for the 2007 Rugby World Cup).

AGE NO BARRIER FOR ORMAECHEA

A legend in Uruguay's rugby history, Diego Ormaechea became the oldest try-scorer in Rugby World Cup qualifying history when, on 3 April 1999, at the tender age of 39 years 195 days, he scored a try during his side's crucial 33–24 first-round repechage victory over Portugal in Lisbon. The veteran No.8 also holds the all-time record for the most appearances as captain in Rugby World Cup qualifying matches, having led Uruguay on 11 occasions between 1993 and 1999.

RECORD FOR MOST TRIES IN A MATCH BY A SINGLE PLAYER

The main beneficiary of Hong Kong's 164–13 demolition of Singapore in the Asian section Rugby World Cup qualifying match at Kuala Lumpur on 27 October 1994 was Ashley Billington. The full-back ran in ten tries during the match – a record in international rugby.

MOST DROP GOALS (OVERALL)

The record for the most drop goals in a single Rugby World Cup qualifying match is four, by Uruguay's Juan Menchaca during his side's 34–23 victory over Chile at Montevideo on 7 September 2002. Menchaca also holds the record for the most drop goals in all Rugby World Cup qualifying matches, with five in 13 matches between 1999 and 2007).

MOST PENALTIES (IN A MATCH)

The record for the most penalties in a Rugby World Cup qualifying match is eight, held by two players: Diego Dominguez, for Italy against Romania at Catania on 1 October 1994; and Roger Warren, for Samoa against Tonga at Apia on 29 May 2004.

RIGHT: Italy's Diego Dominguez (with ball against England in a Rugby World Cup qualifying match at the McAlpine Stadium, Huddersfield in 1994) is one of only two players to have slotted eight penalties in a qualifying match.

PART IV
INTERNATIONAL RUGBY

International rugby denotes any match played between any of the International Rugby Board's (IRB) 95 full member or 19 associate member countries. It all started on 27 March 1871 when Scotland beat England in the first-ever international rugby match played, at Raeburn Place in Edinburgh, and has grown steadily ever since. By the end of the nineteenth century, 130 international matches had been played; by 1950, that number had risen to 725; and, remarkably, by October 2011, more than 7,300 international fixtures had been contested in a variety of competitions.

In Europe, the elite playing nations contest the Six Nations Championship, while those in the second and third tiers take part in the European Nations Cup. The southern hemisphere giants (Australia, New Zealand and South Africa) compete in the Tri-Nations on an annual basis. In the Americas, there is the South American Championship; in Africa, the Africa Cup and the CAR Development Trophy; and in Asia and Oceania, teams play in the various divisions of the Asian Five Nations Championship and the Oceania Cup. Add to these the numerous continental Rugby World Cup qualifying competitions, the Rugby World Cup itself, as well as tours from representative teams (such as the British Lions) and it does not take long to discover that the modern international fixture list has become a congested one – in 2010 alone 220 international matches were contested around the globe.

This section deals with the all-time record holders in international rugby, from overall team records (such as the largest victories and the most matches won) to team records (with statistics for the leading try-scorers, points-scorers and appearance records), and includes records from the major annual competitions in both the northern and southern hemispheres – the Six Nations Championship (which has been contested in its many guises since 1883) and the Tri-Nations (which has been played since 1996).

BELOW: The French (left) and New Zealand teams line up before the start of the 2011 Rugby World Cup final at Eden Park, Auckland, won 8–7 by the All Blacks.

CHANGING POINTS SYSTEMS

The first 18 years of international rugby (covering 118 international matches) were played under a points system whereby a team scoring a try earned the chance to kick at goal, with the winning team being the one that kicked the most goals. The first international match to use a different points system (try = 1 point; conversion = 2; penalty = 2; drop goal = 3; goal from mark = 3) was England against the New Zealand Natives at Blackheath, London, on 16 February 1899 (the last match of the New Zealand Natives' tour – they had played Ireland and Wales in matches using the old points system). England scored five tries and one conversion to win the match 7–0. But that was only an experiment: the following year's Four Nations tournament reverted to the tried-and-tested points system of old, and the 'new' system was implemented only in 1890. Remarkably, it wasn't until 1971 that a try became the most rewarded source of points – and the modern points system (try = 5 points; penalty = 3; drop goal = 3; conversion = 2) was introduced for the first time in 1992.

ABOVE: Argentina add to Ireland's record-breaking tally of defeats (325) at the 2007 Rugby World Cup.

FEWEST MATCHES PLAYED BY A TEAM

Apart from the African Leopards representative side, the only other team in history to have played one international match and lost is Tokelau – a small territory in the South Pacific belonging to New Zealand – who played against Papua New Guinea in Apia in 1983 and lost their one and only international 28–15.

ENGLAND HAVE AN EYE FOR A DRAW

England have drawn more matches than any other team in international history. The first of their record-breaking 49 draws (in 638 matches) came against Scotland on 3 March 1873 (0–0); their most recent stalemate was also against the Scots (15–15 in their 2010 Six Nations clash).

MIXED FORTUNES FOR THE MEN IN GREEN

They may now be sixth in the IRB world rankings and considered among the stronger teams on the global rugby stage, but success in the international arena did not always come easily to Ireland. As their fortunes have risen and fallen over the years, they have lost 325 (out of 611) matches – an all-time record in international rugby.

MOST MATCHES AND MOST WINS

France hold the distinction of having played more international matches than any other rugby-playing nation. *Les Bleus* opened their international rugby account on 1 January 1906 (with a 38–6 defeat to New Zealand) and have gone on to play 677 matches. France also hold the record for the most wins in international rugby (375).

RIGHT: The sweet taste of victory as France celebrate grand-slam glory. Les Bleus have registered more wins (375) than any other team in international rugby history.

LEOPARDS, LIONS AND OTHERS

A combined South America side played in eight internationals against South Africa between 1980 and 1984, winning one of the matches and losing seven. The African Leopards (a representative side made up of players from CAR development countries): played one match (for which they received international caps) against a South Africa Students XV in Johannesburg on 23 July 2005 and lost 30–15. Other representative sides to have played international rugby (featured elsewhere in the book) are the British Lions and the Pacific Islanders.

ESTABLISHING THE GAME'S GOVERNING BODY (THE IRB)

It was not long before the other Home Nations countries – Ireland, Scotland and Wales – began to challenge England's self-proclaimed role (as founders of the game) as rugby's rule-makers, and the situation came to a head in 1885. A year earlier, Scotland had questioned the legitimacy of a match-winning England try, only to be told, in no uncertain terms, that those were the rules. Understandably unhappy, the Scots refused to honour their 1886 Home Nations Championship match against England and, the following year, along with Ireland and Wales, formed the International Rugby Football Board (the IRFB) – a body tasked with governing the game and its rules. England, unwilling to relinquish their control over the game, refused to take part; the IRFB forbade its members to play against England until they joined; and the stand-off continued until 1890, when England became the IRFB's fourth member nation. A few angry words had been exchanged along the way, but the game's global governing body was born – and, by 2010, now known as the International Rugby Board (IRB), it had 95 full members, 19 associate members and six regional associations.

HARD TO BEAT

Of all teams in international rugby to have played 50 matches or more, New Zealand have the highest winning percentage. The All Blacks have won 364 of 484 matches played – 76.96 per cent – between 1903 and 2011. There are, however, three countries with a 100 per cent record: Macau, who won their only international against Cambodia, 46–,7 in 2005; Algeria, who won their only two matches (both in 2010) and Qatar, who also won their only two matches (also in 2010).

FIRST MATCH IN THE SOUTHERN HEMISPHERE

Twenty long years passed between the first-ever international rugby match – Scotland's victory over England at Raeburn Place, Edinburgh, on 27 March 1871 – and the first international match to be played in the southern hemisphere. On 30 July 1891, a touring team from Great Britain beat South Africa 4–0.

RIGHT: Argentina's legendary fly-half Hugo Porta not only played for South America in a series of matches against South Africa, but also for the South African Barbarians when they played two matches against the touring British Lions in South Africa in 1980.

LOWEST WINNING PERCENTAGE

Winning rugby matches has not come easily to Jamaica: in 21 matches played since 1975, they have won only three of them. Their winning percentage of 16.66 is the lowest of any country to have played 20 internationals or more.

SIDES STILL AWAITING FIRST INTERNATIONAL VICTORY

Country (Span)	Matches played
Costa Rica (2006–11)	14
Mauritania (2003–04)	7
Guadeloupe (1977–99)	3
St Vincent and Grenadines (2005–11)	3
Estonia (2010–)	2
Libya (2010–	2
Mongolia (2009–10)	2
Turks and Caicos Islands (2002–08)	2
Tokelau (1983)	1

ALL BLACKS PROVIDE TRUE MEASURE OF GREATNESS

New Zealand made a blistering entrance on to the international rugby scene, losing only once in their first 15 matches between 1903 and 1910 and, notwithstanding their many Rugby World Cup disappointments prior to 2011, have remained the standard against which other teams have been judged ever since. The All Blacks hold the all-time records for: the most points scored (12,568 in 484 matches between 1903 and 2011 – an average of 25.97 points per match); best points difference (+6,440 – the next best is Argentina with +3,672); most tries (1,654); most conversions (1,060); most matches won at an away venue (147 in 219 matches between 1906 and 2011); and best winning percentage in away matches of all teams to have played 20 internationals or more (69.63).

BELOW: New Zealand captain Richie McCaw with the Tri-Nations trophy and the Bledisloe Cup in 2007. The All Blacks have scored more points (12,568) than any other country in international history.

ABOVE: Georgia celebrate overall victory in the 2006–08 European Nations' Cup. The Lelos' form is among the most impressive in world rugby.

STEADFAST SWISS HOLD AN UNLIKELY ALL-TIME RECORD

Switzerland may be relative newcomers to the international rugby scene (they played their first match, a 4–23 defeat to Portugal, in April 1973) and currently locked in the third tier of European rugby, but they hold a unique record: they have conceded the fewest points (1,953 in 116 matches between 1973 and 2011) of any country to have played in 100 internationals or more.

THERE'S NO PLACE LIKE HOME FOR GEORGIA

Georgia have built their reputation as one of international rugby's most improving nations on their performances at home. The Lelos have recorded 41 wins in 49 home matches between 1989 and 2011, at a winning percentage of 85.71 – the highest by any country to have played 20 or more home internationals.

FLAWLESS RECORD

Their time on the international rugby stage may only have been brief, but Algeria have earned a unique place in the game's all-time record books: they have won both of their matches – 50–0 against Libya and 50–0 against Egypt (both matches were played in October 2010) – and are the only team in international rugby history never to have conceded a point.

PLENTY OF PROBLEMS FOR POOR PARAGUAY

Paraguay have not enjoyed the best of times in South American rugby: they lost the first 14 matches in their history; have gone on to win only 18 of their 89 matches; have been on the wrong end of two of the four heaviest defeats in history (152–0 and 144–0, both times against Argentina); and have the worst points difference (-2,450) of any international team on the world rugby circuit.

RUGBY GLORY EVADES GUADELOUPE

Guadeloupe may be renowned for several things – it is the place where Christopher Columbus is credited with discovering the pineapple (in 1493) and has since become a popular location for an exotic getaway – but the islanders are not known for their prowess on the rugby field. They have played three matches in international rugby between 1977 and 1999 and lost all of them (3–30 against Bermuda; 6–47 against Trinidad and Tobago; and 0–52 against Bermuda). Their overall total of nine points scored is the fewest by any team in international rugby history.

THE KUALA LUMPUR TRY-FEST

If tries were the order of the day, there would have been no better place to be than at Hong Kong's Rugby World Cup qualifying match against Singapore in Kuala Lumpur on 27 October 1994. Hong Kong ran in a remarkable 26 tries – one every three minutes – during their thumping 164–13 victory. Their performance set new records for the most tries and the most points scored by a team in an international match.

A LONG LIST OF RECORDS FOR *LES BLEUS* ... NOT ALL OF THEM GOOD

As a consequence of having played more international matches than any other nation (677, as opposed to the All Blacks' 484), France hold numerous all-time records in international rugby. *Les Bleus* have won the most matches at home (208) and have kicked the most penalty goals (1,051) and drop goals (217), but they have also conceded more points than any other team in history (9,839).

FAILING TO BREAK THE DEADLOCK

There have been 19 0–0 draws in international rugby, the most recent of which came between Togo and Nigeria in an African CAR Championship match at Lomé, Togo, on 3 July 2004.

RIGHT: Thomas Castaignede (10) celebrates his match-winning drop-goal against in England in 1998, one of the all-time record 217 kicked by Les Bleus.

BELOW: Full-back Percy Montgomery gave South Africa great attacking options and outstanding defence.

BIGGEST VICTORIES: TOP TEN

Pos	Winner	Score	Opponent	Venue	Date
1	Argentina	152–0	Paraguay	Mendoza	1 May 2002
=	Japan	155–3	Chinese Taipei	Tokyo	7 Jul 2002
3	Hong Kong	164–13	Singapore	Kuala Lumpur	27 Oct 1994
4	Argentina	144–0	Paraguay	Montevideo	27 Apr 2003
5	Australia	142–0	Namibia	Adelaide	25 Oct 2003
6	Argentina	147–7	Venezuela	Santiago	1 May 2004
7	England	134–0	Romania	Twickenham	17 Nov 2001
8	Korea	135–3	Malaysia	Hong Kong	20 Sep 1992
9	South Africa	134–3	Uruguay	East London	11 Jun 2005
10	New Zealand	145–17	Japan	Bloemfontein	4 Jun 1995
=	Japan	134–6	Chinese Taipei	Singapore	27 Oct 1998

TRY-SCORING RECORDS

FIRST TRY IN INTERNATIONAL RUGBY HISTORY

Scotland's Angus Buchanan holds the distinction of scoring the first-ever try in international rugby. The Inverary-born forward touched down for a push-over try against England at Edinburgh on 18 March 1871, a try that William Cross converted to hand Scotland the first victory in international rugby history.

FEW AWAY-DAY BLUES FOR CAMPESE

Given his consistently incisive try-scoring performances over the years against the world's top rugby-playing nations, Australia's David Campese is viewed by many as the deadliest finisher ever to have played the international game. He made a typically bullish try-scoring debut against New Zealand in Christchurch on 14 August 1982 and continued to bewitch opposition defences for the next 14 years. He appeared in three Rugby World Cups, notably as a key member of the Wallabies' triumphant squad in 1991, and bowed out of international rugby in December 1996 having scored a then record 64 tries – a total since passed by Japan's Daisuke Ohata. Campese does, however, still have one all-time record to his name: he has scored more tries in away matches than any other player – 24 in 39 matches between 1982 and 1996.

RIGHT: Australian winger David Campese scored more tries in away matches (24) than any other player in international rugby history

MOST TRIES BY A PLAYER IN A LOSING CAUSE

The record for the most tries in a match by a player whose team has gone on to lose is three, a feat achieved by ten players: Robert Montgomery (Ireland v Wales on 12 March 1887); Howard Marshall (England v Wales on 7 January 1893); Roland Raymond (Australia v New Zealand Maori on 24 June 1922); Sevaro Walisoliso (Fiji v Wales on 26 September 1964); Vilikesa Mocelutu (Fiji v New Zealand Maori on 31 August 1974); Yuji Matsuo (Japan v England on 20 May 1979); Ray Mordt (South Africa v New Zealand on 12 September 1981); Emile Ntamack (France v Wales on 6 March 1999); Josh Taumalolo (Tonga v Georgia on 28 March 1999); and Goncalo Malheiro (Portugal v Barbarians on 10 June 2004).

BILLINGTON'S RECORD-BREAKING DAY IN THE SUN

The stand-out performer during Hong Kong's 26-try, 164–13 demolition of Singapore at Kuala Lumpur on 27 October 1994 was Ashley Billington. The full-back ran in ten of his team's tries during the game – a record for a player in a single international match.

JAPAN'S TRY-SCORING GEM

Although he established a glowing reputation in the World Sevens Series as a player with both enormous natural ability and searing pace, few would have expected Daisuke Ohata to evolve into the most prolific try-scorer international rugby has ever seen. He made his debut for Japan against Korea on 9 November 1996, scoring a hat-trick of tries, and went on to become a constant presence in the Cherry Blossoms' line-up from that moment on. He appeared at the 1999 Rugby World Cup and caught the eye with a blistering try against Wales. On 7 July 2002, he scored a sensational eight tries during Japan's world-record-equalling 155–3 demolition of Chinese Taipei in Tokyo and ended the calendar year with 17 tries to his name (a record equalled by New Zealand's Joe Rokocoko in 2003). He made his second Rugby World Cup appearance in 2003, scoring against France and the USA. On 14 May 2006, to great acclaim from the Japanese public at least, he scored his 65th try (his second of three in the Cherry Blossoms' 32–7 victory over Georgia in Osaka) to break David Campese's all-time record for

ABOVE: Daisuke Ohata is the most prolific try-scorer in international rugby history with 69 tries in 58 appearances for Japan,

the most tries in international rugby. He made the last of his 58 appearances for Japan in November 2006 and bowed out of the international game having scored 69 tries. He also holds the all-time records for: the most tries by a player in home matches (43) and the most tries by a player at a single ground (28, at Chichibunomiya in Tokyo).

MOST TRIES: TOP TEN

Pos	Tries	Player (Country, span)
1	69	Daisuke Ohata (Japan, 1996–2006)
2	64	David Campese (Australia, 1982–96)
3	59	Shane Williams (Lions/Wales, 2000–11)
4	50	Rory Underwood (Lions/England, 1984–96)
5	49	Doug Howlett (New Zealand, 2000–07)
6	46	Christian Cullen (New Zealand, 1996–2002)
=	46	Brian O'Driscoll (Lions/Ireland, 1999–2011)
=	46	Joe Rokocoko (New Zealand, 2003–10)
9	44	Jeff Wilson (New Zealand, 1993–2001)
10	43	Hirotoki Onozawa (Japan, 2001–11)

ABOVE: Former Uruguay captain Diego Ormaechea is the oldest-ever try-scorer in international rugby history.

YOUNGEST AND OLDEST TRY-SCORERS

Diminutive 5ft 8in (1.73m) fly-half Robin Bredbury made rugby history on 25 October 1994 when he scored the first of his two tries (and his team's 14 tries) during Hong Kong's emphatic 93–0 victory over Thailand in Kuala Lumpur: aged 17 years 141 days, he had become the youngest try-scorer in international rugby history. The oldest try-scorer is Uruguay's Diego Ormaechea, who was 40 years 13 days old when he scored against Spain at Galashiels during the 1999 Rugby World Cup.

A WEEK TO REMEMBER

Uriel O'Farrell's international career was as brief as it was splendid. Remarkably, the Argentine winger scored 13 tries in two matches in the space of five days: seven during Argentina's 62–0 victory over Uruguay in Buenos Aires on 9 September 1951 and six during the Pumas' 72–0 victory over Brazil in Buenos Aires on 13 September 1951. He played in only one more match for his country – a try-scoring appearance during Argentina's 13–3 victory over Chile on 16 September 1951 – and ended the calendar year having scored 14 tries. It was a record which stood for 51 years (until Japan's Daisuke Ohata scored in 17 tries in 2002).

MOST TRIES BY A REPLACEMENT

The record for the most tries scored by a replacement in an international match is three, a feat achieved by seven players. The record for the most tries scored by a replacement in international history is six, achieved by two players: Jeremy Paul in 38 replacement appearances for Australia between 1998 and 2006; and Petrisor Toderasc in 22 replacement appearances for Romania between 2002 and 2007.

CAPTAIN MANS LEADS BY EXAMPLE

Appointed captain of the Namibia national team for their first post-independence international, against Zimbabwe on 24 March 1990 in Windhoek, just 26 days short of his 38th birthday, speedy winger Gerhard Mans gave his all for the Welwitschias in his 25-match Test career (all of them as captain). By the time he lowered the curtain on his international career in August 1994, aged 42 years 127 days, he had scored 27 tries – the most by any captain in international rugby history.

TRYLESS PERUGINI SETS ALL-TIME MARK

A powerful prop forward who made his debut in Italy's Six Nations Championship match against Ireland at Lansdowne Road in 2000, Salvatore Perugini has been the cornerstone of a consistently impressive Italian pack for more than a decade. In 83 appearances, however, he has never scored a try – a record in international rugby.

BELOW: An impressive peformer for Italy for more than a decade, Salvatore Perugini played in 83 internationals without scoring a try.

ALL-TIME LEADING TRY-SCORERS: BY POSITION

Position	Player (Teams, Span)	Tries
Full-back	Christian Cullen (New Zealand, 1996–2002)	40
Winger	Daisuke Ohata (Japan, 1996–2006)	62
Centre	Brian O'Driscoll (Lions/Ireland, 1999–2011)	46
Fly-half	Dan Carter (New Zealand, 2004–11)	24
Scrum-half	Joost van der Westhuizen (South Africa, 1993–2003)	38
No.8	Zinzan Brooke (New Zealand, 1990–97)	14
Flanker	Colin Charvis (Lions/Wales, 1996–2007)	19
	Richie McCaw (New Zealand, 2001–11)	19
Lock	Mamuka Gorgodze (Georgia, 2004–08)	13
Prop	Levan Tsabadze (Georgia, 1994–2002)	10
	Martin Castrogiovanni (Italy, 2002–11)	10
Hooker	Keith Wood (Lions/Ireland, 1994–2003)	15

POINTS-SCORING RECORDS

THE MAN WITH THE GOLDEN BOOT

Wales's points-gatherer-in-chief for over a decade (between 1991 and 2002), Neil Jenkins divided opinion throughout his career. No one questioned the golden nature of his right boot, but did he have the attacking flair required for a No.10, the rugged defence of a centre or the pace of a full-back? In short, his ability to garner points made him the first name on the teamsheet, but where to play him? Jenkins simply got on with his game while the debate raged around him and for a while in the late 1990s he was the most prolific scorer in world rugby. In 1999, he smashed Gavin Hastings' record for the most points in a calendar year (263 to the Scot's 196, set in 1995) and when he retired in 2002, he did so as the only player in history to have scored more than 1,000 international points (1,090). Jonny Wilkinson and Dan Carter have since passed that mark, but Jenkins will go down in rugby history as the game's first true points-scoring machine.

LEFT: Wales's Neil Jenkins was the first player to score 1,000 points in international rugby.

WORLD-RECORD POINTS HAUL FOR KURIHARA

As Japan ran riot against Chinese Taipei in Tainan on 21 July 2002, winning the match by the colossal margin of 120–3, Toru Kurihara helped himself to a place in the record books. The winger contributed 60 points to his team's total (with six tries and 15 conversions) – an all-time record for a player in a single international match.

DEFEAT FOR TEIXEIRA WITH ALL GUNS BLAZING

Thierry Teixeira produced an almighty performance for Portugal against Georgia in Lisbon on 8 February 2000, scoring nine penalties and a drop goal, but the visitors still ended up winning the match 32–30. The fly-half's contribution of 30 points is the most ever by a player in international rugby who has ended up on the losing side.

ENGLAND'S MOST PROLIFIC POINTS-SCORER

English rugby has had no greater hero than Jonny Wilkinson and it was highly appropriate that the mercurial fly-half's magical boot nailed the match-winning points to secure the greatest moment in England's rugby history – victory over Australia in the 2003 Rugby World Cup final. Wilkinson burst on to the international scene in 1998 as an 18-year-old and, as a result of his relentless accuracy with the boot, his eye for a gap with ball in hand and his formidable defence – not to mention an almost obsessive training regimen – soon established himself as England's first-choice No.10. When free from injury – his catalogue of ailments has brought tears to the eyes of every England fan – he has been a consistent source of points and stands second on all-time points-scoring list (1,246 in 97 matches). He does hold the records for most penalty goals (255), most points at a single ground (650 in 42 matches at Twickenham) and most drop goals in a career (36).

MOST PENALTIES IN A MATCH

Four players have kicked nine penalties in a match, but only New Zealand's Andrew Mehrtens has done so twice, against Australia at Auckland on 24 July 1999 and against France at the Stade de France on 11 November 2000. The three other players to achieve the feat on one occasion are: Keiji Hirose (for Japan against Tonga at Tokyo on 8 May 1999); Neil Jenkins (for Wales against France at the Millennium Stadium on 28 August 1999); and Thierry Teixeira (for Portugal against Georgia at Lisbon on 8 February 2000).

BELOW: England's Jonny Wilkinson stands second on international rugby's all-time points-scoring list with 1,246.

MOST POINTS: TOP TEN

Pos	Points	Player (Country, span)
1	1250	Dan Carter (New Zealand, 2003–11)
2	1246	Jonny Wilkinson (Lions/England, 1998–2011)
3	1090	Neil Jenkins (Lions/Wales, 1991–2002)
4	1075	Ronan O'Gara (Lions/Ireland, 2000–11)
5	1010	Diego Dominguez (Argentina/Italy, 1989–2003)
6	970	Stephen Jones (Lions/Wales, 1998–2011)
7	967	Andrew Mehrtens (New Zealand, 1995–2004)
8	911	Michael Lynagh (Australia, 1984–95)
9	893	Percy Montgomery (South Africa, 1997–2008)
10	878	Matt Burke (Australia, 1993–2004)

MOST POINTS IN A CALENDAR YEAR: RECORD PROGRESSION (TEN POINTS PLUS)

Points	Player (Country)	Year
263	Neil Jenkins (Wales)	1999
196	Gavin Hastings (Scotland)	1995
181	Neil Jenkins (Wales)	1994
140	Grant Fox (New Zealand)	1987
132	Hugo Porta (Argentina)	1985
113	Eduardo Morgan (Argentina)	1973
89	Guy Camberabero (France)	1967
45	Michel Vannier (France)	1957
43	Lewis Jones (Lions/Wales)	1950
32	Bot Stanley (Australia)	1922
25	Dickie Lloyd (Ireland)	1913
24	Daniel Lambert (England)	1911
23	Reggie Gibbs (Wales)	1908
22	John Gillespie (Scotland)	1901
17	Charlie Adamson (England)	1899
17	Lonnie Spragg (Australia)	1899
16	Fred Byrne (England)	1896
12	Dicky Lockwood (England)	1894

ABOVE: Dan Carter overtook Jonny Wilkinson during the 2011 Tri Nations Tournament to be come the leading points-scorer in international rugby history with (with 1,250).

THE KING OF MODERN FLY-HALVES

In recent times, Dan Carter has taken over the mantle from Jonny Wilkinson as the most lethal fly-half in world rugby. Blessed with a searing turn of pace, an ability to read the game in front of him at lightning speed and an unerringly accurate left boot, he is perhaps the main reason why New Zealand remain the team to beat in international rugby. Aided in no small part by Wilkinson's lengthy absences through injury, Carter heads the England fly-half on the all-time points-scoring list (1,250 to 1,246) and also holds the all-time records for: the most conversions (224 in 85 matches) and scoring the most points against a single opponent (270 in 21 matches against Australia between 2003 and 2011).

MAKING AN IMPACT FROM THE BENCH

It was the one bright moment in what was otherwise a fairly ordinary eight-match career spread over six years. On 27 October 1998, Keisuke Sawaki came off the bench for Japan (to win only his second cap) during the Cherry Blossoms' comprehensive 134–6 mauling of Chinese Taipei and scored one try and seven conversions. His haul of 19 points in the match is an all-time record for a replacement in international rugby.

THE MOST PROLIFIC REPLACEMENT

No player has scored more points as a replacement in international rugby than David Humphreys. The Belfast-born fly-half, who spent the twilight years of his international career fighting Ronan O'Gara for Ireland's No.10 jersey, scored an all-time record 62 points in 28 appearances as a replacement between 1997 and 2005.

MOST DROP GOALS IN A MATCH

Only one player has notched up five drop goals in a match on two separate occasions: Portugal's Goncalo Malheiro, first against Georgia at Lisbon on 16 February 2003 and then again against Russia at Krasnodar on 29 March 2003. South Africa's Jannie de Beer is the only other player to achieve the feat of scoring five drop goals in a match, famously against England in the 1999 Rugby World Cup quarter-final at the Stade de France, Paris.

PUMAS POWERED BY CAPTAIN'S BOOT

Considered one of the finest fly-halves in in history, Hugo Porta defined the Argentina national rugby team for more than two decades. It was clear the Pumas had unearthed a points-scoring diamond from the moment he made his debut, against Chile, in October 1971. Appointed captain in June 1977, he continued to lead by example, registering 496 points in 46 matches as skipper – an all-time record for a captain in international rugby.

BELOW: David Humphreys holds the distinction of having scored more points as replacement (62) than any other player in history.

A REGULAR TASTE OF DEFEAT FOR TRONCON

While Italy fought to establish themselves in the upper echelons of world rugby – a struggle that continues to this day – Alessandro Troncon remained one of the Azzurri's constant bright lights. The canny scrum-half made his debut against Spain in 1994 and went on to form a much-respected half-back partnership with Diego Dominguez, becoming the first Italian in history to win 100 caps. But there were plenty of low points along the way: for the Treviso-born No.9: he ended up on the losing side on 67 occasions – the most by any player in history.

ABOVE: Alessandro Troncon is the only player to appear in 100 internationals for Italy, but he found himself on the losing side on a record 69 occasions.

ONLY PLAYER TO HAVE PLAYED FOR THREE COUNTRIES

Fifty-four players have played international rugby for two countries, but only one player has represented three countries: Enrique Edgardo Rodriguez won 13 caps for Argentina between 1979 and 1983 and 26 caps for Australia between 1984 and 1987. In 1981, he also made a one-off appearance for Tahiti in their match against France on 13 July.

INTERNATIONAL RUGBY'S MOST CAPPED PLAYER

A shrewd rugby brain and the quickest service in the business helped George Gregan to represent Australia with distinction for over 13 years and secure his place among the game's all-time greats. He made his debut in 1994, played for the Wallabies at the 1995 Rugby World Cup, was appointed vice-captain in 1997 and was a key member of Australia's Rugby World Cup-winning team in 1999. But he was just getting started. A natural successor as captain to John Eales, he led the Wallabies to a second successive Rugby World Cup final – where they suffered an agonizing loss to England – in 2003 … and on he went. On 17 June 2006, a replacement appearance against England at Melbourne saw him win his 120th cap to overtake Jason Leonard as international rugby's most capped player. He made a fourth Rugby World Cup appearance in 2007 and bowed out of international rugby following the Wallabies' quarter-final defeat to England with an incredible 139 caps to his name. He also holds all-time records for: the most appearances on a winning side (93) and the most appearances against a single opponent (30 against South Africa between 1995 and 2007).

BELOW: George Gregan won an all-time record 139 international caps for Australia in a 13-year period between 1994 and 2007.

MOST APPEARANCES: TOP TEN

Pos	Caps	Player (Country, span)
1	139	George Gregan (Australia, 1994–2007)
2	123	Brian O'Driscoll (Lions/Ireland, 1999–2011)
3	119	Jason Leonard (Lions/England, 1990–2004)
4	118	Ronan O'Gara (Lions/Ire, 2000–11)
5	118	Fabien Pelous (France, 1995–2007)
6	111	Philippe Sella (France, 1982–95)
=	111	John Smit (South Africa, 2000–11)
8	110	Stephen Jones (Lions/Wales, 1998–2011)
=	110	Victor Matfield (South Africa, 2001–11)
=	110	George Smith (Australia, 2000–09)

MOST APPEARANCES: BY POSITION

Position	Player (Country, Span)	Appearances
Full-back	Mils Muliaina (New Zeaand, 2003–11)	84
Winger	Rory Underwood (Lions/England, 1984–96)	91
Centre	Brian O'Driscoll (Lions/Ireland, 1999–2011)	122
Fly-half	Stephen Jones (Lions/Wales, 2000–11)	98
Scrum-half	George Gregan (Australia, 1994–2007)	134
No.8	Sergio Parisse (Italy, 2002–11)	73
Flanker	Richie McCaw (New Zealand, 2001–10)	99
Lock	Victor Matfield (South Africa, 2001–10)	110
Prop	Jason Leonard (Lions/England, 1990–2003)	116
Hooker	John Smit (South Africa, 2000–11)	96

A UNIQUE CASE

Hugh Ferris is a unique case: he played only two matches in international rugby, both of them for different countries – one match for Ireland (against Wales at Swansea on 16 March 1901) and the other for South Africa (against Great Britain at Cape Town on 12 September 1903).

CROSSING THE HOME NATIONS DIVIDE

There is only one instance in history of a player representing two Home Nations countries. As a medical student in Edinburgh, Dr James Marsh played twice for Scotland in 1889. He went on to settle in the Manchester area and played for England against Ireland in 1892.

BELOW: Australian hooker Jeremy Paul holds the all-time record of having made more appearances in international rugby as a replacement (38) than any other player.

INTERNATIONAL RUGBY'S YOUNGEST PLAYER

When George Chiriac came on as a replacement for Romania in their match against Belgium in Bucharest on 20 April 1996 (which the home side won 83–5), it marked a moment of rugby history: aged 16 years 141 days, the Bariad-born forward became the youngest player in international rugby history. Not that it was a prelude to greater things: Chiriac had to wait five years before winning his second cap and would go on to make a total of only 19 appearances for his country – the last coming against Namibia at the 2003 Rugby World Cup.

ONE-CAP WONDERS

Of the 14,737 players to have played in international rugby, 3,252 of them only won one cap – a remarkable 22 per cent.

JONES A MILLENNIUM STADIUM REGULAR

No player has made more international appearances at one ground than Stephen Jones has done for Wales at the Millennium Stadium in Cardiff. The long-serving fly-half – the most capped No.10 in world rugby – made his first appearance there against Canada on 21 August 1999 and has since gone on to make a record-breaking 58 appearances at the stadium, three more than England's Jason Leonard made at Twickenham.

OLDEST DEBUTANT

Although the month of his birth remains uncertain, what is known is that, on 22 January 1923, Frederick Gilbert (born in 1884) made history when he made his debut for England against Wales at Twickenham. At 39 years of age he became, and remains, the oldest-ever debutant in international rugby.

RECORD-BREAKING REPLACEMENT

Jeremy Paul holds the all-time record for making the most appearances as a replacement in international rugby history. The New Zealand-born Australian hooker, who appeared in both the 1999 and 2003 Rugby World Cup finals (both times as a replacement), made 38 appearances for the Wallabies from the replacements' bench between 1998 and 2006.

ABOVE: England's legendary prop – a 2003 Rugby World Cup winner – Jason Leonard played 55 international matches at Twickenham and 119 in all, 116 of which were at prop, the most by any forward in world international rugby.

INTERNATIONAL RUGBY'S OLDEST PLAYER

Kevin Wirachowski made his international debut as a replacement during Canada's 26–13 defeat to England at Wembley on 17 October 1992 and, although he failed to become a regular in the Canucks' line-up, he remained in and around the national squad for the next decade, bowing out of international rugby in record-breaking fashion. When the prop forward from British Columbia came on as a replacement to win his 17th and final cap during Canada's 16–11 defeat to the United States in Vancouver on 18 June 2003, he became, aged 40 years 198 days, the oldest player ever to have made an appearance in an international rugby match.

MOST CONTESTED FIXTURE

There has been no more contested fixture in international rugby history than matches between Australia and New Zealand. The two southern hemisphere giants faced off for the first time in 1903 (New Zealand won the match 22–3) and they have since played a further 166 matches. The two countries compete for the Bledisloe Cup on an annual basis (as part of the Tri-Nations schedule).

For the record, New Zealand lead the way with 115 wins to Australia's 47, with five matches drawn.

YELLOW CARD BITS AND PIECES

A total of 912 yellow cards have been issued in international rugby history: the first was shown to Australia's James Holbeck during the Wallabies' clash with South Africa at Pretoria on 23 August 1997, a match the visitors went on to lose 61–22.

A DAMAGING EFFECT

Statistics prove that a team's chances of winning an international rugby match are significantly reduced if one of its players is dismissed: 111 red cards have been issued in international rugby history and on only 33 occasions has a team with a player sent off gone on to win the match – a lowly 29.73 per cent.

ABOVE: Australian centre James Holbeck (with ball) achieved the unfortunate distinction of becoming the first player in international rugby history to receive a yellow card.

MOST YELLOW CARDS (COUNTRY): TOP TEN

Pos	Yellow	Team
1	77	Georgia
2	72	South Africa
3	67	Italy
4	47	Australia
=	47	Wales
6	46	Argentina
7	45	Romania
8	42	Fiji
9	41	Canada
10	40	New Zealand

DOUBLE TROUBLE FOR FIJI

Fiji carved out an unwanted place for themselves in international rugby history during their clash with England at Twickenham on 4 November 1989: the islanders had two of their players sent off (centre Noa Nadraku and winger Tevita Vonolagi) by referee Brian Stirling – the first time that two players from one team had ever been sent off in a single match – and went on to lose 58–23.

MOST YELLOW CARDS IN A MATCH

The record for the most yellow cards issued in a single match is seven, during Uruguay's encounter with Georgia at Montevideo on 30 October 2004: Federico Capo Ortega, Nicolas Brignoni and Ignacio Lussich all spent ten minutes in the sin bin for Uruguay, while Irakli Ninidze, David Zirakashvili, Mamuka Gorgodze and Giorgi Jghenti all received yellow cards for Georgia. Uruguay went on to win the fractious match 17–7.

MOST YELLOW CARDS AND GONE ON TO WIN THE MATCH

The record for the most yellow cards received by a team that has gone on to win the match is three, a feat achieved by three teams: Canada against Italy at Rovigo on 11 November 2000 (Canada won the match 22–17); Uruguay against Georgia at Montevideo on 30 October 2004 (Uruguay won the match 17–7); and Romania against Portugal at Lisbon on 20 March 2010 (Romania won the match 20–9).

LEFT: Australia celebrate a rare victory over New Zealand in the two countries' Bledisloe Cup match played in Hong Kong on 30 October 2010. James O'Connor (leaping) scored a last-minute try to equalise and his conversion made it 26–24.

ALL BLACK BROWNLIE THE FIRST TO SEE RED

England's match with New Zealand at Twickenham on 3 January 1925 promised to be a titanic struggle. The home side came into the match off back-to-back grand slams, while the visitors were unbeaten since 1921 and were reaching the end of a 32-fixture tour during which they had swept all before them – but nobody expected the fiery clash that ensued. It was a battle from the first whistle, so much so that, after only eight minutes, referee Albert E. French brought the forwards together for the third time and issued a final warning. To little effect: moments later, New Zealand loose-forward Cyril Brownlie stamped on a prostrate England player and was duly ordered from the field, thus becoming the first player in history to be sent off in an international match.

RED CARDS GALORE IN PORT ELIZABETH

It was perhaps the only black mark for South Africa during what was otherwise a glorious march to the Rugby World Cup crown in 1995. Ten minutes from time during the Springboks' final pool match, against Canada at Port Elizabeth on 3 June, what had already been a bruising encounter degenerated into a mass brawl. As a result, South Africa's John Dalton and Canada's Gareth Rees and Rod Snow all received their marching orders. It is the only time in international rugby history that three players have been expelled from the field of play during a single match.

OTHER RED CARD BITS AND PIECES

One hundred and eleven players have been sent off in international rugby matches over the years, although, interestingly, no player has been sent off more than once in his international career. The team to have received the most red cards is Italy, with ten.

BATTLE RAGES AT CARDIFF ARMS PARK

For over 100 years, no player had ever been sent off in a Home Nations Championship match, but that all changed on 15 January 1977 when Wales played Ireland at Cardiff Arms Park. Thirty-eight minutes had passed in an unexpectedly tight contest (the score was locked at 6–6) and Ireland were getting the better of the forward confrontations. And then it all kicked off: when another Welsh line-out was disrupted, Wales prop Geoff Wheel vented his frustration on Ireland's Stuart McKinney; Ireland's Willie Duggan reacted by taking a swing at Welsh lock Alan Martin and a mêlée ensued. When the dust settled, Scottish referee Norman Sanson showed red cards to both Wheel and Duggan – it was the first time in history that two players had been sent off in a single international.

ABOVE: Cyril Brownlie (third row, fourth player) was the first player ever to be sent off. The All Black stamped on an England forward and referee Albert E. French – having warned both sets of players three times in the first ten minutes of the match – issued the ultimate sanction on the All Blacks loose-forward.

SMIT: A NATURAL-BORN LEADER

John Smit was presented with one of international rugby's ultimate tests when he was handed his first start for South Africa (after six appearances as a replacement) for their match against Argentina in the cauldron of the River Plate Stadium in Buenos Aires on 12 November 2000. When he performed with distinction during the visitors' 37–33 victory, it seemed as though the Springboks had unearthed another front-row gem. But, by 2001, a dip in form saw him dropped from the Springbok squad and a subsequent shoulder injury left him on the fringes for the next 18 months. He returned for South Africa's 2003 Rugby World Cup campaign, playing in all of his country's five matches and captaining his country for the first time in their match against Georgia. South Africa's poor performance in the tournament – coupled with the fallout surrounding the team's preparation for it – prompted a change of coach; and new incumbent Jake White, seeking to rebuild the side, handed Smit the captaincy on a permanent basis early in 2004. It was an inspirational choice: South Africa won the Tri-Nations that year and by 2007 had developed a team capable of challenging for the game's greatest prize – which they duly achieved, winning all seven matches at the 2007 Rugby World Cup, including a 15–6 victory over England in the final. Further honours were to follow – a 2–1 victory over the British Lions in 2009 followed by a further Tri-Nations crown later that year – and by 2011 Smit had led the Springboks on 83 occasions and recorded 54 wins as captain. The former is an all-time record in international rugby.

LEFT: Some questioned his appointment, but John Smit has gone on to become an inspirational leader for South Africa. His 83 apperances as captain are an all-time record in international rugby.

RBS

GRAND SLAM

SIX NATIONS CHAMPIONSHIP

The oldest competition in world rugby, it all started in 1893 when the four Home Union countries (England, Ireland, Scotland and Wales) contested the first of what would become the annual Home Nations Championship. It became the Five Nations Championship in 1910 with the inclusion of France and, bar a period of 15 years when France were excluded from the competition (amid rumours of professionalism in the French game), remained that way until 2000, when Italy joined the party and the competition was renamed the Six Nations Championship.

BELOW: France celebrate grand slam glory in the 2010 Six Nations Championship, their third since the competition expanded with the inclusion of Italy in 2000.

NATIONS®

CHAMPIONS 2010

TEAM RECORDS

ENGLAND WIN INAUGURAL CHAMPIONSHIP

The first-ever Home Nations Championship – contested between December 1882 and March 1883 – was played under the game's old points system, with matches decided by goals: a goal was awarded for a successful conversion after a try, from a drop goal or from a goal from mark. If the scores were level at the end of play, any unconverted tries were counted to produce a winner; if the scores were still level at that point, the match was declared a draw. The 1882–83 championship came down to a final-match, winner-takes-all showdown between Scotland (who had beaten Wales 3–1 and Ireland 1–0) and England (2–0 winners against Wales and 1–0 conquerors of Ireland) in Edinburgh on 3 March 1883. After the match ended in a 0–0 draw, England won on count-back by two tries to one to become the competition's first winners.

RIGHT: England celebrate a grand-slam-winning 2003 Six Nations Championship campaign. Eight months later they would go on to lift the Rugby World Cup.

OVERALL RECORD

Country (Span)	Home Nations		Five Nations		Six Nations	Overall		Grand Slam	Triple Crowns
England (1883–)	5	(4)	17	(6)	5	27	(10)	12	23
Wales (1883–)	7	(3)	15	(8)	2	24	(11)	10	19
France (1910–31, 1947–)	–		12	(8)	5	17	(8)	9	–
Scotland (1883–)	9	(2)	5	(6)	0	14	(8)	3	10
Ireland (1883–)	4	(3)	6	(5)	1	11	(8)	2	10
Italy (2000–)	–		–		0	0	(0)	0	–

Note: *outright wins (shared wins)*

FIVE NATIONS CHAMPIONSHIP (1910–31, 1947–99)

The expanded Five Nations Championship (following the inclusion of France) was contested 71 times between 1910 and 1999, with England and Wales leading the way with 23 tournament victories (England with 17 outright wins and six shared titles; Wales with 15 outright wins and eight shared), followed by France (with 20 wins, 12 outright and eight shared) and Ireland and Scotland (11 wins each – Ireland with six outright and five shared titles, and Scotland with five outright wins and six shared titles).

RIGHT: Captain Brian O'Driscoll lifts the 2009 Six Nations Championship trophy after Ireland recorded their first grand slam for 61 years.

HOME NATIONS CHAMPIONSHIP (1883–1909, 1932–39)

The Home Nations Championship was contested 22 times between 1883 and 1909 – the competition was started but not completed on five occasions (in 1885, 1888, 1889, 1897 and 1898) – and Scotland led the way with eight tournament victories (six outright and two shared), followed by Wales (seven wins – six outright and one shared), England (five wins – three outright and two shared) and Ireland (four wins – three outright and one shared). The championship reverted to the Home Nations Championship between 1932 and 1939, following the exclusion of France, with England claiming four victories (two outright and two shared), Ireland and Wales three each (both one outright and two shared) and Scotland two (both outright).

SIX NATIONS WINNERS

2000	England
2001	England
2002	France (grand slam)
2003	England (grand slam)
2004	France (grand slam)
2005	Wales (grand slam)
2006	France
2007	France
2008	Wales (grand slam)
2009	Ireland (grand slam)
2010	France (grand slam)
2011	England

CHAMPIONS 2003
RBS The Royal Bank of Scotland

CHAMPION The Roy of Scotland

CONSECUTIVE GRAND SLAMS AND TRIPLE CROWNS

The record for the most consecutive grand slams is two, held by England (who have achieved the feat three times, in seasons 1913–14, 1923–24 and 1991–92) and France (in 1997–98). Diehard Wales fans also lay claim to the feat, stating that back-to-back triple crowns in the 1908 and 1909 Home Nations Championship, coupled with a pair of victories over France in the same years, equate to a grand slam. France, however, did not join the championship until 1910, so the Welsh claim is merely unofficial. Two teams have won four consecutive triple crowns: Wales (between 1976 and 1979) and England (between 1995 and 1998).

HEAD-TO-HEADS: WINS/DEFEATS/DRAWS

	England	France	Ireland	Italy	Scotland	Wales
England	X	43/32/7	62/46/7	12/0/0	63/38/13	51/52/12
France	32/43/7	X	50/27/5	11/1/0	45/34/2	39/40/3
Ireland	46/62/7	27/50/5	X	12/0/0	55/58/5	45/61/6
Italy	0/12/0	1/11/0	0/12/0	X	5/7/0	2/9/1
Scotland	38/63/13	34/45/2	58/54/5	7/5/0	X	48/64/3
Wales	52/51/12	40/39/3	61/45/6	9/2/1	64/48/3	X

1973: A UNIQUE CHAMPIONSHIP

Shared championships were a common feature of the Home Nations and Five Nations tournaments – there were 19 of them – until 1994, when points difference was used for the first time to break ties between teams, but on only one occasion did all five teams share the spoils. In 1973, England, France, Ireland, Scotland and Wales all finished with a record of won two, lost two to finish locked on four points apiece.

TEMPORARY FIVE NATIONS AU REVOIR FOR LES BLEUS

Sporadic wins over Ireland and Scotland apart, it took time for France to find their stride in the Five Nations after they had been admitted to the fold in 1910: they had to wait until 1927 to record their first victory over England and until the following year before they did the same to Wales. But just when it seemed as though French rugby was on the up, rumours of professionalism in the French domestic game started to emerge and, as a result, in 1932 France were banished from the competition – the only team ever to suffer such a fate. Les Bleus were reinstated to the fold in 1947 and have been part of the championship ever since. They won their first title outright in 1959.

THE AZZURRI ENTER THE FRAY

By the mid-1990s, Italy had developed a squad of players that swept all before them in European rugby's second tier and were starting to string together some impressive performances against the world's elite rugby-playing nations, including home-and-away victories over Ireland in 1995 and 1997. It was only right, therefore, that the Azzurri should be given the chance to test their mettle on a regular basis against Europe's elite and, in 2000, they were invited to join an expanded Six Nations Championship. They have found life much tougher on the bigger stage, winning only eight of 60 matches played in the competition, although in 2011 they did enjoy their first ever Six Nations victory over France.

ABOVE: Wales did not lose to England, Scotland or Ireland between 1976 and 1979, and they beat England 27–3 in this 1979 encounter at Cardiff Arms Park.

BELOW: Diego Dominguez was one of Italy's brightest stars in their early years in the Six Nations Championship.

GRAND SLAMS AND TRIPLE CROWNS

Team	Grand slams	Triple crowns
England	12	23
Wales	10	19
France	9	n/a
Scotland	3	10
Ireland	2	10
Italy	0	n/a

AZZURRI STILL FINDING THEIR FEET

Surprisingly, Italy hold the all-time Six Nations record for averaging the most points scored per match (with 15.12), but that is where the good news ends. The Azzurri have struggled since joining Europe's premier competition in 2000, winning only eight of 60 matches (with only one of those victories achieved away from home) and hold unwanted all-time tournament records for: the lowest winning percentage (14.16 – including a 15–15 draw away to Wales in 2006); the worst points difference (-1,075); and conceding the most points in a single tournament (228 in their debut season).

WALES FORMIDABLE AT HOME

There is no stronger home team in Six Nations Championship history than Wales. The Welsh, who have used five home venues in the competition – St Helens, Swansea; Rodney Parade, Newport; Cardiff Arms Park; Stradey Park, Llanelli; and the Millennium Stadium, Cardiff – have recorded more home victories (138 in 214 matches) than any other team in the tournament's history.

SERIAL RECORD-BREAKERS

England have been the championship's (in all its guises) most dominant team over the years. They have collected the most grand slams (12) and triple crowns (23) and hold the all-time tournament records for: the most wins (231); most draws (39); highest winning percentage (57.19); best winning percentage at home (68.57); most matches won away (93); best winning percentage away (46.11 in 219 matches); most points scored (5,808); best points difference (+1,358); most tries scored (840); most penalties (562) and most conversions kicked (438); and most conversions in a single match (nine – from ten attempts – against Italy at Twickenham on 7 February 2001), which they won 80–23 (it was the biggest margin of victory in Five/Six Nations Championship history).

BELOW: Will Greenwood crosses the line for England during their convincing 44–15 victory over Wales in 2001. England ended as Six Nations Championship winners and scored a tournament-record 229 points.

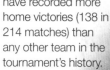

ABOVE: Bill Beaumont led England to grand slam glory in the 1980 Five Nations Championship – one of a record 12 grand slams won by England in the history of the Five/Six Nations Championship.

PLENTY OF LOWS FOR THE MEN IN GREEN

Ireland have enjoyed numerous good times in the Six Nations Championship over the years, with 19 tournament victories (11 outright and eight shared), two grand slams (in 1948 and 2009) and ten triple crowns, but there have been plenty of low points, too: the men from the Emerald Isle – who started out in the tournament with ten straight defeats – share with Scotland the all-time record for most defeats in tournament history, both having been beaten on 231 occasions.

A DARK CLOUD WITH A RECORD-BREAKING LINING FOR ENGLAND

Although England bowed out of the extended 2001 Six Nations Championship in disappointing fashion – losing 14–20 to Ireland in Dublin in the final round of matches (delayed by five months because of an outbreak of foot-and-mouth disease) to miss out on a grand slam (if not the tournament) for a second consecutive year – their performances up until that point, including victories over Wales (44–15), Italy (80–23), Scotland (43–3) and France (48–19), had been nothing short of scintillating. During the course of that championship, England set all-time records for: the most points scored in a single tournament (229), the most tries scored in a single tournament (29) and the most conversions scored in a single tournament (24).

BIGGEST MARGINS OF VICTORY: TOP TEN

Pos	Margin	Winner	Score	Opponent	Venue	Date
1	57	England	80–23	Italy	Twickenham	17 Feb 2001
2	51	France	51–0	Wales	Wembley	5 Apr 1998
3	47	Ireland	60–13	Italy	Lansdowne Road	4 Mar 2000
=	47	England	59–12	Italy	Rome	18 Mar 2000
5	46	England	59–13	Italy	Twickenham	12 Feb 2011
6	44	Ireland	54–10	Wales	Lansdowne Road	3 Feb 2002
7	43	France	56–13	Italy	Rome	19 Mar 2005
8	42	France	50–8	Italy	Rome	21 Mar 2009
9	41	England	50–9	Italy	Rome	15 Feb 2004
10	40	England	46–6	Ireland	Lansdowne Road	15 Feb 1997
=	40	England	43–3	Scotland	Twickenham	3 Mar 2001
=	40	England	50–10	Wales	Twickenham	22 Mar 2002

THE SCOREBOARD TELLS ONLY HALF THE STORY

The history books record that Scotland beat Wales by four goals to nil in the two sides' Home Nations Championship match at Raeburn Place in Edinburgh on 26 February 1887, but few of them describe the devastating manner of their victory. Scotland scored a tournament record 12 tries in the match (five of them by George Lindsay, another all-time tournament record), of which only four were converted. In modern scoring terms, the Scots would have run out 68–0 winners.

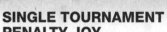

ABOVE: Iain Balshaw scored two of England's ten tries during their record-breaking 80–23 win over Italy at Twickenham in February 2001.

LEFT: Dan Parks nails one of Scotland's record-equalling five drop goals during the 2010 Six Nations Championship. This one came against Wales during the Scots' 31–24 defeat at the Millennium Stadium, Cardiff.

SIX NATIONS DROP GOAL BITS & PIECES

France are the Five/Six Nations drop goal kings, having nailed a record 109 attempts in 339 matches since 1910. In 1967, Les Bleus also became the first team to drop five goals in one tournament, a record since equalled by Italy in 2000, Wales in 2001, England in 2003 and Scotland in 2010. The Six Nations record in a match is three, against Scotland, by Italy in 2000 and Wales in 2001.

SINGLE TOURNAMENT PENALTY JOY

The record for the most penalty kicks scored by a team in a single tournament is 20, set by Ireland in 2001 (the men in green finished second to England on points difference) and equalled by France the following year (as *Les Bleus* helped themselves to the seventh grand slam in their history). The record for the most successful penalty attempts in a match is seven, a feat achieved on seven occasions.

THE MOST POROUS DEFENCE

No side in the competition's history has conceded more points than Scotland. The Scots have leaked 5,372 points in 439 matches since the inaugural Home Nations Championship in 1882–83 – an average of 12.24 points per match.

TRY-SCORING RECORDS

THE FLYING SCOTSMAN STEAMS INTO THE RECORD BOOKS

Born in Australia and raised in New Zealand, Ian Smith was educated in England (at Winchester College and Oxford University, where he first played rugby) and eventually played for Scotland (he qualified through relatives in the Scottish Borders). Scotland were delighted to secure his services. Nicknamed the 'Flying Scotsman', he made his debut in 1924, helped Scotland to their first grand slam in 1925 (during which he equalled Cyril Rowe's record of most tries in one tournament – 8) and was a mainstay of the Scotland side until 1933. He stands second on the all-time tournament try-scoring list with 24 (behind Ireland's Brian O'Driscoll) and shares the record (with O'Driscoll) for most tries scored in home matches (15).

A SPECIAL DAY FOR THE HEWITTS

Ireland's Home Nations Championship match against Wales at Cardiff on 8 March 1924 was one of the most memorable in the tournament's history – and particularly for the Hewitt family. That day, two brothers, 18-year-old Tom Hewitt (on the wing) and his younger brother Frank (at fly-half), both made their international debuts and both scored a try as Ireland edged to a slender 13–10 victory. During the match, Frank, at 17 years 156 days, had become not only the youngest-ever player to appear in the tournament but also the youngest-ever player to score a Six Nations try.

BELOW: Ireland's Brian O'Driscoll hunts down the tryline en route to becoming the Six Nations' all-time leading try-scorer.

DREAM DEBUT FOR LLEWELLYN

A winger with the unfashionable second-tier Welsh club Llwynpia, Willie Llewellyn launched what would become one of the great careers of Wales's greatest era in spectacular style. On 7 January 1899, against England at Swansea, he scored four tries – a record for a player making their Six Nations debut – as Wales cruised to a convincing 26–3 victory. Llewellyn went on to make a further 19 appearances for Wales and ended his international career in 1905 having scored 16 tries for his country – to stand 12th on Wales's all-time try-scoring list.

LEFT: Shane Williams scored 14 tries in 22 Six Nations Championship appearances for Wales at Cardiff's Millennium Stadium – record for one player at signle ground.

THERE'S NO PLACE LIKE HOME FOR SHANE WILLIAMS

Shane Williams made his international debut when he came on as a replacement for Wales during their opening 2000 Six Nations match against France at the Millennium Stadium on 5 February 2000 (the first Six Nations match ever played at the venue) and ended up on the losing side, as France romped to a 36–3 victory. But disappointments at the new home of Welsh rugby have been few and far between for the wing wizard: he went on to score 14 tries in 22 matches there – a Six Nations record for a player at a single ground – before bowing out after the 2011 tournament.

NO AWAY-DAY BLUES FOR HICKIE

No player has enjoyed as much try-scoring success in away matches in the Six Nations Championship as Ireland's Denis Hickie. The Leinster wing crossed the line 11 times in 18 away matches for Ireland between 1997 and 2007 – an all-time championship record.

MOST TRIES: TOP TEN

Pos	Tries	Player (Country, Span)
1	25	Brian O'Driscoll (Ireland, 2000–11)
2	24	Ian Smith (Scotland, 1924–33)
3	22	Shane Williams (Wales, 2000–11)
4	18	Gareth Edwards (Wales, 1967–78)
=	18	Cyril Lowe (England, 1913–23)
=	18	Rory Underwood (England, 1984–96)
7	16	Ben Cohen (England, 2000–06)
=	16	Gerald Davies (Wales, 1967–78)
=	16	Ken Jones (Wales, 1947–57)
=	16	Willie Llewellyn (Wales, 1899–1905)

AITKEN HAULS SCOTLAND OVER FIRST GRAND SLAM HURDLE

It may have been the only try of his seven-year, 24-match international career, but when the Scotland captain crashed over the line against Wales at Cardiff Arms Park on 21 January 1984, it was a crucial and record-breaking moment: aged 36 years 60 days, Jim Aitken had become the oldest try-scorer in the tournament's history but, more importantly, his try secured Scotland's first victory (15–9) of a season that would end with the Scots celebrating grand slam success for the first time since 1925.

RIGHT: Scotland captain Jim Aitken (sitting) receives the praise from teammates John Rutherford (left) and David Leslie (right), with Finlay Calder looking on, after scoring a match-winning try against Wales at Cardiff Arms Park in January 1984.

TOP TRY-SCORING CAPTAIN

The leading Ireland player of his generation (and arguably the best of all time), Brian O'Driscoll has captained Ireland a record 40 times in Six Nations Championship matches between 2003 and 2011, and to great effect, too: his 14 tries as captain – out of a total of 25 (to stand top of the tournament's all-time try-scoring list) – are the most by a captain in the competition's history.

MAKING AN IMPACT FROM THE BENCH

Tom Shanklin (Wales) holds the record for the most Six Nations Championship tries by a replacement with three in five appearances between 2003 and 2007. The Wales centre holds another record, too: on 22 February 2004, against Ireland at Lansdowne Road, he became only the second replacement in the tournament's history to score two tries in a match. The only other player to achieve the feat is another Welshman: Mike Rayer, against Scotland at Cardiff on 15 January 1994.

THE LONGEST TRYLESS STREAK

Jason Leonard enjoyed numerous champagne moments during his illustrious 13-year Six Nations Championship career with England – with four grand slams (1991, 1992, 1995 and 2003) and eight triple crowns (1991, 1992, 1995, 1996, 1997, 1998, 2002 and 2003) but, in 54 matches in the championship between 1991 and 2004, he never had the satisfaction of scoring a try. It is the most matches played without scoring a try in the tournament's history.

RIGHT: Emile Ntamack did his bit, scoring a hat-trick of tries, but it was not enough when France entertained Wales at the Stade de France in March 1999. Although outscored four tries to three, Wales prevailed 34–33.

HOME/FIVE/SIX NATIONS CHAMPIONSHIP ALL-TIME LEADING TRY-SCORERS: BY POSITION

Position	Player (Country, Span)	Tries
Full-back	Serge Blanco (France, 1983–91)	11
Winger	Ian Smith (Scotland, 1924–33)	24
Centre	Brian O'Driscoll (Ireland, 2000–11)	25
Fly-half	Ronan O'Gara (Ireland, 2000–11)	8
Scrum-half	Gareth Edwards (Wales, 1967–78)	18
No.8	Imanol Harinordoquy (France, 2002–11)	8
Flanker	Jim McCarthy (Ireland, 1948–55)	8
	Cherry Pillman (England, 1910–14)	8
Lock	Jack Whitfield (Wales, 1920–24)	5
Prop	Bruno Brown (England, 1911–22)	4
	Marco Castrogiovanni (Italy, 2004–11)	4
	Robert Paparemborde (France, 1976–83)	4
Hooker	Eric Evans (England, 1950–58)	5
	Keith Wood (Ireland, 1995–2002)	5

MOST TRIES IN A LOSING CAUSE

The record for the most tries by a player whose team has gone on to lose the match is three, achieved by three players: Robert Montgomery (Ireland) against Wales at Birkenhead on 12 March 1887; Howard Marshall (England) against Wales at Cardiff on 7 January 1893; and Emile Ntamack (France) against Wales at the Stade de France, Paris, on 6 March 1999.

POINTS-SCORING RECORDS

THE TOURNAMENT'S FIRST POINTS-SCORER

It may not have been the most convincing kicking display in the championship's illustrious history, but when England's Welsh-born three-quarter Arthur Evanson, making his international debut, slotted two conversions in six attempts during England's 2–0 victory over Wales at Swansea on 16 December 1882 (the competition's inaugural match), he became the tournament's first-ever points-scorer.

MOST POINTS IN A LOSING CAUSE

Ireland's sensational 27–25 Six Nations victory over France at the Stade de France, Paris, on 19 March 2000 is best remembered as the match in which Brian O'Driscoll scored a hat-trick of tries to announce himself to the rugby world as a player blessed with a special talent. For France fly-half Gerald Merceron, however, the match was a bitter-sweet affair: he scored 20 points (six penalties and a conversion) but still ended up on the losing side – a Six Nations Championship record.

MOST POINTS: TOP TEN

Pos	Points	Player (Country, Span)
1	551	Ronan O'Gara (Ireland, 2000–11)
2	546	Jonny Wilkinson (England, 1998–2011)
3	467	Stephen Jones (Wales, 2000–11)
4	406	Neil Jenkins (Wales, 1991–2001)
5	403	Chris Paterson (Scotland, 2000–11)
6	288	Gavin Hastings (Scotland, 1986–95)
7	270	David Humphreys (Ireland, 1996–2005)
8	232	Paul Grayson (England, 1996–2004)
9	207	Michael Kiernan (Ireland, 1982–91)
10	201	Andy Irvine (Scotland, 1973–82)

SERIAL RECORD-BREAKER

Jonny Wilkinson embarked on what would become one of the most stellar careers in international rugby history when, on 4 April 1998, aged 18 years 314 days, he came on as a replacement for England during their Five Nations Championship victory over Ireland (35–17) at Twickenham. And, despite missing three seasons (2004–06) through injury, the mercurial fly-half went on to break numerous championship records. He leads the way for: the most points in a tournament (89 in 2001); the most points in a single match (35, against Italy at Twickenham on 17 February 2001); the most conversions in a match (9, against Italy at Twickenham on 17 February 2001); the most points at a single ground (329 in 22 matches at Twickenham); the most conversions (89); and the most drop goals (11); and stands second (behind Ronan O'Gara on the tournament's all-time points-scoring list (with 546 points compared to O'Gara's 551).

CAPTAIN KICKS HIS WAY INTO THE RECORD BOOKS

A flawless kicking display from Scotland captain Chris Paterson in the Scots' 2007 Six Nations match against Wales at Murrayfield secured his side a surprise 21–9 victory and him a place in the record books. The long-serving winger's 21 points in the match (thanks to seven successful penalty kicks) is an all-time record for a captain in a Six Nations fixture.

TOP-SCORING REPLACEMENTS

David Humphreys spent the latter stages of his international career locked in a battle with up-and-coming fly-half Ronan O'Gara for Ireland's No.10 shirt, with one of the two starting the match only, invariably, to be replaced by the other. Consequently both players racked up a significant number of replacement appearances. The pair share the record for the most points in Six Nations matches as a replacement (30) and Humphreys holds the record for the most points scored in a single Six Nations match by a replacement – 14 (one try, three conversions and a penalty), against Scotland at Lansdowne Road on 19 February 2000.

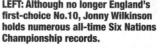

LEFT: Although no longer England's first-choice No.10, Jonny Wilkinson holds numerous all-time Six Nations Championship records.

LEFT: Ireland's Ronan O'Gara tops the Five/Six Nations Championship's all-time points-scoring list with 551 in 56 matches.

O'GARA: SIX NATIONS POINT-SCORING KING

No player has scored more points in Six Nations Championship matches than Ronan O'Gara. The Ireland fly-half, who also holds the all-time tournament record for kicking the most penalties (107) has amassed 551 points in 56 Six Nations Championship matches between 2000 and 2011. O'Gara has 10 tries, 81 conversions and six drop goals to his name.

MOST DROP GOALS IN A MATCH

The record for the most drop goals in a Six Nations match is three, a feat achieved by four players: Pierre Albaladejo (France) against Ireland at Colombes, Paris, on 9 April 1960; Jean-Patrick Lescarboura (France) against England at Twickenham on 2 February 1985; Diego Dominguez (Italy) against Scotland at Rome on 5 February 2000; and Neil Jenkins (Wales) against Scotland at Murrayfield on 17 February 2001.

JARRETT'S DAY IN THE CARDIFF SUN

Brought into the Welsh line-up for the final match (against England at Cardiff) of what had been a disastrous 1967 Five Nations campaign for Wales – they had lost their first three matches – Keith Jarrett enjoyed a day to remember. The Newport full-back scored 19 points (one try, five conversions and two penalties) – the most by a debutant in the tournament's history – to help Wales to a morale-boosting 34–21 victory. Jarrett went on to win a further nine caps for his country before switching to rugby league (with Barrow) in 1969.

MOST PENALTIES IN A MATCH

The record for the most penalties in a Six Nations match is seven, a feat achieved by six players: Simon Hodgkinson (England) against Wales at Cardiff on 19 January 1991; Rob Andrew (England) against Scotland at Twickenham on 18 March 1995; Jonny Wilkinson (England) against France at Twickenham on 20 March 1999; Neil Jenkins (Wales) against Italy at the Millennium Stadium, Cardiff, on 19 February 2000; Gerald Merceron (France) against Italy at the Stade de France, Paris, on 2 February 2002; and Chris Paterson (Scotland) against Wales at Murrayfield on 10 February 2007.

LEFT: Wales's Neil Jenkins (10, playing against Scotland in 2001), is one of only four players to have dropped three goals in a Six Nations Championship match

ABOVE: Chris Paterson equalled the Six Nations Championship record by kicking seven penalties against Wales in Scotland's 21–9 victory at Murrayfield in 2010.

APPEARANCE RECORDS

ONE OF IRELAND'S ALL-TIME GREATS

Born and raised in Belfast and educated at Cambridge University, Mike Gibson is many critics' choice as the finest Irish player of all time (until Brian O'Driscoll came along, that is). A player of great versatility – he won caps in four different positions in his country's backline – he made his debut (at fly-half) during a 18–5 Five Nations defeat of England at Twickenham on 8 February 1964. With a professional approach to the game years before the concept appeared on world rugby's radar, his quick hands, innate ability to break an opponent's backline and tearaway defensive tactics soon marked him out as a special talent. Over a 15-year career that included five tours with the British Lions, he represented Ireland on 69 occasions – a record that lasted until February 1995 – and his record for most appearances in the Five/Six Nations Championship, 56 between 1964 and 1979, was matched by compatriot Ronan O'Gara in 2011.

THAT RECORD-BREAKING LOSING FEELING

A veteran of 46 matches in the Six Nations Championship (who has played in every campaign for Italy since they joined the competition in 2000), prop Salvatore Perugini has the unfortunate distinction of having appeared on the losing side more than any other player in the Six Nations – 39 times.

VICTORY A COMMON EXPERIENCE FOR ENGLAND'S LEONARD

No player has enjoyed the sweet taste of Six Nations success on more occasions than England's most capped player, Jason Leonard. The long-serving World Cup-winning prop forward found himself on the winning side 44 times in 54 Six Nations matches between 1991 and 2004.

FAMILIAR FOES

Two players hold the record for the most Six Nations appearances against a single opponent (12): prop Jason Leonard (for England against Wales between 1991 and 2003) and centre Philippe Sella (for France against Wales between 1983 and 1995).

MOST APPEARANCES: TOP TEN

Pos	Caps	Player (Country, Span)
1	56	Mike Gibson (Ireland, 1964–79)
=	56	Ronan O'Gara (Ireland, 2000–11)
3	55	Brian O'Driscoll (Ireland, 2000–11)
4	54	John Hayes (Ireland, 2000–10)
=	54	Jason Leonard (England, 1991–2004)
6	53	Willie-John McBride (Ireland, 1962–75)
=	53	Chris Paterson (Scotland, 2000–11)
8	51	Martyn Williams (Wales, 1998–2010)
9	50	Stephen Jones (Wales, 2000–11)
=	50	Philippe Sella (France, 1983–95)
=	50	Rory Underwood (England, 1984–96)

BELOW: In his 14-season career, England prop Jason Leonard experienced more Home/Five/Six Nations Championship victories (44) than any other player in the history of the competition.

LEFT: A legendary figure in Irish rugby history, and considered among the finest players his country has ever produced, Mike Gibson made a joint-record 56 appearances in the Five Nations Championship.

MOST APPEARANCES: BY POSITION

Position	Player (Country, Span)	Appearances
Full-back	Tom Kiernan (Ireland, 1960–73)	44
	J.P.R. Williams (Wales, 1969–81)	44
Winger	Rory Underwood (England, 1984–96)	50
Centre	Brian O'Driscoll (Ireland, 2000–11)	55
Fly-half	Stephen Jones (Wales, 2000–11)	47
Scrum-half	Gareth Edwards (Wales, 1967–78)	45
No.8	Mervyn Davies (Wales, 1969–76)	31
	Willie Duggan (Ireland, 1975–84)	31
Flanker	Fergus Slattery (Ireland, 1970–84)	49
Lock	Willie-John McBride (Ireland, 1962–75)	53
Prop	John Hayes (Ireland, 2000–10)	54
	Jason Leonard (England, 1991–2004)	54
Hooker	Colin Deans (Scotland, 1978–87)	37

THERE'S NO PLACE LIKE HOME FOR SCOT CHRIS PATERSON

One of only ten players to have contested 50 or more Six Nations matches, and standing at fifth in the Championship's all-time points-scoring list (with 392), Scotland's long-serving utility back Chris Paterson holds the unusual distinction of of having played more Six Nations matches at one ground than any other player – 27 at Murrayfield between 2000 and 2011.

THE TOURNAMENT'S OLDEST DEBUTANT

His exact date of birth may remain unknown (it was in 1894), but when Frederick Gilbert made his debut for England in their Five Nations Championship match against Wales at Twickenham on 20 January 1923, he became the first, and to date only, 39-year-old to play in the competition (England won the match 7–3). The full-back made only one further appearance for England, against Ireland later that season.

RIGHT: Philippe Sella (white shirt) holds the France record for most Five/Six Nations Championship appearances with 50.

MOST APPEARANCES: BY COUNTRY

Country	Player (Span)	Appearances
England	Jason Leonard (1991–2004)	54
France	Philippe Sella (1983–95)	50
Ireland	Colin Gibson (1964–79)	56
	Ronan O'Gara (2000–2011)	56
Italy	Mirco Bergamasco (2000–11)	46
	Salvatore Perugini (2000–11)	46
Scotland	Chris Paterson (2000–10)	50
Wales	Martyn Williams (1998–2010)	51

LEFT: Scotland's Chris Paterson holds the distinction of having played the most Six Nations matches at one ground, with 27 appearances at Murrayfield.

SUPER SUB GRIMES SETS ALL-TIME MARK

Stuart Grimes's first four appearances for Scotland in the Six Nations Championship (his first coming against Ireland at Lansdowne Road on 7 February 1998) were as a replacement. The lock went on to make 15 Six Nations appearances from the bench – an all-time tournament record – before he bowed out of international rugby in 2005.

ONE-MATCH WONDERS

Of the 4,683 players to have appeared in the Six Nations Championship in 130 years of competition, 930 of them – a surprising 19.86 per cent – only ever appeared in one match.

THE RED MIST RISES IN PARIS

England's Five Nations Championship match against France at the Parc des Princes in Paris on 15 February 1992 always promised to be a fractious affair. Barely four months had passed since England had out-muscled and out-fought the French to win a tense Rugby World Cup quarter-final at the same venue, and France were out to avenge the defeat. They failed in their mission and, as the clock ticked down, their frustration grew, they imploded, with both Gregoire Lascube and Vincent Moscato being shown red cards. It remains the only instance in the tournament's history in which a team has had two players sent off in a match. For the record, England went on to win 31–13 to secure their second grand slam in two years.

TOURNAMENT RED CARDS

Player	Team	Opponent	Venue	Date
Willie Duggan	Ireland	Wales	Cardiff	15 Jan 1977
Geoff Wheel	Wales	Ireland	Cardiff	15 Jan 1977
Paul Ringer	Wales	England	Twickenham	16 Feb 1980
Jean-Pierre Garuet-Lempirou	France	Ireland	Parc des Princes	21 Jan 1984
Kevin Moseley	Wales	France	Cardiff	20 Jan 1990
Alain Carminati	France	Scotland	Murrayfield	17 Feb 1990
Gregoire Lascube	France	England	Parc des Princes	15 Feb 1992
Vincent Moscato	France	England	Parc des Princes	15 Feb 1992
John Davies	Wales	England	Cardiff	18 Feb 1995
Walter Cristofoletto	Italy	France	Stade de France	1 Apr 2000
Alessandro Troncon	Italy	Ireland	Rome	3 Feb 2001
Scott Murray	Scotland	Wales	Millennium Stadium	12 Feb 2006

CAPTAIN FANTASTIC

Not only is Brian O'Driscoll the longest-serving captain in Six Nations history (having led Ireland on a record 40 occasions in the championship), he is also the tournament's most successful leader: Ireland have recorded 31 victories under his charge between 2003 and 2011 – the most wins by a team under a single captain. Most notably, O'Driscoll led Ireland to grand-slam success in 2009, the country's first since 1948.

BELOW: Irish referee Stephen Hilditch made Six Nations history when he sent off France's Gregoire Lascube and Vincent Moscato during Les Bleus' 1992 clash against England at the Parc des Princes, Paris.

ABOVE: One of the Six Nations Championship's stand-out players for more than a decade, Brian O'Driscoll has led Ireland a record 40 times in the tournament.

FAMILIAR FOES

The Six Nations Championship's most contested fixture is that between Ireland and Scotland. The two countries met for the first time in Belfast on 19 February 1883 (a match Scotland won by one goal to nil) and have gone on to contest the fixture on 117 occasions, with Scotland recording 58 wins to Ireland's 54, with five draws.

REDUCING THE CHANCE OF VICTORY

Beware the yellow card! It has been shown to players on 113 occasions in the Six Nations Championship since its introduction in 2000 and statistics reveal that, of teams with a player yellow-carded, only 30.90 per cent have gone on to record a victory – a success rate of less than one in three.

THE TOURNAMENT'S FIRST RED CARDS

In nearly 100 years of Six Nations Championship matches (in all its guises) there had been tussles, scuffles, full-blown fights and limitless bad behaviour that raised many an eyebrow, but no player had ever been shown a red card. That all changed on 15 January 1977 at Cardiff Arms Park when, after the match had descended into a mass brawl, Scottish referee Norman Sansom dismissed Wales's Geoff Wheel and Willie Duggan (Ireland) for fighting. For the record Wales went on to win the fractious 14-a-side encounter 25–9.

MOST RED CARDS (BY TEAM)

The record for the most red cards received by a team in all Six Nations Championship matches over the years is four, shared by two teams. The Wales Hall of Shame has Geoff Wheel, against Ireland in 1977, Paul Ringer, against England in 1980, Kevin Moseley against France in 1990, and John Davies against England in 1995. France's men to see red are Jean-Pierre Gauret-Lempirou, against Ireland in 1984, Alain Carminati, against Scotland in 1990, and Gregoire Lascube and Vincent Moscato, both against England in 1992.

ABOVE: Hard-nosed hooker Vincent Moscate is one of four Frenchman to have seen red in a Six Nations Championship match – an unwanted all-time tournament record Les Bleus share with Wales.

MOST YELLOW CARDS

Pos	Yellow	Country
1	34	Italy
2	23	Scotland
3	21	Wales
4	16	England
5	10	Ireland
6	9	France

LEFT: When Scott Quinnell recieved the first yellow card in Six Nations Championship history, it added to a disappointing day for Wales as they were crushed 36–3 by France at the Millennium Stadium, Cardiff in February 2000.

HISTORY-MAKING MOMENT ON A DAY TO FORGET FOR SORRY WALES

The first-ever Six Nations Championship match to be played at the new Millennium Stadium in Cardiff – Wales against France on 5 February 2000 – ended in disaster for the home side. Wales opened the scoring through a Neil Jenkins penalty, but things went rapidly downhill for the home side from there. France rallied to lead 9–3 at half-time and were at their rampaging best in the second half. As Welsh indiscipline grew under the mounting pressure, Scott Quinnell was shown a yellow card by referee Chris White – becoming the first player in history to suffer the penalty – and France went on to record a resounding 36–3 victory.

MOST YELLOW CARDS RECEIVED

The all-time record for the most yellow cards received by a player in Six Nations Championship matches is three, achieved by six players: Mauro Bergamasco (Italy), Carlo Checchinato (Italy), Danny Grewcock (England), Scott Quinnell (Wales), Simon Taylor (Scotland) and Martyn Williams (Wales).

MOST YELLOW CARDS AND GONE ON TO WIN THE MATCH

The most yellow cards given to a team that has then gone on to win the match is two, a feat that have been achieved by three teams on four occasions: France (who lost Jean Daude and Emile Ntamack for ten-minute spells but still beat Scotland 28–16 at Murrayfield on 4 March 2000); Wales – the only team to achieve the feat twice (Mike Phillips and Martyn Williams being yellow-carded but going on to beat Ireland 16–12 at Croke Park, Dublin, on 8 March 2008, and in the 2011 Championship, losing Lee Brne and Bradley Davies against Scotland at Murrayfield, but still going on to record a comfortable 24–6 victory); and England (who saw Shane Geraghty and James Haskell sent to the sin bin but still went on to register a 36–11 victory over Italy at Twickenham on 7 February 2009).

A GENEROUS SIX NATIONS HOST

No stadium has hosted more Six Nations Championship matches than Twickenham. The south-west London stadium has hosted 181 matches in the tournament since 1910.

TRI-NATIONS

Considered the toughest competition in world rugby, the annual Tri-Nations championship – contested between the three giants of southern hemisphere rugby, Australia, New Zealand and South Africa – was staged for the first time in 1996 as the game embarked on a new era of professionalism. New Zealand have been the tournament's dominant team, winning the championship on ten occasions, while both South Africa and Australia have claimed the title three times.

BELOW: Australia's players celebrate winning the 2011 Tri-Nations Championship, the third time the Wallabies had triumphed, but their first since 2001.

OVERALL RECORD (1996–2010)

Team	P	W	L	D	%	For	Aga	Diff	Tries	Conv	Pens	Drop
Australia	72	29	42	1	40.97	1531	1721	−190	152	102	180	9
New Zealand	72	50	22	0	69.44	1936	1395	+541	186	128	242	8
South Africa	72	28	43	1	39.58	1480	1831	−351	134	93	190	18

LEFT: New Zealand celebrate victory in the inaugural Tri-Nations Championship in 1996. the All Blacks have gone on to collect nine futher titles and have set a whole host of records along the way.

DOMINANT ALL BLACKS SET WHOLE HOST OF RECORDS

New Zealand have been the dominant team since the Tri-Nations' inception in 1996. They won the tournament's first-ever match (thumping Australia 43–6 in Wellington on 6 July 1996) and went on to win their remaining three matches to claim the inaugural title with a 100 per cent record. It set the tone for things to come. New Zealand have claimed ten titles, registered a record 50 wins (with a winning percentage of 69.44) and also hold the all-time competition records for: the most tries (186), the most points scored (1936), the best points difference (+541) and kicking the most conversions (128).

FIRST TRI-NATIONS TITLE FOR THE SPRINGBOKS

Having endured miserable campaigns in the 1996 and 1997 Tri-Nations championships (winning only two of their eight matches), reigning world champions South Africa finally hit their stride in the tournament in 1998. They opened their account with a hard-fought victory over Australia in Perth (14–3), beat New Zealand in Wellington (13–3, to hand a first-ever defeat to the All Blacks in the competition) and battled to their first-ever Tri-Nations title with home wins over New Zealand (24–23 at Durban) and Australia (29–15 at Johannesburg).

RIGHT: South Africa, the reigning world champions at the time, collected the first of their three Tri-Nations titles in 1998.

STALEMATE IN SUBIACO

The third round of matches in the 2001 Tri-Nations championship saw defending champions Australia meet South Africa at the Subiaco Oval in Perth, with both sides – each on a record of won one, lost one – desperate to register a victory. Neither side got their wish: with the scores level at 14–14 as the match entered its dying moments, Australia were awarded a penalty within kicking range, but the Wallabies missed and the final whistle blew. It is the only match in Tri-Nations history to have ended in a draw.

TRI-NATIONS WINNERS

1996	New Zealand
1997	New Zealand
1998	South Africa
1999	New Zealand
2000	Australia
2001	Australia
2002	New Zealand
2003	New Zealand
2004	South Africa
2005	New Zealand
2006	New Zealand
2007	New Zealand
2008	New Zealand
2009	South Africa
2010	New Zealand
2011	Australia

HEAD-TO-HEADS: WINS/DEFEATS/DRAWS
Tri-Nations only

	Australia	New Zealand	South Africa
Australia	X	11/25/0	18/17/1
New Zealand	25/11/0	X	25/11/0
South Africa	17/18/1	11/25/0	X

A GOLDEN AGE FOR THE WALLABIES

Australia did not enjoy the best of starts to life in the Tri-Nations, finishing bottom in 1996 and 1997, but they recorded two wins for the first time in 1998, repeated the feat in 1999 (including a morale-boosting 28–7 victory in their final match against champions New Zealand) and used their improved performances as a platform from which to launch the most successful period in their history. They won the Rugby World Cup (for the second time) later that year and carried that form into the 2000 Tri-Nations, winning three and losing one of their matches to claim the title for the first time. They defended their crown the following year thanks to a pulsating 29–26 final-match win against New Zealand in Sydney. They would have to endure a ten-year wait before collecting a third title.

ALL BLACKS BOUNCE BACK IN STYLE

Having suffered the ignominy of surrendering the Tri-Nations crown for the first time in four years in 2009 (to South Africa), New Zealand bounced back with considerable relish in 2010. They won all six matches – becoming the first team to do so in the tournament's expanded six-match format, used for the first time in 2006 and permanently from 2008 – and scored an all-time tournament record 184 points to reclaim their crown.

ABOVE: Back-to-back tournament wins in 2000 and 2001 marked a zenith in Australia's Tri-Nations form; and then came a ten-year wait for a third crown.

AUSTRALIA RETURN TO WINNING WAYS

If back-to-back crowns in 2000 and 2001 signified a Tri-Nations golden era for Australia, then the nine tournaments that followed were the Wallabies' dark ages: 14 wins from 41 matches meant they could only watch on with envy as New Zealand and South Africa took the spoils. But that all changed in 2011: an impressive 39–20 opening win against South Africa may have been followed by a 30–14 defeat to New Zealand, but the Wallabies rallied to win their final two matches.

MOST POROUS DEFENCE

South Africa hold the unwelcome distinction of having conceded more points than any other team in Tri-Nations history (1,831 in 72 matches – an average of 25.43 per match), compared to Australia's 1,721 and New Zealand's 1,395. They also hold the record for having conceded the most points in a single tournament (194 in six matches in 2010 – an average of 32.33 per match).

BELOW: South Africa's Joe van Niekerk dives over Australia's line to score the Springboks' second try in their title-clinching 23–19 win in 2004.

A CAMPAIGN TO FORGET FOR SORRY SOUTH AFRICA

South Africa embarked on the defence of their Tri-Nations title in 1999 with a disappointing 28–0 defeat to New Zealand in Christchurch and, a week later, crashed 32–6 to Australia in Brisbane. Things barely improved for the Springboks at home when New Zealand beat them 34–18 in Pretoria, but at least they recorded a face-saving victory in their final match of the campaign against Australia in Cape Town (10–9). However, the victory did not prevent them from finishing bottom of the table and, to compound their misery, their tournament haul of 34 points is the lowest in Tri-Nations history.

SPRINGBOKS RALLY TO CLAIM THRILLING TRI-NATIONS CROWN

The ninth edition of the Tri-Nations (in 2004) turned out to be a cliffhanger. New Zealand opened up with two straight home victories (16–7 against Australia in Wellington and 23–21 against South Africa in Christchurch) to head the table. Then Australia won both of their home matches (23–18 against New Zealand at Sydney and 30–26 against South Africa in Perth). The state of play was simple: victory for either Australia or New Zealand in their final match (away to South Africa) would virtually guarantee them the title; the Springboks, on the other hand, had to win both of their remaining home matches to stand any chance of lifting the crown. They started well, beating New Zealand in Johannesburg (40–26), and then pipped Australia in a pulsating winner-takes-all showdown at Kings Park, Durban (23–19), to win the most closely fought Tri-Nations in history.

WALLABIES CUT LOOSE IN BRISBANE

A week after losing 32–12 to New Zealand in Christchurch in their opening match, it seemed as though Australia had got their 2006 Tri-Nations campaign back on track in spectacular fashion against South Africa at Brisbane, running in six tries en route to a thumping 49–0 win to set the record for the biggest victory (by points difference) in the tournament's history. The Wallabies went on to register only one further win, however, and finished second in the final table behind the All Blacks.

ABOVE: Matt Giteau dives over the line to score one of Australia's six tries in the Wallabies' championship-record 49–0 victory over South Africa in the 2006 Tri-Nations.

FORTRESS EDEN PARK

New Zealand have a 100 per cent record at Eden Park, Auckland, in Tri-Nations matches: they have won all 11 of the fixtures they have played there – the most matches won by a country at a single ground in the competition's history. The other grounds where a team has a 100 per cent record are those that have hosted only one Tri-Nations fixture: Australia, at the Sydney Football Stadium (where they beat South Africa 21–16 on 13 July 1996); Australia, at the Woolloongabba (the Test cricket ground), Brisbane (where they beat South Africa 38–27 on 27 July 2002); and South Africa at Olympic Park, Rustenberg (where they beat New Zealand 21–20 on 2 September 2006). Given their overall record it is not surprising that New Zealand also hold the records for most home wins in the Tri-Nations (30) and most away wins (20, compared to seven for Australia and six for South Africa).

BIGGEST MARGINS OF VICTORY: TOP TEN

Pos	Winner	Score	Opponent	Venue	Date
1	Australia	49–0	South Africa	Brisbane	15 Jul 2006
2	South Africa	53–8	Australia	Johannesburg	30 Aug 2008
3	South Africa	61–22	Australia	Pretoria	23 Aug 1997
4	New Zealand	43–6	Australia	Wellington	6 Jul 1996
5	New Zealand	52–16	South Africa	Pretoria	19 Jul 2003
6	New Zealand	40–7	South Africa	Wellington	30 Jul 2011
7	New Zealand	50–21	Australia	Sydney	26 Jul 2003
=	New Zealand	39–10	Australia	Auckland	2 Aug 2008
9	New Zealand	28–0	South Africa	Dunedin	10 Jul 1999
10	New Zealand	33–6	South Africa	Christchurch	14 Jul 2007
=	New Zealand	33–6	Australia	Wellington	19 Sep 2009

SPRINGBOKS SET TRY-SCORING MARK

South Africa are not renowned for being one of world rugby's most free-scoring sides, having settled on an established game plan over the years based more around forward aggression and brute physical power than finesse, so it may come as something of a surprise to learn that the Springboks hold the all-time record for the most tries scored by a team in a Tri-Nations match: eight, which they have achieved on two occasions (both against Australia) – at Pretoria on 23 August 1997 (61–22) and at Johannesburg on 30 August 2008 (53–8).

ABOVE: Stephen Larkham (15, middle) and Australia found themsleves on the back foot against South Africa in Pretoria in the 1997 Tri-Nations. The Springboks romped to a 61–22 victory, scoring a competition joint-record eight tries in the process, Percy Montgomery (right) grabbing two of them. The other player is centre André Snyman.

ZERO POINTS SCORED IN A GAME

Team	Score	Opponent	Venue	Date
South Africa	0–28	New Zealand	Dunedin	10 Jul 1999
South Africa	0–49	Australia	Brisbane	15 Jul 2006
New Zealand	0–19	South Africa	Cape Town	16 Aug 2008

TRY-SCORING HIGHS AND LOWS

New Zealand's impressive march to the 2010 Tri-Nations crown, during which they won all six of their matches, saw them cross the try-line on 22 occasions to set an all-time tournament record. South Africa hold the unwanted record for the fewest tries scored in a single Tri-Nations campaign: in 2001, admittedly a low try-scoring year, they crossed the line just twice in four matches and, not surprisingly, finished the tournament bottom of the table.

LOWEST TRI-NATIONS TRY COUNT

Although the 2001 Tri-Nations championship – won by Australia following their pulsating final-match victory over New Zealand in Sydney (29–16) – may have been one of the most exciting campaigns of recent times, it will not be remembered for the participants' try-scoring exploits: the three teams scored only 13 tries in the tournament's six matches – the fewest in Tri-Nations history.

ONE-POINT WINNING MARGIN

Team	Score	Opponent	Venue	Date
South Africa	14–13	Australia	Perth	18 Jul 1998
South Africa	24–23	New Zealand	Durban	15 Aug 1998
South Africa	10–9	Australia	Cape Town	14 Aug 1999
Australia	24–23	New Zealand	Wellington	5 Aug 2000
Australia	19–18	South Africa	Durban	26 Aug 2000
South Africa	21–20	New Zealand	Rustenberg	2 Sep 2006
New Zealand	19–18	Australia	Sydney	22 Aug 2009
New Zealand	23–22	Australia	Sydney	11 Sep 2010

MOST DROP GOALS

Overall:	18	South Africa
Match:	2	South Africa v New Zealand, Johannesburg, 19 July 1997
		South Africa v Australia, Pretoria, 30 July 2005
		South Africa v Australia, Cape Town, 16 June 2007
Tournament:	4	South Africa in 2005

MOST PENALTIES

Overall:	242	New Zealand
Match:	9	New Zealand v Australia, Auckland, 24 July 1999
Tournament:	29	South Africa in 2009

MOST CONVERSIONS

Overall:	128	New Zealand
Match:	6	South Africa v Australia, Pretoria, 23 August 1997
Tournament:	14	South Africa in 1997
		New Zealand in 2006

VINTAGE CULLEN SETS ALL-TIME TRY-SCORING MARK

Considered in some quarters as the finest full-back in New Zealand's distinguished history, and nicknamed the 'Paekakariki Express' for his scintillating speed, Christian Cullen was international rugby's most dazzling player for a period in the late 1990s and early 2000s. And in the 2000 Tri-Nations, despite the fact that Australia ultimately pipped the All Blacks to the title, he was at his free-flowing, try-scoring best, notching up seven tries in four matches – a record by a player in a single tournament. Cullen is also the leading try-scorer in Tri-Nations history, registering 16 tries in 24 matches between 1996 and 2002.

THERE'S NO PLACE LIKE HOME

Born and raised in Auckland, Doug Howlett enjoyed a lengthy and highly successful 62-Test career with the All Blacks and ended his international stint as his country's all-time leading try-scorer, with 49. A winger with a searing turn of pace – he once ran the 100m in 10.68s – he enjoyed considerable success in Tri-Nations fixtures at Eden Park, once scoring three tries in a match there (against Australia in 2005) and five overall in four matches at Auckland's main stadium (it is an all-time tournament record for a player at a single ground).

TRY-SCORING DEBUTS

Only two players have scored a try on their debut in the Tri-Nations: Warren Brosnihan (South Africa) against Australia at Pretoria on 23 August 1997 (a match South Africa won 61–22); and Lloyd Johansson (Australia) against New Zealand at Auckland on 3 September 2005 (a match New Zealand won 34–24).

BELOW: One of the most incisive runners international rugby has ever seen, New Zealand's Christian Cullen tops the Tri-Nations all-time try-scoring list (with 16).

DRAWING A BLANK

New Zealand prop Greg Somerville enjoyed several champagne moments in the Tri-Nations. He was part of six title-winning teams – in 2002, 2003, 2005, 2006, 2007 and 2009 – but also set an unwanted record, as he played in the most matches (30) without ever scoring a try.

NO AWAY-DAY BLUES FOR THE ALL BLACKS' ROCKET MAN

One of the most lethal finishers in world rugby (he has scored an incredible 46 tries in 68 Tests for New Zealand between 2003 and 2010), Joe Rokocoko, nicknamed the 'Rocket Man', proved a deadly weapon for the All Blacks when they were on their travels in Tri-Nations matches. The Fiji-born winger racked up a tournament best 11 tries in 15 away matches, with a best of three tries in a match when the All Blacks beat Australia 51–21 in Sydney on 26 July 2003.

SUPER-SUB ROGERS

No player has made more of an impact coming off the replacements' bench in Tri-Nations matches than Australia's Mat Rogers. The utility back scored three tries in eight appearances as a replacement in Tri-Nations fixtures between 2002 and 2006 – an all-time tournament record.

BELOW: New Zealand's Joe Rokocoko has scored more tries in away games (11) than any other player in the Tri-Nations.

MOST TRIES: TOP TEN

Pos	Tries	Player (Country, Span)
1	16	Christian Cullen (New Zealand, 1996–2002)
2	15	Joe Rokocoko (New Zealand, 2003–10)
3	13	Doug Howlett (New Zealand, 2001–07)
4	11	Richie McCaw (New Zealand, 2002–11)
5	9	Jaque Fourie (South Africa, 2005–10)
=	9	Justin Marshall (New Zealand, 1996–2004)
=	9	Stirling Mortlock (Australia, 2000–09)
=	9	Lote Tuqiri (Australia, 2003–08)
9	8	Adam Ashley-Cooper (Australia, 2005–11)
=	8	Mils Muliaina (New Zealand, 2003–11)
=	8	Ma'a Nonu (New Zealand, 2008–11)
=	8	Joe Roff (Australia, 1996–2003)

ALL-TIME LEADING TRY-SCORERS: BY POSITION

Position	Player (Country, Span)	Tries
Full-back	Christian Cullen* (New Zealand, 1996–2002)	13
Winger	Joe Rokocoko (New Zealand, 2003–10)	15
Centre	Jaque Fourie (South Africa, 2005–10)	9
Fly-half	*Dan Carter (New Zealand, 2005–11)	5
Scrum-half	Justin Marshall (New Zealand, 1996–2004)	9
No.8	Toutai Kefu (Australia, 1998–2003)	2
	Kieran Read (New Zealand, 2009–11)	2
	Bobby Skinstad (South Africa, 2001–07)	2
Flanker	Richie McCaw (New Zealand, 2002–10)	11
Lock	Mark Andrews (South Africa, 1996–2001)	3
	Victor Matfield (South Africa, 2001–10)	3
Prop	Tony Woodcock (New Zealand, 2005–10)	7
Hooker	Keven Mealamu (New Zealand, 2003–11)	5

* Cullen scored three of his 16 Tri-Nations tries as a winger

NOKWE MAKES HIS MARK FOR THE BOKS

They may have finished bottom of the pile in the 2008 Tri-Nations, but South Africa rounded off what had otherwise been a disappointing campaign in style. The star of their comprehensive 53–8 victory over Australia in Johannesburg on 30 August was Jongi Nokwe. Making only his third appearance for the Boks, the winger scored four tries in the match before leaving the field through injury in the 51st minute. It remains the most tries by a player in one Tri-Nations match.

YOUNG GUN O'CONNOR SETS NEW RECORD

Currently one of the most exciting prospects in world rugby, James O'Connor became Australia's second youngest Test player when he made his debut against Italy at Padova on 8 November 2008. Despite his tender years, he is already being compared to Aussie great Tim Horan, and he made history on 5 September 2009 when he scored Australia's second try in their 21–6 victory over South Africa at Brisbane to become, aged 19 years 62 days, the youngest-ever try-scorer in a Tri-Nations match.

ABOVE: Jongi Nokwe's third match for South Africa was a very special one. Despite having to be taken off with an injury after only 51 minutes, the flying winger had already scored a Tri-Nations Championship record four tries in the Springboks 53–8 rout of Australia at Johannesburg in August 2007.

AGE NO BARRIER FOR BRILLIANT BUNCE

Among a handful of players in the history of the game to have represented more than one country (he played with distinction for Western Samoa at the 1991 Rugby World Cup), Frank Bunce will be remembered as one of the all-time greats of New Zealand rugby. A stand-out performer at centre into his mid-30s, he made history on 26 July 1997 when he scored New Zealand's opening try in their 33–18 victory over Australia at Melbourne to become, aged 35 years 172 days, the oldest-ever try-scorer in a Tri-Nations match.

RIGHT: A Rugby World Cup-winning All Black and one of the finest centres in rugby history, Frank Bunce holds the distinction of being the Tri-Nations Championship's oldest-ever try-scorer.

MAGICAL McCAW

The only player in history to win the IRB's International Player of the Year award on three occasions is New Zealand flanker Richie McCaw, in 2006, 2009 and 2010). He has been a shining light for New Zealand ever since he made his debut for the All Blacks against Ireland in November 2001. And McCaw has enjoyed considerable success in the Tri-Nations, too, scoring 11 tries in 39 matches – the most by any forward in the tournament's history.

MOST OVERALL TRIES AGAINST A SINGLE OPPONENT

Opponent	Tries	Player (Country)	Matches
Australia	8	Doug Howlett (New Zealand, 2001–07)	11
New Zealand	6	Matt Burke (Australia, 1996–2004)	14
South Africa	9	Christian Cullen (New Zealand, 1996–2002)	11

POINTS-SCORING RECORDS

CARTER LEADS THE WAY

Dan Carter's Tri-Nations debut was as a try-scoring replacement during New Zealand's 50–21 defeat of Australia at Sydney on 26 July 2003, but he had to wait almost a year for his second appearance. Since 2004, however, the man who stands at the top of international rugby's all-time leading points-scoring table, has been the creative, driving force behind a dominant All Blacks team that has collected five Tri-Nations titles in seven years. He has also set many Tri-Nations records: most points (461 in 33 matches); most points in one tournament (99 in 2006); most points at one stadium (86 in six matches at Wellington's Westpac Stadium and the same number in five at Eden Park, Auckland); most penalties (100); most conversions (61); and most conversions in one tournament (14 in 2006).

MOST POINTS BY A REPLACEMENT

The history books will show that New Zealand's 34–24 victory over Australia at Auckland on 3 September 2005 was enough to carry them to their sixth Tri-Nations title in ten years, but the match was significant for another reason, too: when Luke McAlister came on as a replacement and kicked three penalties, his match haul of nine points set a new record for the most points by a replacement in the history of Tri-Nations matches.

ABOVE: South Africa's Morne Steyn enjoyed a stellar debut season in the 2009 Tri-Nations Championship and broke a host of records as the Springboks went on to claim the title.

THE HIGHEST POINTS-SCORING CAPTAIN

A combative centre who became the 73rd player to lead the Wallabies when he was appointed captain in 2006, Stirling Mortlock holds the all-time Tri-Nations records for the most overall points scored in the competition by a captain (49 in 11 Tri-Nations matches between 2007 and 2009) and for the most points scored by a captain in a single Tri-Nations match (14 – one conversion and four penalties – during Australia's 24–19 defeat against South Africa at Cape Town on 16 June 2007).

LEFT: New Zealand's kicking machine Dan Carter is the only player in the history of the Tri-Nations Championship to have scored more than 400 points.

SENSATIONAL STEYN MAKES HIS TRI-NATIONS MARK

Bulls fly-half Morne Steyn burst on to the international rugby scene when he nailed a last-gasp penalty for South Africa against the British and Irish Lions at his home ground, Pretoria, on 27 June 2009 to secure a 28–25 win and an unassailable 2–0 series lead. He carried this form into the 2009 Tri-Nations championship, scoring all of his side's points in their 31–19 victory over New Zealand at Durban (to break Andrew Mehrtens' record for the most points scored by a player in a single Tri-Nations match), and ended South Africa's title-winning campaign having set the new tournament mark for the most penalties in a single tournament (23) and for the most drop goals in a single tournament (3). In 2010, he scored 24 points in South Africa's 39–41 defeat to Australia in Bloemfontein to break yet another Tri-Nations record: it is the most points scored by a player who has finished on the losing side.

MOST POINTS IN A TOURNAMENT: TOP FIVE

Pos	Points	Player (Country)	Year
1	99	Dan Carter (New Zealand)	2006
2	95	Morne Steyn (South Africa)	2009
3	84	Carlos Spencer (New Zealand)	1997
4	82	Dan Carter (New Zealand)	2008
5	77	Morne Steyn (South Africa)	2010

MOST TRI-NATIONS CAREER DROP-GOALS FOR SPRINGBOK PRETORIUS

A creative fly-half for South Africa who prospered in attack but was often criticized for his defence, Andre Pretorius made 31 appearances at No.10 for the Springboks between 2002 and 2007. He won 12 caps in Tri-Nations matches and shares the record for the most drop goals in a Tri-Nations career, four, with another Springbok fly-half, Morne Steyn.

KICKING MASTERCLASS PROPELS MEHRTENS INTO RECORD BOOKS

New Zealand fly-half Andrew Mehrtens was the main architect behind his side's comfortable 34–15 victory over Australia at Auckland on 24 July 1999. The South African-born Canterbury fly-half scored 29 points in the match (a Tri-Nations record since broken by Morne Steyn), including nine penalties (a tournament record that stands to this day) and a conversion.

MOST POINTS AGAINST A SINGLE OPPONENT

Opponent	Points	Player (Country, Span)
Australia	230	Dan Carter (New Zealand, 2003–11)
New Zealand	155	Matt Burke (Australia, 1996–2004)
South Africa	231	Dan Carter (New Zealand, 2004–11)

ABOVE: Andrew Mehrtens kicked a Tri-Nations record nine penalties in a match during New Zealand's 34–15 victory over Australia at Auckland in July 1999.

KING OF THE REPLACEMENTS POINTS-SCORERS

Australia's Mat Rogers holds the all-time Tri-Nations record for scoring the most points after coming on as a replacement. The versatile three-quarter, who has represented his country at both rugby union and rugby league, scored 15 points in eight Tri-Nations Championship appearances as a replacement between 2002 and 2006.

THE DEADLY BOOT OF JANNIE DE BEER

Famed for his exploits in South Africa's 1999 Rugby World Cup 44–21 quarter-final victory over England in Paris, in which he kicked a staggering five drop goals, Jannie de Beer made his mark in Tri-Nations matches, too. He holds the all-time competition record for the most conversions in a match (six, against Australia at Pretoria on 23 August 1997) and shares the record, with compatriot Francois Steyn (who achieved the feat against Australia in Cape Town on 16 June 2007), for the most drop goals in a match (with two against New Zealand at Johannesburg on 19 July 2007).

LEFT: Australia's Matt Burke has the distinction of having scored more points against New Zealand in Tri-Nations matches (155) than any other player.

MOST POINTS: TOP TEN

Pos	Points	Player (Country, Span)
1	461	Dan Carter (New Zealand, 2003–11)
2	328	Andrew Mehrtens (New Zealand, 1996–2004)
3	271	Matt Burke (Australia, 1996–2004)
4	257	Matt Giteau (Australia, 2003–10)
5	210	Percy Montgomery (South Africa, 1997–2008)
6	198	Stirling Mortlock (Australia, 2000–09)
=	198	Morne Steyn (South Africa, 2009–11)
8	153	Carlos Spencer (New Zealand, 1997–2004)
9	94	Braam van Straaten (South Africa, 1999–2001)
10	80	Christian Cullen (New Zealand, 1996–2002)

INTERNATIONAL RUGBY'S MARATHON MAN

As the most capped player in international rugby history (with 139 appearances for Australia between 1994 and 2007), it is no surprise that George Gregan set many Tri-Nations appearance records. The scrum-half has played in more matches in the competition than anyone else (48 between 1996 and 2007); made the most appearances on a losing side (27); made the most appearances against one opponent (25, against South Africa); and jointly holds, with compatriot Nathan Sharpe, the record for the most Tri-Nations appearances at one ground (ten, at Stadium Australia in Sydney).

BELOW: International rugby's most-capped player, George Gregan, played in 14 Tri-Nations champoinships and a set a number of all-time appearance records.

MOST APPEARANCES: TOP TEN

Pos	Caps	Player (Country, span)
1	48	George Gregan (Australia, 1996–2007)
2	44	Victor Matfield (South Africa, 2001–11)
3	43	Mils Muliaina (New Zealand, 2003–11)
4	41	Nathan Sharpe (Australia, 2002–11)
=	41	George Smith (Australia, 2001–09)
6	40	John Smit (South Africa, 2000–11)
7	39	Richie McCaw (New Zealand, 2002–11)
8	38	Stephen Larkham (Australia, 1997–2007)
=	38	Keven Mealamu (New Zealand, 2003–11)
10	37	Matt Giteau (Australia, 2003–10)

SUPER SUB PAUL

No player has made more Tri-Nations appearances as a replacement than Australia's Jeremy Paul. The Wallabies hooker (who won 72 caps for his country, with 38 of those coming from the substitutes' bench) made 13 of his 26 tournament appearances as a replacement.

THE LONGEST OF WAITS FOR DALE SANTON

After a long domestic career with Boland and then Western Cape-based franchise Eagles (during which he established a reputation as a fiery hooker), as well as a few outings with the Emerging Springboks (whom he captained against the British and Irish Lions as long ago as 1997), Dale Santon was finally handed his senior debut for South Africa in their Tri-Nations clash with Australia at Cape Town on 12 July 2003. He thus became, at 33 years 328 days, the oldest debutant in the tournament's 15-year history.

ONE-CAP WONDERS

Of the 440 players to appear in Tri-Nations matches, 46 of them have only ever made one appearance in the competition – a lowly 10.45 per cent.

ALL BLACK MULIAINA CANNOT SHAKE THAT WINNING FEELING

Born in Western Samoa, raised in Invercargill (his family emigrated there when he was two) and a member of the Junior All Blacks team that won the U21 World Championships in 2000 and 2001 and the New Zealand Sevens side that struck gold at the 2002 Commonwealth Games, Mils Muliaina made his senior debut for the All Blacks (as a replacement) in their 15–13 defeat to England at Wellington on 14 June 2003. His blistering pace, awareness of space and devastating counter-attacking abilities soon marked him out as a player of enormous potential and he went on to become an integral part of a New Zealand side that dominated world rugby – particularly the Tri-Nations championship. Muliaina has appeared on the winning side in 32 out of the 43 matches he has played in the competition – an all-time record.

LEFT: Mils Muliaina has tasted victory in 32 of his 43 Tri-Nations matches for New Zealand – an all-time tournament record.

THE TRI-NATIONS' YOUNGEST PLAYER

One of the most exciting young talents in world rugby, James O'Connor became the second youngest Australian debutant in history when, aged 18 years 126 days, he came on as a replacement against Italy at Padova on 8 November 2008. He made his first full start for his country, also against Italy, at Canberra on 13 July 2009 (and scored three tries in the match), but he was named as a replacement for the Wallabies' 2009 Tri-Nations opener against New Zealand in Auckland on 18 July. However, when he came on as a 61st-minute replacement for Berrick Barnes, he became, aged 19 years and 13 days, the youngest player in Tri-Nations history. Not that his first experience in the tournament was a winning one: the All Blacks won the match 22–16.

BROOKE, BUNCE AND FITZPATRICK BOW OUT IN STYLE

The 1996 and 1997 Tri-Nations Championships – the first two editions of the tournament ever played – provided the perfect stage for three legendary and long-serving All Blacks – Zinzan Brooke, Frank Bunce and Sean Fitzpatrick – as they brought down the curtains on their stellar international careers. With New Zealand romping to back-to-back titles, without losing a match, the trio set the record for the most Tri-Nations matches played without ever experiencing defeat – eight.

RIGHT: Zinzan Brooke (with ball) in Tri-Nations action for New Zealand against Australia at Dunedin in 1997. The All Black No.8 played eight matches in the early days of the competition and was on the winning side in all of them, this time 36–24.

APLON'S LOSING RUN

The all-time Tri-Nations record for the most matches played without ever being on the winning side is seven, set by South Africa's Gio Aplon (in 2010–11). The full-back made his competition debut as a 72nd-minute replacement during the Springboks' 32–12 defeat to New Zealand at Auckland on 10 July. A week later, he played during the 31–17 defeat to the All Blacks at Wellington.

He made his first start during South Africa's 30–13 defeat to Australia in Brisbane on 24 July, kept his place for the Boks' 29–22 loss to New Zealand in Johannesburg on 21 August and rounded off a miserable campaign when he came on as a replacement in South Africa's 41–39 reverse to Australia. Aplon's miserable run continued in 2011, when he appeared in both of of South Africa's defeats against Australia.

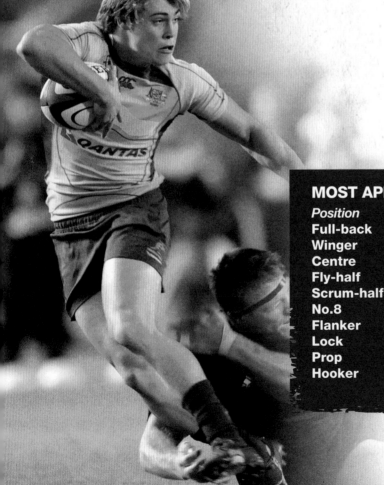

MOST APPEARANCES: BY POSITION

Position	Player (Country, Span)	Appearances
Full-back	Mils Muliaina (New Zealand, 2003–11)	37
Winger	Joe Rokocoko (New Zealand, 2003–10)	28
Centre	Jean de Villiers (South Africa, 2005–10)	23
Fly-half	Stephen Larkham (Australia, 1998–2007)	33
Scrum-half	George Gregan (Australia, 1996–2007)	48
No.8	Pierre Spies (South Africa, 2006–11)	20
Flanker	Richie McCaw (New Zealand, 2002–11)	39
Lock	Victor Matfield (South Africa, 2001–11)	44
Prop	Tony Woodcock (New Zealand, 2005–11)	32
Hooker	Keven Mealamu (New Zealand, 2003–11)	36

LEFT: Australia's rising star James O'Connor is the youngest player to appear in the Tri-Nations Championship and also the competition's youngest-ever try-scorer.

OTHER RECORDS

SOUTH AFRICA'S LONG-SERVING CAPTAIN

John Smit captained South Africa for the first time, against Georgia, at the 2003 Rugby World Cup and, to the surprise of many, was new coach Jake White's choice as permanent captain the following year. He may have tasted defeat when he led South Africa for the first time in a Tri-Nations match, during the 23–21 defeat to New Zealand at Christchurch on 24 July 2004 (also his first start for the Springboks in the competition), but he demonstrated his admirable leadership skills as South Africa rallied to win two of their remaining three games and collected the title for the first time in six years. He has gone on to lead the Boks in 31 Tri-Nations matches – an all-time tournament record.

TOURNAMENT RED CARDS

Player	Team	Opponent	Venue	Date
Andre Venter	South Africa	New Zealand	Auckland	9 Aug 1997
Marius Joubert	South Africa	Australia	Johannesburg	17 Aug 2002
Drew Mitchell	Australia	New Zealand	Melbourne	31 July 2010

TRI-NATIONS JOY FOR KIWI HENRY

Although Graham Henry's tenure as New Zealand coach will ultimately be judged on whether or not he can end his country's long Rugby World Cup drought, his record in the Tri-Nations is exemplary. The All Blacks have taken the title five times since Henry's appointment in 2004, comfortably making him the most successful coach in the tournament's history.

McCAW BRINGS THE BEST OUT OF THE ALL BLACKS

Bar one glaring omission on an otherwise glittering rugby résumé (a lack of Rugby World Cup honours, which New Zealand will hope to redress when they host the tournament in 2011), Richie McCaw has enjoyed an exceptional run of success as the All Blacks captain. Since his appointment in 2006, New Zealand have consistently been the best team in world rugby and the All Blacks have collected the Tri-Nations title four times in five years, winning 22 of 28 matches under McCaw's leadership – an all-time tournament record.

YELLOW IS THE COLOUR IN BRISBANE

The most yellow cards shown in a single Tri-Nations match came during Australia's 2002 Tri-Nations clash with South Africa at Brisbane on 27 July 2002. Four players were yellow-carded: Justin Harrison and Jeremy Paul (for Australia) and Werner Greeff and Faan Rautenbach (for South Africa) all spent ten minutes in the sin bin in a fractious match that Australia went on to win 38–27.

PERCENTAGE OF MATCHES WON WITH YELLOW CARD

Statistics show that only 16 teams (in 50 matches) have gone on to win a Tri-Nations tie after one of their number has received a yellow card – just 32 per cent.

ABOVE: Five Tri-Nations titles in seven years bears testimony to Graham Henry's substantial impact on New Zealand rugby, but he would swap every one of them – and his numerous Beldeisloe Cup successes – for victory at the 2011 Rugby World Cup.

SPRINGBOKS SUFFER A RED CARD BUT STILL SEE OFF THE WALLABIES

South Africa are the only side in Tri-Nations Championship history of to have won a match despite having had a player sent off. The Springboks' Marius Joubert was red-carded in their match against Australia at Ellis Park, Johannesburg, on 17 August 2002, but still held on to win 33–31. In both other cases, the team with a player sent off has gone on to lose.

LEFT: John Smit has led South Africa in a record 31 Tri-Nations Championship matches and, notably, to the title in both 2004 and 2009.

MOST YELLOW CARDS (COUNTRY)

Pos	Yellow	COUNTRY
1	26	South Africa
2	17	Australia
3	10	New Zealand

SOUTH AFRICA'S VENTER THE FIRST TO SEE RED

New Zealand's clash with South Africa at Eden Park, Auckland, on 9 August 1997 was fraught with tension from the moment the Springboks refused to face the All Blacks' traditional pre-match haka, and the match was on a knife-edge when the second half kicked off with the home side holding a slender 23–21 lead. And then came a history-making moment that changed the course of the match: South Africa's Andre Venter became the first-ever player in the Tri-Nations to be sent off (for stamping). The floodgates duly opened and New Zealand romped to a 55–35 victory.

STADIUM AUSTRALIA: A GENEROUS HOST

No ground has hosted more Tri-Nations matches than Stadium Australia in Sydney. The arena, built in 1999 and used for the 2000 Summer Olympics, has played host to 14 Tri-Nations fixtures between 1999 and 2011. The Wallabies have a decent record at the venue, winning nine of the matches – a winning percentage of 64.28

THE TRI-NATIONS' FIRST YELLOW CARD

The first player in Tri-Nations history to be shown a yellow card was Australia's James Holbeck in the Wallabies' final match of the 1997 campaign, against South Africa in Pretoria on 23 August. The Springboks went on to record a comfortable 61–22 victory, condemning the Wallabies to a bottom-place finish.

SURVIVING THE YELLOW-CARD ODDS

The Tri-Nations record for the most yellow cards received by a team that has gone on to win the match is two, a feat achieved on three occasions: by Australia (Justin Harrison and Jeremy Paul) against South Africa at Brisbane on 27 July 2002 – won 38–27; by South Africa (Percy Montgomery and Breyton Paulse) against Australia at Durban on 21 August 2004 – won 23–19; and by South Africa for a second time (Bakkies Botha and J.P. Pietersen) against New Zealand at Durban on 1 August 2009 – won 31–19.

PLAYERS TO HAVE RECEIVED TWO YELLOW CARDS

Player (Country)	Yellow cards against
De Wet Barry (South Africa)	v Australia at Johannesburg on 17 August 2002; v Australia at Cape Town on 12 July 2003
Bakkies Botha (South Africa)	v New Zealand at Durban on 1 August 2009; v New Zealand at Auckland on 10 July 2010
Richard Brown (Australia)	v South Africa at Cape Town on 8 August 2009; v New Zealand at Sydney on 22 August 2009
Victor Matfield (South Africa)	v Australia at Brisbane on 15 July 2006; v New Zealand at Dunedin on 12 July 2008
Breyton Paulse (South Africa)	v Australia at Durban on 21 August 2004; v Australia at Perth on 20 August 2005
Pedrie Wannenburg (South Africa)	v New Zealand at Durban on 23 June 2007; v New Zealand at Christchurch on 14 July 2007

RIGHT: Victor Matfield sees yellow against New Zealand at Dunedin on 12 July 2008 – a match South Africa went on to win 30–28. The Springbok lock is one of only six players in Tri-Nations history to have received two yellow cards.

PART V
OTHER PRINCIPAL IRB TOURNAMENTS

One of the main challenges for the game's administrators has been to create a structure in which the game's second- and third-tier nations at senior level and all of the world's teams at junior level can compete against each other on a regular basis. The ad hoc fixture list of the sport's early years, in which teams new to international rugby (or lesser-established nations) played sporadic fixtures against neighbouring countries or the occasional touring side, was never going to be enough to sustain either public interest in the game or its future growth. And it wasn't doing

much for the teams, either: Argentina and Japan, both dominant forces on their home continents, crashed out of the inaugural Rugby World Cup in 1987 at the first hurdle having recorded only one win between them. Many lessons were learned from the first World Cups, but the starkest problem – and one that continues to this day – was how to close the enormous gap between the game's haves and have-nots. The answer has been to establish annual continental-based tournaments: in Europe, there is the Six Nations B Championship (also known as the European Nations Cup), a multi-division event with promotion and relegation; and in Asia there is the Asian Five Nations (which includes all three of the Pacific Island nations – Fiji, Samoa and Tonga – who also compete in the annual Pacific Nations Cup). There are also annual competitions in Africa (the CAR Development Trophy) and in South America (the South American Championships). Rugby at junior international level, an essential breeding ground for the stars of tomorrow, is also well served: the world's U20 international teams have competed for the IRB Junior World Championship on an annual basis since 2008 (replacing the former U19 and U21 Rugby World Championships); and, in Europe, an U20 equivalent of the annual Six Nations Championship has also been running since 2008.

BELOW: New Zealand rugby fans are hoping that the success of their Under-20 team in winning the 2010 IRB Junior World Championship in Argentina will be repeated with the seniors in the 2011 Rugby World Cup.

WORLD JUNIOR RUGBY TOURNAMENTS

Introduced in 2008 to replace the Under-21 and Under-19 Rugby World Championships (which had been running from 2002 and 2004, respectively), the IRB Junior World Championship is restricted to players under the age of 20. The tournament consists of 12 teams and is the upper of two levels; the lower level of the competition is the eight-team IRB Junior World Rugby Trophy, which involves a selection of the world's developing rugby nations.

IRB JUNIOR WORLD CHAMPIONSHIP: WINNERS

Year	Winner	Score	Runner-up	Host
2008	New Zealand	38–3	England	Wales
2009	New Zealand	44–28	England	Japan
2010	New Zealand	62–17	Australia	Argentina

BABY BLACKS DOMINATE

The New Zealand Under-20 team – known as the Baby Blacks – have been unbeatable in the IRB Junior World Championship since its inception in 2008, recording a hat-trick of title wins. In the process, they have set all-time tournament records for the most points (719), the most tries (99) and the most conversions (67).

HOMER'S POINTS-SCORING ODYSSEY

Born in Salisbury and educated at Milton Abbey School in Dorset, Tom Homer played his early rugby with Andover, progressed through the England junior teams and signed for Guinness Premiership outfit London Irish in June 2008. A versatile back whose preferred position is full-back, he marked himself out as a player of great potential with England at the 2009 and 2010 IRB Junior World Championships, scoring 118 points – the most in the competition's history.

BELOW: New Zealand defended their IRB Junior World Championship title in 2009 and completed a hat-trick of titles in 2010.

MOST RUNNERS-UP FINISHES

It's been a case of so near and yet so far for England at the IRB Junior World Championship. In the inaugural tournament in 2008 in Wales, they beat Fiji (41–17), Canada (60–18) and Australia (18–13) to finish top of their group. England then recorded a hard-fought victory over South Africa (26–18) in the semi-finals, but they came unstuck against New Zealand in the final, suffering a 38–3 defeat. They finished on top of their group yet again in 2009 – notching up comfortable victories over hosts Japan (43–0), Scotland (30–7) and Samoa (52–7) – and romped to a comfortable victory over South Africa in the semi-finals (40–21). But despite faring much better this time round, they lost to New Zealand in the final for the second successive year (44–28).

BELOW: Tom Homer (with ball) amasssed 118 points for England at the 2009 and 2010 IRB Junior World Championships – an all-time record.

IRB TOSHIBA JUNIOR WORLD CHAMPIONSHIP 2009, JAPAN
CHAMPIONS

MOST OVERALL CONVERSIONS, PENALTIES AND DROP GOALS

Score	Total	Player (Country)
Conversions:	24	Francois Brummer (South Africa)
Penalties:	28	Matthew Jarvis (Wales)
Drop goals:	2	Sias Ebersohn (South Africa)
		Ignacio Rodriguez Muedra (Argentina)

MOST POINTS (OVERALL): TOP FIVE

Pos	Points	Player (Country)
1	118	Tom Homer (England)
2	116	Matthew Jarvis (Wales)
3	105	Francois Brummer (South Africa)
4	82	Tyler Bleyendaal (New Zealand)
5	75	Patrick Lambie (South Africa)

GUILDFORD TOPS THE TRY-SCORING CHARTS

A prolific try-scorer for Hawke's Bay in the 2007 Air New Zealand Cup, Masterton-born Zac Guildford made an impact with the Hurricanes at provincial level in 2008 and was a part of the Baby Blacks side that cantered to the inaugural IRB Junior World Championship title in 2008, scoring two tries. The winger made his Super 14 debut for the Hurricanes the following year and first came to the attention of the international rugby audience with some stellar performances for New Zealand at the 2009 IRB Junior World Championship in Japan. Along with team-mate Julian Savea, the newly crowned IRB Junior Player of the Year, he scored eight tries in the tournament – including two in the 44–28 final victory over England – as New Zealand defended their title. His overall haul of ten tries is an all-time tournament record. He made his senior debut for the All Blacks against Wales at the Millennium Stadium, Cardiff, on 7 November 2009 and has gone on to win four caps.

BELOW: Zac Guildford's ten tries in two IRB Junior World Championship tournaments (in 2008 and 2009) are an all-time competition record.

SOUTH AFRICA RUN RIOT IN WREXHAM

South Africa got their 2008 IRB Junior World Championship campaign off to a spectacular and record-breaking start against the United States at the Racecourse Ground, Wrexham, on 6 June 2008, running in 16 tries (three of them by Pieter Janse van Vuuren) on their way to a crushing 108–18 victory, the biggest in the tournament's history. Sadly for the Baby Boks, however, their interest in the competition ended at the semi-final stage when they lost 26–18 to England.

MOST PENALTIES AND DROP GOALS

No team has kicked more penalties in IRB Junior World Championship matches than Wales. The Welsh, whose best performance in the tournament came when they reached the semi-finals in 2008, have nailed 39 penalties in 15 matches. Argentina hold the competition record for the most drop goals, with four.

THE OAKS FINISH TOP OF THE TREE

After finishing the inaugural IRB Junior World Rugby Trophy in fourth place (following a 34–10 third-place play-off defeat to Georgia), Romania made amends in the best possible way the following year when the tournament was staged in Kenya. They beat Papua New Guinea (50–17), Korea (65–14) and 2008 runners-up Chile (26–20) to top their pool before beating the United States (25–13) in the final.

MOST TRIES (OVERALL): TOP FIVE

Pos	Tries	Player (Country)
1	10	Zac Guildford (New Zealand)
2	8	Ryuhei Arita (Japan)
=	8	Julian Savea (New Zealand)
4	7	Nemani Nadolo (Australia)
5	6	Tomas De La Vega (Argentina)

BLEYENDAAL BOOTS THE BABY BLACKS TO GLORY

Captain of the New Zealand Under-20 side for the 2010 IRB Junior World Championship in Argentina, Tyler Bleyendaal led the Baby Blacks in record-breaking fashion. The Canterbury fly-half scored an all-time high 82 points in the course of the tournament as New Zealand completed a hat-trick of titles.

LEFT: Baby Blacks captain Tyler Bleyendaal showed himself to be a player of huge potential at the 2010 IRB Junior World Championship, scoring a tournament-record 82 points.

IRB JUNIOR WORLD RUGBY TROPHY: WINNERS

Year	Winner	Score	Runner-up	Host
2008	Uruguay	20–8	Chile	Chile
2009	Romania	25–13	USA	Kenya
2010	Italy	36–7	Japan	Russia

INAUGURAL CHAMPIONS

The first-ever IRB Junior World Rugby Trophy final, held at the Stade Francais in Santiago, was an all-South American affair between hosts Chile and Uruguay. And it was Uruguay who came out on top, winning the match 20–8 to become the first-ever champions and to earn promotion to the following year's IRB Junior World Championship (in which they failed to win a single game).

ABOVE: The inaugural IRB Junior World Rugby Trophy was played in Chile in 2008 and the trophy stayed in South America as Uruguay defeated the hosts 20–8 in the final in Santiago.

PROLIFIC PATRASCU TOPS POINTS-SCORING LIST

Scoring 15 of his country's 25 points in the final against the United States, a match they won 25–13, impressive fly-half Stefan Patrascu was the star of Romania's march to the 2009 IRB Junior World Rugby Trophy crown. He holds the all-time record for the most points scored in the second-tier world championship with 82.

BACK-TO-BACK JOY FOR THE BABY BLACKS

Having won the competition for the first time in England in 2003, following a 21–10 victory over Australia in the final at Oxford, New Zealand became the first team in history to collect back-to-back Under-21 Rugby World Championship titles when they beat Ireland 47–19 in the 2004 final which was played at Hampden Park, Glasgow.

UNDER-21 RUGBY WORLD CHAMPIONSHIP: WINNERS

Year	Winner	Score	Runner-up	Host
2002	South Africa	24–21	Australia	South Africa
2003	New Zealand	21–10	Australia	England
2004	New Zealand	47–19	Ireland	Scotland
2005	South Africa	20–15	Australia	Argentina
2006	France	24–13	South Africa	France

ITALY TAKE TITLE AT FIRST ATTEMPT

Italy's first appearance in the IRB Junior World Rugby Trophy in 2010, which saw the third edition of the second-tier world championship staged in Russia, was a successful one. The junior Azzurri beat Papua New Guinea (74–0), Romania (48–12) and Uruguay (16–12) to win their group and then downed Japan (36–7) in the final at the Slava Stadium in Moscow to take the title at the first time of asking and to earn promotion to the IRB Junior World Championship for 2011.

SOUTH AFRICA ARE THE FIRST TO LIFT UNDER-21 CROWN

Seeded seventh at the start of the 2002 Under-21 World Championship (the forerunner of the IRB Junior World Championship), hosts South Africa, with future Rugby World Cup-winning coach Jake White at the helm, were the surprise package of the tournament, beating Romania (135–0), France (28–9), Ireland (42–22), New Zealand (19–18) and Australia (24–21) in a tense final at Ellis Park, Johannesburg, to take the title. The Baby Boks won the title for a second time – beating Australia 20–15 in the final – in Argentina in 2005.

JUNIOR WALLABIES TRIUMPH IN DUBAI

The 2006 Under-19 Rugby World Championship was a tournament of firsts: it was staged in Dubai for the first time (it was the first world 15-a-side competition to he held in Asia) and Australia, thanks to a nail-biting 17–13 victory over New Zealand in the final won the tournament for the first time in their histor; and the Baby Blacks – the inugural champions in 2004 – were the first team to lose in consecutive finals.

UNDER-19 RUGBY WORLD CHAMPIONSHIP: WINNERS

Year	Winner	Score	Runner-up	Host
2004	New Zealand	34–11	France	South Africa
2005	South Africa	20–15	New Zealand	South Africa
2006	Australia	17–13	New Zealand	United Arab Emirates
2007	New Zealand	31–7	South Africa	Northern Ireland

HOSTS FRANCE MAKE THEIR HOME ADVANTAGE COUNT

France entered the 2006 Under-21 Rugby World Championship, as hosts, keen to erase the bitter memories of their semi-final defeat to Australia in the previous tournament. They opened up with victories over Ireland (26–8) and Wales (32–3), but then lost their final pool match against South Africa (14–10). The result left them facing a semi-final showdown with Australia for the second consecutive year. This time, though, they won – 32–17. Buoyed by the victory and full of confidence, they went on to beat South Africa in the final (24–13) to become the tournament's first and last winners from the northern hemisphere.

KIM SHINES FOR STRUGGLING KOREA

Korea may not have enjoyed the best of times at the IRB Junior World Rugby Trophy, finishing sixth out of eight teams in the inaugural edition of the event, in Chile in 2008, but, for their No.8 Kim Hyun Soo, the competition was an unqualified success. He scored seven tries in four matches to become the tournament's all-time leading try-scorer. Despite winning only once in the competition, Korea still finished as the third-highest points-scorers (with 123).

RIGHT: Kim Hyun Soo (right) made his mark in a struggling Korea side at the 2008 IRB Junior World Rugby Trophy. The imposing No.8 scored an impressive seven tries in just four matches as his team finished in sixth place in the competition.

BABY BLACKS ARE THE CLASS ACT OF THE SHOW

New Zealand were in a class of their own at the inaugural Under-19 Rugby World Championship in 2004, beating Ireland (30–6), Georgia (81–12) and Australia (30–5) to win their pool, before seeing off hosts South Africa (30–23) in the semi-final and France (34–11) in the final to take the crown. Worthy winners, the Baby Blacks scored 40 per cent more tries and made 30 per cent more passes than any other team in the tournament, with over one-third of their tries scored from inside their own half. In 2007, they beat South Africa (31–7) in the final to become the only team to win the event for a second time.

SECOND TIME LUCKY FOR HOSTS SOUTH AFRICA

Having failed to make home advantage count at the 2004 Under-19 Rugby World Championship, when they crashed out of the tournament at the semi-final stage following a disappointing 30–23 defeat to New Zealand, South Africa made amends when they hosted the competition for the second successive year in 2005. The Baby Boks, seeded third, held off wave after wave of New Zealand attack in the final to win the match 20–15 and become the first host nation to take the title.

UNDER-20
SIX NATIONS CHAMPIONSHIP

Established by the International Rugby Board in 2008, and mirroring the senior edition of the tournament, the Six Nations Under-20 Championship is an annual event featuring six teams – England, France, Ireland, Italy, Scotland and Wales. The first three editions of the competition have seen three different winners, with England taking the inaugural title, France winning in 2009 and Ireland in 2010.

OVERALL TABLE

Pos	Team	P	W	L	D	PF	PA	TF	TA	Points
1	England	20	17	3	0	614	277	80	28	34
2	France	20	13	6	1	484	311	55	28	27
3	Ireland	20	12	7	1	386	356	36	41	25
4	Wales	20	10	9	1	470	388	53	38	21
5	Scotland	20	4	15	1	211	385	19	58	9
6	Italy	20	2	18	0	204	545	16	67	4

ENGLAND ROMP TO GRAND SLAM GLORY

England found their stride in the inaugural Six Nations Under-20 Championship in 2008 in record-breaking fashion, beating Wales (25–18), Italy (22–13), France (24–6), Scotland (41–15) and Ireland (43–14) to record the first, and to date only, grand slam in the competition's history.

On the march to the title, England scored 21 tries and a total of 158 points – both all-time tournament records.

FRANCE RALLY TO CLAIM FIRST TITLE

After losing the opening game of the 2009 Six Nations Under-20 Championship to Ireland (9–6), it seemed as though France were set to suffer a second successive disappointing tournament (they had finished third in 2008 following three wins and two defeats), but they rallied in exemplary style, beating Scotland (30–3), Wales (40–20), England (33–11) and Italy (43–10) to deny the Irish take the title for the first time on points difference.

BELOW: England players celebrate after their 43–14 defeat of Ireland at Kingsholm, Gloucester, gave them not only the inaugural Six Nations Under-20 Championship in 2008, but also they completed the grand slam.

THE TOURNAMENT'S DOMINANT TEAM

England have been the most successful side in the first four years of the Six Nations Under-20 Championship, recording the only grand slams (in 2008 and 2011); winning the most matches (17); scoring the most and conceding the fewest points (614 and 277); scoring the most and conceding the fewest tries (80 and 28); and scoring the most tries in a single match – 11, during their 74–3 defeat of Italy at Bath on 11 February 2011.

McKINNEY FIRES IRELAND TO MAIDEN TITLE

Fly-half James McKinney was on the top of his game as Ireland won the Six Nations Under-20 Championship for the first time in 2010. The Ulster No.10 notched up what was then an all-time record 54 points for a single tournament, including 19 in Ireland's title-clinching 44–15 victory over Scotland at Athlone on 19 March.

SIX NATIONS UNDER-20: WINNERS

Year	Winner
2008	England (grand slam)
2009	France
2010	Ireland
2011	England (grand slam)

THIRD TIME LUCKY FOR IRELAND

Ireland's progress in the tournament may have been gradual – they finished fourth in 2008 and second (on points difference) a year later – but it all came together in title-winning fashion in 2010. They opened up with a 39–0 victory over Italy (the biggest in the tournament's history) and, despite losing to France (20–15) in their second match, bounced back with three closing victories – against England (25–10), Wales (24–17) and Scotland (44–15) – to win the championship on points difference ahead of England.

HONOURS EVEN AT INVERNESS

When Toulon wing Jeremy Sinzelle scored for France after three minutes against Scotland at Inverness on 5 February 2010, it seemed as though the French were well on their way to recording a third consecutive victory over the Scots. But the home side had other ideas, with fly-half Alex Blair crossing the line to level the scores. A penalty apiece in the second half saw the match end 8–8. It was the first draw in the Six Nations Under-20 Championship (Wales and Ireland drew 25–25 in 2011).

MOST TRIES IN A MATCH

The record for the most tries in a match by a single player is four, and it was achieved by two players in the same contest: Elliott Daly and Andy Short of England touched down four times in the 74–3 victory against Italy at Bath on 11 February 2011.

TOUGH TIMES FOR THE AZZURRI

Just as their senior counterparts have struggled in the Six Nations Championship over the years, so Italy's junior side has found wins hard to come by in the Under-20 tournament. They have won just twice in 20 matches, both against Scotland – 14–13 at Venice on 14 March 2008 and 9–7 at Stirling on 18 March 2011. Italy have also conceded the most points in a single tournament (180 in 2011) and suffered the heaviest defeat in the competition's history (74–3 against England at Bath on 11 February 2011).

BARRAUD SHINES FOR FRANCE

Aristide Barraud had a match to remember for France against Italy at Chieto on 20 March 2009. The Stade Francais fly-half scored 23 points (one try, three conversions and four penalties) – a tournament record for a player in a single match – as France romped to a convincing 43–10 away victory.

CATO CRUISES TO TRY-SCORING RECORD

Noted for his pace and flair, Saracens wing Noah Cato played for England at the 2007 Under-19 Rugby World Championship and for their senior sevens side, but captured the attention of a wider audience with some impressive performances in the 2008 Six Nations Under-20 Championship. As England romped to grand slam glory, he achieve the rare feat of scoring tries against all four opponents, twice against Scotland, to register five in all. It was a single-season record for a player in the Six Nations Under-20 Championship, until Elliott Daly grabbed seven in England's 2011 grand slam run.

RIGHT: Noah Cato shows his off electric pace, going past a French defender in Grenoble during the 2008 Under-20 Six Nations Championhip match. England won the match 24–6.

WINS BY ONE POINT

Winner	Score	Opponent	Venue	Date
Italy	14–13	Scotland	Venice	14 Mar 2008
Scotland	18–17	Wales	Perth	6 Feb 2009
Ireland	19–18	England	Athlone	27 Feb 2009

OTHER MAJOR CUPS

Today, the world's second- and third-tier nations are well served when it comes to regular, competitive rugby. In Asia and Oceania, the Pacific Nations Cup has been contested on an annual basis since 2006; Europe's lesser lights play in the Six Nations B Championship (also known as the European Nations Cup), with promotion and relegation between the many divisions; and the multi-division Asian Five Nations Championship has been running since 2008.

IN A LEAGUE OF THEIR OWN

New Zealand teams – the Junior All Blacks and, in 2008 only, the New Zealand Maoris – proved the class act of the Pacific Nations Cup in the tournament's formative years, claiming the first four titles (between 2006 and 2009) with a record of: played 19, won 19 (scoring a colossal 690 points and conceding just 222). However, perhaps accepting that their presence in the competition was doing little to further the cause of the likes of Fiji, Samoa and Tonga (for whom it was intended), they were not included in the revamped 2010 edition of the tournament, which was won by Samoa.

PACIFIC NATIONS CUP: WINNERS

Year	Winner
2006	Junior All Blacks
2007	Junior All Blacks
2008	New Zealand Maori
2009	Junior All Blacks
2010	Samoa

THE TOURNAMENT'S LEADING POINTS-SCORER

Full-back Taniela Rawaqa Maravunawasawasa scored three points (a penalty) on his international debut for Fiji during their slender 8–3 defeat to Samoa in the Pacific Nations Cup match at Apia on 19 May 2007 and has gone on to enjoy considerable success in the competition, scoring 95 points (three tries, 19 conversions and 14 penalties) in ten matches between 2007 and 2010 to top the tournament's all-time points-scoring list.

ELECTRIC HOSEA GEARS UP FOR A SPECTACULAR FUTURE

Hosea Gear may have set tongues wagging when an explosive burst of pace brought him his first international try, against England at Twickenham on 6 November 2010, but his eye-catching performance came as little surprise to those who had seen him in action for the Junior All Blacks in the 2009 Pacific Nations Cup. The electric winger scored nine tries in four matches – not only the record for the most tries in a single tournament but also the most tries by any player in the tournament's history – as a New Zealand team took the title for the fourth successive year.

SIX NATIONS B CHAMPIONSHIP: WINNERS

Year	Winner
2000	Romania
2001	Georgia
2001–02	Romania
2003–04	Portugal
2004–06	Romania
2006–08	Georgia
2008–10	Georgia

PROLIFIC PAVEL TOPS POINTS-SCORING LIST

A legend in Georgian rugby who made his international debut in 1995, Pavel Jimsheladze was the first player from his country to reach the 50-cap milestone and retired in 2007 as the Lelos' all-time leading points-scorer. He was equally prolific in Six Nations B matches, scoring a tournament record 227 points in 28 matches between 2000 and 2007.

A VERY SPECIAL TALENT

A mountain of a man who is one of the most underrated forwards in world rugby, Georgia's giant No.8 Marmuka Gorgodze is the Six Nations B Championship's all-time leading try-scorer. Standing 6ft 5in (1.98m) tall and weighting 18st 6lb (118.5kg), Gorgodze scored 18 tries in 22 matches for the Lelos between 2003 and 2009 – a remarkable try-scoring strike rate for a forward in international rugby.

ABOVE: As well as a highly-potent attack. Romania also used a stifling defence to good effect as the Oaks won the 2004–06 Six Nations B Championship. Portugal's scrum-half Cardoso Pinto (red shirt) is under pressure from Danut Dumbrava (middle) and Gabriel Brezoianu (15) as he passes out of a tackle in Romania's 14–10 win in Bucharest.

RECORD-BREAKING WIN PUTS THE OAKS BACK ON TRACK

Having suffered a narrow defeat to their main 2004–06 Six Nations B Championship rivals Georgia (20–13) in Tbilisi on 12 March 2005, Romania were desperate to put their campaign back on track when they faced Ukraine in Bucharest a week later. They did so in magnificent style, scoring 15 tries en route to a 97–0 victory – the largest in the tournament's history – and went on to win five of their remaining six matches (losing only 25–24 away to Russia) to become the first team to win the tournament three times since it was revamped in 2000.

LELOS USE THE EVENT TO FURTHER THEIR CAUSE

Georgia's consistent rise up the IRB world rankings (they currently lie in a very commendable 14th place) has been reflected in their performances in the Six Nations B Championship. The Lelos won the tournament for the first time in 2001, finished second in 2001–02 and 2004–06 and took the title in 2006–08 and again in 2008–10 to become the first team in the competition's new format to win back-to-back titles.

ASIAN FIVE NATIONS CHAMPIONSHIP: WINNERS

Year	Winner
2008	Japan
2009	Japan
2010	Japan

TOURNAMENT LEADERS IN POINTS AND TRIES

Japan's New Zealand-born fly-half Shaun Webb, who qualified for the Cherry Blossoms through residency, has enjoyed plenty of good times in the Asian Five Nations Championship. Webb has scored an all-time tournament record 108 points (ten tries and 29 conversions) in eight appearances in the competition for Japan between 2008 and 2010, and is second on the Asian Five Nations Championship's all-time try-scoring list behind team-mate Hirotoki Onazawa, who scored 11 tries in seven matches between 2008 and 2009.

JAPAN ARE AN UNSTOPPABLE FORCE

Japan have dominated the Asian Five Nations Championship since its inception in 2008, winning all three titles contested, with a record of played 12, won 12. They have scored the most points in the tournament's history (907 – an average of 75.6 points per match) and the most tries (139 – Korea, the second-placed team on the list, have scored 11); and, not surprisingly, they also hold the record for the biggest victory: 114–6 – Japan against the Arabian Gulf in Osaka on 3 May 2008.

RIGHT: Japan's captain Hitoshi Ono proudly displays the Asian Five Nations Championship trophy after his team had crushed Hong Kong 94–5 in Tokyo to win the 2010 tournament, the Cherry Blossoms' second successful defence of the Cup.

PART VI
SEVENS RUGBY

Sevens rugby is a seven-a-side variant of the 15-a-side game. It is played under the same laws, on a full-size pitch and with two halves each of seven minutes' duration. Sevens rugby originated at Melrose Rugby Club, in Scotland, in 1883 (an annual tournament is contested at the club to this day) and has gone on to become an extremely popular form of the sport that is played on every one of the world's continents. Initially, at least, tournaments sprang up on an ad hoc basis around the globe, with some – particularly the Hong Kong Sevens, which was contested for the first time in 1976 – soon attracting the world's best teams and, with them, a loyal crowd of followers, who would descend on the event year after year looking forward to the rugby festival that lay ahead.

In the 1990s, the International Rugby Board (IRB), recognizing not just the sport's immense popularity but also its potential as a vehicle to spread the rugby gospel to the furthest corners of the globe, sanctioned the first Rugby World Cup Sevens event, which took place in Edinburgh, Scotland, in 1993 – the tournament was won by England. It has been held on a four-yearly basis ever since, and in the 1999–2000 season the IRB combined long-standing events (such as Hong Kong, Wellington and Dubai) into the IRB Sevens World Series – a year-long series of sevens events staged around the world to determine the year's best teams. It is not only the rugby authorities who have registered the enormous interest generated by sevens rugby: in 1998, the sport became part of the Commonwealth Games roster (and has been contested at the last four events – with New Zealand picking up gold on each occasion) and, from 2018, it will form part of the Olympic Games schedule.

BELOW: Wales celebrate their unexpected victory at the 2009 Rugby World Cup Sevens staged in Dubai.

RUGBY WORLD CUP SEVENS

The Rugby World Cup Sevens is the premier sevens competition in world rugby. Organized by the IRB and contested every four years, it was first staged in Scotland, the birthplace of the seven-a-side game, in 1993, with England taking the inaugural title. The five competitions held to date have yielded four different winners, with Fiji the only side to have lifted the Melrose Cup on two occasions (they won in 1997 and again in 2005).

INAUGURAL CHAMPIONS

Twenty-four teams contested the first-ever Rugby World Cup Sevens competition staged in Edinburgh, Scotland, in 1993. And it was England who came away with the spoils: they may have finished second in their pool (after losing 28–10 to Samoa) and lost to Australia in the second qualifying pool, but they did enough to progress to the semi-finals and found their form when it really mattered, beating Fiji (21–7) in the last four and then exacting revenge on Australia in the final (winning the match 21–17) to become the first team in history to win the Melrose Cup.

FABULOUS FIJI WIN IN HONG KONG

The fourth edition of the Rugby World Cup Sevens tournament, hosted by Hong Kong (the spiritual home of sevens rugby) in 2005, was the most memorable of the five tournaments held to date and it was Fiji, inspired by the great Waisale Serevi, who walked away with the crown. The South Pacific islanders topped Pool C thanks to victories over Japan (47–0), Portugal (31–0), Canada (29–14), Hong Kong (38–0) and Australia (31–5); beat Argentina (22–14) in the quarter-finals; held off a strong challenge from England in the semi-finals (winning 24–19 after extra time); and beat New Zealand (29–19) in the final to become the first, and to date only, team to win the competition for a second time.

BELOW: They weren't many people's pre-tournament pick, but England, led by Andrew Harriman (front row, middle) and containing Lawrence Dallaglio (front, far right) ran out winners at the inaugural Rugby World Cup Sevens, beating Australia in the final at Murrayfield in 1993.

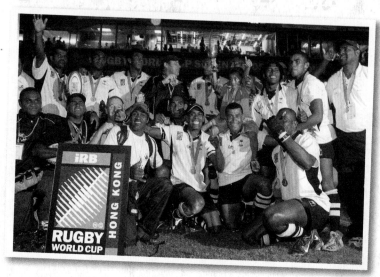

THIRD TIME LUCKY FOR THE ALL BLACKS

Having fallen at the quarter-final stage of the competition in 1993 (they failed to progress beyond the protracted quarter-final group stage, winning only one of three matches) and in the semi-finals four years later (losing 31–7 to South Africa), New Zealand finally confirmed their status as the world's premier sevens side when the competition was held in Mar del Plata, Argentina, in 2001 – the only time a major international rugby competition has ever been staged in South America. The All Blacks beat Australia in the final to win the event for the first, and to date only, time in their history.

ABOVE: Fiji became the first country in history to win the Rugby World Cup Sevens title twice with their victory at the 2005 tournament in Hong Kong.

FIJI ROMP TO TITLE IN HONG KONG

Fiji stormed to the Rugby World Cup Sevens title in 1997. They beat Portugal (59–0) and hosts Hong Kong (45–0) on the first day of competition, and Namibia (66–0) and Wales (35–0) on day two to reach the knock-out stages. Fiji then defeated South Korea 56–0 in the quarter-finals and Samoa 38–14 in the semi-finals (the first points they had conceded in the tournament). In a tense final, the Fijians downed South Africa 24–21 to clinch their first world sevens crown.

TOURNAMENT WINNERS

Year	Winner	Runner-up	Host
1993	**England**	Australia	Scotland
1997	**Fiji**	South Africa	Hong Kong
2001	**New Zealand**	Fiji	Argentina
2005	**Fiji**	New Zealand	Hong Kong
2009	**Wales**	Argentina	Dubai

MOST POINTS (PLAYER): TOP FIVE

Pos	Points	Player (Country)
1	297	Waisale Serevi (Fiji)
2	115	Marika Vunibaka (Fiji)
3	101	Brian Lima (Samoa)
4	100	Amasio Valence (New Zealand)
5	95	Glen Osbourne (New Zealand)

SUPER SEREVI'S RECORD-BREAKING POINTS HAUL

Inspired to take up rugby following Fiji's memorable 25–21 victory over the touring British and Irish Lions side in Suva in August 1977, Waisale Serevi developed into many people's pick as the greatest-ever exponent of sevens rugby. Noted for his sleight of hand and, in his prime, his blistering pace and eye for a gap, the two-time tournament winner holds the Rugby World Cup Sevens all-time records for the most points (297) and for the most goals/conversions (101).

POINTS DON'T NECESSARILY MEAN PRIZES FOR NEW ZEALAND

They may have lifted the Melrose Cup only once in five attempts (in Argentina in 2001), but New Zealand hold the Rugby World Cup Sevens all-time records for the most points (1,106) and the most tries (172) in the competition's history.

MOST TRIES (PLAYER): TOP FIVE

Pos	Tries	Player (Country)
1	23	Marika Vunibaka (Fiji)
2	19	Waisale Serevi (Fiji)
3	17	Brian Lima (Samoa)
4	14	Roger Randle (New Zealand)
5	13	Brendan Williams (Australia)
=	13	Tevita Tu'ifua (Tonga)

ABOVE: Marika Vunibaka has found his stride in Rugby World Cup Sevens matches for Fiji over the years, scoring an all-time competition record 23 tries.

VUNIBAKA TOPS ALL-TIME TRY-SCORING CHARTS

One of only a handful of players to have appeared in three separate Rugby World Cup Sevens tournaments (he represented Fiji in the 1997, 2001 and 2005 events and picked up a winners' medal on two occasions), winger Marika Vunibaka is the leading try-scorer in the competition's history with 23 tries.

SURPRISE WIN FOR WALES IN DUBAI

Even after they had reached the quarter-final stages of the 2009 Rugby World Cup Sevens event in Dubai, few thought Wales capable of mounting a challenge for the title: they had, after all, shown little previous form in the tournament and had already been beaten by Argentina (14–0) in the group stages. But Wales silenced their many doubters in spectacular fashion, beating New Zealand (15–14) in the quarter-finals and Samoa (19–12) in the semi-finals before avenging their earlier defeat to Argentina by beating the Pumas (19–12) in the final to walk away with the title for the first time in their history.

NO HOME COMFORTS FOR ARABIAN GULF

Hosts Arabian Gulf endured a torrid time at the 2009 Rugby World Cup Sevens tournament. They lost all four of their matches in the event, staged in Dubai, and they conceded 103 points while scoring just 27 – setting a record for the fewest points scored by a team in one tournament in the competition's 17-year history.

LEFT: Waisale Serevi has confirmed his status as the best sevens player in world rugby with some stellar performances for Fiji in Rugby World Cup Sevens tournaments.

COMMONWEALTH GAMES

Rugby sevens made its first appearance at the Commonwealth Games in Kuala Lumpur, Malaysia, in 1998 and is now considered a core sport by the tournament's organizing committee. It is one of only two all-male events contested at the Games (the other being boxing). New Zealand have proved the team to beat in the competition, claiming the gold medal on all four occasions and winning all 25 of the games they have played.

THE UNBEATABLE ALL BLACKS

New Zealand have been an unstoppable force in the rugby sevens competition, winning the event on each of the four times it has been contested. In 1998, in Kuala Lumpur, Malaysia, they beat Fiji 21–12 in the final; four years later, in Manchester, England, they beat the South Pacific islanders in the final for the second successive time (33–15) to defend their title. They completed a hat-trick of tournament wins in Melbourne, Australia, in 2002, beating England (29–21) in the final; and struck gold for the fourth time in a row in Delhi, India, in 2010 when they beat Australia (24–17) in the climax to the competition. The All Blacks hold the all-time tournament records for: the most points (973), most wins (25), the best points difference (+771) and the most points in a single tournament (345, in 1998).

OVERALL RECORD (RANKED BY WIN PERCENTAGE)

Country (Span)	P	W	L	D	PF	PA	PD	Win%
New Zealand (1998–2010)	25	25	0	0	973	202	+771	100.00
Fiji (1998–2006)	19	15	4	0	715	186	+529	78.95
South Africa (1998–2010)	23	17	6	0	676	262	+414	73.91
England (1998–2010)	23	17	6	0	604	290	+314	73.91
Australia (1998–2010)	25	17	8	0	814	292	+522	68.00
Papua New Guinea (1998, 2010)	13	8	5	0	378	233	+145	61.54
Scotland (2002–10)	17	9	8	0	341	267	–74	52.94
Samoa (1998–2010)	24	12	11	1	618	318	+300	50.00
Wales (1998–2010)	20	10	10	0	526	415	+111	50.00
Cook Islands (1998–2006)	16	8	8	0	380	351	+29	50.00
Tonga (1998–2010)	23	11	12	0	510	449	+61	47.83
Canada (1998–2010)	21	10	10	1	448	318	+130	47.62
Uganda (2006–10)	10	4	6	0	143	278	–135	40.00
Kenya (1998–2010)	21	8	13	0	327	463	–136	38.10
Malaysia (1998–2002, 2010)	14	4	10	0	159	559	–400	28.57
Bahamas (1998)	5	1	4	0	60	269	–209	20.00
Namibia (2006)	4	0	4	0	31	138	–107	0.00
Guyana (2010)	4	0	4	0	14	146	–132	0.00
India (2010)	4	0	4	0	21	197	–176	0.00
Cayman Islands (1998)	5	0	5	0	17	270	–253	0.00
Swaziland (1998)	5	0	5	0	26	298	–272	0.00
Nieu Islands (2002–06)	8	0	8	0	32	342	–310	0.00
Sri Lanka (1998–2010)	17	0	17	0	108	513	–405	0.00
Trinidad and Tobago (1998, 2002)	9	0	9	0	26	512	–486	0.00

BELOW: No country can come close to matching the New Zealand record in the Commonwealth Games. They have won all four tournaments and their the gold medal performance in Delhi in 2010 meant they were still unbeaten after 25 matches.

BIGGEST WINS: TOP FIVE (PIC)

Score	Team	Opponent	Year
93–0	New Zealand	Bahamas	1998
85–0	Samoa	Trinidad and Tobago	1998
82–0	South Africa	Sri Lanka	2002
80–0	New Zealand	Sri Lanka	1998
79–0	South Africa	Swaziland	1998

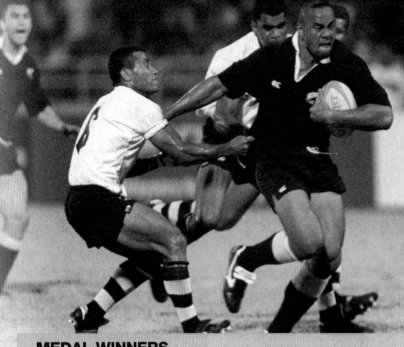

TEAMS WITH NO WINS

Eight of the 24 countries that have taken part in the rugby sevens competition at the Commonwealth Games are still waiting to record their first victory: Cayman Islands, Guyana, India, Namibia, Nieu Islands, Swaziland, Sri Lanka and Trinidad and Tobago.

RIGHT: Playing as a prop forward, rather than a winger, Jonah Lomu provided a powerful presence for New Zealand in their march to the inaugurural Commonwealth Games title in 1998.

MOST MATCHES PLAYED WITHOUT A VICTORY

No side better illustrates the old adage that it is taking part rather than winning that matters than Sri Lanka. Not considered a force in world rugby (their 15-a-side team is currently 42nd in the IRB world rankings), the Sinhalese hold the record for having played in the most Commonwealth Games ties without ever recording a win – 17 matches between 1998 and 2010. They have lost seven of those encounters by more than 50 points.

WORST PERFORMANCE BY HOSTS

Competing in the Commonwealth Games rugby sevens tournament for the first time in their history at Delhi in 2010, home side India set a new record when they became the first host nation not to record a single victory in the tournament. They lost all four of their matches: against Wales (57–6), South Africa (59–0), Tonga (38–5) and Canada (43–10).

BELOW: India (in blue) lost 57–6 to Wales in their opening match of the 2010 Commonwealth Games and never recovered, going on to lose all four of their matches by a combined 197–21.

MEDAL WINNERS

Year	Gold	Silver	Bronze	Host
1998	New Zealand	Fiji	Australia	Malaysia
2002	New Zealand	Fiji	South Africa	England
2006	New Zealand	England	Fiji	Australia
2010	New Zealand	Australia	South Africa	India

ABOVE: Sean O'Farrell of Trinidad and Tobago is halted by Australian duo Cameron Pither (left) and Richard Graham in a 59–0 defeat at the 2002 Commonwealth Games in Manchester. On paper, it was only a little more than an average reverse, because, in nine matches– all defeats – Trinidad and Tobago have conceded an average of 57 points per game and lost by 54 points per game.

ONLY DRAWN MATCH

There has only ever been one drawn match in the history of rugby sevens at the Commonwealth Games. In the 1998 Games at Kuala Lumpur, Malaysia, Samoa and Canada drew their opening Pool C contest 12–12.

DIFFICULT TIMES FOR TRINIDAD AND TOBAGO

Trinidad and Tobago have endured a torrid time in rugby sevens at the Commonwealth Games. In 1998, they lost all five of their matches, scoring 19 points and conceding an all-time tournament record 293. Four years later, in Manchester, England, they lost all four of their matches, scoring a paltry seven points (an all-time tournament low) and conceding 219. Trinidad and Tobago has appeared in only two Commonwealth Games, but the team still has the record for the worst overall points difference (–486) in the competition's history.

IRB SEVENS WORLD SERIES

Introduced in the 1999–2000 season, the IRB Sevens World Series is a year-long circuit of events contested by national sevens teams, with points awarded for their performances at each (there are eight on the current roster) to determine an overall winner. Created to develop sevens rugby as a viable commercial product for the IRB, the tournament has been a huge success: by 2008–09 it was being broadcast to 139 countries in 15 languages.

ALL BLACKS HAVE FUN IN THE DESERT SUN

New Zealand hold the record for the most victories at a single event, claiming the Dubai Sevens title on six occasions over the years (1999–2000, 2000–01, 2001–02, 2002–03, 2007–08 and 2009–10).

ALL-TIME HIGHEST AGGREGATE MATCH SCORE

The record for the most points scored in an IRB World Sevens Series match is 85, during Canada's 78–7 victory over Mexico at the United States Sevens tournament in Los Angeles on 11 February 2006.

RIGHT: New Zealand were inaugural champions of the IRB Sevens World Series and, from left, Orene Ai'i, Brad Fleming, Craig De Goldi and coach Gordon Tietjens, return to Auckland with the trophy in 2000. The team won the final of 10 events in Paris, their fifth of the series, to pip Fiji to the title.

SIX IN A ROW FOR NEW ZEALAND

New Zealand dominated the competition's early years, claiming six consecutive overall titles in six years. In the inaugural tournament in 1999–2000 they won five of the year's ten events; six out of nine in 2000–01; eight out of 12 in 2001–02 – a record number of event wins for a team in a single year; two out of seven in 2002–03; two out of eight in 2003–04; and two out of six in 2004–05. The All Blacks' magnificent run came to an end in the 2005–06 season, when Fiji took the title.

BACK IN BLACK

New Zealand responded to losing their IRB World Sevens Series crown to Fiji in 2005–06 by licking their wounds, dusting themselves down and bouncing back in style. They won four of the year's eight events in 2006–07 (those in South Africa, New Zealand, England and Scotland) and six out of eight events the following year (including the first four – in Dubai, South Africa, New Zealand and Hong Kong) to rack up overall victories numbers seven and eight. They remain the only team in the competition's history to have won back-to-back overall titles.

SERIES WINNERS

Host	Dubai	South Africa	Uruguay	Argentina	New Zealand	Hong Kong	Fiji	Australia	Japan	France	England	Wales	Malaysia	China	Singapore	Chile	USA	Scotland	Series Winner
1999–00	NZ	FIJ	NZ	FIJ	FIJ	NZ	NZ	FIJ	FIJ	NZ	–	–	–	–	–	–	–	–	New Zealand
2000–01	NZ	NZ	–	–	AUS	NZ	–	–	NZ	–	NZ	NZ	AUS	AUS	–	–	–	–	New Zealand
2001–02	NZ	ENG	–	NZ	NZ	NZ	–	SA	–	–	AUS	NZ	NZ	NZ	FIJ	NZ	–	–	New Zealand
2002–03	NZ	FIJ	–	–	ENG	NZ	–	SA	–	–	ENG	ENG	–	–	–	–	–	–	New Zealand
2003–04	SA	ENG	–	–	NZ	ENG	–	–	–	NZ	ENG	–	–	–	SA	–	ARG	–	New Zealand
2004–05	ENG	NZ	–	–	NZ	–	–	–	–	FRA	ENG	–	–	–	–	–	NZ	–	New Zealand
2005–06	ENG	FIJ	–	–	FIJ	ENG	–	–	–	SA	FIJ	–	–	–	FIJ	–	ENG	–	Fiji
2006–07	SA	NZ	–	–	NZ	SAM	–	FIJ	–	–	NZ	–	–	–	–	–	FIJ	NZ	New Zealand
2007–08	NZ	NZ	–	–	NZ	NZ	–	SA	–	–	SAM	–	–	–	–	–	NZ	NZ	New Zealand
2008–09	SA	SA	–	–	ENG	FIJ	–	SA	–	–	ENG	–	–	–	–	–	ARG	FIJ	South Africa
2009–10	NZ	NZ	–	–	FIJ	SAM	–	SAM	–	–	AUS	–	–	–	–	–	SAM	SAM	Samoa

FIRST SUCCESS FOR FABULOUS FIJI

Given their love for, and undoubted talent at, sevens rugby, Fiji could only have looked on in horror – and with a sense of wounded pride – as New Zealand strolled to six successive titles in the IRB World Sevens Series' first six years. But that all changed in 2005–06 when the islanders won four of the year's eight events – in South Africa, New Zealand, England and Singapore – to end the All Blacks' long reign as champions and win the title for the first, and to date only, time in their history.

ABOVE: It was seventh time lucky for Fiji in 2005–06, as they won four of the Series' eight events (in South Africa, New Zealand, England and Singapore) to win the IRB Sevens World Series for the first time. Despite being generally recognised as one of the elite sevens nation in world rugby, it remains their only success in this competition.

HOLDING THE REINS IN RECORD-BREAKING FASHION

One of the least known names in world rugby, Gordon Tietjens, has in recent years nurtured some of the greatest talents in the game, from Christian Cullen and Jonah Lomu to Joe Rokocoko. The long-serving New Zealand sevens coach is also the most successful coach in IRB World Sevens Series history, having led the All Blacks to eight overall titles and 38 event wins in 11 years.

BIGGEST VICTORIES: TOP FIVE

Pos	Score	Winner	Opponent	Venue	Date
1	84–0	South Africa	Malaysia	Tokyo	1 Apr 2000
2	82–0	Scotland	Singapore	Hong Kong	1 Apr 2006
3	80–0	Fiji	China	Hong Kong	24 Mar 2000
4	78–0	New Zealand	Wales	Wellington	9 Feb 2002
=	78–0	South Africa	Mexico	Los Angeles	11 Feb 2006

LEFT: Murrayfield hosted the final event in the IRB Sevens World Series in 2009–10 and Samoa, who won it and three other events, went home with the trophy – their first overall success in the competition.

BELOW: Three event victories (from the eight contested) were enough for South Africa to clinch their first IRB Sevens World Series title in 2008–09.

TENTH TIME LUCKY FOR SOUTH AFRICA

Never considered a real force in the IRB World Sevens Series – although they finished overall runners-up on two occasions (in 2001–02 and 2007–08) they had never claimed more than two event wins in a year (in 2003–04, when they finished fifth) – the Springboks finally found their stride in 2008–09, winning three events (Dubai, South Africa and Australia) to take the title for the first time in their history. Not that they managed to maintain their good form: they finished sixth the following year.

SAMOA'S YEAR IN THE SEVENS SPOTLIGHT

In ten years of participating in the IRB Sevens World Series, Samoa had only ever recorded one event victory (in England in 2007–08) and a best overall placing of third (twice, in 2006–07 and 2007–08). It was hardly the pedigree of future champions. But in 2009–10, Samoa finally turned what had always been considered undoubted promise into tournament-clinching success, winning four of the year's events (United States, Australia, Hong Kong and Scotland) to edge New Zealand to the title and become champions for the first time.

PESAMINO PICTURE PERFECT FOR SAMOA

Renowned for his electric turn of pace, Mikaele Pesamino was a major factor in Samoa's surprise success in the 2009–10 IRB World Sevens Series: the Upolo-born winger scored an impressive 56 tries in the year – second only to Vilimoni Delesau's 83 on the all-time single-season list. Pesamino ended Samoa's victorious campaign by receiving the accolade as the IRB Sevens World Series Player of the Year for 2009–10.

MOST POINTS: TOP FIVE

Pos	Points	Player (country)
1	2374	Ben Gollings (England)
2	1310	Waisale Serevi (Fiji)
3	1178	Santiago Gomez Cora (Argentina)
4	1174	Uale Mai (Samoa)
5	1124	Amasio Raoma (New Zealand)

INAUGURAL PLAYER OF THE YEAR

Famed for leading the England sevens team to three successive triumphs at the Hong Kong Sevens – the jewel-in-the-crown event of the IRB World Sevens Series – between 2002 and 2004, and considered one of the finest exponents of sevens rugby in history, scrum-half Simon Amor, a former Cambridge Blue, holds the distinction being the first man to win the competition's first-ever Player of the Year award in 2003–04. The sevens expert was never selected for a full international.

ABOVE: In 2009–10 Mikaele Pesamino became the second Samoan (after Uale Mai in 2005–06) to collect the IRB Sevens World Series' coveted Player of the Year award

MOST POINTS SCORED IN A GAME

The IRB Sevens World Series record for the most points by a player in a single match is 32. It was set by Saula Rabaka during Fiji's 71–0 victory over Malaysia in Shanghai on 7 April 2001, the final event of the second Sevens World Series. Fiji were third in the final standings, behind New Zealand and Australia.

LEFT: A standout performer for England in sevens rugby, scrum-half Simon Amor was the first player (in 2003–04) to win the IRB Sevens World Series Player of the Year award.

PLAYER OF THE YEAR

Series	Player
2003–04	Simon Amor (England)
2004–05	Orene Ai'i (New Zealand)
2005–06	Uale Mai (Samoa)
2006–07	Afeleke Pelenise (New Zealand)
2007–08	D.J. Forbes (New Zealand)
2008–09	Ollie Phillips (England)
2009–10	Mikaele Pesamino (Samoa)

GOLLINGS: A LEGEND IN SEVENS RUGBY

Ben Gollings may have been a genuine journeyman in the sport's 15-a-side format, plying his trade in club rugby in England, Australia, New Zealand and Japan, but the Cornwall-born fly-half has been a regular feature in the England sevens line-up since 2000 and has forged a reputation as one of the finest exponents of the seven-a-side game on the planet. He holds the IRB World Sevens Series records for the most points in a career (2374 – he is the only player in the competition's history to have amassed more than 1350 points) and for the most points in a single season (with 343 in 2005–06).

CORA LEADS THE WAY FOR THE PUMAS

When it comes to pondering who might be the finest sevens player of all time, most people would fail to progress beyond the names of Fiji's Waisale Serevi or England's Ben Gollings, but another outstanding candidate is Argentina's Santiago Gomez Cora. The current Pumas sevens captain has scored an astonishing 230 tries in IRB World Sevens Series matches, an all-time competition record. He is one of only two players, Gollings is the other, to have passed the 200 try mark, and he stands third – behind Gollings and Serevi – on the tournament's all-time points-scoring list with 1,178 points.

RIGHT: No player has scored more tries in IRB Sevens World Series matches than the 230 scored by Argentina's legendary captain Santiago Gomez Cora.

MOST TRIES: TOP FIVE

Pos	Tries	Player (country)
1	230	Santiago Gomez Cora (Argentina)
2	202	Ben Gollings (England)
3	179	Fabian Juries (South Africa)
4	151	Mikaele Pesamino (Samoa)
5	132	Uale Mai (Samoa)

MOST APPEARANCES

No player has played in more IRB World Sevens Series matches than Uale Mai. The Samoan fly-half, the first player from his country to have won the IRB Sevens Player of the Year award and the most capped sevens player of all time, has made 62 appearances in the competition.

DEVASTATING FIJIAN VILIMONI DELASAU SETS WORLD SERIES TRY-SCORING MARKS

A barn-storming winger or centre, who has also won 31 caps for Fiji and three for the Pacific Islanders in the 15-a-side format of the game, Vilimoni Delasau first made his name playing for Fiji on the IRB World Sevens Series circuit. In the 1999–2000 campaign, he scored 83 tries (second in the list is Samoa's Mikaele Pesamino with 56) and set the record for the most tries by a player in a single game – six in Fiji's match against China in Hong Kong on 24 March 2000.

LEFT: Vilimoni Delasau was in electric form for Fiji in the 1999–2000 IRB Sevens World Series. He scored a single-season record of 83 tries in the inaugural competition – and a single-game record six – but it was New Zealand who claimed the trophy.

SEVENS RUGBY
HONG KONG SEVENS

The jewel in the crown of the IRB World Sevens Series and the most prestigious sevens event in world rugby, the Hong Kong Sevens was first contested in 1976 and was already attracting the game's best teams within a few years of its inception. Played in the impressive Hong Kong Stadium since 1994, the popularity of the tournament with players and fans alike did much to trigger the relatively recent explosion of interest in seven-a-side rugby around the globe.

BIRTH OF THE HONG KONG SEVENS

The origins of the world-famous Hong Kong Sevens lie in a pre-lunch drinks conversation in the spring of 1975 between A.D.C. 'Tokkie' Smith, a South African entrepreneur who was the chairman of the Hong Kong Rugby Football Union, and Ian Gow, the promotions manager of a tobacco company, who thought it would be a great idea to sponsor a sevens tournament that attracted the best teams from around the world. A year later, the Hong Kong Sevens was contested for the first time, with New Zealand representatives Cantabrians winning the inaugural title.

MOST TOURNAMENT WINS

12	**Fiji** (1977–78, 1980, 1984, 1990–92, 1997–99, 2005, 2009)
9	**New Zealand** (1986–87, 1989, 1994–96, 2000–01, 2008)
5	**Australia** (1979, 1982–83, 1985, 1988)
4	**England** (2002–04, 2006)
3	**Samoa** (1993, 2001, 2010)
1	**Cantabrians** (1976)
1	**Barbarian FC** (1981)

FABULOUS HONG KONG FUN FOR FIJI

No side has enjoyed more success at the Hong Kong Sevens than Fiji. The South Pacific islanders have won the biggest prize on the annual sevens circuit on 12 occasions. They also hold the record for being the only team in the tournament's history to have taken three successive titles on two occasions (between 1990 and 1992, and 1997 and 1999). The only other teams to have won the prestigious competition three times in a row are New Zealand (between 1994 and 1996) and England (between 2002 and 2004).

NON-NATIONAL GLORY

Only two non-national teams have walked away with the Hong Kong Sevens title over the years: Cantabrians (from New Zealand), who took the inaugural title in 1976 when they beat the Wallaroos (from Australia) 24–8 in the final; and British representative side Barbarian FC, who beat Australia 12–10 in the 1981 final.

BELOW: Fiji have enjoyed more success in the Hong Kong Sevens than any other country, winning 12 titles – the last of which came in 2009.

HONG KONG SEVENS VENUES

The Hong Kong Sevens has been contested at three venues over the years: at the 2,750-capacity Hong Kong Football Club stadium between 1976 and 1981; at the 28,000-capacity Government Stadium, situated in So Kon Po, Wanchai, between 1982 and 1992; and at the 40,000-capacity Hong Kong Stadium – the redeveloped Government Stadium, which has been the new home of the Hong Kong national football team – since 1994.

LEFT: Skyscrapers form a stunning backdrop to the Hong Kong Stadium.

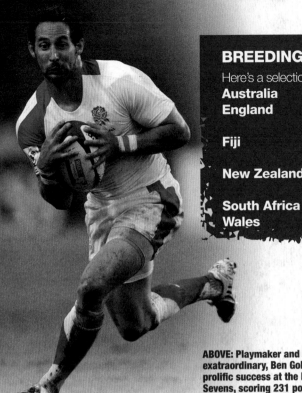

BREEDING POOL OF TALENT

Here's a selection of players who have cut their international rugby teeth at the Hong Kong Sevens:

Australia	George Gregan, Joe Roff, Ben Tune
England	Lawrence Dallaglio, Matt Dawson, Austin Healey, Josh Lewsey, Mathew Tait, David Strettle
Fiji	Rupeni Caucau, Napolioni Nalaga, Sireli Bobo, Noa Nadruku, Joeli Vidiri, William Ryder, Marika Vunibaka, Vilimoni Delasau
New Zealand	Jonah Lomu, Christian Cullen, Zinzan Brooke, John Schuster, Mils Muliaina, Rodney So'oialo, Joe Rokocoko, Rico Gear
South Africa	Jean de Villiers, Bryan Habana, Ricky Januarie, Brent Russell, Kabamba Floors
Wales	Jamie Roberts, James Hook

ABOVE: Playmaker and kicker exatraordinary, Ben Gollings enjoyed prolific success at the Hong Kong Sevens, scoring 231 points, kicking 73 goals (both all-time records) and helping England to a hat-trick of titles between 2002 and 2004.

ALL-TIME LEADING POINTS-SCORER

England's sevens legend Ben Gollings holds two all-time records at the Hong Kong Sevens: he has accumulated more points at the event than any other player in history (231) and has kicked the most goals (73) – 'goals' being the term used in sevens rugby for conversions.

ALL BLACKS ARE HONG KONG'S ALL-TIME TRY KINGS

Fiji may have outstripped them in terms of titles (winning the event 12 times as opposed to nine), but no side has scored more tries in Hong Kong Sevens matches than New Zealand. The All Blacks have crossed the tryline a record 294 times in the tournament's history.

RUGBY WORLD CUP SEVENS COMES TO HONG KONG

In 2005, for the first and only time in the tournament's history, the Hong Kong Sevens tournament doubled as the Rugby World Cup Sevens, with teams competing for the coveted Melrose Cup. Fiji, led by sevens legend Waisale Serevi, won the day, beating Argentina (22–14) in the quarter-finals, England (24–19) in the semi-finals and New Zealand (29–17) in the final to take the title.

BELOW: China's 'Johnny' Zhang is the surprise name at the top of the Hong Kong Sevens' all-time try-scoring list with 25.

JOHNNY ZHANG TOPS ALL-TIME TRY-SCORING LIST

Given the vast number of big-name players to have graced the tournament over the years (from David Campese and Jonah Lomu to Bryan Habana and Mils Muliaina), it may come as something of a surprise to learn that the leading try-scorer in Hong Kong Sevens history hails from China. Zhang Zhiqiang, known as 'Johnny' Zhang – who was once on the playing staff at the famous Leicester Tigers club in England – has scored an event record 25 tries.

ONLY NO SHOW FOR NEW ZEALAND

The year 1982 was a history-making one for the Hong Kong Sevens … and all because of a row. The argument started when the tournament's organizers requested that New Zealand send an official team, as opposed to a representative side, to the event. The New Zealand Rugby Union refused to comply, the organizers said they would not allocate a place in the event for an unofficial team and, as a result, it was the only time in history that New Zealand did not send a team to the Hong Kong Sevens.

PART VII
WOMEN'S RUGBY

Although women have been playing rugby since the 1880s, the problems that would arise to impede the game's growth were apparent as early as 1891, when a planned tour to the United Kingdom by an all-female team from New Zealand was scrapped after a public outcry. Women should not be participating in this highly physical, rough-and-tumble game, so the argument ran. And for years, the odd match apart – notably a well-documented women's charity match at Cardiff Arms Park on 16 December 1917 which saw Cardiff Ladies beat Newport Ladies 6–0 – women's rugby remained on the backburner. It wasn't until the 1960s that widespread interest was revived. It began among young women in the

universities of Western Europe and, after this new breed of player had graduated and taken her interest in the game with her, adult teams started to spring up. In 1990, the first international tournament took place – the Rugbyfest, held in Christchurch and contested by New Zealand, the United States, the USSR and the Netherlands, which saw the home side take the spoils.

The first Women's Rugby World Cup (an unofficial event) took place in Wales the following year (with the United States taking the inaugural title), but it wasn't until the mid-1990s, by which time the game had the full backing of the International Rugby Board, that women's rugby really started to take off: in 1996, the first Women's Home Nations Championship took place (by 2002 it had become the Women's Six Nations Championship); in 1997, the first Hong Kong Women's Sevens was staged; and, a year later, the first fully sanctioned Women's Rugby World Cup was contested. Women's rugby is still an amateur sport and, in terms of development, a long way behind the men's version of the game, but it is very much on an upward curve.

BELOW: New Zealand made it four Women's Rugby World Cup triumphs in a row when they beat England 13–10 in a hard-fought final in 2010.

WOMEN'S RUGBY
WORLD CUP

First staged in 1991, when 12 teams descended on Wales and the title was claimed by the United States, the Women's Rugby World Cup did not really get off the ground until 1998, by which time it had received the full backing of the IRB (and its significant marketing capabilities). In 2010, the sixth edition of the tournament, 30 teams fought for the title with matches screened to 227 million homes in 127 territories around the world.

UNITED STATES STRIKE GOLD

It may have been unofficial, but the inaugural Women's Rugby World Cup in Wales in 1991 was a pivotal moment in the women's game: it was the first time it had been brought to a global audience. Twelve teams fought for the title and it was the United States who emerged as the tournament's top dogs, beating the Netherlands (7–0) and the USSR (46–0) to top their pool, then edging to victory over New Zealand (7–0) in the semi-finals and beating England (19–6) in the final to become women's rugby's first world champions.

OVERALL RECORD (RANKED BY WIN PERCENTAGE)

Team	P	W	L	D	For	Against	Diff	Win%
New Zealand	22	21	1	0	980	132	+848	95.45
England	28	23	5	0	902	260	+642	82.14
United States	28	22	6	0	1028	285	+743	78.57
France	27	17	10	0	652	327	+325	62.96
Samoa	9	5	4	0	131	114	+17	55.56
Australia	19	10	9	0	369	285	+84	52.63
Canada	29	14	14	1	620	469	+151	48.28
Spain	19	9	10	0	272	357	−85	47.37
Netherlands	13	6	7	0	264	238	+26	46.15
Kazakhstan	25	11	14	0	395	504	−109	44.00
Wales	17	6	10	1	293	300	−7	35.29
Ireland	23	8	15	0	262	487	−225	34.782
Japan	9	3	6	0	68	402	−334	33.33
Italy	13	4	9	0	187	246	−59	30.77
South Africa	10	2	8	0	90	414	−324	20.00
Sweden	16	3	13	0	127	518	−391	18.75
Russia/USSR	8	1	7	0	37	286	−249	12.50
Germany	9	1	8	0	65	540	−475	11.11
Scottish Students	5	0	5	0	37	160	−123	0.00

BELOW: There was disappointment for England as they created an unwanted piece of Women's Rugby World Cup history: their defeat against New Zealand was a third consecutive loss in the final.

WORLD CUP-WINNING WAYS FOR PALMER

Having dabbled with rugby in her youth, Farah Palmer first took up the sport seriously in 1992 while studying at Otago University. By 1994 she was also a regular for Otago in provincial rugby, playing at hooker. Palmer made her debut for the Black Ferns against Australia in Sydney on 31 August 1996 and was appointed New Zealand women's captain the following year. In 1998, she led the Black Ferns to their first-ever Women's Rugby World Cup triumph and on to a successful defence of their crown four years later. In 2006 she became the only person in history to captain a side to three Women's Rugby World Cup final victories and announced her retirement from international rugby at the end of the tournament.

ABOVE: Farah Palmer was an outstanding captain for New Zealand, leading the Black Ferns to three Women's Rugby World Cup titles in a row (in 1998, 2002 and 2006.

FOUR IN A ROW FOR THE BLACK FERNS

New Zealand have been the tournament's dominant team since the 1998 Women's Rugby World Cup – the first edition of the event to receive the full backing of the IRB. In 1998, in the Netherlands, the Black Ferns beat the United States (44–12) in the final to take the crown for the first time. Four years later, in Spain, they beat England (19–9) in the final to become the first team to defend their crown. They made it three in a row in Canada in 2006, beating England (25–17) in the final for the second successive time, and completed a hat-trick of final victories over England in 2010 (winning 13–10) to claim their fourth title in a row.

RUSH ROARS INTO THE RECORD BOOKS

The younger sister of All Black Xavier Rush and a member of the famous Marist Brothers Old Boys Rugby Club in Auckland (a club that has nurtured 29 male All Blacks and 29 Black Ferns over the years), Annaleah Rush had a dream Women's Rugby World Cup in 1998, scoring a tournament record 73 points as the Black Ferns romped to the world title for the first time in their history.

LEFT: New Zealand coach Jed Rowlands is flanked by Black Ferns captain Farah Palmer (left) and Rochelle Martin as the team returned to New Zealand after winning the Women's Rugby World Cup for the third consecutive time in 2006, once again beating England in the final.

TOURNAMENT WINNERS

Year	Winner	Host
1991	United States	Wales
1994	England	Scotland
1998	New Zealand	Netherlands
2002	New Zealand	Spain
2006	New Zealand	Canada
2010	New Zealand	England

TOURNAMENT WOES FOR GERMANY

Germany's first-ever match at the Women's Rugby World Cup, against New Zealand in Amsterdam on 2 May 1998 (a supremely difficult assignment anyway), turned out to be a miserable and record-breaking affair: they slumped to a 134–6 defeat – the heaviest in the tournament's history. And things hardly improved for the Germans: they lost their final two fixtures (34–5 against Italy and 55–12 against Wales) and crashed out of the competition having conceded 308 points – a record for a team in a single tournament. They also hold the record for the most points conceded in all Women's Rugby World Cup matches, with 540.

DOCTER'S TRIES ARE NO CURE FOR THE NETHERLANDS

The 1998 Women's Rugby World Cup may not have been the happiest of occasions for hosts Netherlands – they effectively finished in tenth place after winning the Shield competition – but for one of their players, Minke Docter, it was a competition to remember: she scored nine tries, an all-time record for a player at a single Women's Rugby World Cup tournament.

ALL-TIME LEADING POINTS-SCORERS

No side has scored more points in Women's Rugby World Cup matches than the United States. The winners of the inaugural championship in 1991 have scored 1,028 points in 28 matches in the tournament to date. They also hold the record for the most points at a single Women's Rugby World Cup tournament, with 397 in 1994.

ENGLAND TAKE SPOILS AT TROUBLED SECOND WORLD CUP

Debates as to whether the IRB would give its official backing to the tournament marred the second Women's Rugby World Cup. Originally scheduled to be played in the Netherlands in 1995, the tournament was brought forward a year to avoid clashing with the men's edition of the event being played in South Africa. The tournament was then placed under a shadow when the IRB threatened to penalize any union that sent a team to the competition. As a result, only 90 days before the opening match, the Dutch withdrew as hosts. Scotland duly stepped in to host the event and a hastily arranged tournament saw 11 national teams – all from the northern hemisphere (plus a Scottish Students XV) – contest the second Women's Rugby World Cup. England won the title following a 38–23 victory over defending champions United States in the final.

LEFT: Annaleah Rush's tournament-record 73 points powered the Black Ferns to Women's Rugby World Cup glory in 1998.

BIGGEST VICTORIES: TOP FIVE

Winner	Score	Opponent	Venue	Date
New Zealand	134–6	Germany	Amsterdam	2 May 1998
United States	121–0	Japan	Melrose	15 Apr 1994
New Zealand	117–0	Germany	Barcelona	13 May 2002
United States	111–0	Sweden	Melrose	11 Apr 1994
France	99–0	Japan	Edinburgh	17 Apr 1994

WOMEN'S RUGBY
INTERNATIONAL RUGBY

Compared to men's international rugby, which was up and running as early as 1871, women's international rugby is a relatively recent affair. After years of battling the universal stereotype – that the rough-and-tumble world of the rugby pitch was no place for a lady – the first official match finally took place on 13 June 1982. Although the growth of the women's game has been steady, it has been far from rapid: it wasn't until 2006 that 50 internationals were played in a year for the first time.

MOST CAPPED PLAYER: DONNA KENNEDY (SCOTLAND)

Despite having only one year's experience under her belt (playing for the Biggar club in Scotland), Donna Kennedy made her international debut, against Ireland, on 14 February 1993, and went on to become a permanent fixture in the Scotland women's side for the next 17 years. The No.8 was part of the Scotland side that won the grand slam in 1998, appeared at five Women's Rugby World Cups and bowed out of the international game after the 2010 tournament as the most capped player in women's international rugby history (with 112 caps).

STILL WAITING FOR THAT WINNING FEELING

There are 12 countries still active in women's international rugby that have yet to record their first victory: Denmark (five matches played), Brazil (one), Portugal (one), Zimbabwe (one), Bahamas (two), Kyrgyzstan (two), Malaysia (two), Rwanda (two), Tonga (two), St Vincent and the Grenadines (three), Bosnia and Herzegovina (four) and Serbia. The Soviet Union contested six internationals between 1990 and 1991 without ever recording a victory.

RIGHT: England's Gill Burns grabs a lineout during the 1994 Women's Rugby World Cup final, the most important of her country's 107 international victories.

MOST WOMEN'S INTERNATIONALS PLAYED BY A TEAM

England have played more official matches (128) than any other side in women's international rugby. They also hold the record for the most victories (107) and for the most points scored (4,631 – the next best on the list is France with 2,488 points).

UP AND RUNNING

The day, 13 June 1982, was a historic one for women's international rugby. To celebrate the 50th anniversary of the Dutch Rugby Union, a match was organized between the Dutch national women's team and the French national women's team in Utrecht. France won what would come to be considered the first-ever women's international 4–0.

LEFT: A legend in women's rugby, Scotland's Donna Kennedy won more international caps than any other player in history (112) before retiring in 2010

BIGGEST VICTORIES: TOP FIVE

Score	Team	Opponent	Venue	Date
141–3	Netherlands	Denmark	Toulouse	2 May 2004
134–6	New Zealand	Germany	Amsterdam	2 May 1998
121–0	United States	Japan	Melrose	15 Apr 1994
117–0	New Zealand	Germany	Barcelona	13 May 2002
113–0	Netherlands	Denmark	Amsterdam	8 May 2003

WALES STRUGGLE TO PUT EARLY WOES BEHIND THEM

Wales got off to the worst of starts in women's international rugby, losing 13 and drawing one (9–9 against Canada at the 1991 Women's Rugby World Cup) of their first 14 matches. A pattern was set and although the gloom may have lifted, or at least lessened over the years, Wales still hold the record in women's international rugby for the most defeats (65) and the most points conceded (2000).

MOST DEFEATS IN A ROW FOR ONE TEAM

Three countries share the unwanted record for the most consecutive defeats in women's international rugby with ten losses: Germany were the first (between 24 August 1996 and 9 May 1998); Spain followed (between 18 May 2002 and 7 April 2003); and the most recent is Ireland (between 9 March 2003 and 1 May 2004).

ALL-TIME GREAT: ANNA RICHARDS (NEW ZEALAND)

Former New Zealand fly-half Anna Richards had arguably the most successful career in women's international rugby. A talented sportswoman, she first played rugby at university in Christchurch and, in 1989, was selected to appear in the Black Ferns' first-ever international. It was the start of a long and fruitful relationship with the national team: in a career spanning 17 years (she was still playing for the Black Ferns aged 40), she appeared in six Women's Rugby World Cups (picking up a winners' medal in 1998, 2002, 2006 and 2010) and bowed out of the sport as the Black Ferns' most capped player of all time.

BELOW: Kelly Brazier and New Zealand gained revenge on England in the 2010 Women's Rugby World Cup final after the Black Ferns' unbeaten run had been halted at 20 matches at Twickenham in 2009.

ABOVE: Four Women's Rugby World Cup-winners medals and a career that spanned 17 years pay testament to Anna Richards' status as one of the finest women players of all time.

THE BLACK FERNS' ALL-TIME RECORD-BREAKING RUN

New Zealand's response to a 22–17 home defeat at the hands of England at North Shore City on 16 June 2001 was a record-breaking run. The Black Ferns bounced back by winning all four matches at the 2002 Women's Rugby World Cup (and defended their crown with a satisfying 19–9 victory over England in the final) and embarked on a staggering winning streak that included a third World Cup triumph and stretched 20 matches and 8 years 158 days. The unbeaten run finally came to an end on 21 November 2009 when they lost 10–3 to England at Twickenham.

UNOFFICIAL WORLD RANKING

Although the International Rugby Board produces a continually updated rankings list for the men's game, there is no equivalent for women's international rugby. However, given that the IRB bases its seedings for tournaments on a side's performance at the previous event, a list of the top ten from the 2010 Women's Rugby World Cup is the closest thing to an official rankings list one can find. The top ten would currently read:

1	New Zealand	6	Canada
2	England	7	Ireland
3	Australia	8	Scotland
4	France	9	Wales
5	United States	10	South Africa

SIX NATIONS CHAMPIONSHIP

The Women's Six Nations is an annual event that started life as the Home Nations in 1996 (with England, Ireland, Scotland and Wales). It became the Women's Five Nations in 1999 (with the addition of France – and Spain, who replaced Ireland between 2000 and 2002) and has been known as the Women's Six Nations since 2002 (with the reintroduction of Ireland in 2002 and Italy, who replaced Spain, since 2007).

IN A LEAGUE OF THEIR OWN

England have dominated the championship in all its forms since the very start in 1996, claiming 12 titles in 16 attempts, including the last six, with 11 grand slams. They hold the all-time records for the most points scored (2,886); the most match victories (66); the highest winning percentage (92.96 – they have lost only five times in 71 matches); and the most points scored in a single tournament (264 in 2003 en route to claiming a grand slam and triple crown).

SEASON TO FORGET FOR SCOTLAND

The Women's Six Nations Championship record for the most points conceded by a team in a single tournament is 231, set by Scotland in 2011. The Scots' season to forget, losing 58–3 to France, 41–12 to Wales, 22–5 to Ireland, 89–0 to England (the heaviest defeat in the tournament's history) and rounded out a sorry campaign by losing 26–0 to Italy to finish bottom of the table.

ABOVE: England made it five Women's Six Nations Championships in a row in 2010 and they would make it six in 2011. Back-rowers (left to right) Heather Fisher, Catherine Spencer, Margaret Alphonsi and Karen Jones celebrate with the trophy.

TOURNAMENT WINNERS

Year	Winner
HOME NATIONS (1996–98)	
1996	England – grand slam/triple crown
1997	England – grand slam/triple crown
1998	Scotland – grand slam/triple crown
FIVE NATIONS (1999–2001)	
1999	England – grand slam/triple crown
2000	England – grand slam/triple crown
2001	England – grand slam/triple crown
SIX NATIONS (2002–)	
2002	France – grand slam
2003	England – grand slam/triple crown
2004	France – grand slam
2005	France – grand slam
2006	England – grand slam/triple crown
2007	England – grand slam/triple crown
2008	England – grand slam/triple crown
2009	England
2010	England – grand slam/triple crown
2011	England – grand slam/triple crown

FRANCE FINALLY FIND THEIR FEET

Three runners-up finishes in their first three Women's Five Nations Championship campaigns (between 1999 and 2001) may not have represented the worst of starts, but France, who (along with the Netherlands) are the oldest side in women's international rugby, wanted more. It all came together in 2002 when they romped to a 46–0 victory over Ireland to complete the grand slam and record their first-ever title win. And although they slipped to third overall in 2003, they bounced back with successive grand slams in 2004 and 2005. They have not, however, won the title since, but ran England close in 2011.

LEFT: France have won two Women's Six Nations Championship titles since 1999, most recently in 2005.

WHEN IRISH EYES AREN'T SMILING

Ireland endured a torrid time in the Home Nations (and then the Five Nations) Championship between 1996 and 1999, winning only one of 13 matches – 22–6 against Wales in March 1996. Such was the battering they had taken that they withdrew from the tournament between 2000 and 2001. Although their form may have improved since their return to the fold in 2002, winning 16 of 48 matches (including consecutive third-place finishes in 2009–11), Ireland still hold the unwelcome record of having suffered the most defeats in the competition's history 46 in 63 matches.

BELOW: Amy Davis of Ireland throws out a pass against Italy during a 2011 match between the countries with the two worst records in the Women's Six Nations Championship.

OVERALL RECORD (RANKED BY WINNING PERCENTAGE)

Team (Span)	P	W	L	D	For	Against	Diff	Win%
England (1996–)	71	66	5	0	2886	374	+2512	92.96
France (1999–)	62	46	16	0	1261	662	+599	74.19
Scotland (1996–)	71	28	42	1	850	1382	−532	39.44
Wales (1996–)	71	25	45	1	802	1529	−727	35.21
Spain (2000–06)	33	10	22	1	240	899	−659	30.30
Ireland (1996–99, 2002–)	63	17	46	0	547	1294	−747	26.98
Italy (2007–)	25	4	20	1	281	684	−402	12.00

WOEFUL WALES HIT ROCK BOTTOM

Wales have not enjoyed the best of times in the Women's Six Nations Championship (in all its forms) over the years, finishing last on six occasions and recording a best finish of second (three times), but they hit rock bottom in 2001, when they lost all four of their matches and scored an all-time tournament low points tally during the campaign (with three).

SCOTLAND SNEAK TO GRAND SLAM SUCCESS

Having finished second in the Home Nations Championship in 1996 and 1997, Scotland discovered tournament-winning ways in 1998, beating Ireland in Dublin (15–0), Wales in Cardiff (22–12) and defending champions England in a tense match at Stewarts Melville (8–5) to complete a memorable grand slam. It was their first and to date, only title in their history.

ITALY'S SIX NATIONS STRUGGLES

As has been the case with the men's team, Italy's women have struggled since joining the Women's Six Nations Championship in 2007, winning only four of 25 matches (31–10 against Scotland on 16 March 2008, 19–15 against Wales on 21 March 2010, 12–8 against Wales on 2 February 2011 and 26–0 against Scotland on 20 March 2011). It is the worst return in Six Nations history.

BELOW: Maria Grazia Cioffi and Italy have found victories hard to come by in the Women's Six Nations Championship but they doubled their win tally in 2011.

BIGGEST MARGINS OF VICTORIES: TOP FIVE

Winner	Margin	Score	Opponent	Venue	Date
England	89	89–0	Scotland	London	13 Mar 2011
England	83	86–3	Spain	Madrid	11 Feb 2006
England	79	79–0	Ireland	Worcester	17 Feb 2002
England	76	76–0	Spain	London	12 Mar 2005
England	70	76–6	Italy	Rome	9 Feb 2008
England	69	72–3	Scotland	London	15 Mar 2009

WORLD CUP SEVENS

It was a pivotal moment in the women's game: after a series of qualifying events that had been staged around the world since 2008, 16 national teams descended on Dubai in March 2009 to contest the first-ever Women's Rugby World Cup Sevens (which was held alongside the men's tournament). Australia won the day, beating New Zealand (15–10) in a momentous final to walk away with the inaugural title.

THE QUALIFIERS

Sixteen teams qualified for the inaugural Women's Rugby World Cup Sevens tournament in Dubai: South Africa and Uganda (from Africa); Japan, Thailand and China (Asia); England, Netherlands, Russia, Spain, France and Italy (Europe); Australia and New Zealand (Oceania); Canada and the United States (North America); and Brazil (South America).

BELOW: Australia celebrate their last-gasp 15–10 victory over New Zealand at the inaugural Women's Rugby World Cup Sevens event in Dubai in 2009.

AUSTRALIA EDGE OUT NEW ZEALAND IN THRILLING FINAL

Australia rallied from the disappointment of finishing second in their pool – they beat China (50–12) and the Netherlands (36–0) but suffered a surprise defeat to France (14–10) – in memorable style, beating England (17–10) in the quarter-finals and South Africa (19–10) in the semi-finals to set up a final showdown with Oceania neighbours New Zealand. And what a final it turned out to be: Nicole Beck and Debby Hodgkinson scored for Australia to give them a 10–0 lead; Justine Lavea and Carla Hohepa crossed the line for New Zealand to level the scores; and the final whistle blew. The match went into sudden-death extra time and a mere 50 seconds had passed before Australia's Shelly Matcham crossed the line to clinch a stunning victory.

PLATE/BOWL FINALS

One of the great attractions of sevens rugby is that teams who struggle in the main competition are then placed in secondary competitions: the Bowl for the lowest-placed teams, and the Plate for those teams that drop out at the quarter-final stage. The results of the Bowl and Plate finals at the 2009 Women's Rugby World Cup Sevens were as follows:

Bowl: China 10–7 Brazil
Plate: England 12–0 Canada

NO FUN IN THE SUN FOR UGANDA

Despite losing the match to South Africa (24–0), Uganda's reward for reaching the final of the Africa qualifying tournament for the 2009 Women's Rugby World Cup Sevens was a place in the tournament proper in Dubai. Once they were there, however, they enjoyed very little fun in the desert sun. Uganda lost all four of their matches and they scored a paltry 14 points – the fewest by any team in the tournament.

BIGGEST VICTORIES: TOP FIVE (BY WINNING MARGIN)

Pos	Score	Winner	Opponent	Year
1	50–0	New Zealand	Uganda	2009
2	47–0	England	Japan	2009
3	52–7	Canada	Thailand	2009
=	45–0	New Zealand	Italy	2009
5	50–12	Australia	China	2009
=	38–0	Canada	Brazil	2009

BLACK FERNS TOP TRY-SCORING LIST

It may have come as scant consolation – given the dramatic nature of their defeat to Australia in the final – but New Zealand were the leading try-scorers at the first-ever Women's Rugby World Cup Sevens tournament in 2009. They scored 29 tries, four more than the champions Australia managed.

MOST TRIES IN A MATCH (TEAM)

The record for most tries in a Women's Rugby World Cup Sevens match by a team is eight, achieved by: Australia (during their 50–12 victory against China); Canada (during their 52–7 win over Thailand); and New Zealand (during the Black Ferns' 50–0 rout of Uganda).

MOST TRIES IN A MATCH (PLAYER)

The record for the most tries in a match by one player is four, set by two players: Debby Hodgkinson (during Australia's 36–0 win against the Netherlands), and Mandy Marchak (during Canada's 52–7 romp against Thailand).

HOHEPA SHOWS WORLD CLASS FORM

Blessed with great pace and a skill set that would see her go on to star at the 2010 Women's Rugby World Cup and earn her that year's IRB Women's Personality of the Year award, Carla Hohepa shone for New Zealand at the 2009 Women's Rugby World Cup Sevens competition, finishing as the tournament's leading try-scorer with nine tries.

MOST POINTS: TOP FIVE

Pos	Points	Player (Country)
1	52	Selica Winiata (New Zealand)
2	45	Carla Hohepa (New Zealand)
3	40	Yang Hong (China)
4	38	Ashley Patzer (Canada)
5	35	Debby Hodgkinson (Australia)

ABOVE: New Zealand's Selica Winiata contributed a record 52 points to her country's cause at the 2009 Women's Rugby World Cup Sevens tournament, but she was on the losing side against Australia in the final.

LEFT: The world got its first glimpse of Carla Hohepa's talent at the 2009 Women's Rugby World Cup Sevens. The New Zealand flyer topped the try-scoring charts with nine tries.

LEADING POINTS-SCORER

Manawatu star Selica Winiata, who doubles as a police officer in Palmerston North, New Zealand, when she isn't playing rugby, was the leading points-scorer at the inaugural Women's Rugby World Cup Sevens tournament in Dubai in 1999. The Black Ferns fly-half scored 52 points.

LEADING TRY-SCORER: TOP FIVE

Pos	Tries	Player (Country)
1	9	Carla Hohepa (New Zealand)
2	8	Yang Hong (China)
3	7	Debby Hodgkinson (Australia)
4	5	Brooke Hilditch (Canada)
=	5	Jess Watkins (USA)

IRB WORLD RANKINGS AND AWARDS

The IRB World Rankings, introduced on 9 September 2003, is a system used to rank the world's international teams based on their results, with all teams given a rating between 0 and 100. The rankings are based on a points-exchange system in which sides take or gain points off each other depending on the result of a match. The points gained or lost in a match depend on the relative strengths of each team and the margin of defeat or victory, with an allowance made for teams who have home advantage. Due to the singular importance of the event, points-exchanges are doubled for Rugby World Cup matches. When the system was introduced, England, as a result of their 2003 Rugby World Cup victory, were installed at no.1, but New Zealand, thanks largely to their dominance in the Tri-Nations championship, have been the most consistently ranked no.1 team, holding the top spot for approximately 75 per cent of the time between 2003 and 2011. First presented in 2001, the IRB Awards are bestowed annually by the game's world governing body to honour significant achievements in the sport, with the Player of the Year award considered the most prestigious accolade.

BELOW: Richie McCaw has won the IRB Player of the Year award on three occasions (in 2006, 2009 and 2010). No other player has received the accolade more than once.

Pos	Member Union	Rating Point	Pos	Member Union	Rating Point
1	New Zealand	91.43	25	Belgium	56.50
2	Australia	87.42	26	Morocco	56.13
3	France	84.70	27	Hong Kong	54.34
4	South Africa	84.34	28	Moldova	54.09
5	England	81.58	29	Brazil	54.04
6	Ireland	80.65	30	Poland	53.67
7	Argentina	80.28	31	Kazakhstan	53.62
8	Wales	80.18	32	Korea	53.36
9	Tonga	76.63	33	Ukraine	53.22
10	Scotland	76.20	34	Czech Republic	52.99
11	Samoa	75.81	35	Zimbabwe	52.40
12	Italy	73.99	36	Tunisia	52.35
13	Canada	72.92	37	Germany	51.81
14	Georgia	71.09	38	Sweden	51.34
15	Japan	70.45	39	Lithuania	51.14
16	Fiji	68.78	40	Kenya	49.18
17	United States of America	65.63	41	Paraguay	48.84
18	Romania	63.98	42	Netherlands	47.71
19	Namibia	61.24	43	Uganda	47.69
20	Portugal	60.67	44	Ivory Coast	47.52
21	Russia	60.54	45	Sri Lanka	47.03
22	Uruguay	60.00	46	Papua New Guinea	46.19
23	Chile	59.52	47	Bermuda	45.94
24	Spain	59.43	48	Trinidad and Tobago	45.85
			49	Singapore	45.66

BELOW: John Afoa scored the last of New Zealand's five tries during the All Blacks' 37–25 victory over Walles at the Millennium Stadium, Cardiff, on 27 November 2010.

BOTTOM: Dan Parks kicked all of Scotland's points in their unexpected 21–17 victory over South Africa at Murrayfield on 20 November 2010.

Pos	Member Union	Rating Point	Pos	Member Union	Rating Point
50	Croatia	45.56	74	St Vincent and	
51	Venezuela	45.36		the Grenadines	39.30
52	Senegal	45.24	75	India	39.19
53	Malta	45.23	76	Barbados	39.13
54	Cook Islands	44.61	77	Solomon Islands	39.06
55	Madagascar	44.31	78	Cameroon	38.33
56	Switzerland	44.22	79	Bulgaria	37.36
57	Chinese Taipei	43.62	80	Austria	36.79
58	Andorra	42.83	81	Swaziland	36.68
59	Latvia	42.69	82	Botswana	36.68
60	Guyana	42.54	83	Jamaica	36.35
61	Israel	42.02	84	Bahamas	36.33
62	China	41.78	85	Tahiti	36.25
63	Malaysia	41.75	86	Guam	36.24
64	Peru	41.64	87	Bosnia & Herzegovina	36.18
65	Thailand	41.46	88	Nigeria	35.29
66	Cayman	41.23	89	Monaco	35.17
67	Niue Island	41.11	90	Norway	34.81
68	Denmark	40.81	91	Vanuatu	34.77
69	Serbia	40.81	92	Luxembourg	32.26
70	Slovenia	40.20	93	Finland	27.70
71	Hungary	40.10			
72	Zambia	39.94			
73	Colombia	39.59			

ABOVE: Chris Ashton scores the second of his team's tries during England's eye-catching 21–20 victory over Australia at Sydney on 19 June 2010.

BELOW: Hong Kong (with Jamie Hood passing the ball) – ranked in the 30s – were strong favourites to beat Malaysia – ranked in the 50s – at the 16th Asian Games at Guangzhou, China, in November 2010. The form book held up as Hong Kong triumphed 38-10.

APPENDIX II
IRB AWARDS

ABOVE: Ireland's Keith Wood picked up the inaugural IRB Player of the Year Award in 2001.

2001

IRB International Player of the Year: **Keith Wood (Ireland)**
IRB International Team of the Year: **Australia**
IRB International Coach of the Year: **Rod Macqueen (Australia)**
IRB International Young Player of the Year: **Gavin Henson (Wales)**
IRB International Women's Player of the Year: **Shelley Rae (England)**
IRB Referee Award for Distinguished Service: **Ed Morrison (England)**
IRB Spirit of Rugby Award: **Tim Grandadge (India)**
IRB Distinguished Service Award: **Tom Kiernan (Ireland)**
IRB Development Award: **Jorge Brasceras (Uruguay)**
IRB Chairman's Awards: **Kath McLean, Sir Terry McLean, Albert Ferrasse, John Eales**

2002

IRB International Player of the Year: **Fabien Galthié (France)**
IRB International Team of the Year: **France**
IRB International Coach of the Year: **Bernard Laporte (France)**
IRB International U19 Player of the Year: **Luke McAlister (New Zealand)**
IRB International U21 Player of the Year: **Pat Barnard (South Africa)**
IRB International Sevens Team of the Year: **New Zealand**
IRB International Women's Player of the Year: **Monique Hirovanaa (New Zealand)**
IRB Referee Award for Distinguished Service: **Colin Hawke (New Zealand)**
IRB Distinguished Services Award: **Allan Hosie (Scotland)**
IRB Spirit of Rugby Award: **Old Christians Club (Uruguay)**
IRB Development Award: **John Broadfoot (England)**
IRB Chairman's Awards: **Bill McLaren, George Pippos (posthumously)**

2003

IRB International Player of the Year: **Jonny Wilkinson (England)**
IRB International Team of the Year: **England**
IRB International Coach of the Year: **Sir Clive Woodward (England)**
IRB International U19 Player of the Year: **Jean Baptiste Payras (France)**
IRB International U21 Player of the Year: **Ben Atiga (New Zealand)**
IRB International Sevens Team of the Year: **New Zealand**
IRB Spirit of Rugby Award: **Michael and Linda Collinson (Swaziland)**
IRB Award for Distinguished Service: **Bob Stuart (Australia)**
IRB Referee Distinguished Service Award: **Derek Bevan (Wales)**
IRB International Women's Personality of the Year: **Kathy Flores (United States)**
IRB Development Award: **Tan Theany and Philippe Monnin**
IRB Chairman's Awards: **Vernon Pugh (Wales)**

2004

IRB International Player of the Year: **Schalk Burger (South Africa)**
IRB International Team of the Year: **South Africa**
IRB International Coach of the Year: **Jake White (South Africa)**
IRB International U19 Player of the Year: **Jeremy Thrush (New Zealand)**
IRB International U21 Player of the Year: **Jerome Kaino (New Zealand)**
IRB International Sevens Team of the Year: **New Zealand**
IRB International Sevens Player of the Year: **Simon Amor (England)**
IRB Spirit of Rugby Award: **Jarrod Cunningham (New Zealand)**
Vernon Pugh Award for Distinguished Service: **Ronnie Dawson (Ireland)**
IRB Referee Award for Distinguished Service: **Jim Fleming (Scotland)**
IRB International Women's Personality of the Year: **Donna Kennedy (Scotland)**
IRB Development Award: **Guedel Ndiaye (Senegal)**
IRB Chairman's Award: **Marcel Martin (France)**

2005

IRB International Player of the Year: **Daniel Carter (New Zealand)**
IRB International Team of the Year: **New Zealand**
IRB International Coach of the Year: **Graham Henry (New Zealand)**
IRB International U19 Player of the Year: **Isaia Toeava (New Zealand)**

LEFT: England fly-half Jonny Wilkinson's stellar performance at the 2003 Rugby World Cup saw him pick up that year's IRB Player of the Year Award.

IRB International U21
Player of the Year: **Tatafu
Polota-Nau (Australia)**
IRB International Sevens
Team of the Year: **Fiji**
IRB International Sevens
Player of the Year: **Orene
Ai'i (New Zealand)**
IRB Spirit of Rugby Award:
**Jean Pierre Rives
(France)**
Vernon Pugh Award for
Distinguished Service:
Peter Crittle (Australia)
IRB Referee Award for
Distinguished Service:
**Paddy O'Brien (New
Zealand)**
IRB International Women's
Personality of the Year:
**Farah Palmer (New
Zealand)**
IRB Development Award:
Robert Antonin (France)
IRB Chairman's Award: **Sir
Tasker Watkins (Wales)**

2006

IRB International Player of
the Year: **Richie McCaw
(New Zealand)**
IRB International Team of
the Year: **New Zealand**
IRB International Coach of
the Year: **Graham Henry
(New Zealand)**
IRB International U19
Player of the Year: **Josh
Holmes (Australia)**
IRB International U21
Player of the Year: **Lionel
Beauxis (France)**
IRB International Sevens
Team of the Year: **Fiji**
IRB International Sevens
Player of the Year: **Uale
Mai (Samoa)**
IRB Spirit of Rugby Award:
Polly Miller
Vernon Pugh Award for
Distinguished Service:
**Brian Lochore (New
Zealand)**
IRB Referee Award for
Distinguished Service:
**Peter Marshall
(Australia)**
IRB International Women's
Personality of the Year:
**Margaret Alphonsi
(England)**
IRB Development Award:
Mike Luke (Canada)
IRB Hall of Fame inductees:
**William Webb Ellis and
Rugby School (England)**

2007

IRB International Player of
the Year: **Bryan Habana
(South Africa)**
IRB International Team of
the Year: **South Africa**
IRB International Coach
of the Year: **Jake White
(South Africa)**
IRB Under-19 Player of
the Year: **Robert Fruean
(New Zealand)**
IRB Sevens Player of the
Year: **Afeleke Pelenise
(New Zealand)**
IRB Sevens Team of the
Year: **New Zealand**
IRB Women's Personality of
the Year: **Sarah Corrigan,
referee (Australia)**
IRB Referee Award for
Distinguished Service:
**Dick Byres, retired
(Australia)**
Vernon Pugh Award for
Distinguished Service:
**José María Epalza
(Spain)**
Spirit of Rugby Award:
**Nicolas Pueta
(Argentina)**
IRPA Try of the Year:
**Takudzwa Ngwenya
(United States)**
IRPA Special Merit Award:
Fabien Pelous (France)
IRB Development Award:
**Jacob Thompson
(Jamaica)**
IRB Hall of Fame
inductees: **Pierre de
Coubertin (France);
Wilson Whineray (New
Zealand); Danie Craven
(South Africa); Gareth
Edwards (Wales); John
Eales (Australia)**

2008

IRB International Player of
the Year: **Shane Williams
(Wales)**
IRB International Team of
the Year: **New Zealand**
IRB International Coach of
the Year: **Graham Henry
(New Zealand)**
IRB Junior Player of the
Year: **Luke Braid (New
Zealand)**
IRB International Sevens
Player of the Year: **D.J.
Forbes (New Zealand)**

IRB Spirit of Rugby Award:
**Roelien Muller and
Patrick Cotter**
IRB Referee Award for
Distinguished Service:
**Andre Watson (South
Africa)**
IRB International Women's
Personality of the Year:
**Carol Isherwood
(England)**
IRPA Special Merit
Award: **Agustin Pichot
(Argentina)**
IRB Development
Award: **TAG Rugby
Development Trust and
Martin Hansford (South
Africa)**
IRPA Try of the Year: **Brian
O'Driscoll (Ireland)**

2009

IRB International Player of
the Year: **Richie McCaw
(New Zealand)**
IRB International Team of
the Year: **South Africa**
IRB International Coach of
the Year: **Declan Kidney
(Ireland)**
IRB Junior Player of the
Year: **Aaron Cruden
(New Zealand)**
IRB International Sevens
Player of the Year: **Ollie
Phillips (England)**
IRB Spirit of Rugby Award:
L'Aquila Rugby (Italy)

IRB International Women's
Personality of the Year:
**Debby Hodgkinson
(Australia)**
IRPA Special Merit Award:
Kevin Mac Clancy
IRPA Try of the Year: **Jaque
Fourie (South Africa)**

2010

IRB International Player of
the Year: **Richie McCaw
(New Zealand)**
IRB International Team of
the Year: **New Zealand**
IRB International Coach of
the Year: **Graham Henry
(New Zealand)**
IRB Junior Player of the
Year: **Julian Savea (New
Zealand)**
IRB International Sevens
Player of the Year: **Mikaele
Pesamino (Samoa)**
IRB Spirit of Rugby Award:
Virreyes RC (Argentina)
IRB International Women's
Personality of the Year:
**Carla Hohepa (New
Zealand)**
IRB Development Award:
Brian O'Shea (Ireland)
IRB Referee Award for
Distinguished Service:
Colin High

**BELOW: New Zealand's Aaron Cruden,
IRB Junior Player of the Year in 2010.**

**BELOW: England's Carol
Isherwood received the
IRB International Women's
Personality of the Year
Award in 2008.**

2011 IRB AWARD WINNERS

The latest winners of the prestigious IRB Awards were announced on 24 October 2011 at the Vector Arena in Auckland, New Zealand, one day after the Rugby World Cup final. The recipients were:

ABOVE: Thierry Dusautoir led by example as France reached the 2011 Rugby World Cup final

IRB INTERNATIONAL PLAYER OF THE YEAR: **THIERRY DUSAUTOIR (FRANCE)**

The 2011 season may have ended in the ultimate despair of defeat in the Rugby World Cup final, but otherwise it was a magnificent season for Thierry Dusautoir. The France captain stood tall during a difficult World Cup campaign for Les Bleus, confirmed his status as one of the best back-row players in the game and became the second Frenchman (following Fabien Galthie in 2002) to be voted the IRB Player of the Year.

IRB JUNIOR PLAYER OF THE YEAR: **GEORGE FORD (ENGLAND)**

A standout performer at the 2011 IRB Junior World Championship in Italy, at which, despite being the youngest player in the tournament, he led England to the final (which they ultimately lost 33-22 to New Zealand), fly-half George Ford becomes the first player from his country to win the IRB Junior Player of the Year award.

IRB INTERNATIONAL SEVENS PLAYER OF THE YEAR: **CECIL AFRIKA (SOUTH AFRICA)**

A key performer for South Africa during the Sevens World Series, playmaker Cecil Afrika finished on top of both the points-scoring (385) and try-scoring (40) charts as the Blitzbokke took the titles in Las Vegas, London and Scotland.

IRB INTERNATIONAL COACH OF THE YEAR: **GRAHAM HENRY (NEW ZEALAND)**

For all his success over the years, the one line missing from Graham Henry's rugby CV was success at the Rugby World Cup. The All Black coach finally put that right in 2011, and, after stepping down from the role at the end of the tournament, will surely go down in history as one of the greatest coaches in the game's history.

RIGHT: Graham Henry finished his career as New Zealand coach on the highest of highs – 2011 Rugby World Cup winner.

RIGHT: George Ford's brilliant performances for England during his country's run to the 2011 IRB Junior World Championship final shows that the fly-half position will be in good hands for many years to come.

IRB DEVELOPMENT AWARD WINNER:
ROOKIE RUGBY

Rookie Rugby was designed by USA Rugby to give young players between six and 12 years old a fun, safe and enjoyable sporting experience. It introduced a whole new raft of fans and athletes to the sport through programmes administered through schools, community-based and state-based rugby organizations and USA Rugby national events.

IRB WOMEN'S PERSONALITY OF THE YEAR:
RUTH MITCHELL

Hailing originally from Liverpool in England, Ruth Mitchell played rugby in Hong Kong before becoming an administrator and ultimately reaching the post of Director of Development for the HKRFU. A driving force behind youth rugby, Mitchell has also been instrumental in growing the women's game.

IRB TRY OF THE YEAR AWARD
RADIKE SAMO (AUSTRALIA V. NEW ZEALAND)

The final Tri Nations and Bledisloe Cup match of 2011 between New Zealand and Australia in Brisbane was a breathless encounter won by the Wallabies, inspired on the day by Radike Samo. The Fijian-born 35-year-old forward received the ball on his own 10-metre line and shrugged off a couple of All Black defenders before out-sprinting the cover defence to score a remarkable individual try.

IRB INTERNATIONAL TEAM OF THE YEAR:
NEW ZEALAND

New Zealand may have been pipped to the Tri-Nations title by trans-Tasman rivals Australia, but the All Blacks went on to collect the one trophy that truly mattered in 2011: the Rugby World Cup. The standout team in the tournament, they won all seven of their matches, including a slender 8-7 victory over France in the final, to win the game's most coveted trophy for the first time in 24 years.

IRB REFEREE AWARD FOR DISTINGUISHED SERVICE:
KEITH LAWRENCE

The 2010 IRB Referee Award Keith Lawrence refereed 14 international matches between 1985 and 1991 and went on to become an outstanding rugby administrator in the match official sphere. Lawrence worked as a Referee Manager both within his native New Zealand and for the International Rugby Board as Sevens Referee Manager, a role from which he retired earlier this year.

IRPA SPECIAL MERIT AWARD
GEORGE SMITH

Former captain George Smith is one of the greatest flankers ever to play for Australia and a veteran of 110 Tests for his country. Smith made his international debut against France in 2000 and played his final Test for the Wallabies against Wales nine years later.

VERNON PUGH AWARD FOR DISTINGUISHED SERVICE
JOCK HOBBS

Jock Hobbs was elected chairman of the New Zealand Rugby Union in 2002 and served with distinction, overseeing considerable success on and off the pitch while also securing New Zealand the right to host the 2011 Rugby World Cup. In December 2010, he stepped down from his position as chairman of both the New Zealand Rugby Union (NZRU) and Rugby New Zealand (RNZ) 2011 Limited due to ill health but continues to be an inspirational presence in the rugby-mad country.

ABOVE: With a good job well done, New Zealand players – gold medals around their necks – perform the Haka one final time at the 2011 Rugby World Cup.

IRB SPIRIT OF RUGBY AWARD:
WOODEN SPOON

A charity working for underprivileged children across the United Kingdom, the Wooden Spoon society has been running for the past 25 years and is a hugely deserving recipient of the IRB's Spirit of Rugby Award.

LEFT: George Smith may have lost his dreadlocks towards the end of his stellar international career, but the flanker remained a force in all of 110 appearances for Australia between 2000 and 2009.

PICTURE CREDITS

The publishers would like to thank the following sources for their kind permission to reproduce the pictures in this book.

Action Images: /Reuters: 68TR

Colorsport: 28BR, 55T, 120C, 135TL, 159C, 170BR, 171BR; /Steve Bardens: 159BR; /Colin Elsey: 31L, 54C, 72T, 73BL; /Matthew Impey: 41B; /David Lamb: 206R; /Paul Seiser: 150TR

Getty Images: 51B, 99TR, 102C, 137T, 161BR, 217BC; /Allsport: 100TL, 101BL, 106BL; /Odd Andersen/AFP: 17C, 24B, 92, 118TL, 161BL; /Pierre Andrieu/AFP: 23T; /Al Bello: 43T; /Daniel Berehulak: 35B, 57BR, 195BL; /Torsten Blackwood/AFP: 61BL; /Hamish Blair: 31B; /Patrick Bolger: 163BL; /Lionel Bonaventure/AFP: 26BL; /Shaun Botterill: 25BL, 30TL, 44TL, 52TL, 67TR, 101TR, 107BR, 164R; /Raul Bravo/AFP: 184C; /Gabriel Bouys/AFP: Front Endpaper, 76TR, 155BR; /Jeff Brass: 148BR; /Simon Bruty: 20TL, 72BL, 120BR; /Jon Buckle: 22R, 133T; /Martin Bureau/AFP: 130; /Eric Cabanis/AFP: 33B; /Giuseppe Cacace/AFP: 145BR; /Glenn Campbell/AFP: 63L; /David Cannon: 36B, 79BL, 149TR, 165TR; /Cesar Carrion/AFP: 184TL; /Central Press: 102BL; /Central Press/Hulton Archive: 107L; /Russell Cheyne: 17BL, 21TR, 56BR, 117TL; /Mike Clarke/AFP: 136BL, 200R; /Phil Cole: 58BL, 120BL, 207TR; /Michael Cooper: 33T, 135R; /Mark Dadswell: 131L; /Carl de Souza/AFP: 61T; /Delmas/AFP: 21L; /Adrian Dennis/AFP: 29BR, 42C; /Darren England: 55R; /FPG: 90; /Dante Fernandez/LatinContent: 94R; /Franck Fife/AFP: 63TR, 82-83, 87C, 132T, 140B, 152-153, 219TR; /Julian Finney: 23BR, 75BL; /Stu Forster: 24R, 44BR, 77BL, 99BL, 103BR, 104BL, 119TR, 124TR, 161TL, 186; /Victor Fraile: 200BL, 201TL; /Gallo Images: 114-115; /John Gichigi: 5BCR, 158BL, 183; /Paul Gilham: 28C; /Georges Gobet/AFP: 116; /Francois Guillot/AFP: 129BC; /Steve Haag/Gallo Images: 151B; /Stuart Hannagan: 65BL; /Martyn Hayhow/AFP: 195R; /Richard Heathcote: 66BR; /Mike Hewitt: 8-9, 17TR, 26TR, 48-49, 87BR, 88, 127BR, 192BL, 202-203, 204BL, 207BL, 211BL; /Kent Horner: 94B; /Hulton Archive: 25T; /Martin Hunter: 176B; /Roger Jackson/Central Press: 162B; /Alexander Joe/AFP: 109B; /Hannah Johnston: 133B, 138-139, 171TR, 217BR, 218TL; /Ed Jones/AFP: 150BL; /Keystone/Hulton Archive: 98B; /Junko Kimura: 182B; /Ian Kington/AFP: 214R; /Glyn Kirk/AFP: 146BR; /Toshifumi Kitamura/AFP: 56BL, 129T, 144TR; /James Knowler: 199TR; /Mark Kolbe: 80, 91BL, 212-213; /Patrick Kovarik/AFP: 57BL, 122BL; /Jean-Philippe Ksiazek/AFP: 23BL; /Nick Laham: 52BR, 55BL, 126BL; /Ross Land: 32T, 34C, 86R, 106TR, 109TL, 122C, 136TR, 177TR, 178TR, 178BL, 179TL, 205T; /Emiliano Lasalvia: 180-181, 182R; /Pascal Le Segretain: 81L; /Bryn Lennon: 197BR; /Warren Little: 119BR, 190-191, 210; /Philip Littlejohn/AFP: 75T; /Alex Livesey: 39R, 67B, 93C, 124BL; /Juan Mabromata/AFP: 131TR; /Clive Mason: 187; /John McCombe: 108BR; /Jamie McDonald: 5L, 12-13, 36C, 38BL, 93TR, 160, 162BR; /Chris McGrath: 37TL, 50B, 53BL, 91R, 170TL, 192R, 193BL, 216TL;

/Ian McNicol: 197L; /Marty Melville: 77TR, 219B; /Marty Melville/AFP: 34BR; /Damien Meyer/AFP: 5CL, 87T; /Daniel Mihailescu/AFP: 35TL, 189TL; /Ethan Miller: 198TR; /Jeff J Mitchell: 214B; /Sandra Mu: 128BL, 179BR, Back Endpaper; /Peter Muhly/AFP: 4CL, 27BR, 148T; /Jean-Pierre Muller/AFP: 131BR; /Adrian Murrell: 107T, 109TR, 141BR; /Marwan Naamani/AFP: 211R; /Kazuhiro Nogi/AFP: 57TL, 177BL, 189BR; /Mark Nolan: 59TL, 81TR, 89BR, 216B; /Brendon O'Hagan/AFP: 60B, 142BL; /Park Ji-Hwan/AFP: 69TL; /Peter Parks/AFP: 54B; /Gerry Penny/AFP: 14, 156B; /Tertius Pickard/Gallo Images: 121BR; /Ryan Pierse: 10-11, 86BL; /Popperfoto: 21B, 45BR, 103TL, 157TR; /Stefan Postles: 211TR; /Steve Powell: 156TR; /Adam Pretty: 15R, 22BL, 30BR, 47, 100BL, 121C, 125TR, 175BL; /Ker Robertson: 208BL; /David Rogers: 2, 4L, 4CR, 5BCL, 5R, 16BL, 20BR, 27R, 29T, 37BR, 38T, 38BR, 42B, 53TR, 53BR, 60T, 61C, 64, 66BL, 73TR, 76BL, 78, 79BR, 95L, 95BR, 96-97, 98C, 104R, 108L, 108BC, 113BR, 118BR, 121TL, 123C, 123TR, 125BL, 125R, 126R, 128T, 132B, 137B, 140T, 144B, 145TL, 146T, 147BR, 154R, 154B, 158T, 165BL, 168BR, 169BR, 172BL, 173TL, 173BR, 174TR, 174BL, 193TR, 204BR, 205BL, 208T, 215T, 218BR; /Miguel Rojo/AFP: 134R; /Roberto Serra: 209L, 209BR; /Ross Setford: 196; /Tom Shaw: 5CR, 157BL; /Vano Shlamov/AFP: 135BL; /Qamar Sibtain/India Today Group: 194; /Christophe Simon/AFP: 127C; /Cameron Spencer: 5BC, 110-111, 112R, 112B, 141TL, 166-167, 169TL, 176C, 198BL; /Michael Steele: 89TL; /Billy Stickland: 101BR; /Mike Stobe: 46; /Mrs Dulce R Stuart: 27TL; /Rob Taggart: 15BL; /Rob Taggart/Central Press/Hulton Archive: 43B; /Bob Thomas: 15TL, 16TR, 19T, 19B, 39B, 45L, 74B, 85, 117BR, 163TR; /Bob Thomas/Popperfoto: 151T; /Brendon Thorne: 188; /Touchline: 74R, 143BL, 197T; /Dean Treml/AFP: 69B; /Yoshikazu Tsuno/AFP: 50C; /Phil Walter: 4C, 18, 58R, 59R, 113TR, 113BC, 129BR, 147TL, 149BL, 195TR, 199BL, 218BC; /Anton Want: 105TR; /William West/AFP: 32B, 84, 105BL, 117C, 128BR, 172R; /Nick Wilson: 51T, 91T, 175TR; /Andrew Wong: 65TR, 201BR; /Greg Wood/AFP: 7, 62R; /Jonathan Wood: 62BL; /Sam Yeh/AFP: 185, 215BR

Offside Sports Photography: /L'Equipe: 35C; /Mark Leech: 126C; /Marca Media: 40, 41TL, 41R; /Photosport: 168TL

Press Association Images: 155T; /Shakh Aivazov/AP: 142TR; /Paul Barker: 134C; /Lynne Cameron: 206B; /David Davies: 4R; /Empics Sport: 102T; /Tom Honan: 68BL; /Ross Kinnaird: 70-71, 164BL; /Tony Marshall: 123BL; /Neal Simpson: 143TR

Every effort has been made to acknowledge correctly and contact the source and/or copyright holder of each picture and Carlton Books Limited apologises for any unintentional errors or omissions that will be corrected in future editions of this book.